DESCENDING DRAGON,
RISING TIGER

DESCENDING DRAGON, RISING TIGER

A HISTORY OF VIETNAM

VU HONG LIEN AND PETER D. SHARROCK

REAKTION BOOKS

Published by Reaktion Books Ltd
33 Great Sutton Street
London EC1V ODX, UK

www.reaktionbooks.co.uk

First published 2014
Copyright © Vu Hong Lien and Peter D. Sharrock 2014

Printed and bound by TJ International, Padstow, Cornwall

A catalogue record for this book is available from the British Library

ISBN: 978 1 78023 364 2

CONTENTS

Introduction

Vietnam emerged as a southern extension of the great civilization of China for 1,000 years, and then went its own way for a millennium, evolving into a distinct, cultivated and powerful East–Southeast Asian hybrid whose human and technological resources eventually led to the domination of all its neighbours to the south. A legendary, nationalistic account of the history, whose exotic narratives are recorded here as they are known to all modern Vietnamese, was constructed to enhance a national identity centuries after the separation from the great northern power at the end of the first millennium. The legend underplays Chinese influence and asserts a prehistoric Việt identity long suppressed by a foreign occupier. The thin historical data from the prehistoric period does little to support this view. What we recognize today as the vivid and distinct Vietnamese life and culture was at every level and in every field the result of a fusion of the formidable civilization of the great East Asian Central Kingdom with a vigorous, indigenous, but historically hardly recorded Metal Age culture of the Red River Delta.

The current and pervasive nationalist reading of the history of the Việt people covering 4,000 years of prehistory is mentioned periodically in our narrative as a legendary account. It then assesses the depth of Chinese influence on many aspects of Vietnamese life and supports recent scholarly claims that situate the key period of fusion of Chinese and indigenous language into the distinctive hybrid Vietnamese to the end of the first milliennium. Finally it evaluates the new colours taken on by the young dragon that straddled East and Southeast Asia cultures, as it descended and absorbed Cham and Khmer cultures and French colonialism.

The core of the Vietnamese language was forged by some 40 generations of city-dwelling Han-Tang Chinese speakers who gradually created a provincial Chinese dialect which, after the state's links with the giant neighbour loosened into independent vassalage, encompassed a full merger with the autochthonous Mon-Khmer language of the coastal plain. Thus the bilingualism of the first millennium turned into a single, recognizably Vietnamese language, written in a demotic Chinese script called *chữ Nôm*. China had a parallel relationship with the people of the Korean peninsula in the north, who separated from the centre at the fall of Han China in the third century. Vietnam and Korea hang like jewelled pendants from the central mainland mass – exotic, beautifully different but dependent.

One of China's most precious gifts was written history in the form of dynastic annals, which form an illuminated core narrative richer than in Vietnam's neighbours. They were of course written under pressure at court, but the writers often show themselves to be a trained body of highly cultivated thinkers capable of judging events with perspicuity. The strongest counter to this annalistic Vietnamese account is the Chinese state records of the thirteenth and fifteenth centuries, which were written under similar and even greater pressures. With limited evidence from other sources, any account of the first millennium of the Common Era must strike a balance between these two accounts. Other documents that bear on Vietnam's complex geographical, ethnic and cultural past are scattered in Chinese, French, Russian and Japanese texts as well as in the texts inscribed in stone in the temples of ancient Champa and Cambodia. There is also the dense narrative of legend that winds its way around the documentable history. We have aimed to give them all due weight and in particular focused on the still under-researched Việt annals.

'Bốn ngàn năm văn hiến' – 4,000 years of cultural development is a national slogan that over-interprets the flimsy archaeological evidence, which shows instead a mix of peoples we could not yet identify as Vietnamese occupying the northern part of Vietnam for much longer than that. The popular and scholarly claims to cultural homogeneity in this remote era are a backward revision of the data in the search for national identity.

Humans have populated the high ground north of the Red River for many thousands of years. Evidence of a Hòa Bình culture, named after the province where archaeologists made their finds, overlaps with that of Bắc Sơn, dated to 8,000 to 10,000 years ago and centred on the mountains close to the modern Chinese border. The evidence left in caves by these cultures includes used tools for sophisticated manufacture and agriculture. They were hunter-gatherers as well as agriculturalists and they made decorated ceramics and were spinning cotton and weaving textiles.

Later, in the Đông Sơn era considered to extend from 700 BCE to 100 BCE, they perfected the piece-mould casting of large engraved drums – skills they shared with southern China and Yunnan – that were to find great favour in communities throughout early island Southeast Asia. The Đông Sơn drums were named after the location of the first find in 1924. They appear to have become the most prized object in chieftain exchange and royal burial on the mainland and down through the islands of modern Indonesia. The drums are cast in one piece and superbly decorated with a sun-star and boats carrying men with high feathered headdresses, and they were all made in Vietnam south of the Red River. No other high technology product achieved such a wide distribution across the mainland peninsula and the Malay Archipelago. The function of the drum remains largely mysterious but as well as status and alliance, they may have facilitated and transmitted basic calendrical or monsoonal navigational skills that empowered their owners with participation in the crucial maritime trade. Taylor considers the modern Vietnamese claim to direct linkage back to Đông Sơn 'an exuberant use of evidence'.[1]

The Đông Sơn era ended after Han China first sent its armies into southern China, and in the culmination of a slow expansion further south, Han general Lu Bode in 111 BCE pushed across the mountainous border into Nan Yue ('Nam Việt' in Vietnamese) with an army of 100,000 men, supported by warships in the gulf, to extend the Han territories further south. The new Han province was an accorded three Việt prefectures of Giao Chỉ, Cửu Chân and Nhật Nam.

While the north acquired Han culture, further down the coastal plain a long chain of settlements emerged that the Chinese first called Lin-yi and which the inhabitants eventually called Champa. Such riverine ports were settled by ship-borne migrants probably from Borneo. In the world before the rise of rice-based agricultural empires, these migrants from the islands grew prosperous through their maritime skills and support for the growing maritime trade between China, India and the Arab and European worlds. Although they never congealed into a single state, the networked Cham ports accumulated wealth from shipping forest goods and supplying commercial fleets with fresh water and supplies. They were soon building huge brick temple towers on a scale grander than their neighbours. The Cham towers still dot central Vietnam's coastal strip. We trace the end of what some historians call the thousand-year miracle of islanders surviving on the Indochinese mainland in a fatal alliance with the burgeoning Cambodian Empire across the mountains at Angkor. The Khmer-Cham alliance repeatedly attacked the newly independent Buddhist state of the Việt. When Cambodia declined under less ambitious rulers, the Chams were exposed to the superior technology of the Việt and were set on a gradual but eventually total decline as the hybrid dragon descended.

The astonishing ethnic and cultural diversity of modern Vietnam is the result of the powerful young hybrid dragon of the northern delta gradually discovering its powers in the second millennium, in first defensive then expansionist battle mode against the neighbouring Cham and Cambodian peoples. The long drive south was partly accomplished by adventurous Việt kings and partly at a lower level by pioneering fishermen-farmers who exploited local advantages within declining Cham polities.

The usually courteous relationship with China was rent by repeated Mongol invasions in the late thirteenth century. Chinese settlers from Fujian established a Chinese-based literati culture in the south that grew powerful from the expanding Chinese external trade and eventually weakened the Buddhist dynasty in Thăng Long (Hanoi). One of these southern factions seems to have colluded with the Mongol Yuan dynasty. The Mongol horses suffered in the tropical climate and the management of a new, high technology Chinese fleet was finally humiliated in astute river ambushes that produced a new generation of Việt heroes with reputations that thrive today. But the Mongol defeat came at a high cost as the war must have damaged the water management systems, for many decades of crop failures and starvation followed.

[handwritten margin note: Little Ice Age droughts]

Protracted civil war, rebellions and endless dynastic conflicts gravely unsettled the fifteenth–eighteenth centuries. During a notable twenty-year interlude early in the fifteenth century the expansive new Ming dynasty looked beyond its borders and attempted a return to Han- and Tang-scale sovereignty. Within a generation they invaded Đại Việt on the pretext of restoring a Trần heir and sinicized Việt society in fully fledged Confucian mould. A new class of Việt bureaucrats or 'literati' was schooled to run detailed administrative systems in fifteen *phủ*. Identity papers were issued to all and people registers controlled taxation as well as mining, forestry and pearl-diving duties. Chinese clothing and long pigtails were imposed. The Ming army was pushed out when lesser emperors took the throne and the victor Lê Lợi became another Việt national hero. The Chinese came back briefly in the sixteenth century under the Mạc, but that was the last time.

The remnant Cham cities suffered as the Vietnamese pursued their Nam tiến (movement south) that was to divide the state into two rival Việt cultures that European missionaries would identify as Tonkin in the north and Cochinchina in the south. Christianity and French aristocrats scattered by the revolution in France made quick inroads in this contested period and they directly assisted the formation of the new and final Nguyễn dynasty (1802–1945) at the new capital of Huế in central Vietnam. The Nguyễn flourished, aided by French technology, but by 1885 the French had taken total political control. The resultant road, rail, electrical and plantation infrastructure was the envy of Asia. The deep engagement with French colonial values and technology (followed by the more recent freedom and entrepreneurial flair of the American presence), added another cultural layer that differentiated the more conservative and classical but also more rigid north of Vietnam from the warmth and risk-prone conviviality of the south.

The Second World War collusion between the leaders of the Vichy colony and the Japanese Greater East Asia Co-prosperity Sphere proved a disaster that the Free French subsequently failed to master and France left Vietnam after military humiliation at the mountain battle of Điện Biên Phủ in 1954.

The socialist north, created by the Geneva Conference and led by Le Duan's labour party with poet Hồ Chí Minh as international figure-head, would wage another twenty years of war before achieving total power and independence. After Geneva a million Catholics and non-Catholics headed south rather than live under communism. The new socialist-nationalists in the north went back to war because the post-war American superpower, having blocked the 'Yellow Peril' in Korea, intervened when it foresaw a chain of dominoes collapsing from Vietnam through Malaysia, Indonesia, Australia and maybe California. But the American will broke in the nightly televized Tết Offensive of 1968 and Richard Nixon and Henry Kissinger negotiated a 'decent interval' for the Americans to withdraw. After the hasty departure the false peace soon collapsed and the north swept to victory in 1975. A massive exodus of 'boat people' in small vessels broke through the bolted doors of the new communist state, which soon reduced the 'jewel of the orient' to one of the poorest countries on earth. Only in the late 1980s did Vietnam open its doors with a post-Mao development model for socialist-capitalism, which unleashed the entrepreneurial culture of the south that is powering today's rising economic tiger.

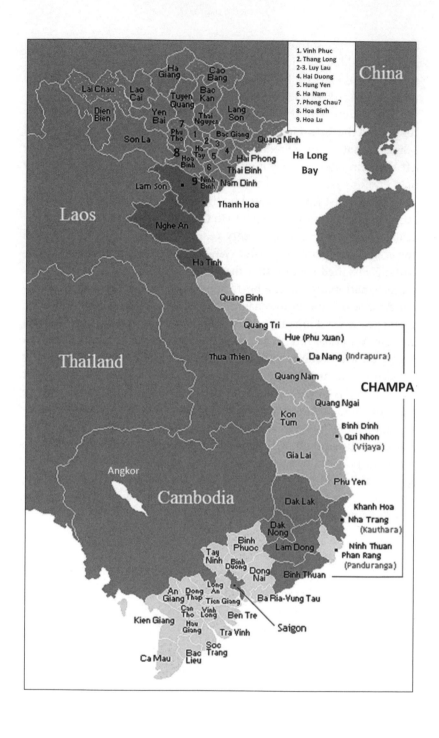

1. Vinh Phuc
2. Thang Long
2-3. Luy Lau
4. Hai Duong
5. Hung Yen
6. Ha Nam
7. Phong Chau?
8. Hoa Binh
9. Hoa Lu

China

Ha Giang
Cao Bang
Lai Chau
Lao Cai
Tuyen Quang
Bac Kan
Lang Son
Dien Bien
Yen Bai
Thai Nguyen
7
Son La
Phu Tho
1
Bac Giang
Quang Ninh
8
Ha Tay
Hoa Binh
5
Hai Phong
Ha Long
6
Thai Binh
Bay
9
Ninh Binh
Nam Dinh
Lam Son
Thanh Hoa

Laos

Nghe An

Ha Tinh

Quang Binh

Quang Tri
Hue (Phu Xuan)
Da Nang (Indrapura)
Thua Thien
Quang Nam

Thailand

CHAMPA

Quang Ngai
Kon Tum
Binh Dinh
Qui Nhon
(Vijaya)
Gia Lai
Phu Yen

Angkor
Dak Lak
Khanh Hoa
Nha Trang
(Kauthara)
Cambodia
Dak Nong
Binh Phuoc
Lam Dong
Ninh Thuan
Phan Rang
(Panduranga)
Tay Ninh
Binh Duong
Dong Nai
Binh Thuan
An Giang
Dong Thap
Long An
Tien Giang
Ba Ria-Vung Tau
Can Tho
Vinh Long
Ben Tre
Kien Giang
Hau Giang
Saigon
Tra Vinh
Ca Mau
Bac Lieu
Soc Trang

1

Prehistory

Recent genetic studies suggest the identity of the early human inhabitants of the Red River delta possibly resulted from a fusion of the first *Homo sapiens* migrants from sub-Saharan Africa some 74,000 years ago and returning hardy hunter-gatherers whose ancestors had walked on further north into what became China, Tibet, Korea and Japan, where their struggle with a severe climate resulted in their developing *Mongoloid* traits like folded eyelids and flat noses.[1] In a purely speculative reconstruction with no base of data, it is possible that during the catastrophic freeze of the Last Glacial Maximum (LGM) some 20,000 years ago, those who had moved north were driven back for survival down the river valleys that their ancestors had traversed thousands of years earlier. The freeze may have sent these hardy northerners back down the Brahmaputra to Assam, east along the Yangtze to southern China and down the Mekong into today's Thailand, Laos, Cambodia and Vietnam. If this did occur, then some travelled down the Hồng River and settled in northern Vietnam, where they presumably cohabited and interbred with those who had stopped there during the original migration. Thousands of years later these people, who may have been early forbears of the Việt, would have their genetic and cultural roots deeply enriched by the arrival of a continuous stream of settlers from China from the second century BCE onwards. The major contribution to life in the Delta region made by these immigrants, who eventually lost touch with their ancestral roots, tends therefore to vindicate the old theory that the Việt came from southern China.

According to genetic studies of the Recent Single Origin Hypothesis (RSOH), after a long journey out of Africa that started about 85,000 years ago, one group from sub-Sahara arrived at the Malay Peninsula some time before 74,000 years ago. At this point, they split into three or more groups. One travelled up the eastern coast of Asia, another walked south to Australia and others stayed put. From the Malay Peninsula, the group that went north travelled up the coast of mainland Southeast Asia and arrived at today's Vietnam before splitting again. Between 35,000 and 70,000 years ago, one group stayed put while another carried on along the coast of China and branched out to Taiwan and on to Korea and Japan. From the river mouths on the Chinese coast, they moved inland to populate China. Those who stayed in Vietnam formed colonies along the coast and rivers like the Mekong, the Thu Bồn in the centre and the Hồng (Red) in the north. From there some migrated into southern China while some followed the Hồng River to Yunnan.

Research into the mitochondrial DNA (mtDNA) that passes from mothers to daughters first affirmed the 'Out of Africa' theory of the ancient Việt, who carried a sub-group of mtDNA (Haplogroup M9b) unique to the area and the Indochina Peninsula that they inherited from their original African female forebears.[2] However, they are not pure descendants of the original settlers but a mixture of the original settlers and some of their former travelling companions from the north, later known as China. In a study into Southeast Asian mtDNA in 1992, a group of international scientists noted that 'of the current populations in Southeast Asia, the Vietnamese have the greatest intrapopulational genetic divergence (0.236 per cent), suggesting that it is the oldest.'[3] Archaeological evidence interpreted by Vietnamese scholars suggests the settlers from Africa were not the only inhabitants at the time of their arrival.[4] The settlers could have lived with or interbred with their *Homo erectus* cousins who arrived earlier. The newcomers left traces in caves and stone dwellings, such as piles of shells in caves in Quỳnh Lưu (Nghệ An province), north of Vietnam and Sa Huỳnh in today's central Vietnam.[5] The period from 75,000 to 8,000 years ago was a time of environmental upheaval when the earth went through great freezes, interspersed by interglacial ice melts. The most dramatic event of this period in Southeast Asia was the massive eruption of Mount Toba in Sumatra which brought about disastrous changes to living things in a vast area stretching from Sumatra to India.[6] The Hồng River delta escaped the skies raining down volcanic ashes that destroyed many human cultures and this probably contributed to their early development of the technology of the Bronze Age[7] and their premium orientation towards coastal and island Southeast Asia.[8]

The great freeze in the northern hemisphere made the sea water in Southeast Asia drop 100–120 m below today's level. The receding sea exposed large stretches of coastal land off the coast of what we now call Vietnam. During the LGM, northern Vietnam was connected by dry land to Hainan Island and lower China, which today is submerged under modern Vietnam's tourist resort of Hạ-Long bay. Further south, today's Vietnam was connected to a vast tract of land called the Sunda continent that linked the Southeast Asian mainland with the many islands of

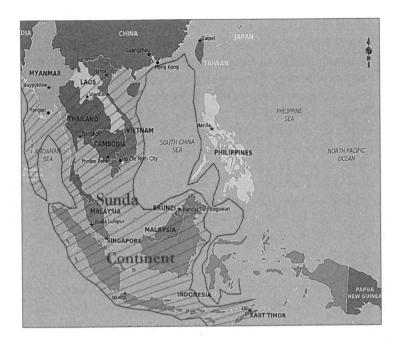

The Sunda continent.

modern Indonesia and Malaysia, stretching as far as today's Bali and included Java, Sumatra and Borneo.[9]

Before the LGM, however, there was a mild period recorded as 40,000–20,500 BCE which affected Southeast Asia. The ice melt probably continued and the water changed the shape of the coastland to some extent, forcing groups of people living by the coast to move inland and upland and re-adapt their cultures.[10] The relatively mild climate must have made life easier for these Stone Age hunter-gatherers. Archaeological evidence assembled by French and Vietnamese scholars since the end of the nineteenth century shows evidence of cultural layers that date back tens of thousands of years.[11] The pre-Việt peoples lived on high ground such as in Lạng Sơn, on the border with China and on mount Đọ in Thanh Hóa. Excavations show an evolution from Stone Age to Bronze Age technology and beyond. After the simple stone tools of Sơn Vì culture (21,000–9000 BCE),[12] came the more developed Hòa Bình culture from 16,000–5500 BCE.[13] Later phases of this are known as the Bắc Sơn (8000–5000 BCE) and Đa Bút (4000–2000 BCE). The Bronze Age came in with the Phùng Nguyên (2000- ±1500 BCE),[14] Hạ Long (2000 BCE), Gò Mun (1000–700 BCE) and culminated in the Đông Sơn culture famous for sophisticated bronze drums from about 1000 BCE that were eventually distributed throughout island Southeast Asia.[15] Further south towards central Vietnam, the earliest identified cultures are called Bàu Tró (2000 BCE) in Quảng Bình province, Sa Huỳnh (2000 BCE–200 CE) in central Quảng Ngãi province and Đồng Nai (2000 BCE) in the south.[16] The three cultures of Đông Sơn, Sa Huỳnh and Đồng Nai make up the prehistorical picture of life in what would become Vietnam.

The cultures were named after the locations where their typical artefacts were first identified. Sơn Vì culture was first identified in 1968 by shaped pebble tools found at Sơn Vì village in Phú Thọ (today's Vĩnh Phú province). Sơn Vì people lived mainly in caves and on high ground sloping down to the banks of small rivers.[17] Theirs was the most widespread as their artefacts have been found in 230 locations – from the high grounds of Phú Thọ, Hà Tây, Bắc Giang, Lao Cai in the north to Quảng Trị and Lâm Đồng provinces in the centre. Similar artefacts have also been found in Lang Rongrien and Moh Khiew in Thailand, as well as in southern China.

Skulls and bones from Sơn Vì caves in Con Moong, between Lai Châu and Ninh Bình provinces indicate Sơn Vì people were *Australonegroid* and *Australoid*, without traces of *Mongoloid*. Only later did *Mongoloid* characteristics indicate the presence of the prehistoric Hòa Bình culture.

Sơn Vì groups shared a communal hearth in the middle of a cave with traces of wood ash mixed with broken pebble tools. Around the rim were animal bones and teeth, crab claws and mollusc shells. The molluscs have been identified as freshwater cockles, oysters and mountain snails, a staple food still favoured by highlanders in modern Vietnam.

The Hòa Bình culture was made famous in 1927 by Madeleine Colani, a French botanist turned archaeologist, who was then a lone female in French colonial archaeology. She named the culture after the province where its distinct artefacts were first classified. They were flaked stone implements of oval, circular or triangular shapes.[18] To date, more than 120 Hòa Bình sites have been discovered in Vietnam, and others have been found in modern Cambodia, Thailand, Laos, Burma, Sumatra and Australia.

The Hoà Bình-ians gradually developed sophisticated stone tools and low-bake pottery as well as agricultre and animal husbandry. Technological breakthroughs included cord-marked pottery, the taming of dogs and nurturing of certain plants.[19] Traces of their primitive agricultural efforts show that they grew root vegetables, fruit trees and a form of rice.[20] They were concentrated mainly in Hòa Bình, Thanh Hóa, Lai Châu, Sơn La, Hà Giang, Ninh Bình, Nghệ An, Quảng Bình and Quảng Trị provinces, with most traces in Hòa Bình and Thanh Hóa provinces.

Although coming on the heels of Sơn Vì culture, the Hòa Bình people were very different. According to Vietnamese archaeologists, they had

Mongoloid features, indicating a degree of crossbreeding with people from as far north as northern China and Tibet.[21] The migrants from the north probably came down the Hồng (Red) River to Hòa Bình when their own land became unhabitable during the LGM. The Hòa Bình people left traces of smaller hearths suggesting smaller communal groups.[22] Animal bones and large quantities of shells were usually present around the hearths.[23] Hòa Bình people also buried their dead in graves lined with stones, shells or ashes.

Bắc Sơn and Đa Bút are two fairly limited but important sub-cultures. Bắc Sơn is sometimes considered as late Hòa Bình. The Bắc Sơn culture had a uniquely shaped stone axe marked with indentations. Bắc Sơn culture was named after a district of Lạng Sơn province and its traces have been found in the northern provinces of Lạng Sơn and Thái Nguyên. Đa Bút flourished in Thanh Hóa province and was named after the village of Đa Bút, Vĩnh Lộc district, where it was first discovered by the French archaeologist E. Patte in 1926–7. Typical artefacts of this culture are early pottery and stone tools, found mainly in two provinces of Thanh Hóa and Ninh Bình. Pottery pieces produced during the time of this culture were very simple and crudely shaped by hand. They place Đa Bút among the earliest sites of pottery production in what became Vietnam.

Phùng Nguyên was a major early culture that brought in the Bronze Age in a marked leap in technology. It flourished from circa 2000 to ±1500 BCE. These people made pottery and experimented with bronze, although no crafted bronze object has yet been found.[24] Most Phùng Nguyên artefacts have been found in Văn Lang, which in current Vietnamese mythology is considered the cradle of Việt civilization. They are dated to the second half of the third millennium BCE. The first were identified in Phùng Nguyên village in Vĩnh Phú province in 1959.[25]

Phùng Nguyên people lived on ground above the confluence of the main rivers Hồng, Đà and Mã.[26] Excavations begun in 1959 uncovered stones, some of them coloured, that were sawn, drilled, shaped and sharpened.[27] Their axes were smaller and finer than their predecessors' and they made arrowheads and jewellery. Arguably the most significant development of the Phùng Nguyên period is the appearance of fine pottery fired at relatively high temperature. The clay was mixed with fine sand and shaped on pottery wheels, which produced thin and even walls that were decorated with a variety of patterns, including cording, combing and rice stalk designs. The pots came in many different sizes and shapes – round and square, vases and urns.

The presence of ceramic pottery spools and shuttles proves they could weave cloth. And they represented key elements of their world in clay models of cows and chickens. The dead were sometimes buried with a pig's jaw. From these findings we can assume that the Stone Age people living in what we now call Vietnam, since the last great freeze, flourished as hunter-gatherers in a slightly cooler climate than the present, using stone tools and sheltering in caves.[28] They hunted deer, elephant, wild boar, tiger, wild cats, monkeys and foxes, and gathered fish and bivalve molluscs along the coast, or from their streams and rivers. They possibly used stone tools to shape bamboo lengths to make other tools and utensils, but these perished without trace. The Sơn Vì culture developed into the slightly more sophisticated Hòa Bình and Bắc Sơn cultures until the last great melt of around 6000–5500 BCE. The most significant event during the Bắc Sơn culture was the appearance of the square axe and some of the first pottery.

The flooding of the coastal land that occurred 8,000 to 7,500 years ago drove these people upland and interrupted the spread of Hòa Bình culture, which, by then, had expanded as far as other areas of Southeast Asia, both mainland and island, and even Australia.[29] At the beginning of the flood, both mainland and island Southeast Asia were still connected to the southern part of Vietnam by the Sunda continent. Traces of Hòa Bình culture, most probably, also existed on the Sunda itself, which have now been submerged under the meltwater. After Hòa Bình, no known major culture has been identified between 5500–4000 BCE, due presumably to environmental upheavals across the earth as the ice melted. The lessening of ice weight in the northern hemisphere presumably disturbed the balance of the earth surface and created cracks on the earth's crust, bringing an unsettled period full of climatic change in earthquakes, tsunamis and recurring floods.[30] Only when the meltwater started receding did new cultures began to appear and such as the Đa Bút, Hạ Long, Phùng Nguyên and Gò Mun cultures. They were the prelude to Đông Sơn culture of 1000 BCE to 100 CE. The sophistication of Đông Sơn is attested in the manufacture of minutely decorated and superbly finished drums which, from their distribution pattern, became the sine qua non of chieftainship across island Southeast Asia. Similar drums have been excavated in Han burials in China in Gangxi, Xilin and Luobowan. The cultural sphere that produced these artefacts – all with boat, house and feathered figure motifs – extended up to southern Yunnan and even parts of modern Burma and Thailand. In modern Vietnam such bronze manufactures have been found over a large area stretching from Đào Thịnh in Yên Bái province, by the right bank of the upper Hồng River and the border with China, down to Quảng Bình province.[31] A famous recent find of an estimated 40 drums was made by Andreas Reinecke at Prohear, Cambodia.

Overlapping with the Đông Sơn culture were the Iron Age cultures of Sa Huỳnh and Đồng Nai. The Sa Huỳnh culture is believed to appear in Chinese archives as 'Lin Yi', from the end of the second century CE. Its inhabitants preceded the Cham people, who possibly arrived in boats from Borneo, and who were to establish a string of culturally innovative enclaves and polities on the river estuaries of the coast of today's central Vietnam. The Chams retained their strong maritime culture and inhabited a narrow strip of the coast stretching from Quảng Binh to Bình Thuận province. The Sa Huỳnh people developed glass beads and sophisticated jewellery and buried their dead in earthen jars. They made pottery, cultivated wet rice and were skilful mariners. Further south a culture known as Đồng Nai has been traced on the high ground, at the base of the central highlands, from whence flow the rivers Đồng Nai, Saigon and Vàm Cỏ. Together, the three cultures Đông Sơn, Sa Huỳnh and Đồng Nai formed the prehistoric life that preceded Việt culture.

POST-GLACIAL PERIOD

In the 12,000 years following the most severe freeze of 20,000 years ago, three periods of interglacial melt occurred, the last one in 6000–5500 BCE. The last great melt was quite rapid and overwhelmed many areas of settlement along the coast, which might explain why traces of the early Sơn Vì and Hòa Binh cultures are only found on higher ground unaffected by the rising sea. The melt of 7,500–8,000 years ago inundated the Sunda continent, separating the mainland from 'Sundaland', several groups of islands that make up today's Indonesian archipelago.[32] One result of this may have been reduced dependence on fishing as suggested in archaeological evidence from eight Da Bút sites (4000–2000 BCE) that mostly show remains of agriculture. Leafy and root vegetables dominate with some fishing in rivers.[33] In the following Phùng Nguyên sites (2000 to ±1500 BCE) there is evidence of stone hoes, axes and sickles for cultivation.[34] They grew rice as rice pollen at Tràng Kênh in Hải Phòng province gave carbon-14 dates of 1500 BCE.

As the meltwater receded, the Phùng Nguyên people moved down to land near present Hanoi and some settled on the coast at Tràng Kênh and Hạ Long in a culture dubbed 'Hạ Long'. The melt submerged Hạ Long bay, leaving exposed only its dragon-back limestone karsts and other islands. Hạ Long culture from 2000 BCE advanced into boat building. Archaeological finds show the people lived by agriculture and fishing with nets and wore woven clothes.

wove textiles

THE LEGEND OF THE ORIGIN OF THE VIỆT PEOPLE

After a long war-time search, the North Vietnamese Committee on Social Science in 1970–74 claimed in an account rich in patriotism and a little science to be able to trace four phases of 2,000 years of early Việt civilization that evolved locally and without outside influence.[35] These culminated in triumph in the bronze Đông Sơn culture and the first coherent 'Văn Lang' polity under the mythical Hùng dynasties dated to 2879 BCE–258 BCE. The early fusions of northern peoples with highland Stone Age inhabitants during the LGM and the melt period are recorded mythically in the story of Lạc Long Quân and Âu Cơ.[36] According to this myth, Lạc Long Quân – The Lạc Dragon King – came from the lineage of the god of Agriculture. He came from the sea and was a just king who taught the Việt people to wear clothes, learn good manners and respect family hierarchy. He met Âu Cơ, a goddess of the highlands, who came to the lowlands with her husband Đế Lai, a king from the north. She was left alone while her husband travelled all over the land and 'caused lots of problems to the Việt people'. The people appealed for help to Lạc Long Quân, who came and married Âu Cơ, taking her to Long-Trang mountain, said to be today's Tản Viên mountain in Vĩnh Phú province. Âu Cơ's husband returned, fought a series of magical battles with Lạc Long Quân and was defeated. He returned to his own land in the north.[37] Lạc Long Quân and Âu Cơ had no less than 100 sons who split into two groups; 50 stayed with their mother on the mountain and the other 50 went with their father to the sea. The 50 highland sons created 'Văn Lang', with a capital in Phong Châu, in today's Vĩnh Phú Province, in an era known as Hồng Bàng. The rulers of this mythical state were called Hùng Vương, or Hùng kings, who ruled over the Lạc people for eighteen dynasties.

The meeting of Lạc Long Quân and Âu Cơ may possibly be a colourful folk memory of a fusion of mountain dwellers with migrants from the north. The 50 sons taking to the sea may represent the Hạ Long culture archaeologists now date to circa 2000 BCE.[38] According to the myth, the Dragon King divided the children 'after some time had elapsed',[39] which could mean after the water had receded far enough to make the lowlands habitable again. The Hùng kings were said to rule over fifteen *bộ* (tribal area or district), where people called Lạc occupied an indeterminate geographical area of southern China and today's North Vietnam.[40] South of Văn Lang's was a polity called Hồ Tôn, which Vietnamese archives identify as Champa.[41] Each group of Lạc was said to be headed by a military lord who provided the Hùng king with wealth and manpower.[42]

The system of autonomous tribes grouped around a chief was similar to that adopted by their southern neighbours in the Sa Huỳnh culture, who later probably merged with the arriving Cham. Archaeologists and historians have noted similarities in artefacts and technologies among the Đông Sơn, Sa Huỳnh and Đồng Nai cultures.[43] For example, Sa Huỳnh earrings were found in the Đồng Nai area, stone artefacts from Đồng Nai appeared in Sa Huỳnh, and Đông Sơn bronze drums and artefacts were found in both Sa Huỳnh and Đồng Nai areas. The three cultural centres used similar agricultural implements, like bronze sickles, stone axes and crescent-shaped knives. Vestiges of linga-like forms suggest a life creation force was venerated and copulating couples are represented on the lid of the Đào Thịnh bronze vat dated to the Đông Sơn era. They all appear to have inherited burial practices and jewellery from the Hòa Bình culture. The groups followed similar political systems until the arrival of sophisticated immigrants from China in the second century BCE drove a cultural wedge between Đông Sơn and Sa Huỳnh and Đồng Nai. The northern alluvial plains became sinicized, while the central coast turned to a new influence from India. In the south the Đồng Nai culture expanded into the Mekong Delta in a new and rapidly advancing Indic-influenced polity known to the Chinese by the second century CE as 'Funan'.

According to the Hùng Vương mythology, in Văn Lang the Hùng king was assisted by civil lords called Lạc Hầu.[44] The Lạc lived in houses on stilts[45] and irrigated their *ruộng Lạc* fields from rivers and streams. They cultivated ordinary and glutinous rice which they cooked with salt in bamboo tubes; they made rice wine, wore tree bark clothes and wove dry grass mats. Flooding occurred regularly, as told by the legend of Sơn Tinh–Thủy Tinh, which tells of why they lived in houses on stilts, even on high ground.

THE FLOOD LEGEND

According to the Sơn Tinh–Thủy Tinh legend, the first recurrent flood after the great melt occurred during the eighteenth Hùng dynasty. Two suitors, Sơn Tinh (Spirit of mountain) and Thủy Tinh (Spirit of water) came to ask for the king's daughter's hand. Unable to choose between them, the Hùng king told them that he would choose the first who arrived at his palace the next day with suitable marriage offerings. The Mountain Spirit, Sơn Tinh, arrived first, got his princess and took her to his home on mount Tản Viên. Thủy Tinh arrived late and became so angry he made the water level rise and rise to drown his rival on the mountain. Sơn Tinh, however, possessed similar magical power and made his mountain rise up always above the level of Thủy Tinh's water, until the

Spirit of water gave up the fight and the water receded. This tale is popularly seen as an account of the annual flood of the Hồng River.

The legendary account says those who moved upland to avoid the rising water evolved into the 54 ethnic minorities of Vietnam today. They share some cultural traditions with the sinicized lowland early Việt people, who still today call themselves the 'kinh', the people of the capital. The language of the non-Chinese speaking lowland inhabitants belongs to the Mon-Khmer group of Austroasiatic languages and is called Proto-Việt-Mường by linguists.[46] The still-surviving nonsinicized remnants of this group, known as the Mường, are viewed by the Việts as relatives and they share the Lạc Long Quân and Âu Cơ myth of their origin. Some of the other minorities have the dark skin and frizzy hair probably typical of the early migrations out of Africa. In appearance they have more in common with mountain peoples in Malaysia and island Southeast Asia than with their lowland counterparts in Vietnam itself. The continuous wars of the twentieth century have restricted research among these people and there are still blockages today.

WHAT THE DÔNG SƠN DRUMS SAY ABOUT LIFE UNDER 'HÙNG VƯƠNG'

Since the Ngọc Lũ drum was uncovered in 1893–4 in Hà Nam Ninh province, southeast of Hanoi, many interpretations have been offered to explain the function of these highly sophisticated cylindrical drums.[47] Their use remains mysterious despite many studies,[48] but their wide distribution across island Southeast Asia, suggests they were considered to have been symbols of wealth and authority and major exchange goods among the region's chieftains.

All drums are engraved with dense and exquisite etchings and some have small animals, often frogs, perched on the tympanum. The later drums, classified as Heger II and III, bear three-dimensional bullfrogs and large lizard-like creatures perhaps related to flooding or rain-making. The bullfrogs are arranged evenly around the outer rim of the tympana at four or six equidistant points, and at times they stand on each other's back. Scholars have usually identified them as frogs, but some Vietnamese historians insist they are toads that signify rain, as in the Vietnamese expression 'the toad is the uncle of the power above'. Both sides agree that these animals, frogs or toads, are associated with rain-making, as they are in ancient rock art and popular rituals still performed in modern northern Thailand.

During the nineteenth and twentieth centuries many were purchased and taken abroad and they appear in considerable numbers in museum

Sông Đà Đồng Sơn Drum. Guimet Museum, Paris.

collections. The four earliest drums, dated to the sixth century BCE, have four curved handles attached to the body. They vary in height from 53 to 63 cm and the tympana measure between 74 and 79 cm in diameter. There is a raised 'solar star' that radiates from its centre. Bands of images encircle the star with patterns similar to those on Phùng Nguyên pots,[49] and progress anti-clockwise. On the body of the drum there are drawings that include boats carrying men in feathered headdresses. Then there are rectangular indentations, elaborately framed in thick borders, with each frame bearing one or two images. Three of the early drums from Ngọc Lũ, Hoàng Hạ and Sông Đà were studied by French scholars Goloubew and Parmentier, among others. The fourth drum, found buried in 1982 in Cổ Loa outside Hanoi, suggests this may have been the mythical capital of Âu Lạc, ruled by An Dương Vương Thục Phán, a polity said to have seized power from the Hùng Kings in the third century BCE. Historians still await the discovery of a Rosetta Stone that will unlock the meaning of the drums. The bulbous part of the drums is assumed to be for resonance and the four handles for transporting them on bamboo poles.

Some of the central solar stars on the drums show ten to sixteen rays – possibly interpretable as the Hùng king and fifteen Lạc lords whose

Model of tribal Communal House. Gia Lai Plateau, Central Vietnam.

heraldic symbols may appear between the rays. The number may have varied like a mandala state with adhesions and secessions. Around the outer band of the tympanum fly majestic birds like stylized egrets – now called Lạc birds. On the Ngọc Lũ drum, there is an extra band of activities, showing a forest with animals around the villages.

Taylor suggests that the men on boats depicted on the drums were envoys sent from the rulers 'to collect rice and other goods, armed with crossbows, spears, swords, and their distinctive bronze pediform axes. They proclaimed their arrival by beating their bronze drums to summon the people to submit what was due.'[50] They could also be warriors travelling out to sea in boats to explore or wage war as some wield axes and point arrows in an aggressive manner. The circular direction of the images may suggest passage through the lunar year. The drums were presumably beaten whenever the authority of the king was invoked, whether in celebration or war. The Đông Sơn drum may therefore be the symbol of the king's authority that is entrusted to the Lạc lord as a snapshot of the realm when the honour is awarded. Life in the Văn Lang realm, as hinted at in the designs of the four earliest drums, resembles that recorded in the primary historical accounts. People apparently lived in houses on stilts, with roofs made of shaped bamboo poles decorated with wooden strips, and covered by woven materials. Similar roofs are still in use in the Vietnamese highlands. On the drums people pound rice in mortars and dignitaries wear feathers on their heads and hold ploughs or hoes, as well as swords, lances and axes. They are accompanied by musicians playing instruments including a bamboo pipe like the *khèn* that is still in use in the highlands. The absence of forest on the Hoàng Hạ, Sông Đà and Cổ Loa drums may indicate that agriculture and domestication of animals was spreading. This may also be implied in the pig in one of the houses on the Cổ Loa drum and a bird and a goat in a house of the Sông Đà drum. They show no sign of forest.

The Việt language as we know it today evolved during the long encounter with Chinese and today remains peppered with Chinese imports. During a thousand years of constant interaction with the empire to the north, speakers of Han-Tang Chinese were always present in numbers in the Red River basin. As immigrants or appointed officials, their vocabulary over time developed into a regional version of Chinese and they would have also spoken the Proto-Việt-Mường of the other locals. 'During the ten centuries of imperial rule, many Chinese words were borrowed into spoken Proto-Viet-Muong and we can reasonably conjecture that there was a significant high level of bilingualism among primary speakers of both languages.'[51] From the tenth century on, when

Đông Sơn drum tympanum.

Bronze-making equipment, Museum of Ethnic Minorities, North Vietnam.

the intimate internal links with China had faded, the regional combination of local Chinese and Proto-Việt-Mường fused with the latter absorbing 'a critical mass of vocabulary and grammatical particles, thus giving rise to the Vietnamese language as we categorize it today'. The Chinese tones stayed for good but were pronounced in a different way to reflect local words.

There was no writing in the mythical 'Hùng Vương' dynasties but there are 'cartouches' on drums dated later than the four primary ones which could contain still-undeciphered pictograms. These dynasties are said in much later reconstructions to have been ended by Thục Phán of the Chinese Thục (Shu) dynasty, in the year 257 BCE. Thục Phán is said to have taken the royal title An Dương Vương and established his capital at Cổ Loa. The Cổ Loa drum is popularly thought to mark his coronation. Its discovery gave rise to a national conference in which scholars discovered an inscription near the bottom edge in a script which was said to be in early Chinese characters. The translation of the characters is disputed between Vietnamese and Japanese scholars; Vietnamese translations[52] read two obscure characters as 'Tây Vu' (Western Ou), the name of the realm led by Thục Phán, who is credited with creating the kingdom of Âu Lạc. In 2011, Japanese scholar Ba Hjo claimed these characters meant 'Việt Tộc' (Việt clan). Read either way, the inscription reads: 'Forty-eighth bronze drum of the Western Ou [or Việt clan]; weight: 281cân [c. 72 kg].'

In 1982 it was claimed that the inscription was a later addition under An Dương Vương or Zhao To (Triệu Đà in Vietnamese), a renegade Chinese general who defeated An Dương Vương and ruled Âu Lạc in 179 BCE. The numbering of the drum indicates an extended lineage.

Tribal pictogram book. Hà Giang province, Museum of Ethnic Minorities.

LATER LEGENDS OF AN DƯƠNG VƯƠNG AND THE KINGDOM OF ÂU LẠC

In the year 257 BCE Thục Phán, said to be a son of the late King of Shu (Ba Thục in Vietnamese), came from the north after several earlier attacks and conquered Văn Lang.[53] The archives say the Hùng king was too busy drinking when Thục Phán attacked. Although Thục Phán is claimed by some sources to be an historical figure, he remains obscure. The Vietnamese annals *Đại Việt Sử Ký Toàn Thư* say he came from the Ba Thục kingdom in Sichuan province, but nineteenth-century scholars considered this impossible.[54] More recently, it has been suggested that he was a remnant of the Shu (Thục) kingdom that was defeated by the Qin a century earlier. Vietnamese historians today suggest he moved south to today's Cao Bằng area close to the current border with China.[55] This area is to the northeast of the Văn Lang realm and is said to have belonged to the tribe Tây Âu (Vu) or Western Ou, one of the *bộ* submitted to the Hùng king.[56] According to this source, Thục Phán defeated the lord of the tribe and became the leader of *bộ* Tây Âu. When in the latter half of the second century BCE, the powerful army of Qin Si Huang came south and attacked southern China (to the north and northeast of Văn Lang), the Hùng king and the then leader of Tây Âu, Thục Phán stopped the Qin army from crossing into Văn Lang but it gained control of a large area of southern of China in Guangdong and Guangxi.[57]

After the Hùng king and Thục Phán proclaimed victory over the Qin army, Thục Phán became a hero among Lạc people, but the Hùng king, without a son, chose his son-in-law as successor, until Thục Phán advanced on Văn Lang with his army and the Hùng king accepted him instead. Thục Phán became An Dương Vương of Âu Lạc, the polity whose name betokens a merger of Tây Âu and Lạc Việt in 257 BCE, according to the reconstructions of the later Vietnamese annals.

CỔ LOA AND THE MAGICAL GOLDEN TURTLE

An Dương Vương is said to have named his capital Cổ Loa, north of today's Hanoi, in Đông Anh district across the Hồng River. According to legend he wanted to build a citadel with fortified walls running around the centre but the walls kept falling down. After three years he prayed to the spirit of the land and an old man appeared and told him to wait for his envoy. The next day a spirit called Kim Quy (golden turtle) appeared who showed An Dương Vương how to kill the bad spirit who damaged his walls. An Dương Vương then completed his citadel in half a month.[58] Kim Quy said goodbye to the king and gave him one of his claws as a parting gift for the protection of the citadel. An Dương Vương made a magic bow out of the turtle's claw and used it to keep his enemies at bay. The state was stable and well-defended by the magical bronze crossbows said to be capable of firing several arrows consecutively. The trigger was said to be the key to the bow and was described by its shape as a turtle's claw. The bow was the magic prop of An Dương Vương in the folklore of Trọng Thủy and Mỵ Châu. In this myth, Mỵ Châu was a princess and the only daughter of An Dương Vương. Trọng Thủy was the son of Zhao To, a Chinese general who marched south to conquer Âu Lạc. He made several attempts and called for truce with An Dương Vương, proposing that his son marry Mỵ Châu as a gesture of goodwill. Furthermore, Zhao To agreed to let his son stay behind in Âu Lạc, so that Mỵ Châu wouldn't have to leave her beloved father. In Cổ Loa Trọng Thủy found out about the magic bow and stole it for his father. With this Zhao To brought his army down to capture Âu Lạc. An Dương Vương rode to the sea on his horse with his daughter behind him. Little did he know that Mỵ Châu was plucking goose feathers from her jacket along the way so her husband could follow her. When An Dương Vương reached the water, he called the Golden Turtle for help. Kim Quy rose up and said his own daughter had betrayed him. An Dương Vương turned around, cut off her head on the beach with his sword and rode into the water, never to be seen again. When Trọng Thủy followed the goose feathers to get to the beach, he found Mỵ Châu's body and took it back to Cổ Loa, where he jumped into the royal well.[59] In Cổ Loa today there is a temple dedicated to Mỵ Châu, in which a headless statue of her is still venerated. Thousands of arrows possibly designed for An Dương Vương's 'magic' bows have been recorded in modern times. In 1959 when a new road was being built, workers uncovered an underground store of tens of thousands of bronze arrows ranging from 6 to 11 cm stacked neatly according to size. Modern Vietnamese archaeologists called them 'Cổ Loa arrows'.[60]

Cổ Loa citadel has been excavated several times. The outer earth rampart with three gates measures 8 km and is reinforced by stone and brick. The inner area was approached by five gates. All three levels are connected by canals and moats and the outer wall guarded by turrets.[61]

From 2004 to 2006 excavations took place in Cổ Loa and Vietnamese archaeologists discovered several layers of habitation at a new site within the innermost area. They found the oldest layer bore traces of stone and pottery that they dated to the Cổ Loa period. They found a number of ancient kilns thought to have been used to make bricks and tiles for the houses and palaces of the citadel. A foundry for arrowheads has been excavated at the southeast corner of the inner citadel. Here they

Cổ Loa arrows and crossbow, History Museum, Hanoi.

found traces of metal ore and cauldrons as well as thousands of stone arrow-moulds.[62]

In 210 BCE, Qin Shi Huang died and China became unstable in the north as the Qin empire collapsed. In southern China, the Qin army lost much of its control. The governor of today's Guangdong rebelled and his general Zhao To declared the area was the independent state of Nan Yueh (Nam Việt in Vietnamese) with himself as king.[63] Meanwhile the Han defeated their rivals in northern China and in 196 BCE sent an envoy to recognize Zhao To. But Zhao continued to defy the Han and seized today's Hunan province in 185 BCE. From his newly established seat of power, Zhao To tried to conquer the land of Âu Lạc several times but was repulsed. The later annals record the demise of An Dương Vương of Âu Lạc and the beginning of the reign of Zhao To in the year 179 BCE.

Some historians see Zhao To as an alien who imposed his rule on the pre-Việt. Others salute his opposition to the Han and his taking a local wife and adopting local customs.[64] He is therefore generally thought of as an early Red and Ma river delta king. Under Zhao To, the Lạc political system is presumed to have survived. 'Outside of a few imperial outposts, local rulers limited the influence of Han officials . . . The local organization of society and politics apparently remained fundamentally unchanged in the transfer from Hung kings to King An Duong to the kingdom of Nan Yue.'[65] The realm was grouped into two prefectures, Giao Chỉ and Cửu Chân, with Giao Chỉ as the Hồng River delta and Cửu Chân as the Mã river delta, further south. Both were governed by legates appointed by Zhao To with the duty of controlling the trade routes. Nan Yueh appeared most interested in the commercial value of the former Âu Lạc. The legates' administrative power centred on the market towns they resided in, while the Lạc people pursued their own affairs outside.

Zhao To is recorded as king of Nam Yueh and the former Âu Lạc for over 70 years until he died in 130 BCE. He was succeeded by his grandson Hu (Hồ), who had earlier been wrongly identified as the son of Trọng Thủy.[66] Hu ruled with the royal name Triệu Văn Vương and died in 124 BCE. His son Yung Chi (Anh Tế) became the new king of Nan Yueh with the royal name Triệu Minh Vương. This king had been sent earlier to live at the Han court as hostage and was married to a Han woman called Cù Thị in Vietnamese. She was later blamed for the demise of Nan Yueh. On Yung Chi's death in 112 BCE, Cù Thị became regent while her young son Hsing (Hưng) reigned as king Triệu Ai Vương. When an old lover of hers was sent as the Han envoy to her court, the Nan Yueh court split into hostile pro-Han and anti-Han camps. The anti-Han camp was led by the prime minister Lu Chia (Lữ Gia). Fearing for her life, Cù Thị appealed to the Han to take over the realm as their vassal. The Han court agreed and announced that they would begin to apply Han laws in Nan Yueh. Prime minister Lu Chia was considered a respectable figure at court with strong connections to former kings. His sons married into the royal family and he was described as a loyal Yueh. Lu Chia tried to talk the queen out of her plan. When the Han despatched an army of 2,000 men to Nan Yueh, Lu Chia rebelled and killed all the Han at court and the young king. Lu Chia then put the late king's half-brother on the throne as king Thuật Dương Vương. The Han army conquered Nan Yueh in 111 BCE.[67]

2

Han Province (111 BCE–40 CE)

In 111 BCE, on the orders of emperor Han Wu Di (141–87 BCE), general Lu Bode (Lộ-Bác-Đức) marched into Nan Yueh with an army of 100,000 men supported by many warships with deck castles (lou-chuan). They defeated prime minister Lữ Gia's army and burned their citadel to the ground at Phiên Ngung (today's Guangdong). Lữ Gia was captured and the citadel surrendered. Three *Lạc Hầu* (civil lords) came to offer Lu Bode 300 buffaloes, 1,000 measures of wine and population registers for their three districts of Giao Chỉ, Cửu Chân and Nhật Nam.[1] The offer of the population registers was the ultimate act of obedience as it meant that the victors could then use them to levy taxes. The offer was accepted and all three lords were appointed *Thái Thú* (prefects) and allowed to rule their districts. Lu Bode did not change established institutions and allowed the Lạc king and all the military chiefs to keep their positions.[2] China under the Han was expanding fast in all directions, westwards along the Silk Route to Rome, eastwards to conquer Korea and southwards to Nan Yueh. To control such a vast area, they adopted rule by proxies and aimed to finance this from the tribute of new vassal states. 'Tribute' was offered in pearl, ivory, rhino horn, spices, coral, pheasants, peacocks and their feathers. Much remained unchanged, but there was a distinct difference in status. Under the Han governor general and his prefects, the Lạc lords functioned as prefectural and district officials, rather than aristocratic rulers with supreme authority over their people.

The 'pacification' of Âu Lạc could not have been easy for the Han army. It was remote, its climate was 'poisonous' and the language was difficult. It 'took two, three levels of translation for the two sides to understand each other'.[3] Resistance no doubt continued in Âu Lạc, especially in the territory of the most powerful Lạc lord, whose territory was known as Tây Vu or Tây Âu that included the old capital Cổ Loa.[4] In 110 BCE, a year after the Han takeover, the king of Tây Vu was recorded as trying to declare independence from the Han, but was killed by a high-ranking

Trấn Quốc Pagoda. Hanoi, view from West Lake.

official or *quan lang* who was subsequently rewarded by Lu Bode with his title.[5] After the death of Tây Vu, the administrative machinery ran unchanged before Lu Bode separated Nan Yueh into nine prefectures under the control of a governor general (Thứ Sử) called Thạch Đái. Two of the prefectures were on Hainan islands, four were in today's Guangdong and Guangxi provinces, and the other three were in today's North Vietnam.[6] Thạch Đái was overall governor of all seven mainland prefectures.[7] Each prefecture was headed by a Han civil governor (Thái Thú), with a Han military deputy (Đô Úy). The Lạc lords controlled their districts under the supervision of these two officials.

In a census in the year 2 CE, the total population of the three prefectures in Vietnam, Giao Chỉ, Cửu Chân and Nhật Nam was recorded as about 1 million, in the *Hán Thư Địa Lý Chí* Han geographical record. Initially, the governor general ruled from an old administrative centre called Luy Lâu, in today's Bắc Ninh province, a short distance from Hanoi. This commercial centre had been created under Zhao To to control the trade routes. With the Han governor occupying Luy Lâu, Lu Bode set a military garrison at Mê Linh to guard the route into the mountains and, presumably, the way on to the Yunnan plateau. At the same time, he created smaller Han military outposts throughout the land. Little more is known about the first century under Han rule as Chinese records rarely mention Giao Chỉ, Cửu Chân and Nhật Nam again until the turn of the millennium.

LUY LÂU, THE GATEWAY SOUTH

Luy Lâu was a commercial centre under Zhao To and later the seat of power for the governor-general of Giao Chỉ prefecture. It was an important location for the Han and became the gateway to the delta area. One of the longest-lasting cultural influences at this time was Buddhism. Whether this influence came from China or from India direct is still unresolved by scholars. Buddhism was promoted by Indian and Chinese monks who came to build pagodas and monasteries at Luy Lâu in later centuries. It was reinforced much later by the Lý emperors of the eleventh century who made it the state religion. Buddhism rapidly absorbed indigenous elements and became a way of life grounded in morality and ethics, focused on the images of Buddha.

Luy Lâu became the largest Han commercial and political centre in Giao Chỉ and was a fortified citadel. Modern French and Vietnamese archaeologists claim to have located the Luy Lâu citadel at Lũng Khê village, Siêu Loại district, Bắc Ninh province, in an area that also housed some of the oldest pagodas of Vietnam. One of these was the Dâu pagoda (also called Pháp Vân pagoda), the first Buddhist monastery and original centre for the dissemination of Buddhism in Vietnam. Japanese archaeologists have questioned the location and are cooperating in excavating the site.[8] At the presumed site of Luy Lâu archaeologists have found a Han-Tang layer of artefacts from China, India and the Middle East, including ceramics, traces of kilns, bronze workshops and tombs.[9] Underneath this layer, the archaeologists found traces of 24 kilns and metal foundries with vats, ladles, moulds and copper ore. Japanese archaeologists concluded that the citadel at the site, whether Luy Lâu or not, was probably built in the second century CE and was active until the latter half of the fifth century CE. Some artefacts appear to be imported and bronze axes and spears were local.[10] An excavation of 1998 at Lũng Khê village remarkably yielded moulds once used for making bronze drums. One piece of mould was found in a layer of soil showing signs of high temperature combustion. The 8.5 × 8 × 6 cm piece is still imprinted with a section of the circular bands normally seen engraved on Đông Sơn Heger I type drums. In 2001 another piece of mould was found, bearing similar engraved images.

Vietnamese and Japanese archaeologists concurred on these pieces of mould being dated to between the second and fourth century, proving that bronze drums were still made in Vietnam during the Western Han occupation. Their status then is unknown but, according to Chinese records, by the year 42–3 CE, the Han general Ma Yuan abolished the authority of all Lạc lords and melted their drums to make a bronze horse, after putting down the uprising of the Trưng sisters of Mê Linh. Evidence from the site does not tally with the dates proposed for the moulds and this issue remains problematic.[11] Under the Western Han, the policy of ruling by proxy continued in Vietnam until the arrival of Hsi Kuang (Tích Quang), a new Giao Chỉ prefect in the first years of the Common Era. Chinese and Vietnamese annals describe him as an administrator who 'civilized' the Việt by making them wear Han clothes and shoes and adopt Han customs and manners. He and Jen Yen (Nhâm Diên), another prefect said to be his choice for Cửu Chân prefecture in the 25 CE, opened schools and enforced marriage rituals in Chinese style. Jen Yen was particularly zealous in his enforcement of Han style. He made local officials pay for the marriage expenses on behalf of those too poor to afford the cost and in one year 2,000 such marriages took place.[12] If we try to set aside the rhetoric of the Chinese and sinicized Vietnamese records, we may conclude that Hsi Kuang and Jen Yen pursued a policy of assimilation that was found acceptable to local lords and the people. The change in customs was also a result of a new exodus of Chinese into the delta region during a chaotic period in China when in 9 CE a high minister called Wang Mang usurped the Han throne. He was not a popular ruler and it was not long before he was overthrown by the Eastern Han in 23 CE, but during his tenure many Western Han officials and scholars moved south to take refuge in Giao Chỉ, where governor Teng Jang openly defied Wang Mang's rule and cut his ties with China.[13]

When the Eastern Han established themselves in China, Teng Jang and Hsi Kuang assumed their role as Han officials.[14] In 25 CE, the Eastern Han appointed Jen Yen as prefect in Cửu Chân, where Chinese and Vietnamese records indicate he was a popular administrator who persuaded many Việt to give up their traditional life of hunting and fishing and settle down to grow rice. One of the major changes under the Eastern Han was that the Han governor-general for Giao Chỉ remained in his post all year round, without being required to travel back annually to the capital to report. He sent an official instead.[15]

Han policy in the Việt zone changed in 34 CE with the appointment of Su Ting (Tô Định), a new prefect described as greedy and cruel even in Chinese records. He is said to have tied up Lạc lords with regulations. One such Lạc lord was Đặng Thi Sách, who ruled Chu Diên district and was married to Lady Trưng Trắc, a strong woman and daughter of a more powerful neighbouring Lạc lord of Mê Linh. According to Chinese records, Su Ting tried to restrain Thi Sách's power by limiting the system of autonomy. In Chu Diên and Mê Linh, the struggle against the Han prefect resulted in the death of Thi Sách. His death has been explained in several ways, according to Chinese and Vietnamese records. One says he plotted a coup with Lạc lords to overthrow Su Ting but the plot was discovered and Thi Sách killed. Another version says that Thi Sách was plotting to overthrow Han rule but the plot was discovered and the uprising went ahead prematurely, resulting in Thi Sách's death. His death became a trigger for rebellion in the year 40 CE, led by his wife Trưng Trắc and her sister Trưng Nhị. These sisters were to achieve heroic status in later Vietnamese accounts of the history for instigating the first armed revolt against Han rule. The uprising briefly forced the Han to withdraw from Vietnam.

3
Tutelage and Dissension (40–939)

TRƯNG SISTERS (*r.* 40–43 CE)

After a century and a half of schooling by the great Han civilization, the year 40 CE marked the first recorded uprising against it by two Lạc aristocratic sisters Trưng Trắc and Trưng Nhị of Mê Linh prefecture. The cause of the rebellion is given in much later Vietnamese historical accounts as the avenging of the death of Trưng Trắc's husband Đặng Thi Sách, who was killed by a cruel Han prefect Su Ting, who restricted the power of the Lạc lords. Prefect Su Ting arrived in 34 CE and tightened the rules. Trưng Trắc is described in Chinese records as a 'tough Giao Chỉ woman who did not cope well with the new restrictions'.[1] In late 40 CE she 'gathered her support from all Lạc lords and aristocrats in the land and marched toward Luy Lâu', the headquarters of the Han authority in Vietnam and the residence of the prefect Su Ting. The Chinese version quoted by Maspéro differs from the Vietnamese in that it says Thi Sách was alive and 'following behind Trưng Trắc' when the rebellion started. On this account he must have been killed in one of the ensuing battles rather than beforehand at the hands of Su Tinh.[2] Otherwise the Chinese and Vietnamese versions agree on the speed with which the revolution ignited.[3] Some 65 fortified garrisons were assaulted and Luy Lâu fell to the Việt. Su Ting and his Han officials fled by sea to Hainan.

Trưng Trắc proclaimed herself queen with her sister Trưng Nhị as her deputy. They established their capital at Mê Linh, their family seat.[4] One of her first acts was to abolish Han taxes for two years.[5] She ruled for just two years until the Han responded.

Early in 41 CE, the Han court appointed veteran general Ma Yuan (Mã Viện) to be the 'Wave-Calming General' (Phục Ba Tướng Quân) to restore Han order in Giao Chỉ and Cửu Chân.[6] Ma Yuan, 56, was an experienced general who had just suppressed a rebellion in An-hui. It took him a year to organize his expeditionary force of 8,000 troops and 12,000 militiamen in Guangdong.[7] In the spring of the year 42, following the plan of Lou Bode in 111 BCE, Ma Yuan first planned to board a fleet of 2,000 junks. He then found he did not have enough ships and switched to a land route. Chinese records say it proved to be an arduous journey through hostile territory with supplies coming in only on occasional ships.[8] Ma Yuan had to build roads and dig tunnels and was recorded as always in peril of landslides. 'Tens of thousands of labourers died', according to Chinese records.[9] Ma Yuan eventually reached Tây Vu, where he faced the Trưng army. He retreated to 'Lãng Bạc' lake[10] – possibly today's West Lake (Hồ Tây) in northwest Hanoi.[11] He faced major obstacles in the tropical climate. Like many Han officials, Ma Yuan complained, after his eventual victory, that 'it rained, the ground was flooded, foul vapours rose high in the air, carrying with it pestilential elements, and the heat was wicked. I even saw a bird trying to rise but fell back into the lake because of the poisonous vapour. I lay down and thought of my cousin's advice on the merit of a simple life and wondered how I could achieve it.'[12]

The Lạc lords and their militia showed no awareness of Ma Yuan's difficulties. To break the impasse, the Trưng sisters launched a disastrous all-out attack against Ma Yuan. Thousands of Việt were killed and the sisters had to retreat to Cấm Khê, a mountainous region to the southwest of Mê Linh, to regroup. The Việt militia deserted in droves 'because they thought a woman would not be able to fight against the Chinese', according to the Vietnamese annals. The war however was not immediately lost because the weather continued to take its toll on the Chinese army that was reduced by sickness.[13] It took another six months for Ma Yuan to reach Cấm Khê and finally defeat them. The Trưng sisters were captured and beheaded along with a thousand of their militia. The 20,000 people on the high ground were recorded as 'at last subdued'. The Vietnamese version of events is curtailed, saying only that the Trưng sisters were defeated in battle and died.[14] The current popular version says the Trưng sisters jumped into the Hát River and drowned when all was lost.

ASSIMILATION

After his victory at Mê Linh, Ma Yuan rested his troops before pursuing the remaining Lạc lords. He later cornered them at Cư Phong district in Cửu Chân, where they surrendered or were beheaded. The general erected two bronze columns to mark the limit of Han territory and abolished the title 'Lạc lord'. The sub-prefects became village chiefs. He then built fortified Chinese garrisons at important locations and divided the large Tây Vu prefecture into Phong Khê and Vọng Hải districts. A round, fortified citadel was constructed in Phong Khê and another in Vọng Hải. To increase his control at ground level he settled a number of his soldiers in villages, appropriating Lạc fields for them to farm. This was done under an order to dig irrigation ditches for those living in his walled garrisons.[15] Giao Chỉ became a place where 'the men worked the fields and attended to commerce and the women raised silkworms and wove cloth. Their manner and speech were mild and they were not ambitious. Visitors were treated with care, and offered betel nut to chew. These people ate pickled things and sea food.'[16] Although no extant document records this, Ma Yuan must have listed the 'tribute' the Việt people had to send to the Han court, for *An Nam Chí Lược* recorded two centuries later that after his departure 'all seven districts of Giao Chi transported their dues by boat.' *An Nam Chí Lược* also notes that the prefect Sĩ Nhiếp (Shi-xie) of Giao Chỉ sent his son with tribute to the Wu court. 'Every year without fail, he sent an embassy to China with a large amount of tribute that included spices, pearls, jade, coral, amber, peacocks, rhino horns, ivory and all manners of rare and valuable goods and fruits such as bananas and longhan.'

Ma Yuan left Giao Chỉ for China in 44 CE and was received like a hero in the Wu capital. Chinese records say he brought back considerable amounts of bronze, which was melted to make a bronze horse at Lu-Pan gate outside the capital.[17] He had already shown his love of bronze with the two pillars. Where did the bronze come from? Vietnamese accounts speak of Ma Yuan melting down the bronze drums of the Lạc people to erase their authority. Perhaps he made an inventory of all the bronze drums and other objects he confiscated during this time, and listed the Cổ Loa drum as number 48. This drum possibly escaped being melted by being buried where it was uncovered nearly two millennia later in 1982. Other drums and bronze objects from the period that French and Vietnamese archaeologists uncovered during the last century may also have been hidden by the Lạc lords. Ma Yuan left behind a Chinese system of direct administration through Han officials which governed the region for the next 140 years, until the Eastern Han lost control of China in 184. During this period, Giao Chỉ became a part of the Han maritime trading network that linked China with the Roman Empire via India. The Greek geographer Ptolemy in the second century mapped out the shipping routes, including the commercial centres along the coast of today's Vietnam. The presence of Roman coins bearing the image of Antoninus Pius at Oc Eo, in the lower Mekong, nearer the border with today's Cambodia, is evidence for East–West maritime trade during the Han dynasty in Vietnam.[18] In 166, a group of ambassadors from the court of Marcus Aurelius made a stopover in Giao Chỉ on their way to the Han court.[19] This so-called Nanhai trade through the South China Sea, known in Vietnam as Biển Đông, flourished and expanded into modern times.[20]

Along with the flow of trade, Indian influence began to seep into the ports along the coast of today's Vietnam, most notably at the stop-overs further south from Giao Chỉ and Cửu Chân in Nhật Nam prefecture and was especially strong in today's Quảng Trị-Thừa Thiên and Quảng Nam area. In a rebellion in 192 the son of a district official called Ou Lien (Khu Liên) killed the local Han representative and proclaimed him-self king of a new state. The Chinese later identified this as Lin Yi (Lâm Ấp), a predecessor of later Champa.

In 184 China descended into chaos as rival warlords led the state into the Three Kingdom Era. The three strongest warlords proclaimed themselves the emperors of Wu, Shu and Wei. All three were locked into a bloody contest that lasted until 263, when one by one they fell to the Jin. In Giao Chỉ and Cửu Chân, after 140 years of cohabitation between the Việt and two major waves of Chinese settlers during the Wang Mang era and after Ma Yuan's expedition, a new class began to emerge of edu-cated Việt-Han marriages. These Han-Việt opted for classical Chinese education to gain entry to the upper social echelon.[21] In a report to the Jin court, Đào Hoàng, who served as governor general of Giao Châu under both the Wu and the Jin, said 'customs are not uniform, languages are mutually unintelligible so that several levels of interpreters are needed to communicate'. Over time it is assumed that bilingualism spread, with Han Chinese reserved for the educated class and for special events.[22] Meanwhile, the local Mon-Khmer language of Proto-Việt-Mường became peppered with Han vocabulary and expressions, while the educated Han-Việt class spoke their own version of Chinese, with multiple expressions of Proto-Việt-Mường. Most prominent among the Han-Việt was the

Đoan Môn, the Main Gate of Old Thăng Long Imperial Citadel, Hanoi.

Chùa Thầy or Thầy Pagoda.

family of Shi-xie (Sĩ Nhiếp), whose members became the best known prefects of Giao Chỉ and Cửu Chân. After the Han fragmented in political turmoil, the administration of Giao Chỉ and Cửu Chân was firmly in the hands of Han-Việt officials. The prefect Shi-xie had a title that included the Chinese character Wang (king).

SHI-XIE (187–226 CE)

Shi-xie's ancestors arrived six generations back from Wen-Yang, in the state of Lu, during the Wang Mang era.[23] During the years 147–67 CE, his father Shi-Ci served as prefect for the Je Nan (Nhật Nam) district, the southernmost tract of land held by the Han. Shi-xie received a classical Chinese education and became the prefect of Giao Chỉ in 186 after the governor general Chu-Fu of Giao Chỉ was killed by rebels. Shi-xie chose Luy Lâu as his seat, and ruled in a 'kind and praiseworthy way, his humility well respected among his scholars and officials', according to his own biography. Shi-xie was supported by his younger brothers Shi-Yi (Sĩ Vỹ), Sĩ Nhất and Sĩ Vũ.[24] Sĩ Nhất was prefect of Hợp Phố, Sĩ Vũ was prefect of Nam Hải and Sĩ Vỹ was prefect of Cửu Chân. Together, the brothers had surpreme influence. Shi-xie's power has been described as majestic and awe-inspiring: 'Shi-xie ruled strongly in one corner of the world, whenever he went in and out (of his office/residence), orders were shouted, bells, drums and stone chimes were sounded, and the noise echoed far and wide. His horses and carriages took up entire roads, flanked by Hu (Indian or central Asian monks) who carried fragrant incense and the entourage was usually a few dozen strong. His wives and concubines travelled in curtained off carriages while his children rode by their sides, guarded by soldiers. Everybody was in awe, not even Zhao To could be compared to this spectacle.'[25] Under his leadership, Giao Chỉ was strong and relatively stable. In 203 he asked the Han emperor to upgrade Giao Chỉ prefecture to Giao Châu (province) and the request was accepted. From then on, Giao Chỉ was also known as Giao Châu and had the same status as other 'châu' in Han China.[26] Later on, the boundaries of Giao Châu encompassed all northern Việt prefectures. When the Han disintegrated, Shi-xie distanced himself from the warring lords in China. Giao Châu became a land of refuge for many who found themselves masterless and stateless during the fierce contest among the warlords. 'Hundreds of learned people came from China and took refuge with him.' In 210 Shi-xie decided for the Wu dynasty, which sent newly appointed governor general Bộ Chất to visit him in Giao Châu. Shi-xie paid lavish annual tribute to the Wu court and sent his son Khâm or Hâm as hostage. The tribute included thousands of valuable products like spices, fine fabrics, pearl, tortoise shell, rhino horn and ivory. He also sent longhan, bananas and coconut. His brother Shi-Yi sent hundreds of horses. Relations between Việts and Wu were good under Shi-xie. His son and his brother's son were given Wu titles and Shi-xie passed away in 226 at the age of 90, after 40 successful years as ruler of Giao Chỉ. His son, Shi-Hui (Sĩ Huy), succeeded him as prefect.

When the news of Shi-xie's death reached the Wu court, the Wu emperor decided to rearrange the boundaries of Giao Chỉ and Cửu Chân to establish two new prefectures. The area from Ho Pu (Hợp Phố) to the north went to Guangzhou and was headed by governor general Lu Tai (Lữ Đại). Southern Ho Pu became Giao Châu with Tai Liang (Đái Lương) as governor general. A third man, Chen Shi (Trần Thì) was sent to Giao Chỉ as the new prefect to replace Shi-xie. This new appointment triggered an internal conflict between Shi-Hui, who had taken over as prefect of Giao Chỉ when his father died, and some of his own officials. However, even when the disagreement was resolved, Shi-Hui found himself being confronted by the Wu army of Lu Tai, the new governor of Giao Châu. Hui surrendered and was beheaded along with five of his brothers. The remaining three Shi brothers submitted later and were pardoned as ordinary citizens. Two were later killed for obscure offences and the third died of illness.[27] Lu Tai then took his army to Cửu Chân to 'pacify' the prefecture, having killed tens of thousands of soldiers and civilians. The Wu emperor then restored Giao Châu as it was, with Lu Tai as governor general. Giao Châu under the Wu was considered calm until 248 when the next popular uprising occurred in Thanh Hóa and rapidly became a major event in Giao Châu; the uprising of Lady Triệu.

THE UPRISING OF BÀ TRIỆU (248 CE)

Like the Trưng sisters, Lady Triệu Thị Trinh is described in Chinese records as a rough and tough woman who was well-versed in martial-arts. It was said 'she had enormous breasts which she flipped over her shoulder in combat while riding atop an elephant'.[28] This description was resented even in the nineteenth century by the Nguyen royal chroniclers, but it remains embedded in Vietnamese folklore. Lady Triệu was born in Mount Nưa, Triệu Sơn district, Thanh Hóa. Some accounts say she killed her sister-in-law when she was nineteen and went to live in a cave, where she gathered an army 1,000 strong and practised for battle.[29] When her brother rose up against the local prefect, she came to help him and took over the leadership of the resistance when he was killed. Under her direction, the uprising spread from Cửu Chân to Giao Châu, arousing terror among Wu officials. The prefect of Giao Châu and many district officials were subsequently killed and the rest fled. Lady Triệu took over the country briefly but her army soon faced a large force from China under the leadership of Lu Yin (Lục Dận), a new governor general appointed by the Wu. Lu Yin arrived with 8,000 regular troops and after several months of fighting, the uprising was crushed and she died or was killed on Mount Tùng in Thanh Hóa. The Việt were again subjects of the Wu.

UNDER NANJING (248–589 CE)

During the 'Period of Disunity' (220–589), the Việt lands were a colony of a succession of dynasties. Having been governed by the Han and Wu for four centuries, they became a vassal to the Western Jin, who unified China from 265 to 317. But when China divided into Northern and Southern Dynasties (317–589), Giao Châu and Cửu Chân were subject to the Southern dynasties in Nanjing: the Eastern Jin (317–420), Liu Song (420–79), Southern Qi (479–502), Liang (502–57) and Chen (557–89). Although they paid tribute to Nanjing local governor generals, the prefects had free control of the Việt zone.

THE LÝ TRƯỜNG NHÂN UPRISING (468–85 CE)

Under the Song, of the Six Dynasties in Nanjing, local chief Lý Trường Nhân took advantage of a power vacuum left by the death of a Chinese governor in 468 and rose up, killing all Chinese officials and declaring himself governor general. He sent an embassy to Nanjing seeking official recognition, but the Song only accepted him as administrator. After his death his cousin Lý Thúc Hiến took over the administration of Giao Châu and rejected a newly appointed Chinese governor general. In 479 the Song were overpowered by the Qi (479–502), who appointed Lý Thúc Hiến governor general of Giao Châu. When he stopped sending tribute, the Qi despatched an expeditionary force. He offered twenty sets of silver hats adorned with peacock feathers, but these were rejected and Lý Thúc Hiến subsequently disappeared on the road to Nanjing, while a new Chinese governor took over Giao Châu.

During the next century, the volatile situation in China usually affected the Việt. When the Qi were ousted by the Liang (502–57), Lý Nguyên Khải in Giao Châu declared independence in 505. He was killed and Liang envoy Lý Tắc only pacified the region in 516. Little was known about Giao Châu for several decades after that date, until a major uprising in 541, led by Lý Bí, (or Lý Bôn), who proclaimed the Việt state of Vạn Xuân.[30]

LÝ BÍ AND THE EARLY LÝ (541–7 CE)

Lý Bí was born in Long Hưng district, Thái Bình and became a mandarin at the Liang court.[31] Taylor places his home district on the north side of the Hồng River in the shadow of Mount Tam Đảo.[32] Lý Bí is always portrayed as a Việt but he was in fact of Han origin. His ancestors left the late Western Han during the Wang Mang usurpation and settled in Giao Châu. After seven generations his family was seen as high-born locals, part of the Han-Việt class. When he led the uprising against the Liang, he was known as talented in civil and military affairs and was military overseer for Cửu Đức, a southern district in today's Hà Tĩnh province. Giao Châu was then ruled by the cruel governor Xiao Tzu (Tiêu Tư). Lý Bí allied himself with disaffected scholar Tinh Thiều, who had been refused a mandarin post because his family were not scholars. They won the backing of Phạm Tu, military chief of Chu Diên and marched on the Long Biên seat of the governor to proclaim the province's independence. Chinese governor general Xiao Tzu bribed his way out to Guangzhou.

Lý Bí first dealt with an army sent by the Liang in 542, then stopped an advance in the south by a Lin-Yi army, and in 544 declared the creation of the polity of Vạn Xuân (Ten-thousand Springs or Eternal Spring).[33] Lý Bí crowned himself king of Nam Việt (Nam Việt Đế), a name later shortened with inclusion of his name as Lý Nam Đế. Lý Nam Đế established a court of a hundred mandarins under prime-minister Triệu Túc, with civil mandarin Tinh Thiều and military mandarin Phạm Tu. Lý Nam Đế reigned over the state of Vạn Xuân under the royal title Thiên Đức (Heavenly Virtue). He created a separate monetary unit called Thiên Đức money and built the first national pagoda called Khai Quốc or Trấn Quốc (The Establishment of the Nation or Guarding the Nation). Relics of the old pagoda are still traceable on the bank of Hanoi's West Lake. Lý Nam Đế built a shrine to commemorate the uprising of Lady Triệu and awarded her a posthumous title that made her the Heroic First Lady.[34]

The state of peace under Lý Nam Đế lasted only a year before the Liang sent an army. In 545, having consolidated their own affairs, the Liang again despatched an army to Giao Châu, this time headed by a newly appointed governor general for Giao Châu called Yang Biao (Dương Thiêu), and a military commander Chen Ba-xian (Trần Bá Tiên). This strong force was supported by another army under the governor Xiao Bo (Tiêu Bột) of Ting, an area in today's Guangxi. The combined Liang army spearheaded by Chen Ba-xian entered Giao Châu near the end of the summer of 545 and was confronted by Lý Nam Đế's army of 30,000 men on the Hồng River plain.[35] The Lý army lost the battle of Chu Diên and was defeated again in today's Hanoi area. The king took his army to Gia Ninh Citadel, his stronghold at the head of the Hồng River plain. The Liang army was recorded as pursuing him there and laying siege to the citadel.[36] Gia Ninh eventually fell to the Liang in the spring of 546. Lý Nam Đế withdrew into the mountains and took refuge with a Lao tribe. Meanwhile, the Liang army under Chen Ba-xian made camp by Gia Ninh, across the river. The situation dramatically changed when Lý Nam Đế brought his army of 20,000 men, reinforced by soldiers of the Lao people, to camp beside a natural reservoir called Điển Triệt lake. The Liang army camped on the opposite shore and 'watched in awe as the Việt army built so many boats they covered the surface of the lake'. As a natural reservoir connected to a river, the lake water rose and ebbed with the river tide. At high water one night, Chen Ba-xian launched his attack against the Việt army. Lý Nam Đế's army was routed. He took refuge in a cave and ordered his young military commander Triệu Quang Phục to take over the defence of the country on the Hồng River plain while he himself regrouped in the mountains. During 547 Triệu Quang Phục and his 20,000-strong army fought several battles with Chen Ba-xian without either side gaining the upper hand. However, to avoid confronting the large Chinese army head-on, Triệu Quang Phục retreated to a swamp area in Chu Diên and resorted to guerrilla attacks by night. His success in keeping the Liang army of Chen Ba-xian at bay has been attributed to the celestial power of a dragon claw which he attached to his hat whenever he went into combat with the Liang army. According to popular belief, he was blessed with this claw by the power of heaven which appeared to him in the guise of a legendary figure Chử Đồng Tử, who was once worshipped at the site. The war on the Hồng River plain continued inconclusively until the spring of 548 when Lý Nam Đế died at his refuge. His death was said in Vietnamese accounts to be by natural causes.[37] However Chinese sources, picked up in the pro-Chinese Vietnamese primary historical book *An Nam Chí Lược*, say that he was killed by the Lao of Khuất Liệu and his head sent to the Chinese side.[38] On hearing the news of his death, Triệu Quang Phục proclaimed himself Triệu Việt Vương (The Triệu King of the Việt).

When Lý Bôn died in the mountains, his elder brother, assisted by a Lý general, escaped to Cửu Chân further south and lay siege to a citadel in Ái Châu but they were defeated by the Liang army.[39] The brother Lý Thiên Bảo and general Lý Phật Tử took what was left of their army to the Lao territory and there established a kingdom called Dã Năng. Lý Thiên Bảo proclaimed himself king Đào Lăng Vương and died in 555 without issue, leaving the kingdom in the hands of Lý Phật Tử.

The political situation in China had a direct bearing on the Việt country during this period. In 550, while the war was still inconclusive in Giao Châu, the Liang recalled Chen Ba-xian to deal with trouble at court. When he left Triệu Quang Phục engaged and defeated the Liang army and entered Long Biên victoriously, to begin a new era as king of the Việt.[40]

TRIỆU VIỆT VƯƠNG (*r.* 548–70 CE)

Under Triệu Việt Vương the Việt people were independent for 23 years, yet it is one of the most obscure periods in their history, perhaps because he was not mentioned in Chinese sources and Việt records are lost or confiscated. All we know of this king is that he was much liked and that when he died the people built a temple to honour him.

LÝ PHẬT TỬ - HẬU LÝ NAM ĐẾ (*r.* 571–602 CE)

When Đào Lăng Vương died in 555 Lý Phật Tử took over Dã Năng and marched his army down to the Hồng River plain to challenge Triệu Việt Vương. After several inconclusive battles, Lý Phật Tử asked for a truce. Triệu Việt Vương accepted that Lý Phật Tử was 'a legitimate kinsman of the late king Lý Nam Đế (Lý Bôn), which gave him power over the land to the west of the country', while he ruled in Long Biên.[41] Lý Phật Tử settled in this area and placed his power centre at a citadel alled Ô Diên. The families of Lý Phật Tử and Triệu Việt Vương became close when Lý Phật Tử proposed for his son Nhã Lang to marry a daughter of Triệu Việt Vương called lady Cảo Nương. Nhã Lang stayed with his wife's family so that she wouldn't have to leave her beloved father to follow him home, as required by the Việt custom. The records say that, as in the legend, in 570 Nhã Lang stole the dragon claw from Triệu Việt Vương and gave it to his own father. Lý Phật Tử then launched an attack against Triệu Việt Vương, who lost because he no longer had the celestial power of the claw. He ran away and disappeared into the sea at Đại Nha bay, where a temple was later constructed for him.

Lý Phật Tử became sole king of both regions and ruled under the title of Hậu Lý Nam Đế (Later Lý king of the South) with residence in Phong Châu, the traditional aristocratic land under the Hùng kings. He assigned his nephew Lý Đại Quyền to Long Biên and general Lý Phổ Đỉnh to Ô Diên. Hậu Lý Nam Đế ruled until 602, another long period of 32 years of independence. Little is known about his rule except that he was a strong promoter of Buddhism. His name 'Phật Tử' indicates devotion to the Buddha.[42] The sixth century was a particularly favourable time for Buddhism for the Việt and Chinese peoples. When its popularity grew among the Việt the Zen sect was dominant. Vinitaruci, who came from India then China in 580, resided in the Dâu (or Pháp Vân) pagoda in Luy Lâu, the old commercial centre of Giao Chỉ under the Han. Luy Lâu has always known a strong Buddhist presence, with 20 pagodas and 500 monks. The monks had managed to translate fifteen sets of sutra by the time Vinitaruci arrived.[43] Vinitaruci translated sutras under the direct patronage of king Hậu Lý Nam Đế.[44]

The end of the sixth century marked the arrival of the Sui dynasty (589–618), which defeated the Northern dynasty in 581 and the Southern in 589. In the south of China, the Sui took over from the Chen, whose founder was Chen Ba-Xian, the Liang general who had battled with both Lý Bôn and Triệu Quang Phục before returning to China to deal with strife at court. The Chen had left both Triệu Việt Vương and Hậu Lý Nam Đế in peace for 55 years.

One Pillar Pagoda, Chùa Một Cột.

By 601 the Sui had consolidated enough to look at former colonies. The Lý king was summoned to the Sui court but he asked for postponement. Meanwhile he transferred his capital to the old citadel of Cổ Loa, in the heart of Giao Châu, a move seen by the Sui as open rebellion. The following year a Sui army of 27 battalions led by general Liu Fang entered Việt territory through Yunnan. His army was met by 2,000 Việt troops, who were quickly defeated.[45] Liu Fang's army advanced on the Lý king's residence and asked him to surrender. Lý Phật Tử submitted and was taken to China, where he died. Liu Fang then killed all Việt generals who did not submit. The Việt territory was again under Chinese rule after 61 years of independence.

According to Chinese and Việt records, it took three years for Liu Fang to pacify Giao Châu. From 604 the Sui reorganized the Việt territory into three prefectures;[46] Giao Châu again became Giao Chỉ prefecture, its name under the Han, and the administrative centre was moved to Tống Bình, a location south of the Hồng River, in the vicinity of Hanoi.[47] The three prefectures were Giao Chỉ, on the Hồng River, Cửu Chân on the Mã River and Nhật Nam on the Cả River. The Việt population was given as 56,566 people in the Sui census, which probably did not include the highlanders.[48]

THE VIỆT UNDER THE SUI-TANG (618–938 CE)

Little else is known about the Việt territory under the Sui. In 605 however Sui general Liu Fang was sent to Lin-Yi to fight Cham king Sambhuvarman (Phạm-Chí in Vietnamese and Fan Chen in Chinese). He took away gold and royal gold funerary tablets. The Cham king and his family escaped to sea before returning to rebuild his capital and Liu Fang lost half his men to illness on their way back north. The Sui were not in power for long. The last Sui emperor Yang was judged extravagant in lifestyle and was deposed in 618 by the Li family, who captured Xian and founded the Tang.

The Việt colony was again at the whim of local Chinese officials. Sui governor Chiu Ho (Khâu Hòa) 'liked to travel to the limits of the land to collect valuables for himself' and 'Lin-Yi and others gave him gems, pearls, rhino horn and gold.'[49] When the Tang took over he was retained as administrator of Giao Châu. In 679 the Tang changed the name of the Việt territory to the Protectorate of An-Nam, the pacified south.[50] When the Tang imposed taxes the people had to pay land tax, labour tax and poll tax. On top of these the Việt also paid civil tax on their assets.[51] The Tang also required tributes in rare forest products and local handicrafts.

Court politics was full of disputes under the Tang and courtiers were often killed or severely punished. A frequent punishment was life in exile, or appointment to a protectorate like An-Nam.[52] Among highly educated Chinese officials sent to Giao Chỉ was Liu Yen-yu (Lưu-Diên-Hựu), who was appointed protector-general of Giao Chỉ after a court dispute.

49

REBELLIONS

In 687 the first anti-Tang uprising was recorded in An-Nam which Liu Yen-yu called a peasant revolt. Two local men Lý Tự Tiên and Đinh Kiến protested against the doubling of taxation. As set out under earlier Tang rules, people in border territories, the so-called 'barbarians', paid only half of the usual tax rate, but when Liu Yen-yu arrived in An-Nam, he levied full taxes on all. Liu Yen-yu killed Lý Tự Tiên and set off an even stronger reaction. Under Đinh Kiến, the Việt besieged Liu Yen-yu in his citadel Tử-Thành at Tống Bình and killed him. The Tang court sent the governor of Guangzhou and general Tao Xuan-Ching to An-Nam. They crushed the rebellion and killed Đinh Kiến.

THE MAI THÚC LOAN UPRISING (713–22 CE)

According to the New Book of Tang, in 713 a peasant called Mai Thúc Loan gathered a force of 30,000 men and seized the province.[53] Mai Thúc Loan became king and ruled under the popular title of Mai Hắc Đế (Mai Black emperor) because of his dark complexion. He built a citadel at Vạn An and traces of it can still be found in the province of Nghệ-An, near his tomb. He rallied support from 32 areas and solicited help from Champa, Zhenla and 'Chin-Lin', possibly the Malay peninsula. With their support he defeated the Tang protector-general and took over Giao Châu. He ruled An-Nam until 722 when the Tang sent down an army of 10,000 men to escort their appointed protector-general Kuang Chu-Ke to his new post. Mai Hắc Đế was killed along with many of his followers, 'their bodies piled as high as mountains.'[54]

THE PHÙNG HƯNG UPRISING (?–801 CE)

The Tang were a well-organized and prosperous regime and their golden age was under Emperor Tang Xuanzong. Early in the eighth century they replaced the conscript army with a professional one.[55] Gradually military governors began to challenge the power at the central court and the Tang suffered defeats from southern Manchuria to central Asia and Yunnan. The An Lushan rebellion in Manchuria in 755 was the biggest and although subdued it had lasting effects. After defeats by the kingdom of Nanzhao in Yunnan, the Tang adopted a defensive position and militarized border zones. In 758 An-Nam, the pacified south, became Trấn Nam, the 'guarded south'.[56] The Tang closed the southern trading port of Guangzhou after it was attacked and looted by Arab and Persian merchants who said Chinese officials were corrupt.[57] The port Tống Bình in An-Nam, today's Hanoi, replaced Guangzhou for a time.[58]

In 767 protector-general Chang Po-Yi began to build a new citadel that was less vulnerable to attacks. La Thành began to rise south of the Hồng River but just north of Tô Lịch River, roughly on the site that is today's Hanoi. The name La Thành meant a citadel with ramparts. It had 7-metre walls that were reinforced with a surrounding wall in 808.[59] In 768 the Tang changed the name the Protectorate back to An-Nam.[60] As the Tang were weakened, rebellions sprang up in China and An-Nam. Wealthy An-Nam village dignitary Phùng Hưng rebelled with his brother in 791 and ruled as king until 798. He was venerated as both father (Bố) and mother (Cái) by the people who called him fondly Bố Cái Đại Vương, the great father and mother king, and there is today a large statue dedicated to him in his home village, Đường Lâm. His son Phùng An succeeded him but within two years the Tang sent in a new protector. During the rest of the ninth century, there were some small uprisings in An-Nam but these were not reliably recorded. The Tang, meanwhile, consolidated their power in An-Nam by fortifying the citadel of La Thành in 808 under the protector-general Trương Chu. He built 300 ships to carry 25 soldiers and 23 rowers and rebuilt citadels in Hoan and Ái Châu after attacks by the Chams.

Following a period of severe food shortages, the Việt laid siege to the residence of the protector-general Vương Thức in 858, but their leaders were killed the next day.[61] Two years later Nanzhao troops were supported by the Việt in attacking Tang protector-general Lý Hộ, who fled.[62] It took a large army from China to retake An-Nam. Nanzhao did not give up its plans though and returned to attack in 863 when they captured the citadel, looted it and withdrew, leaving 2,000 men to administer the territory.[63] The Nanzhao force was said to have captured and killed 15,000 people. After some unsuccessful attempts to retake An-Nam during the year, the Tang organized an army in large ships commanded by general Gao Pian, who was appointed protector-general of An-Nam. The preparations took two years and Gao Pian fought several fierce battles before defeating the Nanzhao army at Nam Định, where tens of thousands were said to be killed in 866. The Tang emperor made Gao Pian military governor of Tĩnh Hải Trấn (the Peaceful Military Sea-Post), formerly An-Nam.[64]

Gao Pian stayed for nine carefully documented years. He recorded building roads, bridges, public inns, canals and dykes throughout the territory. He mapped the land, recorded taxes paid and documented all soldiers. He was recorded as having travelled all over the Việt territory to inspect and to view the lie of the land. Popular accounts record him as a skilful magician and Feng-Shui expert.[65] His works included re-building La Thành and the clearing of a maritime route from Guangzhou to the Việt territory. He fortified La Thành citadel, raising the ramparts and adding turrets, giving it the newer and grander name of Đại La Thành, later shortened to become Đại La. Thousands of houses were built inside the citadel for soldiers and it housed officials, the treasury and the rice depot.[66] Another major work was clearing the maritime passage from Guangzhou to An-Nam, which was full of dangerous sub-merged rocks. In 868 he mobilized a force of a thousand soldiers and sailors.[67] 'On the fourth moon, people took up their pick-axes and spades to begin the task of breaking up the rocks.' Most rocks were cleared in a month but two huge boulders resisted all efforts until they were broken by 'mighty loud thunderbolts from the sky'. The cleared route was called 'Thiên Uy', Power from Heaven. This was presumably a romantic descrip-tion of Tang explosives, for by the seventh and eighth centuries the Tang had invented gunpowder and created fireworks and other awe-inspiring spectacles. There has yet been no record of them using explosives during this period but by the end of the ninth century they clearly used gun-powder in warfare. Gao Pian thus restored the economy after several years of war. He is lauded for encouraging farmers to rework abandoned fields, although the Việt account says these fields belonged to his own soldiers, who had been rewarded with them after their victory over Nanzhao. The Việt people worked as their labourers and remained mostly destitute.[68] Two years after the clearing of the maritime route, a stele was erected to record the good works of Gao Pian in An-Nam.[69] In 875 he was recalled to China, leaving An-Nam to his grand-nephew Cao Tầm.

Tang China went into decline in 875 with wars in several regions. For nearly a decade, the country was ravaged by the Huang Chao rebel-lion. Renegade general Huang Chao looted Xian and proclaimed himself the emperor of Qi. The Tang emperor Xizong escaped to Sichuan. The death of Huang Chao in 884 did not improve the situation. Tang power eventually crumbled before the Later Liang in 907 and China fragmented into separate kingdoms in the Five Dynasties and Ten Kingdoms period of 52 years. The Việt territory was as usual left under governors who ruled as they pleased. While the Tang court was plunged into troubles, another uprising took place in the Việt territory and this time it heralded the hazy dawn of lasting independence.

THE DAWN OF INDEPENDENCE (906–38 CE)

In 906 a hitherto unmentioned individual named Khúc Thừa Dụ, from the wealthy Khúc family declared himself to be military governor and the Tang accepted this. The Khúc were a well-established family from Hồng Châu in today's Hải Dương province. Khúc Thừa Dụ is recorded as a kind man of mild nature who was much liked by the people. He died the next year, leaving his son Khúc Hạo as military governor. He was quickly affirmed by the Tang.[70] Khúc Hạo thus came to power in the year the Tang lost their power to the Later Liang. During the ensuing political disruption in China, Khúc Hạo administered the Việt territory independently as he was recorded as 'reorganising the territory into regions, provinces, districts and villages'. He appointed chiefs and officials, established a population register and exempted the people from labour tax. In other words, he had total authority over the territory even though, in name, he was an official appointed by the Tang. It was a peaceful period,[71] but the Later Liang soon appointed a new governor for Guangzhou, Liu Yin (Lưu Ẩn), who was also given an extra title of 'pacifier king of the south'.[72] The two sides opposed each other but no direct confrontation took place during the lifetimes of Liu Yin and Khúc Hạo.

In 917 Liu Yin died and was succeeded by his brother Liu Yan, who promptly declared his own kingdom with the title Great Việt. He ruled from Guangzhou, whose name was later changed to Southern Han. This included Guangzhou, Guangxi, southern Fujian, Hainan island and, in name only at that stage, the Việt territory. Relations between the power in Guangzhou and the Việt ruler Khúc Hạo were still cordial for Khúc Hạo sent his son Khúc Thừa Mỹ to congratulate the new emperor Liu Yan in Guangzhou.

Khúc Hạo died in the same year and his son Khúc Thừa Mỹ became the new military governor of the Việt territory; but instead of paying tribute to the Southern Han, he turned to the Later Liang to ask for affirmation which it was granted. This insult to the Southern Han was duly recorded and as soon as the Later Liang fell in 923 the Southern Han sent general Lý Khắc Chính to the Việt territory. Khúc Thừa Mỹ was captured and taken to Guangzhou and a Han military governor was appointed for the Việt territory. General Lý Khắc Chính stayed on to keep the peace.[73]

It was not long before the Việt again rose up against the Han in 931 under general Dương Đình Nghệ, who had served under Khúc Hạo. Chinese general Lý Khắc Chính was defeated and fled back to China and the Southern Han affirmed Dương Đình Nghệ as the new governor of the Việt territory. He was killed in 937 by his own officer Kiều Công Tiện who made himself governor. His action provoked a former officer, Ngô Quyền, to raise an army to attack him in 938.[74] Kiều Công Tiện called in the Southern Han, for An-Nam at the time was still a Chinese colony in name, and the emperor sent his son Hoằng Tháo. He led a naval force that entered An-Nam up the Bạch Đằng River, the main waterway connecting Hạ Long bay with the Hồng River. But by the time he arrived in An-Nam, Ngô Quyền had killed Kiều Công Tiện and awaited him. Ngô Quyền decided on a simple but effective tactic. He ordered his troops to drive stout stakes onto the bed of Bạch Đằng River and set up an ambush. The high tide covered the stakes and Hoằng Tháo entered the river without any suspicion. Ngô Quyền's army came out in small boats to confront Hoằng Tháo and lured the big Chinese vessels into the staked area. When the tide ebbed the smaller Việt boats escaped into the reeds while the heavy Chinese ships were left stranded on the stakes. In a subsequent battle Hoằng Tháo was captured and killed. The Chinese armada was routed and Ngô Quyền claimed victory. In the spring of 939 Ngô Quyền proclaimed himself king of the Việt and launched the Ngô dynasty and a lasting independence of the Việt.[75]

CONSEQUENCES OF CHINESE RULE

After ten centuries of Chinese tutelage from the second century BCE to 939 CE, the cities of the delta absorbed massive transfers of Chinese customs and practices from a stream of sophisticated immigrants. They brought Chinese political theories, social organization, bureaucratic practices and religious beliefs.[76] The urban population was all but Chinese yet the new isolation from China gradually led to an end to bilingualism and a fusion of the Han-Tang language with the indigenous Proto-Việt-Mường of the countryside. The hybrid language, written in demotic characters not readable by Chinese, made for growing and distinct differences from China. Only at the official level was the bilingualism maintained, for classical literary Chinese was the medium of officialdom as late as 1919.

The remoteness of Giao province was the second factor making for distinctness. Many generations of Chinese settling in this territory had brought their own way of life, language and customs. Taylor says of this period: 'During this millennium, these people were eventually cut off from the north and gradually faded into the local population through a process of mutual absorption that produced what we call Vietnamese.'[77] Nguyễn Thế Anh expresses a similar view with: 'The people who lived in the Red River plain before this time and those who lived there after this time would surely be unrecognizable and unintelligible to each other.' The Việt form of Buddhism is an eloquent example of the fusion. The temples and towers of Giao Buddhist complexes resemble the architectural forms Buddhist architecture created during its transmission through China and they housed a similar pantheon of deities. Yet the names and functions of the Bodhisattvas change and some cults have deep roots in Cham Brahmanical deities and forms that were inspired local forms of deities transferred direct from India.

Throughout the Chinese province period, the Han-Việt residents periodically rebelled in armed uprisings that resulted in brief periods of self-rule. The international awareness of the distant Chinese capital inculcated an abiding international outlook. As Taylor says, 'only a slave can know its master'.[78] This awareness helped forge a tenacity that, over time, developed into a powerful nationalism.

By the tenth century, the cities of the Hồng River plain were culturally far removed from the indigenous inhabitants of the mountains, who lived and dressed in the manner known among the ethnic minorities of northern Vietnam today.

4

Independence

THE NGÔ DYNASTY (939–65 CE)

The arrival of Ngô Quyền seemed to inject new vigour into the Việt that was expressed in their ceramics, literature and religious and political evolution. Their independence brought a protracted ambivalent relationship with China, and harsh lessons in self-government. Ngô Quyền was a nobleman from Đường Lâm, a son-in-law of Dương Đình Nghệ (r. 931–7) and a general who governed the southern province of Ái Châu. After his victory over the Southern Han navy, he proclaimed himself king and chose as his capital the old Cổ Loa citadel, across the river from La-Thành. Evidently he did not want to associate himself with the Chinese by using their La-Thành citadel. The battle of Bạch Đằng, when Ngô Quyền stopped the Han invasion of 938, became a national day that is celebrated today. Nevertheless, to govern the new realm Ngô Quyền followed the Chinese system with court, formal rites and mandarins. Soldiers who aided his victory were given land with joyful tributes, but the euphoric moment passed when he died in 944, aged 47, after just six years in power. His young son Ngô Xương Ngập was to succeed him under the guidance of his uncle Dương Tam Kha, the queen's brother. But the regent proclaimed himself king instead and adopted Ngô Xương Văn, the second son of Ngô Quyền and Ngô Xương Ngập escaped to Hải Dương province.[1] In 950 Ngô Xương Văn was put at the head of an army to crush a rebellion in Sơn Tây province, but he instead turned it to deposing Dương Tam Kha. Ngô Xương Văn reduced his disgraced uncle to citizen status, invited back his brother and they ruled together until Ngô Xương Ngập died in 954. Left alone, Ngô Xương Văn was weaker and the territory disintegrated into warlord fiefdoms. The treachery of regent Dương Tam Kha was rejected by many courtiers who left to establish their own self-ruled domains. Ten years later the surviving brother Ngô Xương Văn found himself alone among powerful lords, each with an army in the region around the capital. He sought recognition from the Southern Han and the Han emperor appointed him Tĩnh Hải Quân Tiết Độ Sứ, a military governor title. These Việt accounts are not corroborated in the Han family history, which says Han envoy Lý Dư was sent to An-Nam seeking submission from the Việt king but was stopped from entering Việt territory on the grounds that 'it was full of bandits'.[2] But this may be the result of confusing Việt names. 'Tribute' missions from vassals were an intricate dance and toe-crushing missteps were frequent, as analysed by O. W. Wolters.[3]

Ngô Xương Văn was killed in battling one of the warlords in Thái Bình in 965.[4] The civil war that ensued lasted two years and is known in Vietnamese history as the twelve warlord era. Đinh Bộ Lĩnh, one of these twelve, managed to reunify the country through both diplomatic alliances and military victories. He proclaimed himself Đại Thắng Vương (king of great victory) and inaugurated the Đinh dynasty.

THE DINH DYNASTY (967–80 CE)

Đinh Bộ Lĩnh was a son of Đinh Công Trứ, another official who served under Dương Đình Nghệ as acting prefect of Hoan Châu, and later, under Ngô Quyền in the same capacity. When his father died, Đinh Bộ Lĩnh was still a young child who followed his mother to Hoa Lư to live with his uncle. As a child he often played soldiers in the many caves of the area. Việt accounts say his skill in strategic warfare had been developed from this period of child play. Đinh Bộ Lĩnh called himself Đinh Tiên Hoàng Đế, later shortened to Đinh Tiên Hoàng, the first Đinh emperor. This title signalled equivalent rank with the Chinese emperor,[5] and he renamed the country Đại Cồ Việt, The Great Big Việt. His capital was in his home town Hoa Lư,[6] and was the first purpose-built capital of the Việt. It was built on a flat stretch of land intersected by rivers and surrounded by the complex of limestone caves he knew from childhood. It was a strategic choice as the location was easier to defend than La-Thành or Cổ Loa further north.

Hoa Lư was built as a group of three fortified citadels in a small valley surrounded by a circle of tall jagged mountains. Đinh Tiên Hoàng built ten sections of wall to bridge gaps between mountains and to complete a circle, leaving only narrow openings for entry and exit. The walls were made of packed earth and were several metres thick at the base. They were reinforced with brick on the inside to reach a height of 10 m,[7] and several sections still stand today. Water was channelled from rivers into moats around a series of citadels. The moats were also used as transport routes between the capital and the River Hoàng Long nearby. The main gate led to the East Citadel (Thành Đông) where the emperor held court. It was connected by a narrow passage to a similar structure

Đinh Lê Temple complex, Hoa Lu ancient capital.

called the West Citadel (Thành Tây) where the emperor resided with his family, mandarins and courtiers. The complex was protected by 3,000 imperial guards.

As a king of a dynasty born of civil war, Đinh Tiên Hoàng kept himself in a high state of readiness. His capital was a military base with defence posts on top of the surrounding mountains. The rivers around the capital were also seen as escape routes to the main river, Hoàng Long, and then out to sea. Guarding the south was the much larger South Citadel (Thành Nam), which was also shielded by mountains and brick walls. The most notable feature of this citadel was a web of waterways flowing through an intricate cave system known as Tràng An. This cave had been among the first used by the ancient Việt 25,000–5,000 years ago.[8] Mollusc shells, ancient hearths, pottery, animal bones and traces of the Hòa Bình and Đa Bút cultures were excavated recently.

Đinh Tiên Hoàng used the caves to store treasure, weapons and rice and to imprison people. In the citadels themselves, Đinh Tiên Hoàng built royal palaces, shrines and temples, established court orders, appointed five empresses and ruled firmly.[9] In 969 Đinh Tiên Hoàng appointed his eldest son Đinh Liễn as Nam Việt Vương – king of the Southern Việt.

In 1997–8 and 2009–10 Vietnamese and Finnish archaeologists uncovered in field campaigns the foundation of a tenth-century palace which included bricks stamped with Chinese characters saying 'for Đại

Việt citadels' and 'Jiangxi bricks'.[10] The archaeologists also found tube-shaped roof tiles, paving stones decorated with phoenix and lotus motifs, a number of stone columns with inscriptions from Buddhist sutras, ceramic objects and a number of farm animal figurines in terracotta.[11] These finds show that the first Việt imperial palaces were built in brick and wood and highly decorated with Chinese and Việt auspicious symbols such as phoenix hens and ducks. In 970 Đinh Tiên Hoàng named his reign 'Thái Bình' (Peace) and issued his own monetary unit, the Thái Bình coin. In the same year he sent his son Đinh Liễn as ambassador to the Song, who, by then, had unified China. It was a diplomatic move to show respect and an early step in intricate diplomacy. The Song rewarded Đinh Liễn with titles and then sent their envoys Cao Bảo-Tự and Vương-Ngạn-Phù on a courtesy visit to Hoa Lư.[12] Next he appointed four senior mandarins as 'the four pillars supporting the throne', and three religious leaders to promote Buddhism as the national religion. The highest ranking Buddhist leader was Khuông Việt đại sư, who served Đinh Tiên Hoàng and later the Lê emperor. The participation of Buddhist monks in the first independent court of the Việt attested the prominence of Buddhism in Việt society and these monks launched a tradition that became the model for Việt literati for many centuries. The ruler also reorganized the army into a pyramid command structure based on units of ten. The army comprised 10 divisions under Lê Hoàn, one of the 'four pillars' with the title Thập đạo tướng quân, similar to today's chief of the armed forces.[13] Đinh soldiers wore hats that were flat on top with brims flaring at the corners.

Đinh Tiên Hoàng regularly sent tribute to the Song such as gold, silk, ivory and rhino horn. Bilateral relations were cordial for the Song emperor sent an ambassador to Hoa Lư in 973 to award Đinh Tiên Hoàng the title of Giao Chỉ Quận Vương (king of Giao Chỉ prefecture).[14] This was a lower title than the imperial one he conferred on himself in 967. In doing so, the Song emperor implied that Đại Cồ Việt did not exist, only the Giao Chỉ prefecture mattered, but neither side expressed concern about the discrepancies. The realm was stable and foreign ships were trading in 976.[15] The peaceful years began to decline in 978 when Đinh Tiên Hoàng made his infant son Hạng Lang Crown Prince, which was greeted with dismay, for his first son Đinh Liễn had been treated as his successor. Đinh Liễn soon paid an assassin to kill the infant Hạng Lang. To atone for the deed and to pray for his half-brother's soul, he ordered 100 blocks of stone to be inscribed with Buddhist sutras and arranged in a hexagon shape by the Hoàng Long River, as described in an inscription found in 1986.[16] Within a year a courtier named Đỗ Thích killed both Đinh Liễn and Đinh Tiên Hoàng while 'the emperor was in a drunken stupor after a banquet'. He died at 56 after twelve years as the first Đinh emperor. The assassin Đỗ Thích was caught, beheaded and his body chopped into thousands of pieces. The throne was left to Đinh Toàn, a child of six, with army chief Lê Hoàn acting as regent and Đinh Toàn's mother Queen Dương Vân Nga as the power behind the throne. She held no other title but Lê Hoàn called himself Phó Vương (deputy king), presumably at the behest of the queen mother. To express their displeasure at this alliance, the three other 'pillars of the throne' launched a number of attacks against Lê Hoàn but all were defeated. One of the former twelve warlords, Ngô Nhật Khánh, allied himself with the Cham king at Đồng Dương (Paramesvaravarman I) for an attack on Hoa Lư. A Cham fleet of more than a thousand ships set sail for Hoa Lư but was battered by a storm before reaching the capital. The Cham king turned back and Ngô Nhật Khánh was drowned. This incident became a *casus belli* for the Việt and the Cham in subsequent years.

The Song meanwhile saw an opportunity to restore their Giao Chỉ prefecture and in 980 the emperor sent an army and a navy force to 'punish the Việt for breaking away from China' and for 'keeping a trained army to support self-rule'.[17] Some 30,000 men were gathered from Hubei and Hunan to launch a surprise attack on Hoa Lư from Guangxi.[18] On hearing of the imminent attack, the Hoa Lư court proposed appointing Lê Hoàn as emperor, to replace the child Đinh Toàn. The queen mother approved and Lê Hoàn became emperor of the Việt and launched the new Lê dynasty.[19] Đinh Toàn was demoted to the lowly royal title of Vệ Vương.

THE EARLY LÊ (980–1009 CE)

Lê Hoàn's first act as the first Lê emperor was to reorganize the army against the Song. Lê Hoàn replied to a Song emissary in the name of Đinh Toàn, and asked the Song to approve his own position as king. The Song emperor demanded that the queen mother, her son Đinh Toàn and the whole Đinh family come to China to pay their respects. It was effectively a declaration of war and there were no further diplomatic moves. The Song force set out from Guangxi on 981 and reached the Việt territory by land via Lạng Sơn province, and along the Hồng and Bạch Đằng Rivers. In the ensuing battles, the Việt navy lost 200 ships, but on land the Song army was routed at Chi Lăng pass on the border between Vietnam and China. More than half of the Song army was killed and two generals captured and taken back to Hoa Lư. The Song emperor recalled his army and severely punished the returning generals. Lê Hoàn was a national hero. He appointed five empresses the following year, including the mother of the child emperor Đinh Toàn whom he had deposed. Some later historians have denounced this move as betraying a cynical ploy concocted with the queen. Lê Hoàn sent an embassy to the Song court in the name of the former child emperor Đinh Toàn while he took an army south to Champa, to avenge the earlier Cham attempt on Hoa Lư and to punish the Chams for jailing his envoys.[20] The magnificent Buddhist complex at Đồng Dương was 'razed to the ground' and the temples looted. The Việt annals say the expeditionary force 'killed the Cham king and captured and took back to Hoa Lư hundreds of Cham court women and dancers and a Tibetan Buddhist monk'. This Cham king was named Bê Mi Thuế and reports of his death are inconclusive. The great Cham temple city of Đồng Dương was left in ruins. Today, this once magnificent complex only has one doorway standing following a B52 raid during the American war in Vietnam.

Over the next two years Lê Hoàn appointed eleven princes as regional rulers and began to build palaces in Hoa Lư, whose interior walls were said in the formal elegy to be lined with gold and silver and whose roof tiles were silver. A Song ambassador in 990 however found them 'small and lowly'. He mentioned a 'crudely built wooden tower at Lê Hoàn's residence' he was invited to inspect.[21] By 985 the Song seemed appeased by lavish tribute in gold and ivory and the Song emperor issued an edict praising Lê Hoàn as a good ruler of a strong state who 'did not forget to obey commands from China'. He compared Lê Hoàn to Shi Xie and Zhao To, the two best-known Chinese prefects appointed during their occupation of Giao Chỉ. They awarded Lê Hoàn the title 'ruler of the country' with 'his own command over the military'.[22] Relations between Hoa Lư and China remained cordial with envoys going back and forth almost annually. In 997 the Song finally accorded Lê Hoàn the royal title of Nam Bình Vương (king of the pacified south), omitting reference to Giao Chỉ,[23] in tacit acknowledgement of true independence.

Lê Hoàn campaigned constantly in the regions around Hoa Lư and in one expedition the former child emperor Đinh Toàn was killed. Lê Hoàn died in his palace bed in 1005 aged 65, after a 24-year reign as emperor of the independent Việt. He was given the posthumous title of Lê Đại Hành and left the throne to his third son, the Crown Prince Long Việt. His firstborn had died young, and the second son, for some reason, was overlooked. This appointment caused a rift at court, for three other sons of Lê Hoàn did not accept Long Việt as king. The four princes then fought for the crown in a bitter eight-month war, before Long Việt ascended the throne in 1005 for a three-day reign before being killed by his brother Lê Long Đĩnh. The assassination drove courtiers away, except for one mandarin, Lý Công Uẩn, who stayed to mourn the death of Long Việt. This noble act was recognized and he was subsequently appointed deputy commander of the imperial army. Lê Long Đĩnh became the new Lê emperor at the age of twenty, and ruled for four years that are known only for cruelty and depravity. He was wont to hold court lying down, which earned him the nickname Lê Ngọa Triều (the prone Lê emperor), and he soon turned to the Song for protection and adjusted court rituals and costume to match Song styles. In 1007 the Song awarded Lê Long Đĩnh the title Giao Chỉ Quận Vương, or military governor. The Song sent an ambassador to Hoa Lư to present Lê Long Đĩnh with the seal of this office and at the same time re-awarded his father Lê Hoàn the posthumous title of Nam Bình Vương. This implied that Lê Long Đĩnh was only an official of the Song and the title Nam Bình Vương was rendered obsolete by being awarded to a dead person. Lê Long Đĩnh died in 1009 leaving young children and no suitable successor.[24] The chief of the imperial guard, Lý Công Uẩn, immediately proclaimed himself emperor. The Lê dynasty thus ended with Lê Long Đĩnh after 29 years and three emperors, one of them for only three days.

The end of the Early Lê concluded an important period for the Việt, during which they experimented with their new independence, while king after king found a long Chinese shadow over the land. At the same time the Việt learned internal unity the hard way, as in the twelve warlord era. The later civil wars among brother princes served as another severe warning against disunity. The Việt remained under military threat from the Song in the north and Champa in the south. But they managed to resist both to retain their precious independence. By the time Lý Công Uẩn seized the throne the Việt had earned 70 years of self-rule and experienced bitter lessons about preparedness and war that the Lý were to take to heart in order to build one of the strongest dynasties in Việt history.

5
The Lý Dynasty (1009–1225)

LÝ THÁI TỔ (*r.* 1009–28 CE)

After three-quarters of a century of uncertain adjustment to their independence, the Việt gained one of the strongest emperors in their entire history who set the model for a series of powerful and successful monarchs. Under this monk-turned-general, Buddhism reached its apogee among the Việt. Lý Công Uẩn took the crown as emperor Lý Thái Tổ with confidence, promptly put behind him his unorthodox accession to power and his own obscure personal history. Vietnamese historians have tiptoed around the first Lý emperor's origins. The *Việt Sử Thông Giám Cương Mục* asks who was his father and what became of him? According to the Việt annals, his mother Phạm went to Tiêu Sơn pagoda in Hà Bắc province where she 'met and copulated with a spirit'. Lý Công Uẩn was born in 974 and lived with his single mother until he was three.[1] She then took him to Cổ Pháp pagoda and gave him for adoption to a monk named Lý Khánh Văn, who gave him his surname Lý. The child grew up among well-regarded monks of the highest educational standards. One of them was the most venerable Vạn Hạnh Thiền Sư, who had been consulted on state policies by Lê emperor Lê Đại Hành.

It is not known how Lý Công Uẩn joined the Lê court, but his propensity for military affairs was noted early.[2] He was judged to be loyal by the last Lê emperor when he stayed and wept over the corpse of the assassinated king Lê Long Việt, when most courtiers had fled. Lê Long Đĩnh eventually made him commander of the imperial guard. When Lê Long Đĩnh then died, Lý Công Uẩn brought 1,000 guards to the throne room and imperial court official Đào Cam Mộc quickly proposed that Lý Công Uẩn be made emperor instead of Lê Long Đĩnh's ten-year-old son. Lý Công Uẩn agreed because he said the venerable Vạn Hạnh Thiền Sư had just predicted this would happen. 'The whole court escorted him to the throne, had him sit and gave him the mandate of heaven as emperor.'

His first acts as emperor Lý Thái Tổ were to change the reign title to Thuận Thiên ('following the will of heaven') and announce a general amnesty. He elevated his unknown father to the royal title of Hiển Khánh Vương, and his mother to queen mother Minh Đức.[3] He gave the title crown prince to his son Lý Phật Mã and raised Đào Cam Mộc, the imperial courtier who called him to the throne, to the title of Nghĩa Tín Hầu and gave him his daughter in marriage. His six wives were made queens. The emperor was a devout Buddhist from his pagoda upbringing and all monks received new robes. Lý Thái Tổ's first year was busy. He sent two envoys to the Song court with tribute seeking acknowledgement. He offered money and silk to all elders of his village of Cổ Pháp on a visit and resolved to leave Hoa-Lư as it was too small. He travelled by boat from Hoa-Lư to the old citadel of the La-Thành (in modern Hanoi) that was fortified in the ninth century by Tang military governor Gao Pian (Cao Biền). On the journey Lý Thái Tổ famously had a vision of 'a golden dragon flying above the citadel' and was inspired to change its name to Thăng Long, or rising dragon.

The emperor moved to Thăng Long and began extensive reconstruction. The citadel was remodelled with three areas inside one other. The innermost circle was the Forbidden City reserved for the emperor and his family. The next layer was the Imperial Citadel of the court and the outer layer was for business. Four main gates opened through the outer walls, which were surrounded by moats and with the Hồng and Tô Lịch Rivers running along two sides. The infrastructure was damaged over the centuries but the layout remained the framework for constructions by his successors such as the Trần and the later Lê dynasties. He built palaces in the city for himself, his queens, princes and princesses, his concubines, and for court affairs. The throne room was in a palace called Càn Nguyên palace and each building was adorned by sets of steps flanked by stone dragon balustrades. Today little is left but foundations and broken phoenix heads, dragon balustrades, decorated flagstones, tiles and architectural ornaments in glazed ceramic have been uncovered in recent excavations. The palaces were completed in record time with the concubine quarters finished on the twelfth moon of early 1011. Taxes were suspended for three years and all old tax debts written off in celebration.

Relations with China were carefully maintained with ambassadors offering annual tribute in gold, silver, silk, rhino horn and ivory. The Song awarded Lý Thái Tổ the title of Giao-Chỉ quận-vương and the status of military governor. He sent envoys to ask the Song for a set of Buddhist canonical texts or *Đại-Tạng* (Tripitaka), and copies of the Song emperor's handwriting and both requests were granted. On each visit the Song awarded the Lý emperor a higher title. In 1017 he received the royal title of Nam Bình Vương, king of the pacified south that they had awarded to Lê Đại Hành, thus recognizing Lý Thái Tổ as a king, and not just an official of the Chinese court. He also maintained good contacts with both Champa and Zhenla (Cambodia), for both sent tribute several times. Usually such a record implied there was active trade being conducted between the parties. Tribute missions were a formal framework for trade.

In internal affairs Lý Thái Tổ issued copper coins, adjusted tax levels and gave his princes and princesses the right to collect taxes for themselves. He split the country into 24 regions called *lộ* and appointed princes to rule provinces. The army was kept strong and he established a Giảng Võ (military academy) west of the capital for training and theory. It has been often noted that wars were few and far between under the first Lý emperor, but there was conflict in outlying areas and in Champa. Lý Thái Tổ led his army against the ethnic Mán Cử Long in Ái Châu in 1011 and Diễn Châu in 1012.[4] He sent princes to fight rebels in 1013 and 1015 and against a Cham threat in 1020. Rebellions were suppressed in Phong Châu and Đô Kim in 1024.

As a devout Buddhist, Lý Thái Tổ started building pagodas, eight of them at his home village of Cổ Pháp, now upgraded to be *phủ* Thiên Đức (Grace from Heaven). He built two imperial pagodas, Hưng Thiên and Vạn Tuế, inside his new citadel and seven pagodas outside the city; and he issued an edict ordering the people to repair and renovate rundown pagodas throughout the country. Each pagoda received donations of land and peasant labourers for the fields. Buddhist monks became the new nobility under the Lý and many high-born men became monks and accessed the highest privileges. More than 1,000 men were ordained monks in the capital in 1016. Bronze temple bells were forged and Buddha images cast for the new pagodas. Almost every year there was some major Buddhist event in the land and some years saw several. The monk-turned-emperor regularly asked the Song for Buddhist sutras and other texts and built an octagonal building to house them in 1021.

Born under the Đinh and a military commander under the Lê, Lý Thái Tổ had a rich experience of strife at court to draw upon as he planned the independent future of the Việt state after a thousand years of submitting to external orders. He knew much about greed, resentment and the power struggles among the lords, princes and kings, and he began work on principles of government that would eventually issue as civil and criminal codes under a national Buddhist ethic. His Buddhism developed into a popular form in a mixture of two Zen schools – Vinitaruci's sixth-century model and 'wall meditation' initiated by the venerable Vô Ngôn Thông (759–826).[5] The Zen sects appealed to the Lý intellectuals through their 'literary and poetical bent'[6] and to the people through narratives coloured with local beliefs and superstition. Việt Zen Buddhism thus soon flowered into the distinctive form that is now re-emerging in strength in modern Vietnam.

Buddhism reached its Việt apogee under the Lý. Buddhist monks rose to eminent positions in Việt society and those also well-grounded in Confucian teaching advanced as mandarins and advisors to the emperor. This privileged status generated some cases of abuse where men profited from pretending to be monks and 'unclean' activities were sometimes recorded in pagodas.[7] The generous and costly gifts to pagodas bred resentment in some quarters and were challenged by fourteenth-century historian Lê Văn Hưu as 'wasteful and excessive extravagance paid for by the people' when 'more than half of the population became monks'. Buddhism flourished throughout the Lý dynasty and under the succeeding Trần dynasty. Many fine pagodas were built during this period and they have been constantly repaired to retain their original features. Lý Thái Tổ ruled for nineteen years and died aged 55 in 1028.[8] He laid firm foundations for an independent Việt state.

His death triggered conflict among his sons, three of whom, Đông Chinh, Dực Thánh and Vũ Đức Vương, rejected their father's choice of crown prince Lý Phật Mã and brought their troops to surround Càn Nguyên palace, threatening the crown prince, who barricaded himself inside. In the ensuing battle Vũ Đức Vương was killed while the other two royal princes escaped. The incident later became known as Loạn Tam Vương, 'three princes' rebellion.

EMPEROR LÝ THÁI TÔNG (r. 1028–54 CE)

Lý Phật Mã became the second and highly distinguished Lý emperor with the reign name Lý Thái Tông. The two defeated princes Đông Chinh and Dực Thánh asked to be pardoned and they were allowed to return to their districts with their titles intact. Emperor Lý Thái Tông appointed a genie to be his supreme spiritual guardian and to inspire the future loyalty of his family. He chose the spirit of Đồng Cổ (Bronze Drum), whom he awarded the title Thiên hạ minh chủ (wise master of the people). The spirit of Đồng Cổ came from a mountain of Thanh Hóa province, cradle of the ancient Đông Sơn bronze culture, south of today's Hanoi. Lý Thái Tông said he had met this spirit on his way to fight the Cham in 1020. The spirit appeared in a dream and helped him to victory. Now he built a temple in Thăng Long to the spirit after he warned the emperor of the princes' rebellion. His mix of powerful commitment to spirits and to fervent Buddhism, along with military prowess and administrative flair made him a representative genius of his people.

Once the spirit's temple was built, Lý Thái Tông set a new calendar of court rituals that called for a pledge of allegiance to the Đồng Cổ spirit. For the pledging ceremony the temple was festooned with flags and guarded by cavalry. Inside, swords and lances were hung before a spiritual tablet to reinforce the pledge. Each mandarin and royal family member entered the temple by the east entrance and solemnly declared that 'if they were not loyal to their family and their emperor, they would be struck dead by the spirit of Đồng Cổ'. They then drank blood in front of the tablet to pledge blood-brother loyalty to the emperor and each other. Those who evaded the pledge were to receive 50 strokes of the cane.[9] Among highly superstitious people such a ceremony was considered to be highly effective in maintaining discipline and restraint, as is shown in its continuing existence throughout the Lý and then through the Trần and Lê dynasties. The choice of the Đồng Cổ spirit as the disciplinary genie is interesting. The spirit of the bronze drum was perhaps thought powerful because it embodied the ancient and mysterious Việt craft for the creating of this high technology object that was to become a key attribute of chieftaincy throughout island Southeast Asia. Or perhaps he compared himself to the Hùng king whose supreme authority was engraved at the centre of the bronze drum for regional lords to pay homage to. Perhaps the pledge temple housed a bronze drum that is now lost? These are intriguing questions that we cannot at present answer.

Lý Thái Tông continued his father's infrastructural development with roads, bridges, state buildings and many more pagodas. He became a patriarch of the Vô Ngôn Thông school of Buddhism, which was then favoured over the Zen school of Vinitaruci.[10] He was an even more zealous Buddhist than his father and built pagodas and temples in the capital and throughout the land. In 1040 he ordered the sculpting of more than 1,000 Buddha statues and 10,000 painted images. He followed his father's model too in relations with the Song. Tribute was regularly sent, along with requests for more Buddhist texts and materials and the Song eventually awarded him the full royal title of Nam Bình Vương in 1038.[11]

Beyond the capital and the surrounding provinces, governed by princes, Lý Thái Tông entrusted security to alliances with ethnic minority chieftains along the borders and the western plateau beneath the Trường Sơn cordillera. They were offered princesses as wives like Princess Bình Dương, for example, who was married to the chief of Lạng district (today's Lạng Sơn) in 1029, Princess Kim Thành who was married to the chief of Phong district in 1036 and Princess Trường Ninh to the chief of Thượng Oai district. Đại Cồ Việt chieftains still however often acted independently and changed their allegiances, especially those on the borders with Yunnan and China. The Nùng were especially disruptive and effective in this. They were a large and wealthy clan thanks to an abundance of gold, silver and copper in their area, and they proclaimed themselves independent kings a number of times. The emperor felt the need to personally lead an expedition against chief Nùng Tồn Phúc in 1039. The chief was killed but one son, Nùng Trí Cao, and the chief's wife escaped to the border with China and reasserted their independence in 1041 in a state they called Đại Lịch. The emperor sent in the army and captured Nùng Trí Cao, who was brought to Thăng Long. The emperor recognized his qualities and pardoned and ennobled him, allowing him to govern his former border lands plus other districts, as an official of the Lý court. However seven years later Nùng Trí Cao rebelled again and repulsed a Lý army sent to suppress him. Nùng Trí Cao offered his allegiance to the Song but the Song refused. Over some years Nùng Trí Cao launched attacks against the Song in Guangxi and ransacked several towns. Only in 1053 was he killed by the people of Dali in Yunnan when he sought refuge there. The Nùng clan later played a pivotal role in relations between the Song and the Lý under Lý Thái Tông's successor.

Lý Thái Tông's major foreign excursion was his invasion of Champa in 1044. He was a seasoned military commander and he launched the invasion because the Chams had sent no tribute for sixteen years. Another reason for his expedition was that Cham kings were fighting each other and crossed into Việt territory for refuge in 1039–40. It is possible that the Lý emperor helped one of the kings return to power. Lý Thái Tông set out in a fleet of 100 ships and ransacked what the annals call the Cham capital of Phật Thệ. This could be a location in Thừa Thiên province[12] or Vijaya in today's Bình Định province.[13] They killed the Cham king Jaya Simhavarman II and took back 5,000 captives, 30 elephants and a large amount of gold and silver. Among the prisoners were the first and second Cham queens, many court dancers, musicians and craftsmen. On the way back, the Cham first queen committed suicide by jumping into the sea – an act highly praised by the emperor himself. The Cham courtiers were housed in a palace specially built for them in 1045 and the dancers and musicians became a national treasure of the Việt for several generations. The Cham craftsmen were drafted into building palaces and pagodas such as the Phật Tích in Bắc Ninh province and Chùa Thầy in today's Hanoi. Their trademarks in pagodas were bricks inscribed with Cham characters, Cham-Sanskrit words like *garuda* and *kinnari* (half bird, half female musician with a drum), some of which are visible today.[14] In subsequent Lý reigns the Chams built the national pagoda of Sùng Khánh Báo Thiên and its renowned Báo Thiên tower in Thăng Long.[15] The melancholy Cham music was later blamed for the Lý neglecting their state duties.[16]

Lý Thái Tông died aged 55 in 1054 after a long and remarkable reign of 26 years. He refined and bolstered Việt statecraft and the political system, moving beyond the long Chinese shadow of the past. Đại Cồ Việt grew to such strength that Lý Thái Tông even offered an army to help the Song in their struggle against Nùng Trí Cao in the 1050s. The Song accepted at first but then thought better of it.[17] Internally, the emperor showed fervent zeal in promoting his version of Buddhism throughout the country, and linked this to maintaining law and order. He regularly adjusted tax levels in line with the fortunes of the people and he prohibited the sale of men of working age into slavery. He is often recalled for building Thăng Long's iconic one-pillar pagoda in 1049. This shrine, supported above a lake on a broad single column, was destroyed and rebuilt several times in later centuries. It was blown up for the last time in 1954 on the day the French withdrew in defeat from Hanoi. This major tourist attraction beside the Ho Chi Minh museum in Hanoi today is a replica built in 1955. A second celebrated innovation was the creation in 1040 of an easy-access court of law manned by prince Khai Hoàng Vương. Anybody could take their dispute to the court directly and explain their problem. The first Vietnamese Penal Code was issued in 1042 and the promulgation of the Code was considered such a joyful occasion that the emperor felt he should change his reign title to Minh Đạo (bright path) and mint new Minh Đạo coins. To pre-empt potential dispute, Lý Thái Tông prudently named five-year-old prince Lý Nhật Tôn crown prince in the first year of his reign, presumably to avoid another bloody succession struggle.

EMPEROR LÝ THÁNH TÔNG (r. 1054–72 CE)

The first imperial act of prince Lý Nhật Tôn when he became emperor Lý Thánh Tông was to rename the country Đại Việt.[18] Aged 31 he came to the throne with a mature understanding of state affairs, learnt from assisting at his father's court assemblies. Lý Thánh Tông ruled confidently from the start and soon earned the reputation of a humane ruler who built on the foundations laid by his father and grandfather. Đại Việt is generally judged to have reached one of the high points of its political and military power in his reign and the next. The Lý expanded their political and commercial reach with territories won from both China and Champa, as recorded in the Việt annals, the Song-shi and Cham inscriptions.

Lý Thánh Tông was accorded the title of Giao Chỉ Quận Vương in 1055[19] and the Lý sent increasingly valuable tribute to the Song to foster relations. One gift caused a real stir. In 1057 they sent the Song a rare animal with single horn called a 'qilin', one of the four most revered fabled animals. The perplexed Song courtiers were deeply shocked, arguing that this mythical beast could be the heavenly intimation of the birth of someone very special, and if this came first to the Lý, accepting it would mean the Song admitting precedence to the Lý. Some argued that since no one had ever seen a qilin in the wild, if they accepted the animal and it turned out to be something other than a qilin, they would be seen to be fools. *Song-shi* devotes several paragraphs to recording the consternation at the Song court. The text says it looked 'like a buffalo with a horn sticking out of its nose'. It was a herbivore but 'one has to beat it with a stick to make it eat!' The Song emperor classified the baffling animal, now presumed to be a rhinoceros, as a 'strange' animal and declined to accept it, much to the disappointment of the Lý. The beast was housed in Guangzhou while the Song rewarded the Lý handsomely for it. The 'strange' animal later became the pretext for otherwise unexplained armed clashes between Chinese and Việt border authorities and the rejection of the animal introduced a new atmosphere of suspicion across the border. The Song province chief of Guangxi started mobilizing troops to fortify the area and in the spring of 1059 the Lý penetrated Guangxi, killed a Song official in a clash and withdrew. The Việt annals say the scuffle occurred 'because the Song were treacherous' and the *Song-shi* recorded a report by the district chief of Ung in Guangxi, saying the Việt attacked and captured people and valuables because he tried to prevent them from taking the 'strange' animal to the emperor's court and he wished to retaliate.[20] The dates of the reports do not tally and the Song said their emperor sent three officials to Guangxi to review the situation but decided against sending troops into Đại Việt. Border incidents persisted and the Song even considered asking Champa to lend a hand. But at the highest level bilateral relations were close and the Song awarded Lý Thánh Tông the full title of Nam Bình Vương in 1067. The reality on the ground, however, was changing somewhat as the Lý grew strong and the Song court weakened and border skirmishes were exacerbated by incidents with minorities. After their bitter experiences with Nùng Trí Cao, the Song realized they needed to be more vigilant. The Nùng continued to control the area to the northwest of today's Cao Bằng after the death of Nùng Trí Cao. In 1057 the chief Nùng Tông Đán and his son advanced into Guangxi territory but were persuaded to return home. In 1060 the Lý army crossed into Chinese territory and the Song offered a high reward to the Nùng for their support. Nùng Tông Đán and son went over to the Song in 1062 with their land; two years later, Lý Thánh Tông sent an envoy to demand their return. Local Song officials called for an attack on Đại Việt but the new Song emperor demurred and returned the two districts, restoring calm to the border. Chief Nùng Tông Đán however remained a Song official.

Foreign trade was growing. Champa sent tribute in 1055, followed by Cambodia in 1056 and Java in 1066.[21] Internally Lý Thánh Tông continued consolidating Đại Việt and propagating Buddhism but he added a sect called Thảo Đường that was exclusive to the royal family, the nobility and women. This modification of the traditional Việt Zen came after the Báo Thiên pagoda and tower were built by Chams in 1056. Two gold statues of Brahma and Indra were also placed in the new Thiên Phúc and Thiên Thọ pagodas. The sect was founded by the emperor Lý Thánh Tông himself to promote the teachings of a Chinese monk of the same name who was captured during his expedition into Champa in 1069.[22] Cham cultural influence continued to be apparent at court, for in 1060 the emperor ordered a translation of Cham songs and incorporated a cylindrical Cham drum called 'trống cơm' into court music exclusively performed by the royal grand ensemble.

The emperor however had a personal problem in that he was still without a son at the age of 40. It was resolved in a noteworthy way. The emperor was travelling with his entourage to various pagodas to pray for an heir when he came across a young woman in a mulberry field, who seemed 'not to care about the royal spectacle' and leaned back nonchalantly against a tree bearing orchids. Intrigued, he took her back to court and appointed her second-rank queen Ỷ Lan (leaning on orchid). To 'help her conceive', the emperor entrusted her to the care of courtier Nguyễn Bông who took her to pray in Thánh-Chúa pagoda outside Thăng Long. Here, the venerable monk of the pagoda 'taught Bông the magic of reincarnation' so that 'he could become Ỷ Lan's child'. The annals add only that the emperor ordered 'Bông to be beheaded after that'. Hoàng Xuân Hãn, a twentieth-century historian, interprets the incident in his book Lý Thường Kiệt as an erotic encounter between the courtier and Ỷ Lan, sanctioned by the head bonze, who said Bông had to die in order to be re-born in the womb of Ỷ Lan. He was beheaded in a field in front of the pagoda that is still known today as Bông field.[23] Thus Ỷ Lan gave birth to a boy in 1066 who was named crown prince Càn Đức the very next day. To celebrate the happy occasion, Lý Thánh Tông renamed his reign Long Chương Thiên Tự, ordered a general amnesty and elevated Ỷ Lan to the much higher position of Thần Phi, which could be translated as 'Goddess' or 'Genius queen'. She was even allowed to preside over state affairs when Lý Thánh Tông went to fight in Champa. Ỷ Lan became the second most important lady at Lý Thánh Tông's court, behind only the official queen – a position she quickly reversed as soon as her son was crowned emperor Lý Càn Đức. During his reign Ỷ Lan became the power behind the throne and the principle decision maker in state affairs. She was the chief benefactor and builder of many pagodas in the land and she was made the subject of a chapter in the important Buddhist historical account *Thiền Uyển Tập Anh,* written during the subsequent Trần dynasty. An area containing twenty pagodas outside Hanoi is still dedicated to her name.

Another cultural change in this period was a resurgence of Confucian teaching in Thăng Long. A temple called Văn Miếu was built and dedicated to Confucius to the south of the Thăng Long citadel in 1070. This Temple of Literature, one of Hanoi's major tourist attractions today, would evolve into the first Việt university. His statue and that of the four sages Yan Hui, Zengzi, Zisi and Mencius Duke of Zhou, and their 72 best students, were erected on stone altars for year-round veneration. The crown prince was sent to study at this temple, which was renovated several times under the Trần and still bears many original features.

Lý Thánh Tông's reign is best known for the victorious campaign he led personally in Champa in 1069. His general Lý Thường Kiệt was one of the most famous generals in the country's history. The general became a eunuch under emperor Lý Thái Tông[24] and served the Lý court for 51 years under three emperors. Under him the Lý army won victories in Champa and in China, accumulating territory to Đại Việt in both. The devastating campaign recorded by the Việt annals in Champa is corroborated in Cham temple inscriptions.[25] Lý Thánh Tông captured the Cham king Rudravarman III who was later released in exchange for three provinces. The Việt campaign lasted four months and occupied the three *châu*, Địa Lý, Ma Linh and Bố Chính, a swathe of land running from today's Quảng Bình to north of Quảng Trị – effectively the Cham kingdom of Indrapura in Cham inscriptions. Lý Thánh Tông returned to Thăng Long victorious and completed the Temple of Literature Văn Miếu before his death, leaving the throne to his son Lý Càn Đức who, at the age of six, succeeded as emperor Lý Nhân Tông.[26]

LÝ NHÂN TÔNG (r. 1072–1127 CE)

All state affairs were held in the hands of his mother, queen Ỷ Lan, now elevated to the rank of queen mother, the official regent Lý Đạo Thành and general Lý Thường Kiệt. Đại Việt reached full maturity as a political power in the region, thanks to the wise leadership of the regent and the powerful army under Lý Thường Kiệt. It was another eventful period, marked by a major war with China and more conflicts with Champa.

The victory over Champa in 1069 drew the military strength of Đại Việt towards the south, a fact immediately detected by the shrewd Wang Anshi, new chief minister of the Song court.[27] Lý Thánh Tông's death in 1072 also left the Lý court exposed to power struggles – one between queen mother Ỷ Lan and the first former queen, and the other between

Drum Pavilion, Temple of Literature, Hanoi.

regent Lý Đạo Thành and general Lý Thường Kiệt, who did not see eye to eye on a number of state matters. The outcome was quickly decided with Ỷ Lan and Lý Thường Kiệt the victors. The former first queen was imprisoned in Thượng Dương palace and put to death with 76 former concubines and palace maids, whose bodies were buried at the tomb of the late emperor. Regent Lý Đạo Thành was exiled to Nghệ An border province, before being restored at court as 'Thái phó Bình chương quân quốc trọng sự', a mandarin entrusted with the crucial duty of speaking the truth to the emperor. Wang Anshi watched these events unfold and advised the Song emperor that the time was ripe for an attack on Đại Việt. After several years of appeasing the Lý on border matters, the new Song emperor approved his suggestion, while on the diplomatic front the Song awarded Lý Nhân Tông the title of Giao Chỉ Quận Vương in 1073. Preparations for war with the Việt went ahead over the next two years. The Song preparations included prohibiting cross-border trade and cultivating support among minorities along the border in today's Cao Bằng and Lạng Sơn provinces. General Lý Thường Kiệt was alert to this and mobilized the Việt army for a pre-emptive strike on land and sea into Guangzhou and Guangxi. The Nùng featured in the strategies of both sides but their help to the Việt was judged important to Lý Thường Kiệt's victory in Guangxi in 1075–6, which was preceded by a Nùng chief laying siege to the citadel of Ung Châu. The siege lasted 42 days before the citadel fell to Lý Thường Kiệt early in 1076. But the strain on the Việt army was beginning to tell and Song reinforcements were on the way, so the Lý general withdrew after taking prisoners. The Nùng took captive thousands of Chinese men and women, and left considerable devastation in a large area of southern China. Several other border minorities switched allegiance back to the Lý.

Lý Thường Kiệt's campaign caused great alarm in the Song court and resulted in harsh punishments for officials, especially in the south. Wang Anshi blamed the failure on his subordinates and an argument between the emperor and his chief minister over the merit of his plan to attack the Việt is recorded in detail in the *Song-shi* before Wang Anshi resigned.

The victory over the Song brought enormous prestige to Lý Thường Kiệt, but the Lý court braced itself for Song retaliation. The Song took several months to muster their land and sea forces and produce the medicines deemed essential to campaigning in the 'pestilential' climate of Đại Việt. The emperor even issued decrees banning raw food and alcohol for soldiers who fell ill.[28] This time the Song aimed at conquering the whole of Đại Việt and sent ambassadors to Champa and Cambodia offering handsome rewards if they would simultaneously attack the Việt southern borders. There is no direct evidence that Champa and Cambodia joined the Song campaign, but their acquiescence may have been the reason Lý Thường Kiệt took an army south to the border with Champa in the autumn. It is recorded cryptically that he mapped out the geography of the three newly ceded provinces, settled people there and went back to court.[29] On his return Lý Thường Kiệt was promoted to Thái Úy, a position equivalent to chief minister.

The Song opened their attack with 10,000 horses in 1077, according to *Song-shi*. The Song navy then sailed up the Cầu River and reached within a few dozen kilometres of Thăng Long before meeting strong resistance. After several bloody battles on land and sea inflicted heavy casualties on both, the Lý emperor called for a truce and the Song accepted.[30] By then thousands of Song troops had fallen in battle and to disease and the Song withdrew, holding on to the contested area of today's Cao Bằng and Lạng Sơn provinces. The Song called it a victory but returned with just half of their troops and 3,174 horses after expending 5,190,000 taels of gold on the campaign, according to the *Song-shi*. In 1078 Lý Nhân Tông sent an embassy with tribute of five elephants and asked for the border land to be restored. The Song agreed on the condition that the Lý returned the people they had captured during their earlier incursion into China. Bit by bit the Song returned the land by 1084 and Lý Nhân Tông was again accorded the full royal title of Nam Bình Vương.

Lý Thường Kiệt was also effective in domestic affairs and the state was strong though the emperor was a child. Law and order were tightened and, most significantly, Confucianism began to rival Buddhism, even though queen mother Ỷ Lan built over 100 more pagodas and the most venerable Khô Đầu was appointed advisor to the emperor. Pagodas were re-classified into small, medium and large with their own land and tied peasants. In 1075 the first nationwide exam was held to choose civil officials for the court and ten mandarins were selected from this first batch. Learned scholars were appointed as teachers and a year later the first university Quốc Tử Giám was opened at the Temple of Literature to train the children of the emperor and the nobility. By 1086 another exam was organized to elect learned men to a National Academy.

In the south in 1104 Cham king Jaya Indravarman II retook the three *Châu* that Rudravarman III ceded to Đại Việt in 1069, but Lý Thường Kiệt soon recovered the territory. Thereafter relations with Champa and Cambodia appeared cordial as visits were exchanged, according to the Việt annals. Some royal family members even sought asylumn from both Champa and Cambodia in 1124. Lý Thường Kiệt died of old age in 1104. Lý Nhân Tông ruled on and further developed the state until his death in 1127 at the age of 63, after a 56-year reign, one of the longest reigns in Việt history. He left no male heir and the crown passed to his nephew Lý Dương Hoán, who ascended to the throne as emperor Lý Thần Tông at the age of twelve.

LÝ LHẦN LÔNG (*r.* 1128–38 CE)

Emperor Lý Thần Tông was born in 1116 and was said to be the re-incarnation of revered Buddhist monk Từ Đạo Hạnh, the most-venerable of the Thầy pagoda outside Thăng Long. At the age of two, he was taken into the imperial palace to be raised as a prince, along with some of his cousins, and was made crown prince in 1118. His reign was a continuation of the previous one with one innovative decree in 1128 ordering soldiers to take turns to work the fields in time of peace.[31] It was the beginning of a policy known as 'Ngụ binh ư nông' that was to be effective under the Trần. The Song came under heavy pressure from the Jin of Manchuria who established a Jin dynasty in 1115, plunging China into domestic strife. The situation was so difficult by 1126 that a Việt embassy bearing tribute to the Song by land was turned back at Guizou because 'the way was unsafe'. The Song were anyway preoccupied with the Jin and could not receive them. Within months the Song were forced to move their capital to Lin'an in today's Hangzhou. A Song envoy reached Đại Việt in 1130 to confer the title of Giao Chỉ Quận Vương on emperor Lý Thần Tông,[32] which was upgraded to Nam Bình Vương two years later. The northern border was quiet in the reign of Lý Thần Tông, but the Khmers of King Suryavarman II, the restless military campaigner made famous by building Angkor Wat, began a serious overland incursion with 20,000 men to the port of Ba Đầu in Nghệ An province in 1128. General Lý Công Bình headed south and repelled the attack, but the Khmers soon returned with 700 warships to attack Nghệ An again. Two Việt generals drove them off but the Khmers came back and left a letter demanding that the Việt emperor send an envoy to Angkor. This was ignored. The period from 1124–50 was one of intense regional interactions among the Đại Việt of Lý Thần Tông and Lý Anh Tông, Cambodia under Suryavarman II and several rulers in Champa. And it was only the prelude to a period of major rivalry and collaboration between the Chams and the Khmers that Cham inscriptions call the thirty-two-year war. Đại Việt was drawn into the struggle when princes from both sides sought asylum there or help regaining lost territory. Different kingdoms of Champa were at war with each other, with Đại Việt or with the Khmers. An inscription at Po Nagar temple in today's Nha Trang summarizes the period as a grand war with the Khmers,[33] during which the Lý recorded the three neighbours engaged in multilateral warfare in nine years between 1123 and 1150, when Suryavarman II disappeared on campaign. Emperor Lý Thần Tông died in the middle of this period in 1138, leaving the crown to his three year-old-son Thiên Tộ.[34]

EMPEROR LÝ ANH TÔNG (r. 1138–75 CE)

Lý Anh Tông's reign marked the beginning of the end for the Lý dynasty. The state was still strong under the leadership of accomplished civil and military mandarins like Tô Hiến Thành, Hoàng Nghĩa Hiền and Lý Công Tín, but rivalry and open hostility broke out at court. The emperor was crowned aged three after a last minute switch when his father changed his will on his death bed and dropped his half-brother Thiên Lộc, who had been the official crown prince for some time. State affairs were managed by his mother, a lady whose surname was Lê and who was elevated to the rank of queen mother. Her alleged lover Đỗ Anh Vũ was appointed 'cung điện lệnh tri nội ngoại sự', mandarin in charge of all affairs in and out of court. Although he battled with a rebel tribal chief on the northwest border adjacent to Yunnan, his position at court aroused discontent among other courtiers. They managed to arrest and jail him once for alleged misdeeds but he was soon pardoned on the queen mother's intervention. Đỗ Anh Vũ's actions at court led to the death of several of his rivals.

Externally, a triangle of hostilities developed with Angkor and Champa. The Song took the unusual step in 1164 of conferring the elevated title of An Nam Quốc Vương to Lý Anh Tông. This for the first time recognized the king of Đại Việt (now called An Nam by the Song) as a true king of an independent state. Previously the highest title accorded a Việt emperor was Nam Bình Vương, king of the pacified south, implying Đại Việt was a southern region of China. While trouble brewed at the court controlled by the queen mother and Đỗ Anh Vũ, Lý Anh Tông made a major commercial move in 1149 by creating the international trading post of Vân Đồn on the island of Cái Bầu in Hạ Long bay. It was the first purpose-built Việt international commercial port that could receive ships from Siam, Java and an unknown state called Lộ Lạc. Vân Đồn was also to become an important military staging post for the Trần during their war against the Mongols in the late thirteenth century. Cái Bầu island in Hạ Long bay is also important for the cave of Soi Nhụ that contains traces of the Việt stone age, before the last ice age, the great melt and the appearance of Hạ Long culture. The island is the remnant of a huge piece of land that once connected the Việt shore with Hainan island.

The tensions of Lý court reduced after the death of Đỗ Anh Vũ in 1158 but cracks had appeared in the foundation of the dynasty that were to grow more visible. A loyal mandarin Tô Hiến Thành became the man the emperors entrusted with keeping order in the south, and he conducted a successful expedition into Champa in 1167. As the Song weakened further and the Jin grew stronger, Đại Việt maintained relations both with the Song in the south and the Jin in the north. These dual relations led to an embarrassing situation in 1168, when Jin and Song ambassadors arrived in Thăng Long at the same time. The Lý courtiers did their best to prevent their meeting each other. Lý Anh Tông had his first son and heir prince Long Xưởng in 1151 and a second son prince Long Trát in 1173.[35] The succession became problematic after Long Xưởng was caught with his father's concubines and he was demoted to ordinary citizenship and imprisoned. Long Trát was made crown prince aged two. Lý Anh Tông fell ill in 1175 after a reign of 37 years and on his death bed appointed Tô Hiến Thành as regent of the infant emperor.

LÝ CAO TÔNG (r. 1175–1210 CE)

Long Trát became emperor Lý Cao Tông despite the objection of the official queen, who supported her own son prince Long Xưởng. The regent died three years later and Đỗ An Di was appointed to replace him. Lý Cao Tông's reign is often blamed for the decline of the Lý, though the problems began under his father. His youth led to internal power struggles. State affairs nevertheless ran fairly smoothly at first. Then prince Long Xưởng gathered an army and attempted to rise up against the infant emperor in 1181, but it seems to have been ineffective.[36] Natural disasters came in the form of floods and earthquakes in 1179–80 and there was widespread famine. The annals say 'almost half of the population died of hunger'. The Song accorded Lý Cao Tông the title of An Nam Quốc Vương in 1186 and foreign trade seemed to flourish at Vân Đồn, indicated by the arrival of merchants from Siam, Champa, Cambodia and Srivijaya. The three-way entanglement between the Việt, the Khmers and the Chams continued with fierce battles flaring up periodically, mainly when Cham kings came to ask the Việt for help. One such incident occurred in 1203 when the then Khmer King Jayavarman VII finally wrested back control of the Cham provinces ceded earlier to Suryavarman II. He drove out Cham protégée Sūryavarman-Vidyānandana, who turned against him by entering Champa with a Khmer army but made himself king instead.[37] The Cham king brought a fleet of 200 ships to the Việt port of Cơ La in Nghệ An province to ask for asylum. The situation was complicated as relations with Angkor were cordial between Lý Cao Tông and Jayavarman VII. When local officials dithered over his request for assistance and even tried to ambush his fleet, the Cham warrior wrecked the Việt navy and disappeared to sea,[38] possibly ending up in Aceh, Sumatra where traces of Cham language have been detected.

Lý Cao Tông had his first son and heir, prince Sảm, in 1194. An amnesty was ordered and a gift of silk presented to all aged over 70 years. He had other sons after that and relations among the princes later became another source of conflict in an already divisive court. Hunger remained a major problem and earthquakes, hailstorms and typhoons occurred almost every year.[39] In 1199 a great flood destroyed most of the crops and many Việt starved to death. The annals say 'banditry was widespread . . . people died of starvation in 1207 and 1208, their bodies falling on top of each other'. The emperor, meanwhile, was busy enjoying himself 'travelling for pleasure with his concubines, building more and more palaces and ignored the problems'. Đại Việt was in turmoil from internal division, natural disaster and an indifferent emperor. The country was divisive in every sense, powerful families and clans began to build their own enclaves and established large estates, some along the coast. At the same time chiefs of minorities ran their areas of settlements as they pleased along the northern and northwestern borders as the centre weakened.[40] As the power at the centre diminished, the estates run by wealthy families, especially those along the coast, became more and more powerful. Some wealthy families such as the Trần operated as autonomous regions with their own estate armies.

The emperor appointed Prince Sảm crown prince in 1208, even as armed conflict among the generals and powerful courtiers spread from their local estates to the capital. For reasons still unknown he suddenly made his second son Thẩm emperor, while he escaped to an estate by the border with Yunnan.[41] Meanwhile crown prince Sảm escaped from court in 1209 and headed for a Trần family estate in today's Nam Định, coastal area southeast of Thăng Long where the fateful entanglement between the Lý and the Trần began. Prince Sảm married Trần Thị Dung, a Trần woman on the estate, and the Trần gathered an army to march on Thăng Long on his behalf. They punished the rebel courtiers and invited Lý Cao Tông to return as emperor. Lý Cao Tông fell ill the next year after asking crown prince Sảm to return to the capital but without his Trần wife. Sảm became emperor Lý Huệ Tông of Đại Việt in 1211 aged sixteen.

LÝ HUỆ TÔNG (r. 1211–26 CE) AND LÝ CHIÊU HOÀNG (r. 1225 CE)

One of Lý Huệ Tông's first acts was to bring his Trần wife to Thăng Long and name her Lady Trần the royal consort. Other Trần members followed, and the Trần family entered the Lý royal household, to the intense displeasure of the queen mother, who even attempted to poison Lady Trần. Lý Huệ Tông suffered many illnesses and relied entirely on incompetent prime minister Đàm Dĩ Mông. Faced with a hostile queen mother, a court in disarray and a country wrecked by conflict, Lý Huệ Tông turned to the Trần and became more and more dependent on them. A princess was born in 1216 and Lý Huệ Tông elevated his wife to the rank of queen and awarded royal titles to her brother Trần Tự Khánh and several other Trần family members. Trần Tự Khánh was a powerful man among the Trần who commanded his own army. When the emperor fell ill he took charge of the affairs of state. Lý Huệ Tông is even recorded as acting insane or being too drunk to know what was going on around him. Conflicts with the Chams and the Khmers continued throughout his reign with Nghệ An province often turned into a battlefield. In 1218 the emperor had another daughter, princess Chiêu Thánh. Trần Tự Khánh died in 1223 and other members of the Trần family took over the running of state affairs, under the direction of a Trần cousin of the queen, Trần Thủ Độ, who commanded the imperial guard. Emperor Lý Huệ Tông ruled officially until 1224 when in an odd gesture he appointed princess Chiêu Thánh 'crown prince'. This appears to indicate that princess Chiêu Thánh was designated heir to the throne, despite her sex and when in 1224 emperor Lý Huệ Tông abdicated to become a monk, she became Empress Lý Chiêu Hoàng of Đại Việt at the age of seven. She was soon married to an eight-year-old Trần boy named Trần Cảnh, the nephew of Trần Thủ Độ and two months later empress Lý Chiêu Hoàng abdicated in favour of her husband. Trần Cảnh thus became the first Trần emperor with the royal name of Trần Thái Tông in 1226. It is deeply ironic that after 216 years the great Lý dynasty collapsed at the hands of a seven-year-old child, made empress by a king not wholly sane, to rule over a highly disturbed realm and a court controlled by the Trần family. The Lý dynasty presided over one of the most prosperous times for the Việt, even though there was much suffering and chaos during their decline. For most of the Lý dynasty, the Việt were strong and Lý emperors acted confidently at the head of a powerful and independent nation as celebrated in the much quoted poem of Lý Thường Kiệt on 'the southern land that belonged to the southern king . . .'.[42] This poem is credited to the general Lý Thường Kiệt during his campaign against the Song in 1076 and was an inspiring work for the Việt for many centuries to come.

Relations with the Chams had haunted the Lý since they went south and killed Cham king Jaya Simhavarman II in 1044. Đại Việt remained embroiled with one or other Cham kingdom through the thirteenth and fourteenth centuries. This added complexity during the invasions of the Mongols in the second half of the thirteenth century. Cham culture, meanwhile, continued to be greatly appreciated at the Việt court. From the time Lý Thái Tông brought back Cham craftsmen, dancers and musicians to Thăng Long in 1044, until Lý Cao Tông's reign, Cham music was played regularly at court. In 1202 when emperor Lý Cao Tông ordered his musicians to compose a Cham air it was said that 'the sound was clear and mournful, typical of a state in turmoil'.[43] The compilers of the annals warned that 'the people were in disorder, the realm unsettled, the state at risk, yet, the emperor preferred to spend time enjoying himself, a sure sign of the decline to come.'

Buddhism in various forms meanwhile evolved from being heavily promoted under the first Lý emperors into one of three main belief systems in Vietnam alongside Confucianism and Daoism. Daoism became widely spread under Lý Nhân Tông, after beng first imported into Giao Chi under the Han. By the end of the Lý dynasty these doctrines had been diluted and blended at grassroots level to form common local religious beliefs. Modern Vietnam still boasts many fine pagodas and temples thanks to the Lý, the Trần and the Lê who maintained and renovated them. The Confucian temple of Văn Miếu still stands in the middle of Hanoi as testament to the rise of Confucianism during the mid-period Lý.

6

The Trần Dynasty (1226–1413)

The Trần dynasty emerged in Đại Việt in 1226 and continued through one of the most significant periods in Việt history. As the histories of the two dynasties Lý and Trần were entwined for a number of years before the Trần took over, modern Vietnamese historians tend to consider them as partners of one long Lý–Trần period. However, the Trần dynasty left their distinctive marks both internally and externally, and a separation of the two helps us to view the Trần on their own merits, just as we have done the Lý. The major events of the Trần period were their repulsion of three Mongol invasions in the second half of the thirteenth century and their descent into a large tract of Cham territory almost immediately thereafter, setting the scene for centuries of mutual hostility.

TRẦN THÁI TÔNG (1226–58 CE)

The year 1226 opened with the first Trần emperor Trần Thái Tông on the throne as a boy of eight, who was given the crown by his wife the Lý empress Lý Chiêu Hoàng who was just seven. Throughout his child-hood the emperor ruled in name only under the control of his uncle Trần Thủ Độ, a clever but ruthless operator according to the annals. One of the first acts of the first Trần emperor was to formalize his uncle's position at court as chief advisor for military matters.[1] Former emperor Lý Huệ Tông had been sent to live as a monk at Chân Giáo pagoda away from court. But with the new emperor secure on the throne, Trần Thủ Độ allegedly forced the former emperor to hang himself at the pagoda. His wife was demoted to princess in rank and was married to Trần Thủ Độ himself. Lý Huệ Tông's former concubines were sent out of the capital to be married to chieftains in outlying areas with a duty to report back on their activities. The policy sometimes failed as in the case of Princess Ngoạn Thiềm, who was married to a troublesome chieftain Nguyễn Nộn in 1228 but was forced to live in isolation so she had nothing to report.

In 1232 Trần Thủ Độ built a false floor in a hall and invited the Lý royal family for a banquet. When the floor was collapsed many of the Lý were buried under the rubble, and any return of the Lý was eliminated.[2]

Relations with the Song in China were going smoothly. The new emperor was accorded the title king of An Nam by the Song emperor in 1229 and he felt ready to embark on internal reforms.[3] One of the first royal edicts by Trần Thái Tông was highly significant but has often been overlooked. Issued in the year 1227 and reinforced in 1237, the edict stipulated that civil contracts, such as title deeds for land and properties, or loan agreements, had to be sealed by fingerprints: 'the witness would put his fingerprints on the first three lines, and the buyer or the borrower on the last four lines of the contract'. Another royal decree at this time stipulated that the former Lý ceremony of 'pledging allegiance to the emperor' at the temple of Đồng Cổ would be upheld, on the same fourth day of the fourth moon. The first ceremony of this kind under the Trần took place in 1227 and continued to be held throughout the dynasty. The punishment for avoiding the pledge was changed though; now the offender would be fined 5 'quan' of money, instead of 50 strokes of cane. In his name, but under the direction of Trần Thủ Độ, the Trần court instigated a series of practices to help sustain the country through natural and man-made disasters. The first was an intense effort to maintain the crucially important irrigation system of the Red River that led to the creation of a minister and vice-minister of dykes in 1248. Their sole duty was to watch over the safety of the main irrigation system of Red and Đà River polders and ensure they were fortified every spring. A man from every household was regularly called upon to perform dyke fortification duty. This initiative provided an effective water management system that still guards the north side of Hanoi today. Thanks to this system Việt agriculture remained manageable despite frequent floods and droughts. Two years after coming to the throne the emperor ordered a census. It was designed to determine the number of men and divide them into three groups: eighteen to twenty, twenty to 60 and those over 60. The primary purpose was to select soldiers, identify taxpayers and set dyke duties. It stipulated that only children of titled families would be eligible for official posts; everyone else, however rich, was eligible for the draft if they were fit enough. Later the Trần modified the mandarin recruitment system to widen their administrative base to the countryside.[4] The Lý first established exams to select men who commanded enough written Chinese to perform 'diplomatic, ceremonial to clerical chores',[5] and the Trần modified the system to elevate able scholars with minor titles to higher administrative posts at the capital. Commoners who passed the exams were now recruited into local administrations. The new system helped to establish a network of well-run local offices throughout the country. The Trần also created a State Academy and maintained the State University and a Military Academy. The historian Lê Văn Hưu, author of the first Việt history *Đại Việt Sử Ký* was selected through the system in 1247 and completed his work in 1272 'to the satisfaction of the Trần emperor'.

The Trần also moved to include commoners in court affairs. This was considered necessary after the Mongols began to pay attention to Đại Việt in the second half of the thirteenth century. Dealing with Mongol tactics was thought to be beyond the ken of courtiers and this proved effective when the Mongols did invade. But when the Mongol threat was over by the end of the thirteenth century, the introduction of commoners into the Trần's court was seen as a factor that divided and weakened the dynasty. Criminal and civil laws were clarified under the first Trần emperor. The court reviewed the penal code of the Lý and reorganized it into a set of twenty books called *Quốc triều thống chế*, which set the punishments for all crimes. The court procedures were clarified in the ten books *Quốc triều thường lễ*. The emperor enlarged the Thăng Long citadel with new buildings and towers and the quarters for royal members more clearly defined. He decreed that, from now on, all temples at resting posts throughout the country would have statues of the Buddha. In 1242 the country was reorganized into twelve administrative regions or *lộ* with a people register.[6] The armed forces were focused in three branches – army, navy and imperial guard with the guards being selected from *lộ* Thiên Trường, the former Trần estate, and the adjacent *lộ* Long Hưng. The exact size of the army was unknown as the Trần continued the Lý policy of allowing soldiers to stay home to cultivate the land in peace time and to be mobilized only for war. Another reform was to allocate estates or *Điền Trang* with their own armies to princes, princesses and other royals. Their estates ringed Thăng Long as an inner defence perimeter. The outer perimeter was formed by the *Trại* or larger estates managed by chieftains. This policy was to prove crucial in repelling the Mongol invasions in 1257–8, 1285 and 1288.

However the young emperor had a marital problem. His wife, who had briefly been child empress Lý Chiêu Hoàng, was demoted in 1237 when she reached the age of eighteen and had still not produced an heir. Trần Thủ Độ chose her elder sister Thuận Thiên to replace her as queen because she was already pregnant by her own husband, the emperor's brother. She was to provide Trần Thái Tông with a ready-made heir. The disgruntled brother promptly staged a rebellion, causing the emperor to run in fear to a pagoda outside the capital and declare that he was too young for state affairs and wanted 'to stop being emperor'. But the regent would not hear of it and insisted he return to court or have a court and capital constructed around him at the pagoda. The young

Trần Thái Tông relented and two weeks after his return to the capital, his brother surrendered and they were at peace again. Despite the upheaval the child born to the emperor's brother's former wife was not chosen to be heir, for a second prince was born in 1240. As the flesh and blood son of the emperor, Prince Hoảng was made crown prince immediately. Other princes were born and they were all given high royal titles. As the emperor grew to manhood the regent continued to maintain an all-encompassing role at court; however, Trần Thái Tông now assumed several duties, such as leading an army to fight at various troubled spots. In 1252 he went into Champa and returned victorious with a queen of a Cham king the Việt call Bố Da La along with other Cham women and men. The emperor focused on clarifying laws and customary regulations, while continuing the repair programme for pagodas and Confucian temples and dyke-building. The country was judged peaceful and prosperous.[7] The royal family enjoyed drinking, dancing and game-playing at their banquets, which some later historians censured.[8] The annals also contain damning comments on inter-marriages and messy entanglements among the highest rank of princes.[9] Although his personal issues are given prominence in the annals, the reign of Trần Thái Tông is primarily remarkable for the first Việt victory over the Mongols. In world history, this signals the first time the all-conquering Mongols have been defeated. Even though the event has clearly been documented in both Việt and Chinese official histories, it is still only known to few specialists.

THE FIRST MONGOL INVASION (1257–8 CE)

In 1257 the Mongols captured Yunnan and were looking at Đại Việt as a passage to southern China in their assault on the Song.[10] The Great Khan Möngke made this plan six years earlier but he could not implement it until he had secured Yunnan under Kublai Khan's command.[11] Kublai Khan left Yunnan for Shensi to join Möngke, leaving his right-hand general Uriyangkhadai to open up the Đại Việt passage to southern China. Uriyangkhadai addressed three letters to Trần Thái Tông in the autumn of 1257 making this demand.[12] The first envoy was spotted by a landowner on the border who informed Thăng Long. The others rode through in the following months, and all three were jailed in the capital.[13] It was an extreme gesture, tantamount to declaring war. Perhaps the Trần still saw the Southern Song as an ally who had accorded Trần Thái Tông the title *An Nam Quốc Vương*. Immediately after the first Mongol envoy was imprisoned the Trần court issued an edict mobilizing the 'whole population to take arms to fight against the Mongols'. The defence of Đại Việt was formally placed under the command of general-in-chief prince Trần

Quốc Tuấn and a joint army and navy force was sent to the border with Yunnan. Another edict ordered citizens to 'repair their weapons and manufacture new ones'. During the last moon of the year of the Snake (January 1258), general Uriyangkhadai led a combined force of Mongol cavalry and Yunnan foot soldiers and camped at the border of Đại Việt.[14] From there he sent two groups of 1,000 men along the Red River into Đại Việt.[15] They intended to encircle the capital in a pincer movement, while Uriyangkhadai's central force pushed directly into Thăng Long. The Mongol general sent his son Aju into Đại Việt to gather intelligence and when Aju reported back that the Việt army was ready and waiting, Uriyangkhadai hurried down with his main force, leaving general Trechecdu and Aju in the rear. The armies clashed at Nỗ Nguyên (according to the pro-Mongol account *An nam Chí Lược,* which modern Vietnamese historians identify as Việt Trì on the Hồng River).[16] The Mongols found the Trần were ready for them with their 'emperor riding an elephant'[17] across the river. The Mongols paused to reflect, for they were not familiar with elephants at this stage. Their wariness about the effect of the elephants on their horses was noted in the Việt annals and the pro-Mongol *An Nam Chí Lược.* The river was another obstacle for the Mongols. The Trần were originally fishermen from coastal Nam Định by the thriving Vân Đồn port and were skilled river and coastal navigators. They had placed boats downstream to provide an escape route, but the Mongols were aware of this and planned to move on the boats first.[18] The Mongols eventually found a way of crossing the river and shot flaming arrows at the feet of the elephants.[19] The battle got underway too quickly and was too fierce for the Mongols to get to the boats, so the Trần emperor and a number of his generals were able to use them to escape when the Mongols started winning. There was another fierce engagement at Phù Lỗ bridge the next day and the Trần army again withdrew by boat and reached the Đông Bộ Đầu east gate of Thăng Long on the south bank of the river. That night the Trần court decided to abandon the capital and an evacuation took place 'in an orderly manner' according to the Việt annals. However, it must have been in some disarray for most of the evacuees left without their weapons.[20] The Trần evacuees took refuge at Hoàng Giang along the Red River and nearer to the coast. The emperor considered surrendering or pleading for asylum with the Southern Song, but the regent Trần Thủ Độ advised against either.[21] With the royal family gone, the Mongols 'entered an empty' Thăng Long to find their three envoys in jail, one of them dead: 'on seeing this, the Mongols went berserk, killing all the people and destroying much of the capital.'[22] The 'emptiness' of the city in courtly rhetoric meant it was empty of royal authority. The 'emptiness' factor has often been cited as a well thought-out strategy by the Trần court to explain the hunger and other difficulties the Mongols encountered in the Việt capital. By focusing on this, other factors affecting the Mongols in Thăng Long have been overlooked. Hunger did indeed affect the Mongols in Thăng Long as they acknowledged.[23] The Việt capital was a small citadel reserved only for the royal family and the imperial guard. Royal princes and high-ranking officials lived on their own estates outside the capital. Food must have been short for an estimated 25,000 Mongol men and horses.[24] Both the men and their horses also suffered from heat and mosquitoes.[25] Dysentery and malaria spread quickly through their ranks in what modern epidemiologists call 'medical threats unique to military service'.[26] In a hot, humid and unhygienic environment following a killing spree, the Mongols became so ill and weak they decided to withdraw after only nine days. Before they left, Uriyangkhadai sent two envoys to the Việt emperor demanding submission but Trần Thái Tông had them bound and sent back.[27] When he heard of the state the Mongols were in, Trần Thái Tông brought back his army and re-entered Thăng Long, where they 'fought the enemy and took the city without much opposition'.[28] The Mongols withdrew to Yunnan 'so weak and demoralised' that they 'went without even thinking of looting along the way'. These retreating Mongols earned the popular title of 'the Buddhist enemies' as they did not loot or kill. Đại Việt was rid of the Mongols. Later, Persian historian Rashīd al-Dīn Hamadānī noted in his *Compendium of Chronicles* that 'to the south of the Qu'an's realm, there was a province called Kafjih-Guh [Tonkin]. It has a separate ruler who is inimical to the Qu'an.'[29]

From the historical accounts of both sides this first Mongol brief incursion came as a surprise to both. Neither expected a war of only nine days, and the Trần had even considered seeking asylum with the Song. The Việt histories hail the events of 1258 as a great victory, but *Yuanshi* and *An Nam Chí Lược* claim a victory for the Mongols as they had captured Thăng Long. Later in the year the Great Khan Möngke sent a letter to the Việt emperor referring to his sending back the two Mongol envoys, and asked the Trần court to submit.[30] This means that the Trần did not submit earlier. It also means the Mongols' reputation for invincibility was broken at that point. *Yuanshi*, the *An Nam Chí Lược* and the Việt annals refer only briefly to this 1258 episode, yet it was a turning point in the history of the world for it was the first setback for the Mongols in Asia and in their worldwide campaign. It was followed by their much better-known defeat by the Mamluks at Ain Jalut in September 1260.[31] As for East Asia, the first Mongol failure there came much later in Japan in their weather-thwarted invasion in 1274.[32]

The Mongol incursion opened a period of intense shuttle diplomacy for the Trần, who were balancing between the Mongols and the Southern Song. Two months after the Mongols left Trần Thái Tông sent an envoy to report to the Southern Song and also announced his abdication in favour of his son Prince Hoảng. At the same time they sent an envoy to the Mongols in Yunnan, whom Uriyangkhadai escorted to Shensi to see the Great Khan Möngke, who was on his way to attack the Southern Song. Möngke was surprisingly reconciliatory in asking the Trần again to submit, and suggested that Trần Thái Tông come to pay him respect.[33] Trần Thái Tông made his excuses but agreed to send tribute 'once every three years'.[34] The incursion and its surprising outcome thus ushered in nearly three decades of diplomatic wrangling between Đại Việt and the Mongols, and later the Yuan dynasty in China under Kublai Khan.

TRẦN THÁNH TÔNG (1258–78 CE)

Prince Hoảng ascended to the Trần throne as emperor Trần Thánh Tông on 30 March 1258 and quickly despatched an envoy to the Southern Song to seek their approval. The Song responded in 1262 by appointing him *An Nam Quốc Vương* and ranking his father as *Đại Vương* (senior king).[35] The abdication of a senior king in favour of his chosen heir was unique to the Trần dynasty, and it was an abdication in name only. The senior king still ruled while his successor sat on the throne as an apprentice-emperor. This practice caused some confusion in Việt and Chinese annals, where Mongol letters were addressed to the senior king, calling him a prince and ignoring the reigning one, because they had not yet approved the change. The Việt annals often refer to 'the two emperors' in its account of the Mongol invasions.

Kublai Khan succeeded in getting himself elected Great Khan in 1260 amid intense rivalry within his family. But despite his pressing domestic agenda the new Mongol leader took up the Đại Việt issue in the following year when he sent reconciliatory letter to Trần Thánh Tông asking for his submission and promising that Mongol troops would not again enter Đại Việt. Kublai Khan awarded the Việt ruler the same kingly title of *An Nam Quốc Vương*[36] he had received from the Southern Song – and this when Kublai Khan and the Southern Song were at war. The double appointment put Trần Thánh Tông in an uncomfortable position, one that he was well aware of. In 1262 Trần Thánh Tông prepared for war, ordering the army and navy to exercise at Bạch Hạc junction, where the Việt first encountered the Mongols in 1258. Next he turned the old Trần estate of *lộ* Thiên Trường in Nam Định province into an alternative capital for the residence of the senior emperor. The Việt army also carried out regular patrols along the upper reaches of the main rivers near the Yunnan border. Envoys were sent back and forth between Đại Việt and China almost yearly and with each visit the Mongol demands became harsher. By 1267 Kublai Khan's tone towards Đại Việt deteriorated, rebuking Trần Thánh Tông that 'while offering tributes regularly, the Trần emperor did not come to Dadu to pay respect, did not submit a population register, nor send hostages, or contribute troops to the Mongol army', whereas 'these have always been among the *six requirements* of vassal states, not something invented specially for Đại Việt'.[37] The other two requirements were to pay taxes and accept a *Daruyaci*, a Mongol overseer that they placed in all of their newly acquired territories. The imperial letter also complained that the appointed *Daruyaci* Nasir-al-Dīn had difficulties at the Việt court and was refused meetings with the emperor. By the end of 1270 Kublai Khan found grounds to suspect the Vietnamese 'vassal's' fidelity and probably realized that the Trần diplomatic courtesies for a decade were only 'appropriate to the protocols of an independent state'. This realization seems reflected in an angry message from Kublai Khan that rebuked the Trần for their 'haughty protocol' when they received Mongol envoys.[38] The Mongol demands were cranked up in the following year after Kublai Khan proclaimed his Yuan dynasty in China. He sent envoys asking Trần Thánh Tông to come to him in person, but the Việt emperor said he was not well enough to travel.[39] Despite the escalating demands the Trần managed to maintain their balancing act between the Mongols and the Southern Song for fourteen years until the Song were defeated by the Mongols at the battle of Xiang-Yang in 1274. Đại Việt became a refuge for Song remnants, and a large group of 'former Song people' arrived in thirty ships and 'opened an emporium selling silk and Chinese herbal medicines' in Thăng Long. This friendly gesture did not escape Kublai Khan's attention, who warned that he was sending an envoy called Ali-haya to demand the Trần emperor to come to him or send his relatives as hostages to Dadu.[40] While Kublai Khan's animosity escalated towards the Trần, the Southern Song were defeated in 1276 at their capital of Hangzhou, destroying one side of the Đại Việt balancing act and fully exposing the Việt to the Mongol threat. Senior emperor Trần Thái Tông died in 1277 and in the same year Trần Thánh Tông abdicated in favour of his son crown prince Khẩm, who took the throne as emperor Trần Nhân Tông.[41]

TRẦN NHÂN TÔNG (1278–93 CE)

The new Trần emperor's reign was studded with diplomatic and military conflict with the Mongols. Kublai Khan's wrath blazed forth from a chastising mission sent just after the coronation. Mongol envoy Sabuqing (Sài Trang Khanh), a ranking member of Yuan protocol, entered Đại Việt through the Guangxi border gate normally used for Trần-Song bilateral exchanges, instead of the usual Mongol route via Yunnan. This caused consternation in the Trần court. The wording of the envoy's letter was alarming, for Kublai Khan made it a blunt declaration of war. The Yuan emperor cast aside diplomatic language and called Trần Nhân Tông an illegal, self-appointed ruler, and a liar. He chastised him for disobeying his *six requirements* and pointed to the Yuan defeat of the Song and its implications for the Trần, the friend of his enemy.[42] Trần Nhân Tông made his excuses and sent two envoys to Dadu with tribute to the Yuan emperor. One of the envoys was detained, while the other was escorted back to Thăng Long by Sabuqing in 1281. Sabuqing, this time, demanded that the Trần emperor come in person to Kublai Khan. The Việt emperor made another excuse and sent his uncle Trần Di Ái to Dadu.[43] A Trần royal at the Yuan court gave Kublai Khan the lever he sought and he received him with honour. Kublai proclaimed his visitor 'King of Annam' in replacement of Trần Nhân Tông and appointed Sabuqing as 'Annam Commissioner and Commander', with the special duty of placing Trần Di Ái on the Việt throne. A force of 1,000 men travelled with Sabuqing to the border, but Trần Di Ái escaped, leaving Sabuqing with a thwarted mission in Thăng Long. Nevertheless, Sabuqing proceeded to the Trần court, where his arrogant demeanour and excessive demands appeared designed to humiliate the Trần. The diplomatic dance was over and war now looked inevitable. But Đại Việt would breathe again, as it proved not to be the next target for Mongol expansion into Southeast Asia. Instead, the newly built Cham-Khmer deepwater port of Sri Banoy (today Quy Nhơn) became the next Mongol objective.

THE SECOND MONGOL INVASION (1283-5 CE)

As soon as Kublai Khan captured the Song capital of Hangzhou he ordered generals Sodu and Mengutai to form a *xingzheng* (mobile administrative unit) in Fujian, whose role was to approach coastal polities on the South China Sea and the Indian Ocean to seek continuing trade with China.[44] The first port of call along the maritime route from China to India was Sri Banoy, so the Chams received the first such invitation. The Cham king Jaya Indravarman ruled over a prosperous if disunited kingdom, where huge temples were regularly endowed with magnificent gifts in gold, silver and bronze, as recorded in Cham inscriptions.[45] The Cham king responded positively to Kublai Khan's invitation and sent the first Cham embassy to the Yuan in 1279 with an elephant, rhinoceros and precious jewellery.[46] Communications between China and Champa intensified with *Yuanshi* noting three 1280 letters from Kublai in January,

June and December.[47] General Sodu brought the first letter in which the Yuan emperor demanded the Cham king come to pay his respects. The second and third letters repeated the demand and added a further request that the Cham king's son come to live at the Yuan court as hostage. The Cham king responded with lavish gifts in the same year but demurred on the hostage. By now Đại Việt and Champa faced the same Mongol demands and this brought the neighbours closer together. In 1282 Cham prince Harijit asked Đại Việt for troops and ships to help him deal with an imminent Chinese attack and Việt troops were later sent in ships to face the Mongol onslaught. *Yuanshi* noted in its Annam section in 1284 that the Trần denied reports they had sent 20,000 men and 500 ships to Champa to help them fight against Sodu's army.[48] The Mongol military campaign against Champa had begun in 1281 when Kublai Khan appointed the Cham king a 'regional prince' and then announced that he had made general Sodu chief of a *xingzheng* for Champa. *Yuanshi* says 'the son of the Cham king, Pu Ti had assumed the ruling of Champa and did not submit'.[49] Pu Ti is the Chinese name for the Cham Crown Prince Harijit, who later became king Jaya Simhavarman III or Chế Mân in Vietnamese. In 1282 Sodu set sail down the South China Sea with 1,000 ships. The delay was partly due to the disastrous Mongol expedition to Japan in 1281, when the *kamikaze* 'divine wind' brought storms that wrecked 75 per cent of the invading fleet. In late 1282 Sodu launched his fleet for Champa[50] with the renowned general Alihaya, who was also experienced at sea.[51] The Mongol fleet arrived at the port of Tchan-Tch'eng Kiang or 'Estuary of Champa' on 30 December 1282, a date omitted in *Yuanshi* but recorded in *Jingshi dadian*,[52] according to Pelliot. Vietnamese historians Hà Văn Tấn and Phạm Thị Tâm came to the same conclusion as Pelliot that Sodu's fleet came into Sri Banoy,[53] the deepwater port constructed a century earlier with the help of Khmer engineers and known today as Quy Nhơn in Bình Định province. Sri Banoy was already playing a major role in the maritime trade and had become the best-known port in the South China Sea as well as being the gateway to Vijaya, the major Cham power centre of the thirteenth century.

Sodu camped on the shore and seven times sent envoys to the Cham king calling for submission, but without effect.[54] After four weeks Sodu launched his first assault against the Cham defences at the top of the bay of Quy Nhơn. By noon the Cham citadel on the north side of the bay fell with the loss of thousands of Cham lives. The remnant escaped inland and Sodu's army marched on to capture Vijaya on 19 February 1283, according to *Jingshi dadian* and *Yuanshi*. The Chinese accounts said the Chams then played tricks on Sodu in the coming months, enticing him into the mountain forest of Đắc Lắc plateau, where he incurred heavy losses in ambushes.[55] During this time, the Chams of

Vijaya sent envoys to plead for help from Đại Việt, Cambodia, Java, and the other Cham kingdoms of Pānduranga and Amaravati.[56] A Yuan envoy was sent to Đại Việt at the same time to ask for a land passage down to Champa. Thăng Long refused.[57] By March 1283 Sodu's army was in severe difficulty: 'his troops being reduced, his situation critical, he had to send for rescue'.[58] Alihaya travelled back to China and was given the task of assembling a rescue force, while Sodu withdrew from Vijaya to his shore camp at Sri Banoy. But the restless Sodu soon struck north, before any supplies or reinforcements arrived by sea, and camped by a large swampy lake called Đại Lăng in the northern part of Champa.[59] Here Sodu 'defeated the local inhabitants, built a camp made of logs, ordered his soldiers to farm for their subsistence and stocked up a rice depôt'. From this camp, Sodu commended to the Yuan court the location of 'Jiaozhi' (Đại Việt) – close to Champa, Yunnan, Cambodia, Siam and Burma. He advised establishing a secretariat there that would eliminate the need for the sea route for moving Yuan troops.[60] Alihaya meanwhile set sail for Champa with his rescue force with three *wanhou* (war commanders); one of them, Omar Batur, was to become a major figure in two subsequent Mongol invasions of Đại Việt.[61] The rescue fleet arrived in Quy Nhơn in April 1284 to find only the burnt-out traces of Sodu's camp. They re-embarked to seek Sodu further north but were battered by a heavy storm and lost most of their ships before joining Sodu.

In Đại Việt, the emperor prepared for war, while sending envoys to sue for peace in Dadu. But at the border the embassy was blocked by a Yuan force of tens of thousands of troops.[62] The Trần hurriedly mobilized land and naval forces and put them into a combined military exercise under general Trần Hưng Đạo. The emperor sent a message suing for peace to Kublai's son Prince Togan, who was commanding the force at the border. Trần Nhân Tông reminded Togan of a 1261 imperial letter from Kublai Khan in which the Yuan emperor promised that his force would not enter Đại Việt.[63] The envoy returned to report that the Yuan emperor had upgraded his son's rank to *Zhen-nan-Wang* (king for the occupation of the south) with Alihaya and Omar Batur as his deputies.[64] In January 1285 prince Togan began the second Mongol invasion of Đại Việt. He broke through border gates and launched his main force against general Trần Hưng Đạo. The Việt were routed and pulled back towards the capital.[65] When emperor Trần Nhân Tông received news of the string of defeats at the border, he travelled by a small boat to Hải Đông in Quảng Ninh province and sent for Trần Hưng Đạo to ask if he should surrender. Trần Hưng Đạo resisted and ordered the Trần royal princes in their estates 'to contribute their private armies; they responded in their thousands'.[66]

Togan's campaign in Đại Việt in 1285 was meticulously planned. The Mongols had learned lessons from their first disastrous incursion in 1258 and this time brought Chinese doctors with them. Togan also established a string of supply depôts from the Chinese border to Thăng Long to maintain supplies from their rear-base at Siming. There were 'hundreds of posts altogether, stationed at 30 *li* [about 15 km] apart'. There were also 'special posts for horses', at 60 *li* (30 km) apart.[67] The Trần sent an envoy to the Mongol camp in early 1285 offering peace terms, but Togan and Omar Batur refused[68] and the next day they met the Trần army in battle on the bank of the Red River. The Mongols won and the Việt withdrew from Thăng Long. General Trần Hưng Đạo escorted both emperors to Thiên Trường, the Trần reserve seat of power in Nam Định province, while Togan entered Thăng Long and held a great victory banquet.[69] Citizens who had remained were massacred.[70] Togan ordered Sodu to advance north from his camp to trap the remaining Việt army and the emperors. Sodu moved up by sea to Thanh Hóa. Several Trần princes tried and failed to stop Sodu's advance. Some surrendered to him, including Emperor Trần Nhân Tông's younger brother, Trần Ích Tắc, whom Kublai made 'king of Annam' when he eventually reached Dadu in 1286. Trần Ích Tắc became an active collaborator of the Yuan court, and acted against his brother and family until his death. Among his entourage was the scholar Lê Tắc, who witnessed some of the Mongol actions and later compiled the pro-Mongol account of *An Nam Chí Lược*.

The Trần emperor faced defeat and sent his youngest sister Princess An Tư as a peace offering to Togan 'in the hope that this action would ease the suffering of the country'.[71] Togan asked Trần Nhân Tông to come himself to surrender, but he refused.[72] Princess An Tư was not heard of again. With Togan moving on Thăng Long, and Sodu battling his way north from Champa, a third Yuan force entered Đại Việt from Yunnan under the command of Nasir-al-Dīn. They travelled down the Red River, defeated Prince Trần Nhật Duật and joined forces with Togan in Thăng Long.[73] Nasir-al-Dīn had earlier been appointed by the Yuan emperor as *Daruyaci* (overseer) of Đại Việt by the Yuan emperor.

The Trần emperors now took refuge in Thiên Trường with remnants of the Việt army. The outcome of the Yuan campaign was however not quite decided, for the Trần policy of establishing princely *trại* and *Điền Trang* estates was still in place, and even as Togan's army went past their areas towards Thăng Long, the princes launched their own attacks from the rear and dug holes in the roads and fields to trap the Mongol horses.[74] Đại Việt was now in a dire state, with their capital lost, their emperors and remaining troops trapped by three Yuan armies. The emperors and their entourage then escaped by boat to a small island called Tam Trĩ in Hạ Long bay.[75] There they narrowly escaped capture in April 1285 and again fled along the coast. They travelled on land and water to Thanh Hoá below Sodu's force. Fighting was breaking out in several areas when

Togan ordered Sodu to return to Champa[76] while he prepared to leave Đại Việt for Siming. The reason given was that 'the weather was too warm and humid . . . [with] disease everywhere'.[77] During this retreat, Omar Batur was sent to join up with Sodu on the Red River. Here they clashed with the Việt and Sodu was killed, while Omar fled back to China. *Yuanshi* says Togan headed north from Thăng Long because 'the Mongol troops and horses could not exercise their familiar skills in battles there; the Yuan ranks were confused and a large number was killed'.[78] *An nam Chí Lược* notes simply that 'Annam troops attacked and retook the capital La Thành (Thăng Long)'.[79] Prince Togan returned to China with only a fraction of his troops.[80] The second Mongol invasion was over for Đại Việt.[81] One outcome of the failed invasion was relief for the Chams, who were no more mentioned as a target in *Yuanshi*. 'The Yuan now concentrated on mobilising 60,000 troops for a campaign against Annam.'[82] Kublai Khan wanted to attack Đại Việt again, but after Togan and the Yuan remnant returned he was persuaded to delay because of the bad climate of Đại Việt.[83]

THE THIRD MONGOL INVASION OF ĐẠI VIỆT (1287–8 CE)

In March 1286 Kublai Khan ordered Alihaya and Omar Batur to formulate a plan for conquering Đại Việt from Yunnan. At the same time, he appointed the defector prince Trần Ích Tắc as king of Annam, with Alihaya as minister on the Left, a decision that was conveyed to emperor Trần Nhân Tông.[84] Kublai Khan massed troops from several provinces in southern China in Guangxi to escort the king of Annam Trần Ích Tắc to sit on his throne. The two Trần emperors returned to a devastated Thăng Long and ordered a census to re-count the population after all the killing,[85] and by May 1286 Trần Hưng Đạo again launched military exercises, built ships and manufactured weapons.[86]

Kublai Khan focused on a naval force for this campaign, with Omar in command. A fleet of 70 transport ships was built to carry food supplies from Hainan to the Yuan troops in Đại Việt under Zhang Wen-hu, son of a former pirate. The Yuan navy and the transports were to enter Đại Việt via Hạ Long bay.[87] The Trần appointed prince Trần Khánh Dư to control Vân Đồn, the main maritime trading post of Đại Việt on an island near the mouth of Bạch Đằng River, the main waterway leading to the Red River and then the capital.

The third Mongol invasion began in November 1287 when a Yuan naval force with 18,000 men in 500 warships and backed by 70 supply ships entered Hạ Long bay. At the same time the Mongol land force advanced down the Red River towards Thăng Long under Togan and

Trần prince Trần Ích Tắc. Lê Tắc was given the title of recorder and many of his entries in *An nam Chí Lược* are eyewitness accounts.[88] Omar launched a successful attack on Vân Đồn and sped towards Thăng Long without caring to protect the laden supply ships behind. When the 70 supply ships reached Vân Đồn they were attacked by prince Trần Khánh Dư's navy and sunk. Zhang Wen-Hu escaped back to Hainan. The loss of supplies was critical for the hay and fodder for their horses went down.[89] Togan advanced on the capital in early 1288 and the Trần emperors again escaped to Thiên Trường. The Mongols were however still without supplies and Kublai Khan again sent Zhang Wen-hu with a transport fleet to Hạ Long bay, which Omar this time was ordered to escort in. Zhang Wen-hu's ships were again sunk. Once more he escaped back to China in a light vessel. The Việt annals record the capture of 300 Mongol ships and *Yuanshi* says: 'the Vietnamese increased their number of ships at the mouth of the River Lục, the Yuan ships were too slow to move because they were laden with supplies, (the ship commanders decided) to throw rice into the sea to lighten the ships to help them escape'.[90] Omar returned to Thăng Long empty handed. With food and fodder in short supply it was not long before heat and the Trần ambushes took a toll on the Yuan in Thăng Long. Togan was furious and wanted to torch the city, but his generals talked him out of it. By May 1288 Togan decided 'Annam is too hot and humid, the troops are too tired' and decided to withdraw. The Mongols planned for Omar to travel down the Bạch Đằng to the sea, while Togan and the rest would go overland to their base in Siming. Trần Hưng Đạo somehow heard of this plan and organized a counter-offensive on land and at sea. His troops destroyed bridges on Togan's retreat route and laid ambushes at border passes. For the ships, he used the same tactics as his predecessor Ngô Quyền in his defeat of the Southern Han in the tenth century. Stakes were driven into the river bed at the mouth of the Bạch Đằng and Việt forces hid in small boats in the reeds.[91] This ambush with stakes was identified as on the Chanh River, a Bạch Đằng tributary and excavated by archaeologists in 1958 and 1969.[92] Some stakes are on display in the Vietnamese Museum of History in Hanoi. When Omar arrived there he was engaged while the tide was still high by Trần Hưng Đạo who lured him above the area with stakes. As the tide receded the Việt commander slipped away in his small boats leaving Omar's fleet stranded on the stakes where they were attacked: 'many boats and men were lost'. The Việt captured 400 ships and several Mongol generals, including Omar.[93] Togan also had problems on land. Many river crossings proved difficult where the bridges were destroyed, and both sides took heavy losses in fighting at the border. Along his route Togan found trenches with spikes set to stop his horses and had to send for the Siming governor to guide him across by another route.[94] The third Mongol invasion of

Đại Việt was over by May 1288. Togan's father Kublai Khan refused to see him again after his second defeat in Đại Việt, as recorded in *Yuanshi*.[95] In July 1288 Kublai Khan ordered the Mongol army to practise naval warfare along with Chinese troops in preparation for another expedition to Đại Việt[96] in 1294.[97] In Đại Việt, on 27 May 1288, almost on the heels of Togan's retreat, Emperor Trần Nhân Tông sent an envoy to Dadu to ask for peace. It was to be the first of many embassies. Each time, Trần Nhân Tông apologised for the war in Đại Việt, saying the Việt were 'animals trapped with no choice but fighting for their survival' and Kublai Khai replied in milder language than before, rebuking him for not opening a passage to Champa and asking for the return of the captured generals Omar and Sodu.[98] Trần Nhân Tông accepted Kublai's letter and entertained his envoy lavishly. The Trần agreed to return Omar by ship in 1289 but halfway to China his vessel was sunk, said to be on the order of Trần Hưng Đạo, and Omar drowned. The Trần emperor told Kublai Khan that Omar was too heavy to be rescued when the faulty ship took in water.[99] The Trần sent tribute to the Yuan court after that. Kublai Khan died in 1294 before he could implement his next invasion plan. His successor Timur Khan decided against invading Đại Việt. Thus the Việt could plan the massive reconstruction task, including the damaged polder systems, which 'exposed the agricultural plains to the hazards of frequent flooding'.[100] Floods brought years of crop failure and almost annual calamities by the middle of the fourteenth century. In 1290 people 'died on the streets' from hunger and 'parents sold off their children for rice'. Emperor Trần Nhân Tông abdicated in favour of his eldest son, Prince Thuyên, in 1293. Prince Thuyên took the crown to become emperor Trần Anh Tông at the age of eighteen and changed the reign era to Hưng Long.

TRẦN ANH TÔNG (1293–1314 CE)

With the death of Kublai Khan in 1294 the Mongol threat receded and Trần Anh Tông ruled in peace while the country struggled through natural disasters and unpredictable harvests. He presided over a gradual disintegration of the Trần court. The Mongol wars opened up the exclusive family circle of the Trần to a new literati class which had been given titles and high status to deal with the Mongols. The inclusion of commoners at court ignited a period of ongoing conflict among courtiers.[101] Commoner-courtiers made fast-track careers like Trần Khắc Chung in foreign affairs and Đoàn Nhữ Hài as the emperor's confidante. The latter had the right to read the royal chronicle prepared by court historians, 'correct what he considered lacking and burn the original copy'.[102] He was only twenty years old and was openly ridiculed in court by the royal princes. By the end of the reign the court had fragmented into factions who blamed each other for the failure to deal with consecutive natural and man-made disasters. Like his predecessors, Trần Anh Tông ruled under the watchful eye of his father, senior king Trần Nhân Tông, even though the latter had become the patriarch of a new Buddhist sect, the Trúc Lâm, and lived on Yên Tử mountain to the northeast of the capital. Apart from being a natural beauty spot and a Buddhist centre, Yên Tử was a natural vantage point from which the senior emperor could look out over the land and sea routes from China. The new emperor had troubles with Laos, where the annals record a number of small-scale wars, but he is most remembered for his intervention in Champa, which precipitated a regional crisis.

The Việt targeted the two Cham provinces of Ô and Lý, which are today's Quảng Trị and Thừa Thiên. Sodu camped in this area in 1284–5 and recommended the construction of a military base to keep watch in three directions. The Việt may possibly have been motivated to obviate any future attempt to implement Sodu's recommendation. The episode was orchestrated by senior emperor Trần Nhân Tông and executed by the emperor's confidante, Đoàn Nhữ Hài. In 1301 the senior emperor visited the court of Jaya Simhavarman III and arranged for his daughter, Princess Huyền Trân, sister of emperor Trần Anh Tông, to marry the Cham king. Đoàn Nhữ Hài went down to Champa in the same year, after being instructed by senior emperor Trần Nhân Tông at Yên Tử.[103] King Jaya Simhavarman III ruled over a peaceful and prosperous kingdom in Champa, maintaining a 'politics of alliances' with Java and a cordial relationship with Yuan China. The port Vijaya was a busy trading post, where 'many commercial ships came and went'.[104] In the last decade of the thirteenth century, Champa was in a better position than its neighbour Đại Việt, which still struggled with natural disasters. Trần Nhân Tông had done well to win over the Cham king as an ally by marriage. The royal marriage took place in 1306 and was recorded in both Việt annals and the Cham inscription of Po-Sah. The Cham inscription is attributed to Jaya Simhavarman III's son, the crown prince Harijitatmaja, who later was called Prince Đa-Da (or *atmaja*) and King Chế Chí by the Việt.[105] In this inscription, the emperor's daughter Huyền Trân is named as the second rank Queen Tapasi, meaning the 'queen of penitence' in old Cham language.[106] In February 1307 the Việt army moved into the two Cham provinces of Ô and Lý despite the protests of local people. Đoàn Nhữ Hài was sent to calm the situation and changed the names of the provinces to Thuận and Hóa châu. The people of these provinces were exempted from taxes for three years, and Đoàn Nhữ Hài appointed some local men to be administrators who were awarded land. According to the Việt annals, the two provinces

Popular impression of Trần Princess Huyền Trân in Huế.

had earlier been given to Đại Việt as the bride price for the princess
Huyền Trân. The Cham king Jaya Simhavarman III died four months
later in 1307, some eight months after Princess Huyền Trân arrived at
his court. Upon news of his death reaching Đại Việt, the Việt navy
under the command of Trần Khắc Chung sailed to Vijaya to 'rescue'
Huyền Trân from the royal pyre during 'a prayer ceremony at sea for
her late husband'. They had a second objective of capturing the Cham
crown prince Đa-Da. No official explanation is given for taking away
this prince. The Việt annals say in 1311 the emperor Trần Anh Tông
led an army to Champa, along with Đoàn Nhữ Hài, to capture the

Cham king Chế Chí.[107] After a difficult war against strong Cham resistance the Việt captured Vijaya in 1312 and made Chế Chí's brother Chế Đà A Bà Niêm the new Cham king. Chế Chí was taken back to Đại Việt, given the titles 'loyal king' and 'submitting king' and was held in Gia Lâm palace, a travel lodge for the Việt royal family across the Red River from the capital. He was presumably a hostage to keep a vassal state under control, in the style of the Yuan court.[108] Chế Chí died in unrecorded circumstances the following year. Northern Champa was clearly under Đại Việt protection for a time[109] and in 1313 a Việt army was sent to protect Chams who had been invaded by Siam.[110] But the death of Chế Chí seems to have led to renewed Cham attacks against Đại Việt.[111] The Yuan court also got involved and in 1316 ordered an investigation by the Jiangshi province chief into 'Đại Việt encroaching borders'. He sent a letter with a terse warning to the Việt emperor saying, 'for some reason, Annam has now acted carelessly in expanding its borders; even if a small piece of land was not a big issue, it was an important matter to the geography of a country'.[112] The letter indicated that the Chams were considered Yuan protégés and by killing or detaining them Đại Việt committed a grave offence against the Yuan. The Yuan missive demanded that the Trần court investigate and take action or 'there will be a war, one day'. Trần Anh Tông responded by sending tribute to the Yuan court but this was refused and bilateral relations remained tense.

Despite the Mongol warning, hostilities continued between Champa and Đại Việt. In 1318 a Việt army under Phạm Ngũ Lão entered Champa and defeated the king Chế Năng, who then escaped to Java to seek help. The Việt installed a Cham chief called Chế A Nan on the Cham throne as a lower rank king and withdrew. But rather than acting as a puppet, Chế A Nan responded with some vigour and sent tribute to the Yuan in 1322 to maintain good relations and demonstrate his independence from the Việt.[113] The following year Chế A Nan sent an envoy to ask the Yuan for help in regaining its territory from Đại Việt. The Yuan despatched two ambassadors to Đại Việt to ask the new emperor Trần Minh Tông to respect Cham sovereignty. In 1326 a Trần prince with the title of Huệ Túc Vương was sent into Champa but to the chagrin of emperor Trần Minh Tông 'did not achieve anything'.[114] In fact his force was defeated by Chế A Nan, who thus regained the full independence for his Cham kingdom after ending nineteen years of being partly under Đại Việt control. The annexation of the two Cham provinces Ô and Lý and the death of Harijitatmaja-Chế Chí in Đại Việt were to remain a thorn in the sides of both Đại Việt and Champa for the next 164 years. Each side won territory and punished each other's capital in an ongoing state of war that prompted the Ming emperor to issue several imperial letters to both sides ordering restraint.[115] Sporadic raids and counter raids continued until Vijaya was definitively captured by Đại Việt in 1471 and the inexorable Việt movement south began.

DECLINE OF THE TRẦN (1314–98)

The reigns of Trần Minh Tông and Trần Hiến Tông (1314–41) are usually grouped together because the senior emperor Trần Minh Tông made all decisions of state affairs and managed external conflicts. Emperor Trần Anh Tông abdicated in 1314 and appointed his fourth son crown prince Mạnh, to become Emperor Trần Minh Tông. The court was riven with disputes and deaths were even recorded as being avenged by persons being 'chopped into thousands of pieces'.[116] Trần Minh Tông was judged a kind but unwise king whose reign was propped up by able mandarins and generals, such as Phạm Ngũ Lão, Mạc Đĩnh Chi, Trương Hán Siêu, Nguyễn Trung Ngạn and Đoàn Nhữ Hài. Relations with the Yuan were maintained but the territorial dispute with the Chams still cast a shadow. In 1324 the new Yuan emperor sent two envoys to Đại Việt to announce his reign. They clashed with the Việt over protocol at court but managed to deliver a letter ordering Trần Minh Tông to respect Cham territory.[117] Trần Minh Tông abdicated in favour of his ten-year-old son, Prince Vượng in 1329, but continued to run the country as before. Prince Vượng became Emperor Trần Hiến Tông and the senior emperor moved to the alternative capital of Thiên Trường. Trần Hiến Tông's reign saw internal and external conflict, with the most persistent problem being the Ngưu Hống rebellion on the upper reaches of the River Đà, adjacent to Yunnan. The senior emperor took an army up there but the trouble continued.[118] Poor harvests continued to curse the land and there was a great famine in 1333. Clashes with the Lao army flared up occasionally and in one action with the Lao Đoàn Nhữ Hài was drowned. After thirteen years of reigning only in name, Trần Hiến Tông died at the age of 23 without an heir. The senior emperor then appointed his brother prince Hạo the next Trần emperor Trần Dụ Tông when he was a boy of six years. Like his brother, Trần Dụ Tông reigned in name only while the senior emperor Trần Minh Tông controlled the affairs of state. The country continued to struggle with natural disasters of flooding, crop failures and famine and at times 'people became monks or domestic slaves to survive'. Famine and food banditry became features of Đại Việt life, but Vân Đồn port continued to thrive with ships calling from China and Java. A mandarin was appointed to control it and an army group to defend it.

Đại Việt experienced repercussions in this period from external events, including rebellions in China against the Yuan, when former Yuan officials sought refuge in 1350. Three years later the Cham king

Ceramic urns, Trần dynasty, Hanoi History Museum.

Chế A Nan died and the husbands of his two daughters battled for the succession. The loser Chế Mỗ came to Thăng Long seeking asylum and help to gain his throne, which senior emperor Trần Minh Tông agreed to, sending him back with a Việt army. The expedition failed and Chế Mỗ later died in Thăng Long. The Chams retaliated with an attack on Hóa Châu, the former Lý territory, but this was repulsed. The senior emperor passed away in 1357 and the still youthful emperor left court affairs in the hands of incompetent mandarins while he amused himself with drinking, theatre, gambling and building more palaces.

In China Zhu Yuanzhang succeeded in defeating the Yuan and establishing a major new dynasty, the Ming, in 1367. He took the title emperor Hong-Wu and sent an envoy to Đại Việt the following year to announce the dynasty and establish relations. Đại Việt was then more preoccupied with its southern border, for the Chams continued to raid Hóa Châu to seize people and property. Emperor Trần Dụ Tông fell ill in 1368 and on his death bed appointed the adopted son of his late elder brother as his successor. The adopted son was an actor named Dương Nhật Lễ, whose family troupe had entertained the court some years earlier. Court scholars expressed their profound disappointment that the emperor, a lowly actor and not a Trần, spent his time acting and drinking. A failed attempt to take his life provoked a bloody assault on his opponents, including the popular queen mother Hiến Từ Tuyên Thánh, who originally supported his appointment but later expressed her regrets. Outraged princes left Thăng Long, including prince Phủ, third son of the senior emperor Trần Minh Tông, who fled to the upper reaches of Đà River. There Trần royal brothers and sisters began to plot against the actor emperor. In 1370 prince Phủ proclaimed himself emperor Trần Nghệ Tông and travelled to Thăng Long with a group of Trần princes and princesses. The actor was jailed and killed on the orders of the new emperor. The mother of the assassinated emperor sought refuge in the Cham court and pleaded for an attack on Đại Việt.

The new emperor faced a formidable foe in Cham king Chế Bồng Nga who made a large-scale attack in 1371 and was to ransack Thăng Long many times. Chế Bồng Nga seized back the Ô and Lý territories for the Cham kingdom and began an extended war against Đại Việt that lasted into the 1380s.[119] The Cham entered Thăng Long in their first attack and burned the archives before withdrawing with many captives.[120] The Trần emperor had fled by boat to Đông Ngàn. In the same year he took a disastrous decision that was to end the dynasty. He promoted a nephew of one of the former emperor's consorts, Lê Quý Ly, to his privy council. The emperor abdicated in the Trần tradition in 1372, leaving the crown to his brother, prince Kính, who became emperor Trần Duệ Tông, while he retired to Thiên Trường. The new emperor came under pressure from both the Ming and the Cham and one of his first acts was to increase the strength of his army and build ships in preparation for war with Champa. In 1374 he banned the use of Chinese-style clothes and hairdos, and Lao and Cham languages. His war preparations were focused under Lê Quý Ly, who was made military chief of staff.[121] The Chams raided Hóa Châu again in 1376 and the emperor ordered an attack on Champa, against the advice of his mandarins. The emperor led the army south and left Lê Quý Ly to organize food supplies and other provisions from the southern provinces of Nghệ-An, Tân Bình and Thuận Hóa. When the Việt army reached Sri Banoy port at Vijaya a month later, they were devastated by Chế Bồng Nga's forces and the Việt emperor was killed. The Việt remnant fled north, pursued by Chế Bồng Nga, who again ransacked Thăng Long in 1377 before pulling back. The senior emperor appointed the deceased emperor's son as emperor Trần Phế Đế at the age of fourteen.[122]

When this youthful new Trần emperor came to the throne, the Ming had consolidated their power and begun expressing displeasure at what was happening between Đại Việt and Champa. The Ming emperor refused to accept the Việt claim that Trần Duệ Tông drowned while inspecting his southern border and renewed their orders to both sides to end the fighting. The conflict however continued with Chế Bồng Nga again destroying Thăng Long in 1378 and 1380.[123] Royal treasure was hidden in temple vaults outside the capital, and even monks were conscripted. Chế Bồng Nga continued to harass the southern Việt southern provinces, but was eventually betrayed into a Việt trap in 1390 and beheaded. The *Mingshi* version says he was killed by his right-hand man, who took the Cham throne in 1390/1,[124] and the Ming refused to accept tribute.[125] Ming demands on Đại Việt also led to strains. In 1384 they asked the Trần to provide food for their troops in Yunnan, with which the Trần complied, and the next year they demanded that twenty monks be sent to China. The Ming demanded fruit-tree seedlings, 50 elephants and passage through Đại Việt to Champa. Faced with these escalating Ming demands, Đại Việt prepared the army and built more ships.

The Trần demise resulted however from internal strife, not external pressure. Trần Phế Đế was a weak ruler and senior emperor Trần Nghệ Tông put all his trust in Lê Quý Ly. The latter often countermanded the emperor's orders and when he sought the senior emperor's approval for dismissing the emperor he succeeded. Trần Phế Đế was imprisoned in Tư Phúc pagoda in late 1388 and killed by strangulation. Prince Ngung, youngest son of the senior emperor was proclaimed emperor Trần Thuận Tông in 1389, under the control of Lê Quý Ly. His reign saw trouble at court, pressure from China and Champa and the revolt of starving peasants. A monk called Phạm Sư Ôn seized Thăng Long with a group of farmers and occupied it for three days before being routed and killed. Lê Qúy Ly was now ruling the country and he began killing princes who opposed him. In 1395 the senior emperor died and Lê Quý Ly appointed himself regent. Lê Quý Ly, by then, was also the father-in-law of emperor Trần Thuận Tông. He signed his decrees 'regent in charge of mentoring the emperor' and brought in new rules on court costume, changed the names of provinces and issued paper money to replace copper coins, as would be expected of a new emperor. He then began building a new capital in the province of Thanh Hóa, causing some alarm at court. He renamed Thanh Hóa *trấn* Thanh Đô (Thanh military capital) and appointed his own men to rule important cities and changed land allocations. The court was ordered to move to Thanh Hóa in 1397 and any who opposed the plan were killed. Thăng Long palaces were dismantled and put on ships to be transported to the new capital, but half were lost at sea. The new capital Tây Đô was built like a citadel surrounded by high stone walls made of slabs weighing from ten to sixteen tons. These still stand and were accorded UNESCO World Heritage status in 2011. Tây Đô was built in only three months and covered an area of 880 sq. m. The rushed work resulted in many deaths and today several temples have been built around the citadel to honour those killed. Lê Quý Ly ordered the emperor Trần Thuận Tông to abdicate in 1398, leaving the crown to his eldest son Prince An, a boy of three. In 1399 Lê Quý Ly ordered the death of the senior emperor.[126] This cleared the way for Lê Qúy Ly to declare himself to be Quốc Tổ Chương Hoàng, the grandfather of the state, a reference to his position as the grandfather of the young emperor. For the next year, he ruled behind the child emperor, with his son as his deputy. This pretence was abandoned in 1400 when Lê Qúy Ly put aside the child emperor and took the crown himself. A bloodbath ensued at court after a plot to kill Lê Qúy Ly was uncovered. More than 370 people were executed in a long purge in which royal family members were drowned, buried alive or made domestic slaves. The search for rebels went on for several years while the country experienced a period of war as opposition groups took up arms.

THE HỒ INTERLUDE (1400–1413 CE)

Lê Qúy Ly changed his surname back to Hồ and proclaimed himself emperor in 1400 and the country's name was changed to Đại Ngu. Ten months later he abdicated in favour of his second son Hồ Hán Thương and appointed himself senior emperor. For the next five years, Hồ Hán Thương and Hồ Qúy Ly issued decrees to revive the economy and restore social order, while eliminating any Trần. They tried to establish diplomatic relations with the Ming by reporting that there was no Trần left. In 1403 the Hồ sent an expedition to Champa to lay siege to Vijaya. They appealed for help from the Ming, but the new Chinese emperor Ming Yong-le, a usurper and professional soldier, preferred his own military solutions and sent nine warships to Champa, where his forces clashed with the Việt who began withdrawing from Vijaya. The Ming complained about the incident and began sending a stream of envoys to protest Hồ actions.

THE MING INVASION

Ming Yong-le rapidly built China into a powerful force in Asia and the beginning of what is sometimes called 'the Chinese century'. His formidable Zhang-He fleet spearheaded a show of force across the South China Sea and beyond to promote state-sponsored trade and draw in the gold, ivory, pearl and perfumes that were in high demand in China. Yong-le presumably saw an opportunity to return to the boundaries of the Han at a time that Đại Việt had no legitimate heir on the throne. Đại Việt was still culturally close to China, for it still officially used classical Chinese, it was ruled by Chinese-style institutions and followed Confucian scholars.[127] Since ancient times it has been an administrative division of China.

In 1406 the Ming emperor acted against the Hồ to restore 'the legitimate Trần', after a Trần named Thiêm Bình arrived at the Ming court and asked for help.[128] The Ming despatched 5,000 troops from Guangxi to take Trần Thiêm Bình home.[129] The Chinese and the Việt armies fought at Chi Lăng border crossing, when the Ming were repulsed and Trần Thiêm Bình captured and executed.[130] Yong-le was said to be furious at the Hồ 'duplicity'. On 11 May 1406 he ordered his commanders

Tay Do Castle, South Gate.

'to take an army to Annam to punish the Hồ'. Yong-le declared 'Annam is secluded in a little cranny in the ocean.'[131] The hostile reference to Annam as a Chinese possession was accompanied by a list of twenty major crimes imputed to the Hồ, including killing two legitimate Trần kings and their many descendants, interfering in Champa and encroaching on the border with China.[132] The army left from Guangxi and Yunnan.[133] The Việt annals record a force of 80,000 men travelling as two groups,[134] while *Ming Shi-lu* speaks of 800,000 men.[135]

The combined Ming forces defeated the Hồ at several locations from the border to Thăng Long. The Hồ fled the old capital and the Ming forces plundered its copper coins, men, boys and women.[136] Some Việt volunteered to go to China to be trained and sent back as Ming officials. As there was 'no Trần left to occupy the throne', the Ming set up the Jiao-zhi regional military commission, a provincial administration and a surveillance commission 'to govern the prefectures and counties'. By mid-1407 the Ming captured the father and son Hồ Quý Ly and Hồ Hán Thương in Thanh Hóa. The Việt army remnant surrendered, both Hồ Quý Ly and Hồ Hán Thương were taken to Yong-le and imprisoned.[137]

THE TRẦN REVIVAL (1407–13 CE)

On the recommendation of Ming commandeer Zhang Fu, the emperor renamed the country Jiaozhi in July 1407[138] and Zhang Fu and commander

Mu Sheng returned to China with their booty.[139] Jiaozhi was assigned to two Ming officials,[140] and one, Huang Fu, was the chief administrator for a decade and was said in the Việt annals to be well respected. The Ming detailed inventory of what they captured included '3,120,000 people . . . 13,600,000 *shi* of grain, 235,900 elephants, horses and cattle, 8,672 ships and 2,539,852 items of military equipment'.[141] The Việt count was lower with 3,129,500 households, 112 elephants, 420 horses, 35,750 head of cattle and 8,865 ships.[142] Pockets of resistance remained under prince Ngỗi, son of the late Emperor Trần Nghệ Tông, who proclaimed himself Emperor Giản Định Đế. From 1407 to 1413 this Trần Emperor Giản Định Đế and later his nephew and successor Trùng Quang Đế, formed a resistance movement that was strong at first, prompting the Ming to send back 40,000 soldiers from Yunnan under Mu Sheng. When Mu Sheng ran into difficulties in 1409, Zhang Fu was sent in with another large force.[143] It took them four years to capture Trùng Quang Đế in the southern province of Hóa Châu according to *Ming Shi-lu*. The Việt annals say Trùng Quang Đế committed suicide in 1414 by jumping into the sea while being shipped to China.[144] *Ming Shi-lu* however says he was executed in the Chinese capital on 16 August 1414.

Thus ended the Trần dynasty. The Trần ruled for 174 years through twelve reigns and survived another seven years in resistance. Ironically the second half of the dynasty gradually unwound the achievements of the first half. During the first 68 years of nation-building, the Trần achieved the unthinkable by three times thwarting Kublai Khan's attempts to expand into Southeast Asia. Thereafter the Trần managed to maintain their independence but permitted a major decline of infrastructure. Natural disasters were made worse by their failure to repair damage to water systems after the Mongols departed. Discontent spread from the highest to the lowest echelons of society and the Chams repeatedly invaded to avenge the losses inflicted by the early Trần. Distrust at court and the incursion by the Chams pushed the last Trần emperors into the arms of Lê Qúy Ly, who eventually schemed his way to pushing aside the Trần boy emperor and founding the abortive Hồ regime. The Hồ took the crown from the Trần much as the Trần divested the Lý, by ingratiating themselves with a tightly knit family by marriage. The difference is the Trần did it quickly and without much bloodshed. The Trần went on to become one of the strongest Việt dynasties and immortalized themselves in the country's history through their series of victories over the hitherto invincible Mongols at the end of the thirteenth century. The brief Hồ interlude is credited with some structural reforms and the introduction of paper money, but it also has a tarnished reputation for its treatment of Trần victims.

7
Ming Invasion and the Rise of
Lê Lợi (1407–27)

Vietnamese historians all condemn the Ming invasion as autocratic, brutal and gloomy while the Chinese account emphasizes rational reorganization and promoted Confucian scholars and administrators. A new class of Việt bureaucrats or 'literati' was schooled to run detailed administrative systems in fifteen *phủ*. Taylor takes the view that 'Ming rule had a transforming effect on the development of Vietnamese culture and politics. For one thing, it completed the destruction of the Trần aristocracy begun by Hồ Quý Ly. For another, it inculcated a generation of students with the Confucianism of Zhu Xi, which thereafter replaced Buddhism as the primary ideological vantage of rulers. And it also aroused a new style of monarchy that built upon the brief experiment of Hồ Quý Ly in Thanh Hóa.'

Following the Ming capture of the Việt capital and the Hồ family, they renamed the territory Jiaozhi in 1407. The Ming invasion came as trade continued to flourish on the maritime route. A new generation of port cities appeared with depots adapted to the increasing volume of goods.[1] At the same time the fifteenth century heralded a new military era when sophisticated firearms and gunpowder became widely available.[2] A thoroughgoing Ming-style bureaucracy was administered by the new class of Việt literati.[3] The Ming sent in erudite monks as well as administrators as a mission intended to be civilizing. Roads and canals were recognized, trade encouraged and taxes kept low. People who had become homeless during the political unrest were settled on land or in the army.[4] Resistance groups opposed them for the next seven years and only when the Trần remnants were finally defeated and the last Trần king died in 1414 could the Ming truly claim to be in full control. For the next thirteen years the Ming ruled with a policy of precise administration and forced assimilation, imposing people registers at all levels down to villages. Each citizen was issued with an identity paper which they had to produce when asked by Ming officials.[5] The registers assisted tax collection and the assigning of duties such as mining for precious metals, collecting forest products, diving for pearls or joining the army. Palace eunuchs at the Ming court were insatiable in their demands for precious metals and pearls.[6] Salt became a state commodity and was taxed and no citizen was allowed to sell it privately.[7] Salt gathered by any means had to be declared and the tax paid before the producer could sell it. Travellers were allowed to carry three bowls of salt each and a small bottle of salted fish sauce (Nước Mắm).[8] Pepper was also tightly controlled. The Việt were obliged to abandon their traditional clothing and ordered to grow pigtails and dress like the Chinese. It was a similar policy that the Nguyễn dynasty would later apply to the Cham. They had to follow the Confucian system of education and to practise only Buddhism and Daoism. The Ming abolished books and stelae written by Việt authors – a policy formulated before the invasion by Yong-le.[9] He sent a secret instruction to commander Zhang Fu prior to his departure to 'burn all written and printed materials within Annam, except for Buddhist and Daoist texts, and anything that promotes Vietnamese rites and customs'.[10] In public in the Ming Shi-lu, Yong-le showed a more benevolent face, saying 'when the army enters Annam and takes prefectural cities, none of the registers, maps or gazetteers obtained are to be destroyed.'[11] But Zhang Fu was chided in private for not destroying the texts. 'I have repeatedly ordered you to destroy all Việt printed and written materials . . . In addition, you were ordered to destroy rather than to preserve every Việt stela encountered.' Yong-le berated Zhang Fu for deploying illiterate soldiers to go through texts and stelae before destroying them and now ordered that he 'immediately burn every Việt work with not a single one to be left behind'.[12] Thousands of books like the Lý penal code and the Trần sets of Quốc triều thống chế in twenty volumes, Quốc triều thường lễ in ten volumes and the first set of Vietnamese history Đại Việt Sử Ký, composed by Lê Văn Hưu in 1272, were taken to China.[13] Taylor observes that 'of the books collected by Ming officials, nothing remains, although today it is possible to encounter myths about hidden texts'.[14] A few books are said to have been recovered by Lê Trừng (Hồ Nguyên Trừng), the eldest son of Hồ Quý Ly, who became a Ming official. He was pardoned after his family was captured and taken to China and then given a position at the Ming court. It is not known when and how he managed to recover these texts and what happened to the originals, but he later claimed that he used them to compose his memoir Nam Ông Mộng Lục.[15] This text was published for the first time in China in 1442 as part of a collection of Chinese writing and was taken back to Vietnam later by ambassador Lê Quý Đôn.[16] The Vietnamese translation of this work was published in Hanoi in 1999 and has been the subject of intense scholarly debate over its authenticity and content of the original facts of Đại Việt Sử Ký. The general conclusion of Vietnamese scholars is that *Nam Ông Mộng Lục* contains a number of stories identical to those in the volumes of *Đại Việt Sử Ký Toàn Thư* by Ngô Sĩ Liên and that both must have shared the same original source. During the Ming occupation under governor Huang Fu, many Chinese officials arrived to man the administration, but the posting was unpopular and the candidates poor. Those entrusted with 'civilizing' the Việt at the Ming Confucian schools complained 'the students are still illiterate'. Better teachers were requested in a report from the colony to the Ming emperor in 1411. Zhang Fu and Mu Sheng were sent back to Jiaozhi to deal with the Trần insurrection and Mu Sheng led in 40,000 troops from Yunnan, but his force was routed.

Less than two months later, Zhang Fu was again sent to Jiaozhi with the title 'General for Subduing the Yi'.[17] The southern provinces of Thuận and Hóa remained troublesome for the Ming, who kept 87,000 soldiers there.[18] Yong-le professed anxiety about the Jiaozhi situation day and night and Zhang Fu was urgently recalled in December 1416 to be replaced by Li Bin (Lý Bân). Li Bin's report of April 1417 said Jiaozhi was full of disaffected native officials, some of them magistrates and battalion commanders: 'they all rose in rebellion, burnt the walls, palissades and buildings of two towns, killed the officials and arrogated titles to themselves. Their followers numbered over 1,000'.[19] The situation would remain unsettled for many years as remnants of the resistance gathered around the new leader Lê Lợi, who rose against the Ming in Thanh Hóa in 1418.

THE RISE OF LÊ LỢI (1418–27 CE)

Lê Lợi was a wealthy landowner born in 1385 in Lam Sơn village in Thanh Hóa province.[20] As an educated man he was asked to take up a position in the Ming local administration but he refused. The Ming only made him a police officer in 1418.[21] Lê Lợi was supported by his nephew Lê Thạch and generals Đinh Bồ, Lê Ngân and Lê Lý. He defeated one Ming force but then his force was crushed and he pulled back to mount Chí Linh.[22] For the next ten years Lê Lợi's army was a thorn in the side of the Ming, who constantly pursued him into the mountains and into Laos. He lost some of his generals but still attracted supporters. Dissatisfied with the situation, Yong-le chastised Li Bin for failing to keep Jiaozhi in order in 1420. Yong-le warned that 'if you neglect your duties and fritter away your time with the result that the bandits grow in strength, it will indeed be difficult to excuse you!' Another imperial order followed asking Li Bin why he had not captured Lê Lợi. By the end of 1422 Yong-le sent more orders castigating officers for their failure to capture Lê Lợi. Li Bin died

Lê Lợi Statue in Thanh Hóa province.

of illness in February 1422 and Chen Zhi took over the Jiaozhi campaign. Lê Lợi's forces meanwhile suffered terrible hunger and were forced to eat their elephants and horses. He eventually sent officers Lê Vận and Lê Trăn to the Ming to seek a truce, which was agreed. Lê Lợi took his troops back to his home village in 1423, where the Ming commander Chen Zhi sent him cattle, salt fish, rice seedlings and agricultural implements. Lê Lợi sent back gold and silver to thank him.

In August 1424 Yong-le died after an expedition and crown prince Ming Ren-zong took over as emperor Hong-xi. It wasn't long before he showed his dismay at the high cost of occupying Jiaozhi. Hong-xi said

Lê Lợi had been forced into becoming a 'bandit' because of official pressure and taxation and proclaimed a general amnesty and 'forgave all Lê Lợi's former crimes'.[23] Two days later, he recalled and replaced Huang Fu. Hong-xi then appointed Lê Lợi prefect of Thanh Hóa. Eunuch Shan Shou was sent to Jiaozhi to make the appointment official but Lê Lợi deferred acceptance until the following year. At the same time he launched attacks on the Ming bases in Nghệ An.[24] By early 1425 the Ming emperor had had enough and he issued an imperial order castigating Chen Zhi and his Commissioner-in-chief Fang-Zheng for 'being tardy in achieving success and thereby assisting the bandits'.[25] Lê Lợi lay siege to the Ming citadel in Nghệ An in 1425.[26] In May Hong-xi died and was succeeded by crown prince Ming Xuan-zong, who took the crown as emperor Xuan-de. Like his father he viewed Jiaozhi with alarm. He sent an ultimatum to his commander Chen Zhi in January 1426 telling him 'to resolve the situation by the spring, if not, blame will be affixed'. While the majority of the Ming force was occupied in Nghệ An, Lê Lợi launched an attack against the former Hồ capital of Tây Đô, forcing the Ming to lock themselves in the citadel while Lê Lợi's army camped outside. In May 1426 the Ming emperor sent in new regional commander Wang Tong to resolve the impasse in a different way. Chen Zhi and Feng Zhang were both stripped of their badges and positions, demoted as officials on probation and sent with an advance force to fight Lê Lợi. Xuan-de complained that Jiaozhi had not been at peace for twenty years and blamed the 'repeated strife and rebellion' on Ming officials who 'plundered insatiably' while not reporting the true situation to the court. He issued a pardon for Lê Lợi and his followers for 'all crimes without regard to their magnitude'. Further, the Việt people 'apart from having to pay land-tax grain, military personnel and civilians will be exempted from other taxes such as the taxes on gold, silver, salt, iron, aromatics, merchandise and fish. It will be permissible to trade gold, silver, copper cash, salt and salted fish within the borders.' It was a more than generous offer, and an unheard of admission of fault on the part of an emperor, but it came too late, for by then the resistance under Lê Lợi had spread far and wide and the Ming force was in defensive posture. The Chinese entrenched themselves in citadels around the country and their Đông Đô headquarters became a target for Lê Lợi. The Đông Đô commander requested help from Nghệ An but that citadel and the Hồ capital of Tây Đô were already besieged. In late 1426 Wang Tong reached Đông Đô with 50,000 soldiers and cavalry but they were defeated by Lê Lợi. Wang Tong reported that he was surrounded in Đông Đô. Lê Lợi meanwhile set about establishing law and order in the countryside and also told the Ming that a Trần heir named Trần Cảo could be put on the throne, even though his Trần lineage had not been fully verified. This was designed as a face-saving gesture for the Ming, whose pretext for invasion was the restoration of the Trần line. Wang Tong first accepted the offer in January 1427 and told his officials that all cities to the south of Thanh Hóa were being put under the command of Lê Lợi. But this was rejected by local Việt collaborators with the Ming[27] and the war continued. Lê Lợi again attacked Ming forces in the southern provinces and set up his headquarters across the Hồng River in today's Gia Lâm district of Hanoi. The Ming emperor sent in a new regional commander Liu Sheng from Guangxi along with the veteran Mu Sheng from Yunnan while Huang Fu was ordered to fall back to be provincial administration commissioner of Jiaozhi. It took nearly ten months for the Ming force to be organized, allowing Lê Lợi time to prepare. Liu Sheng arrived at the border on 1 October 1427 and broke through the Southern Gate and headed south. Mu Sheng camped on the Yunnan border to watch progress. Lê Lợi petitioned Liu Sheng for a truce because he said he had now found a Trần heir, which the Chinese general forwarded to the emperor while continuing his advance into Jiaozhi. When he reached Chí Linh gate, a narrow passage between mountains south of the border, Lê Lợi's army launched a massive ambush and killed Liu Sheng. After two weeks of fighting, the Việt army defeated the remaining Ming troops and captured Huang Fu and thousands of soldiers.[28] On hearing all this Mu Sheng turned back to Yunnan and Wang Tong, marooned in the citadel at Đông Đô, asked for a ceasefire, which Lê Lợi accepted.

On 12 November 1427 Lê Lợi and Wang Tong set up an altar on the south side of the Đông Đô citadel and pledged to cease all hostilities. The two leaders exchanged gifts and the war was over. Lê Lợi ordered his troops to end the sieges at Tây Đô, Cổ Lộng and Chí Linh[29] so that the Ming troops could join with those from Đông Đô and return home early in 1428.[30] On the day the letter Lê Lợi sent to Liu Sheng on the Trần heir arrived at the Ming court Xuan-de accepted Trần Cảo as the new king of Annam.[31] The Ming generals were sent off with a lavish banquet and Wang Tong led 86,640 soldiers and their families back to China by road, according to *Ming Shi-lu*. Lê Lợi allocated 500 ships for those who went by sea and released 20,000 captive men and horses. When all arrived back in China, the emperor sent an envoy to Đông Đô to appoint Trần Cảo as *An Nam Quốc Vương* (king of Annam).

In a famous epic poem *Bình Ngô Đại Cáo* (Great Announcement on the Pacification of the Ngô/Chinese), written in Chinese characters in 1428, Lê Lợi's esteemed counsellor Nguyễn Trãi reviewed the resistance and declared to all, from high to low, that the hard times were over and the people could rest. Soon afterwards Trần Cảo died from poisoning. The details are murky but one account says he took a ship out to sea because Lê Lợi's officials did not want him to be king since he had not helped the resistance against the Ming. He was pursued and caught on the ocean and forced to take poison.[32] His death opened the way for Lê Lợi to become king himself.

After a decade of fighting, Lê Lợi brought the twenty-year Ming incursion to an end. The Ming imposed Chinese ways and burnt or took away texts by Việt authors. In a rapid, forced assimilation, they created a Confucian society that favoured a new literati class at the cost of all others. When they left, the upper echelon of Việt society had been sini-cized and were wearing Chinese dress and growing pigtails. The Ming Jiaozhi had some slight impact within China. In November 1407 alone the Ming brought 9,000 talented Việt to their court to be trained for administrative posts in Jiaozhi.[33] Some remained at the Ming court and were given titles, among them Hồ Quý Ly's son Lê Trừng (Hồ Nguyên Trừng), who was steadily promoted until he became vice minister in the Auxiliary Ministry of Works. Ruan Jun was made vice minister in the Ministry of Justice, while Yan-yi and Si-kai were also promoted to vice ministers. The Ming also brought many children back to China from Đông Đô (former Thăng Long). The Việt boys were castrated to serve as court eunuchs and one of them, called Nguyễn An, became the architect of the Forbidden City in Beijing.[34]

A wider consequence of the Ming invasion of Đại Việt was its effect on Southeast Asia, as a region. 'It alerted all states contiguous with Ming China's southern borders that China was prepared to use force. But, per-haps more important in the long run, it also showed that China neither had the will nor the capacity to conquer and hold territory in the south.'[35]

The Ming in the end proclaimed that their objective was achieved when a Trần heir was restored to the Đại Việt throne. But the true victory was Lê Lợi's, who became a national hero for driving the Chinese out of the country for centuries. Clashes continued at the border and Chinese rule returned briefly in the sixteenth century under the Mạc, but they did not return to occupy.

8

Lê Dynasty: The First 100 Years
(1428–1527)

At the start of the Lê dynasty the ruling Việt literati were considered disgraced by their collaboration. The Chinese customs the Việt were made to adopt were now despised. But no immediate alternatives were available for either. The rise of the Lê gave prominence to the 'southerners' from the mountains of Thanh Hóa and Nghệ An, including Lê Lợi. He was the son of a *kinh* lowlander man and a local woman of the mountains. Many of his generals were from mountain minorities such as the Mường (Lê Lai, Lê Hiến, Lê Hưu), Thái (Lê Cố, Xa Khả Sâm, Cầm Quý) and Tày (Lý Huệ).[1] The Ming dominance of the Hồng River delta had forced the resistance into mountain bases. The armies of the last Trần emperors came from even further south, in the former Cham territories of Thuận and Hóa Châu. As the anti-Ming resistance expanded, more supporters came to Lê Lợi from other areas, and as long as the war was underway all was well between the generals from different ethnic origins. But when peace came the ethnic and regional rivalries showed at court. In 1428 emperor Lê Lợi faced the task of restoring political and social order and redefining Việt identity. During the last years of war, he managed to establish low level administrative bureaus, but now a whole new order was required that would expand and maintain a coherent system that united the people.

LÊ THÁI TỔ RESTORES LAW, ORDER AND EDUCATION
(1428–33 CE)

Lê Lợi proclaimed himself emperor Lê Thái Tổ in 1428, changed the name of the country back to Đại Việt[2] and restored old Thăng Long as his capital. He sent the obligatory envoy to China for official Ming sanction, applying the appeasement strategy with the giant neighbour that had served earlier emperors well. Although he regained Việt territory by force of arms he expressed it as the fulfilment of the Ming policy of restoration and their voluntary departure.

Temple of Literature, Hanoi.

As soon as the Ming army was gone, Lê Lợi sent a memorial to the Ming emperor in the name of emperor Trần Cảo, admitting 'a mountain of crimes' against the Ming and humbly apologizing. Along with regular tribute he sent 'one human figure in gold and one in silver to represent ourselves, offered in acknowledgement of our crimes, together with the memorial and local products'. The tribute offering of gold and silver human figures has been the subject of some speculation among historians, some of whom assumed they were in compensation for the deaths of Liu Sheng and one of his senior generals at the decisive battle of Chi Lăng pass in 1427. Others now see them as representing Trần Cảo and Lê Lợi or the Việt people in general, for the killing of Liu Sheng and his deputy was not mentioned. In June 1428 Lê Lợi reported to the Ming emperor that Trần Cảo had died and requested support as the new ruler. Xuan-de affirmed his pardon for Lê Lợi and granted a general amnesty to Đại Việt but insisted on a search for a Trần heir. For the next three years Lê Lợi sent shuttle missions reporting that no Trần heir could be found and that he was ruling the land to keep order. His face-saving formula for the Ming emperor finally paid off and the Ming approved him as *An Nam Quốc Sự*, caretaker of Annam, on 12 June 1431.[3] Lê Lợi was never awarded the full title of king of Annam but there was an important protocol change in that the Ming ceased to refer to Đại Việt as Jiaozhi in official documents and referred instead to Annam. In diplomatic terms it was a grand gesture indicating that the Ming had at last acknowledged Đại Việt as a separate entity and no longer a province of China.

Lê Thái Tổ meanwhile undertook the enormous task of reorganizing the country. His first act was to declare a two-year tax exemption and his next was to reward his generals and their troops and punish the collaborators who were denounced as 'rogue officials'. Some 227 men, including the confidant Nguyễn Trãi and the generals Trần Nguyên Hãn and Phạm Văn Xảo, were rewarded with high-ranking positions. The state was repartitioned into five *đạo* or circuits, each headed by an executive called *Hành Khiển*. All five *đạo* were placed under a chief executive at court. To select new officials, exams were held in the first year of Lê Thái Tổ's reign. Top grades were awarded to those showing talent in both civil and military affairs; the second were capable linguistically and in attitude and the third were good at writing and calculating. Others who graduated were put in the ungraded category. Lê Thái Tổ also ordered his Imperial Counsellors and mandarins to select deserving candidates for the administration 'based on merit, not because they were family members or friends'. Lê Thái Tổ took the step of putting through an exam system not only for scholars but also for Buddhist and Daoist monks. Those who did not know the sutras or Chinese religious teachings were to be stripped of their titles and reclassified as commoners.[4] A new monetary unit called Thuận Thiên was issued and the senior mandarins were charged with making new laws to control the currency. The early years of the reign were busy with the issue of decrees on law and order and massive land reform. Many were dispossessed of land awarded by the Ming while the emperor's own army was rewarded with land for their years in the resistance. Commodity inventories were created to track resources of copper, iron, mulberry fields, silk stock, beeswax and rattan. In January 1429 a royal decree stipulated that all types of fields, all gold and silver mines and areas producing mountain products had to be registered. The penal code was tightened with severe punishments for vagabonds and gamblers topping the list. Gamblers would have one fingertip chopped off. Those who gathered to drink without an official occasion were to receive 100 lashes. The emperor created a new class of officials called censors (Ngôn Quan), who could speak up or lodge petitions against anybody who did wrong whatever their rank, the emperor included. The army of 250,000 was reduced to 100,000 who rotated duties in between cultivating their land, reverting to the *Ngụ Binh ư Nông* policy of the Lý and Trần.[5] Education and the Việt cultural identity was a major concern because the Ming had burnt or taken to China so many books and artefacts. Only Confucian materials remained. The emperor nevertheless established a national university for sons of the elite and a few gifted commoners. Schools were set up in the regions to teach a curriculum based on Confucian texts.

The Lê court was not as harmonious as it at first appeared. Although the emperor was energetic in trying to engage all in the pursuit of an ideal state 'without putting personal interest above the public good', courtiers formed cliques to obtain privileges and tensions rose between those from Thanh Hóa – the original followers – and the rest.[6] Matters came to a head in 1432 when the emperor was ill and both Trần Nguyên Hãn and Phạm Văn Xảo were killed by their rivals after being accused of plotting to subvert the throne. Lê Thái Tổ died in 1433 aged 49, after only six years on the throne. A month before he died he replaced his first son Tư Tề as heir with his second son Nguyên Long, a boy of eleven.[7]

LÊ THÁI TÔNG (1433–42 CE) AND THE FATAL CONCUBINE

The young crown prince Nguyên Long became emperor Lê Thái Tông under the guidance of the regent Lê Sát, a powerful man of limited intellect who was highly trusted by Lê Lợi.[8] Lê Thái Tổ's reform programme continued and in 1438 those who obtained the first grade in the countrywide state exams were sent to the National University (Quốc Tử Giám) in the capital. Those who studied beyond the age of 25 without passing the exams were sent home as ordinary citizens. Exams were held every five years at circuit level and every six years at the national level in the capital. Later the exams were held every three years. The first doctoral exam was held in the spring of 1442 with 450 candidates registered, 33 of whom were selected as finalists.[9] Of these three reached the first grade as Trạng Nguyên (Doctors *cum laude*), seven passed with the second grade and 23 passed with the third grade as doctors of literature, including the historian Ngô Sĩ Liên. According to an imperial decree, those who passed had their names engraved on stelae erected at the Temple of Literature (Văn Miếu) and National University. The first stelae were raised much later, in 1484, under the emperor Lê Thánh Tông and these are the oldest still standing at Văn Miếu today.

The first imperial seals made of gold and silver were created in 1435. The highest was called *Thuận Thiên Thừa Vận Chi Bảo* and kept solely for the coronation of an emperor. Next came *Đại Thiên Hành Hóa Chi Bảo* for imperial decrees, a third for reward and punishment orders, a fourth one for secret matters and two more for ordinary matters. For everyday court affairs an ivory seal was used. This year also marked the Ming acceptance of the new Việt king. A Ming protocol official was despatched to Đông Kinh in November 1434 to award Lê Thái Tông the position of 'state caretaker' that his father held. Lê Thái Tông was finally awarded the title of *An Nam Quốc Vương* (king of Annam) by the new

Ming emperor Zheng-tong in November 1436. A Ming delegation arrived in Đại Việt in the spring of the next year to convey the Ming emperor's decree and his gold seal to Lê Thái Tông. The gold seal weighed 100 taels and had a handle in the shape of a camel. Foreign relations were cordial under Lê Thái Tông with several embassies calling from China, Laos, Champa and an unknown country called La La Tư Điện beyond Yunnan. Foreign trade flourished with missions from Guangzhou, Laos, Siam and Champa and Javanese vessels came regularly to Vân Đồn port. Unofficial trade developed when Chinese envoys brought their own goods and sold them at high prices when they were sent on official business to the Việt capital. The emperor issued a decree in 1437 ordering all Ming residents in Đại Việt to wear Việt costume and cut their hair. Lê Thái Tông's court also had troublesome factions and Lê Sát made himself the court strongman. Even the Ming emperor noted that Lê Sát had taken over the Lê court, killed off his rivals and acted as he pleased.[10] Lê Thái Tông reigned only in name at first but when he reached the age of fifteen in 1437 he started running state affairs and dismissed Lê Sát. He reinstated a number of former mandarins and appointed new officials. In the autumn of the same year, Lê Thái Tông ordered Lê Sát to commit suicide at home and confiscated his estate to redistribute to other mandarins.

The reign of Lê Thái Tông marked the first time since the Trưng sisters (r. 40–43) and Lady Triệu (248) that women were given official positions. This surprising fact emerges from an imperial decree in 1434 in which the emperor ordered that 'all officials including female ones must be announced first before they enter the throne room to pay respects . . . No female without an official post will be allowed in'. Under this new dispensation lady Nguyễn Thị Lộ was called into court and awarded the title of Lady Scholar in charge of Protocol. Nguyễn Thị Lộ is described as a beautiful and educated young woman who was originally a concubine of the ageing senior counsellor Nguyễn Trãi. As his favourite, she probably accompanied him at official functions and was spotted by the young emperor. In the palace she exerted strong influence and advised the emperor to 'put in jail those women who were not obedient' after a new batch of concubines was selected. Problems among the concubines came to the surface when the emperor demoted one of the distinguished ones called Dương Thị Bí to commoner status in 1441 despite the fact that her son had been appointed heir apparent. After her downfall her son Nghi Dân was downgraded from crown prince to prince of Lạng Sơn. Another consort took over as favourite and her son Băng Cơ was made crown prince. Nguyễn Thị Lộ rose within a year to become the emperor's confidante 'who served him day and night.' In this capacity, Nguyễn Thị Lộ accompanied the emperor on a trip to the east. A few days later emperor Lê Thái Tông died of unknown causes at the age of twenty after an overnight rest at the estate of Nguyễn Trãi. His body was secretly taken back to the capital before his death was announced. Nguyễn Trãi and Nguyễn Thị Lộ were convicted of high treason for his death and were executed, along with three branches of their families. Crown prince Băng Cơ succeeded Lê Thái Tông as Emperor Lê Nhân Tông at the age of two.

LÊ NHÂN TÔNG (1442–59 CE) CREATES THE ANNALS

The infant emperor ruled under the direction of his mother queen Nguyễn Thị Anh, who was elevated to empress dowager in charge of state affairs. Unlike his father and grandfather, Lê Nhân Tông was almost immediately awarded the full title of *An Nam Quốc Vương* by the Ming emperor in January 1444. But the relations with Champa were not so good. The border area had never been truly peaceful since the first Lê, although relations were cordial on the diplomatic front. Cham raids into their former territory of Hóa, today's Thừa Thiên province, occurred intermittently and became more frequent and more serious under Lê Nhân Tông. In 1444 the Lê court sent 10,000 men to Champa and despatched two more forces the next year. Hostilities continued into 1446 when a large Việt army of 60,000 men was sent to fight the Cham king known by the Việt as Bí Cai. (As Cham inscriptions end in the fourteenth century later kings are only known by their Việt names.) They captured the king, his queens, concubines and generals in Vijaya and brought them back to Đại Việt and a new Cham king called Ma Ha Quý Lai was imposed by the Lê. By the end of 1453 Lê Nhân Tông began to take over the affairs of state at the age of fourteen. In 1455 he ordered a professor at the National University, Phan Phu Tiên, to compile a new history called *Đại Việt Sử Ký*, starting from Trần Thái Tông to the end of the Ming incursion.

In 1459 the dismissed crown prince Nghi Dân, son of the disgraced consort Dương Thị Bí, managed to kill the emperor and the empress dowager and proclaim himself emperor. He claimed he was the legitimate heir and that his half brother Băng Cơ became Emperor Lê Nhân Tông only because their father died suddenly. The court was in shock for some months but then courtiers got together and organized a plot to capture Nghi Dân and his supporters. Nghi Dân was demoted to the rank of marquis and told to commit suicide. The fourth son of Emperor Lê Thái Tông, prince Tư Thành, was put on the throne to be the next Emperor Lê Thánh Tông.

LÊ THÁNH TÔNG (1460–97 CE) ANNEXES CHAMPA

Prince Tư Thành was born a year after Băng Cơ and was living quietly in the imperial palaces while his brother reigned as emperor Lê Nhân Tông. At the age of eighteen he took the crown and became the most successful monarch of the Lê dynasty. He reorganized the country into twelve circuits and another was added in 1471 after his victory in Champa in which the Việt acquired a new swathe of land. The emperor remodelled the administration into six ministries and appointed high-ranking imperial officials or *Giám Sát Ngự Sử* (provincial censor) to oversee the provinces. Remarkably Lê Thánh Tông reinstated Nguyễn Trãi and gave a district-level position to his son Anh Vũ. The emperor was himself a highly trained Confucian scholar and it is no wonder that he placed education high in his priorities. Exams were held every three years at the capital to select scholars for the civil service. During the 38 years of his reign, twelve grand exams were held at the capital from which 501 doctors of literature were selected. The number of serving officials under Lê Thánh Tông was 5,370, which possibly included a few women. Of these 2,755 were mandarins at court and 2,615 worked as regional officials.[11] The Việt armed forces were kept well exercised and were organized in specialized branches such as the navy, infantry, elephant corps and cavalry. As well as spears, swords, bows and arrows, their weapons now included firearms and canon. The emperor completed a new legal code called *Quốc Triều Hình Luật* that ranged from criminal law to guidance on civil litigation on marriages, land ownership and inheritance. The code was structured on a Chinese model but managed to include special Việt elements. Inheritance and divorce laws were the most radical of the time. Following his predecessor's practice of honouring women in Việt society, five of his 24 guidances were aimed specifically at women. Women were also employed to do jobs traditionally undertaken by men and in 1471 the new post of female palanquin bearers was created. It is not known what happened to Phan Phu Tiên's history books under Lê Thánh Tông, but another set of Việt history was ordered to be composed, also called *Đại Việt Sử Ký* (*Complete History of Great Việt*), this time by Ngô Sĩ Liên, a highly esteemed scholar and a censor. This set contains two volumes of fifteen books with the first five books starting from the Hồng Bàng era until the time of the twelve warlords; the next ten books from Đinh Tiên Hoàng went up to the first Lê emperor, Lê Thái Tổ. This is the version that is still in circulation today, albeit with some modifications over time. This set of history books was the best example of Lê Thánh Tông's lasting achievements. Initially relations with Ming China were kept on an even keel. In 1462 Lê Thánh Tông was awarded the full title of king of Annam. Relations with Champa, on the other hand, were more problematic. For many years since the beginning of the Lê dynasty, Champa had continued to trouble Đại Việt. This turned into a major war under Lê Nhân Tông when the Cham king Bí Cai was captured and brought back to Đông Kinh. Internal strife between Cham factions then brought hundreds of Cham noblemen to the Lê court seeking asylum.[12]

Economic rivalry in this period focused on pearl-beds. Pearl was a coveted commodity under the Ming and pearl cultivation was an important business. The theft of pearls was a major crime for both the Việt and the Ming courts. In June 1471 a dispute over pearl-bed theft off the coast of Guangdong and Hainan island came to the attention of the Ming court which was told: 'Jiao people had sailed large, double-masted ships across the seas, stolen from the pearl-beds and plundered the goods of merchants.' The Lê emperor was instructed to investigate. Đại Việt's complaint about Champa stealing pearls was also heard by the Ming court. The Việt ruler told emperor Cheng-hua, 'no-one has ever sailed across the sea to steal pearls or plunder property (of Champa) . . . yet Thanh Hóa Guard and other guards in my country have reported over 30 ships of pirates secretly coming to the coast with the desire to steal property and kill people.' Over the years Cham raids into their former territory were often noted in the Việt annals. Champa also reported Việt attacks to the Ming.

By the end of 1470 emperor Lê Thánh Tông mustered a very large army of 260,000 to finally subdue Champa. A naval advance force of 100,000 men left first, followed by the 150,000 infantry ten days later. The emperor led the last 10,000 men to take up the rear. They all headed for Vijaya, then the most prominent kingdom of the Champa group, and its strategic deepwater port in Thị Nại bay. The Việt navy and ground forces reached Vijaya in January 1471 and in two months they defeated the Cham army and captured Cham king Trà Toàn. The king was sent back to Đông Kinh with two of his queens but was said to have died of illness on the journey. His head was severed and presented as booty to the Lê ancestors at their ancestral temple in Thanh Hoá. With this campaign, the Việt controlled 80 per cent of Cham territory. In the south the kingdom of Panduranga (Phan Rang) remained independent under a ruler called Bố Trì Trì and the central highlands remained under the control of two other Cham kings. According to the Vietnamese version of events, these Cham kings also submitted to Việt power and ruled as vassals of the Việt. The Lê emperor annexed the northern Cham territory under the names of Quảng Nam and Thăng Hoa, which were declared the thirteenth *đạo* Quảng Nam of Đại Việt. The Panduranga kingdom was to survive until it was crushed under the Nguyễn dynasty in 1832.

Cham Temple Po Nagar, at Nha Trang.

The devastating Việt assault on Vijaya in 1471 is generally considered as the end of the thousand-year loose confederation of Cham states. The Việt recognized three residual Cham kingdoms: 'three Cham states submitted to the Việt and their kings were then accepted by the Việt.' Apart from these one other Cham king seemed to survive for a while – in a complaint to the Ming court in June 1472 Cham envoy Le-sha said that in early 1471 'Annam troops arrived and attacked our country's capital, carrying off the king Pan-luo Cha-quan (Trà Toàn) and his family members, a total of over 50 persons . . . Now, the king's younger brother Pan-luo Cha-yue has temporarily taken on management of the affairs of state.'[13] Where this temporary Cham king was based and what 'state' he ruled remains obscure but the Ming emperor was persuaded by the claim and sent official Chen-Jun to enfeoff him as the new Cham king on 27 July 1472. The Việt annals offer no corroboration of this but instead identify the Cham king's younger brother as Trà Toại, who escaped into the mountains after the Việt attacked Vijaya but was caught and taken back to Đông Kinh where he was held until his death in 1509. His son Trà Phúc later escaped back to Champa with his father's remains and a number of Cham slaves and eventually built warships and asked the Ming for help against the Việt. When emperor Lê Uy Mục heard of this he ordered Chams in the capital to be killed including female officials *Nữ Sử*.

The crushing Việt victory of 1471 disastrously changed the state of the Cham kingdoms and it also changed the ethnic composition of Đại

Việt, which now reached down to the southern border of today's Bình Định province, bringing culture and genes into the ethnic mix that would eventually make up that of today's Vietnamese population. The Lê emperor was quick to recognize this and produced a policy of assimilation that applied to all non-Việt residents within Việt boundaries. In November 1471 he issued a decree ordering all people of different ethnicities who had surrendered to the Việt, all Lao and Cham people, and all people with Chinese fathers and Việt mothers to register themselves as slaves of the state.[14] At the same time, scholars were selected to teach the people of the newly acquired Cham land 'civilized' ways, that is to follow Việt customs. Việt farmers and estate lords were encouraged to move to and develop the newly acquired Cham lands.[15] By 1488 Cham boys aged fifteen were encouraged to take Việt local exams to qualify for official posts. A new class of Việt-Cham was born at the start of a long period of forced assimilation that all but destroyed Cham culture, language and dress by the time of the Nguyễn dynasty (1802–1945). Today only small, impoverished pockets of Chams survive in the south-central provinces of Khánh Hòa, Phan Rang and Bình Thuận, where popular superstition credits them with black magic power. The Cham diaspora is largely Moslem and lives in Cambodia, Malaysia and the USA.

Emperor Lê Thánh Tông's prestige was enhanced by his victory over the Cham. He had to deal with occasional flare-ups with the Lao and an ethnic minority people called Bồn Man. He legislated against abortion in a detailed decree of 1484, and he implemented an earlier plan for stelae to be erected with the names of those who passed state exams at the Temple of Literature (*Văn Miếu*) and National University in the capital. This tradition continued until 1780 when the last stelae was erected to commemorate the last exam held in the north under the Lê-Trịnh. The 82 stelae attract many Vietnamese and international visitors today. Lê Thánh Tông died from illness aged 56 in 1497 after 38 years on the throne. His death was accompanied by the mysterious loss of the Imperial Seal and the Sword of Mandate. These are the highest ceremonial items to be used for the coronation of a new emperor. His successor was crown prince Tranh (Sanh), the first of his fourteen sons and twenty daughters.

LÊ HIẾN TÔNG (1497–1504 CE), LÊ TÚC TÔNG AND LÊ UY MỤC (1504–09 CE): THE DEMON KING AND THE LÊ DECLINE

Emperor Lê Hiến Tông inherited an enlarged and well-organized Đại Việt and was acknowledged by the Ming. He adjusted taxation and imperial guard duties and allowed women mandarins (*Nữ Quan* and *Nữ Sử*), some of whom were entrusted with the ceremonial task of accompanying the coffin of the late emperor to his tomb. Education continued to feature strongly with grand exams attracting 5,000 candidates in 1499. He appointed his third son heir apparent because 'the first prince liked to dress as a woman and has poisoned his own mother, the second son was too young and might not be firm enough to take on the duty.' Relations with the Ming were nurtured with tribute missions and he was awarded the full title of king of Annam in 1499. In mid-1504 he fell ill after a trip to the western capital (Tây Kinh) and died a month later at the age of 44, leaving the throne to his crown prince Thuần. The short seven-year reign of Lê Hiến Tông marked the beginning of the decline of the Lê.

Prince Thuần became emperor Lê Túc Tông at the age of sixteen but died six months later before leaving any mark. His elder brother Prince Tuấn, earlier written off by their father, was asked by the court to become Emperor Lê Uy Mục. According to Confucian scholar Ngô Sĩ Liên, author of *Đại Việt Sử Ký Toàn Thư*, he was an irresponsible man who enjoyed his drinking parties more than being a reigning monarch. Worst of all, he enjoyed killing people. He executed the senior queen grandmother and two of the highest mandarins Đàm Văn Lê and Nguyễn Quang Bật because they were opposed to his being put on the throne and he sometimes killed servants and concubines for pleasure. The new Ming emperor Zheng-de awarded him the full title of king of Annam, sending an envoy in 1507 with the Ming decree, military uniform and civilian robes. The visit inspired the Ming envoy Hứa Thiên Tích to write a poem expressing his astonishment at Annam's 'demon king'.[16] With disapproval rising against his cruelty at court, Lê Uy Mục turned for support to Mạc Đăng Dung, a powerful fisherman and an outsider from Hải Dương province who had entered the court through the examinations for imperial guards. In 1509 Lê Uy Mục killed or put in jail a number of his relatives whom he considered disloyal. Many disillusioned courtiers went into hiding away from the capital and one of them, Nguyễn Văn Lang, took his Cham slaves and occupied the sea port of Thần Phù. The former Hồ capital Tây Đô also became a stronghold of anti-Lê resistance. One of Lê Uy Mục's jailed cousins called Giản Tu Công Oanh escaped to Thần Phù. Nguyễn Văn Lang welcomed him and organized an army under disaffected military mandarins to confront the emperor in Đông Đô. Lê Uy Mục was captured in early 1510 and made to take poison at the age of 22.

LÊ TƯƠNG DỰC (1510–16 CE), YOUNG AND DECADENT

Giản Tu Công Oanh took the crown and proclaimed himself emperor Lê Tương Dực. He survived a coup attempt and reigned in peace with the Ming title King of Annam. Imperial examinations continued and in 1511 Vũ Quỳnh, court historian and professor at the National University completed the 26 history books called *Đại Việt Thông Giám Thông Khảo* that record events from the Hồng Bàng era to the beginning of the Lê. Although he had been resourceful in removing the 'demon' emperor, Lê Tương Dực soon showed his preference for a decadent lifestyle. He used state resources to build luxurious palaces and pleasure ships for consorting with palace women. A rebellion in late 1511 threatened the capital and many families were evacuated to the countryside. 'The main streets of the capital were deserted.' More rebellions broke out in districts around the capital and as far south as in Nghệ An and Thanh-Hoa. The most serious incident occurred in 1516 when a man named Trần Cao claimed to be the great grand-nephew of the Trần emperor Trần Thái Tông and brought an army to a point across the Hồng River. The rebels were engaged several times without being subdued. The bad situation took a turn for the worse when a disaffected mandarin named Trịnh Duy Sản killed the emperor. He died aged 24 after eight years on the throne. A period of confusion and lawlessness ensued while courtiers fought over who should be the next emperor. Eventually a boy of eight was chosen to be emperor but was killed a few days later. Another boy of fourteen, Prince Ỷ, was then chosen to be emperor while fighting broke out in the capital between rival generals and 'people were fighting with each other to grab whatever valuables they found in the empty palaces'.[17] The new boy emperor was evacuated to Tây Đô. Ten days after the death of Lê Tương Dực, Trần Cao entered the capital and proclaimed himself king, but within days the Lê force from Tây Đô returned and retook the capital. Trần Cao fled north to Lạng Sơn where his son would continue to be a problem for the next Lê.

LÊ CHIÊU TÔNG AND LÊ CUNG HOÀNG (1516–27 CE), RIVAL EMPEROR BROTHERS

Prince Ỷ became emperor Lê Chiêu Tông with a divided court and a devastated capital, while military mandarins fought among themselves. In 1517 a great famine swept the country and bodies piled up, especially in areas of fighting. This was later characterized as a period when 'the dynasty was weak, and people no longer prospered'.[18] The young emperor fled the capital a number of times and finally appealed for help from Mạc Đăng Dung who managed to restore an uneasy calm by 1520. Troubles rumbled on in the province and two years later fighting again wreaked havoc in the capital.[19] By then Mạc Đăng Dung had been promoted four more times to become the most powerful man at court. He consolidated his power by killing the imperial guards and keeping the emperor as a virtual hostage. Lê Chiêu Tông eventually fled to Sơn Tây some 35 km west of today's Hanoi. In his absence, Mạc Đăng Dung promptly installed the emperor's brother Prince Xuân on the throne as Emperor Lê Cung Hoàng. Civil war followed for three years between the rival emperor brothers. In 1525 Mạc Đăng Dung captured Lê Chiêu Tông and killed his protector Trịnh Tuy. Lê Chiêu Tông was stripped of his imperial title while Lê Cung Hoàng continued to reign under the control of Mac Đăng Dung, who then held the title of chancellor (Thái Sư) *An Hưng Vương*. In 1527 Lê Cung Hoàng was asked to abdicate in favour of Mạc Đăng Dung. Before being made to commit suicide, the young emperor read an imperial decree at a grand court assembly which said he was unworthy of the throne and had decided to cede it to a better man, Mạc Đăng Dung.

After Lê Lợi established the independence of Đại Việt with his victory over the Ming the Lê dynasty consolidated and expanded the country for 100 years, reaching its apogee under emperor Lê Thánh Tông. His Hồng Đức reign was a golden era when law and order were firmly established and education was made the universal gateway to prestigious positions. In a radical departure from the sinicized tradition of valuing only the males, the Lê dynasty acknowledged the status of women in society, and gave them positions at court, as well as at lower levels of employment. The reign of Lê Thánh Tông marked the beginning of the southward descent of the Việt dragon, at the expense of the Cham, although it would take another century before the Việt pushed south in a systematic movement later known as the *Nam Tiến* under the Nguyễn Lords. As under the Lý and the Trần, once the initial glory of a new dynasty wore off, internal rivalries weakened the position of the monarchs who turned to outsiders who then seized control of state affairs and the crown. A weak Lý emperor brought in the Trần, who brought in the Hồ when the Trần court fragmented. Under three weak Lê courts, Mạc Đăng Dung made rapid progress through the ranks before taking the throne. The Mạc would cling to power at all costs and survive for a long period, always citing the culture and administrations established by the Lê dynasty as their model.

9
Mạc Usurpation (1527–92)

Most modern Vietnamese historians see the first five years of the Mạc dynasty as a time that restored stability and consolidated the army.[1] Mạc Đăng Dung proclaimed himself emperor of Đại Việt on the fifteenth day of the sixth moon, 1527: the reign era was renamed Minh Đức. The Mạc continued Lê-style civil service exams, selecting 27 candidates from 4,000 applicants in 1529.[2] The inscription on the stelae bearing the names of the new doctors of literature indeed says this year marked 'the dawn of civilization for the empire'. By the time the Mạc erected the stelae of 1536 they said they were set 'firmly in the institutional pattern originated by Lê Thánh Tông seventy years earlier'.[3] But their foreign policy was a failure, especially in their clumsy dealings with Ming China. No tribute was sent to the Ming during twenty years of upheavals under the last three Lê emperors. Ming emperor Jia-Jing expressed displeasure at this in November 1536. The Ming had earlier dismissed Mạc Đăng Dung's claim in 1528 that he had to take over because there was no Lê heir. Mạc Đăng Dung then surrendered Việt sovereignty to the Ming to save his life. He volunteered this action when the Ming offered a prize for his head in 1540. With this surrender Đại Việt lost its status as an independent state (*guo*) and reverted to being a vassal prefecture of Ming China. The Việt annals record this event briefly in contrast with the great detail in *Ming Shi-lu*.

MẠC DĂNG DUNG AND MẠC DĂNG DOANH (1527–37 CE) SURRENDER TO THE MING

Although the Mạc continued in power until 1592, they were independent rulers for only thirteen years before returning Đại Việt to Ming vassalage. Even then, the first years under Mạc Đăng Dung and his son Mạc Đăng Doanh were unsettled with opposition to the usurpation manifesting immediately in many areas and under different banners. A large Lê force rose up in Thanh Hóa to support Lê Ý, a true Lê descendant. This force won the support of several former Lê generals and mandarins and took control of the western capital Tây Đô.[4] In 1529 Mạc Đăng Dung abdicated in favour of his son and proclaimed himself senior emperor. The following year, 1530, they assembled 200 warships to fight the Lê in Thanh Hóa. After several fierce battles Lê Ý was captured and killed and his army dispersed. Some remnants crossed into Laos to join forces with another Lê loyalist, general Nguyễn Kim. Another Lê force headed by former courtier Lê Công Uyên rebelled in Thanh Hoá but was crushed. In January 1533 a new Lê pretender Lê Duy Ninh made his claim to the throne as a son of Emperor Lê Chiêu Tông. He won the support of Nguyễn Kim in Laos. The pretender proclaimed himself Emperor Lê Trang Tông from an exile court in Sam Nua, where Nguyễn Kim was given the title of chancellor for the restoration of the country (Hưng Quốc Công). Lê Ninh sent an envoy to Ming emperor Jia-Jing seeking recognition. The envoy Trịnh Duy Liêu took a party of ten, boarded a merchant ship from Champa to Guangdong and arrived at the Ming court on 13 March 1537. He reported to the Ministry of Rites on Mạc Đăng Dung's usurpation in Đại Việt and appealed for support for the Lê heir in Laos. The Ming were undecided and held the envoy delegation while they investigated their claim. The Ming were at first ambivalent to the Mạc usurpation but, spurred by the pretender's claim in Laos in May 1537, they decided to launch a punitive campaign against the Mạc. A force of 300,000 men was called up from Guangdong, Guangxi and Yunnan while Mạc Đăng Dung was accused of ten grand crimes that called for punishment. He was now called a bandit, while Lê Ninh was considered legitimate and accorded the right to kill the bandit.[5] By 1538 the Ming managed to gather a force of 110,000 men under the command of Qiu Luan and the minister of war Mao Bo-wen. They made camp at Guangxi on the Chinese side of the border. On hearing the news of an imminent invasion, Mạc Đăng Dung sent an envoy to the camp to offer his surrender. The Việt delegation reached the border gate Nam Quan on 14 March 1539 and presented a petition in the name of Mạc Đăng Doanh to Mao Bo-wen. The petition ignited a fierce debate at the Ming court between those who favoured an invasion and those accepting the surrender. The Chinese troops stayed camped at the border until 1540, when emperor Jia-jing finally accepted Mạc Đăng Dung's surrender. By then, Mạc Đăng Doanh had died and been succeeded by Mạc Phúc Hải. According to *Ming Shi-lu*, 'Deng-yong (Đăng Dung) and his nephew Wen-ming as well as 40-plus persons crossed the borders with silk cord tied around the neck.'[6] On reaching the palace erected there they crawled in on bare feet, kowtowed and presented the memorial of surrender. They then went to the military headquarters and crawled in again in obeissance. They provided details of all the land, troops, civilians and officials and asked that arrangements be made for them. On this occasion, Mạc Đăng Dung also offered to return to the Ming a stretch of land at the border that the Việt had occupied since the previous century, and promised to make up for the missing tribute missions with 'gold and silver figures representing ourselves' and the Việt population registers for tax purposes. He declared that 'the territory and people all belong to the (Ming) Court'. This event was relayed to the Ming court in a lengthy memorial and emperor Jia-jing accepted Mạc Đăng Dung's surrender. He ordered that 'the title of king is being abolished and Annam is no longer permitted to refer to itself as a state'. Đại Việt was downgraded to 'Annam Commandery' and Mạc Đăng Dung was its commander, a hereditary post with a silver seal of office.[7] From that date the thirteen *đạo* that made up Đại Việt territory were governed by Ming pacification bureaux. As for the Lê, their claim of legitimacy for Lê Ninh was officially put in doubt.

MẠC AGAINST LÊ: MẠC PHÚC HẢI, MẠC PHÚC NGUYÊN, MẠC MẬU HỢP (1540–93 CE)

As vassal officials of the Minh, the Mạc are not referred to as a dynasty by most Vietnamese historians. They are called the Mạc rulers in Đông Kinh and considered a sideshow to the Lê emperor Trang Tông in exile in Laos. Support for the Lê in exile grew especially after the defection of general Lê Phi Thừa, who took his army to the Lê in 1538.[8] From 1539 to 1543 Lê Trang Tông and Nguyễn Kim launched a series of attacks into Thanh Hoá and Nghệ An provinces, where the Mạc had limited control. They captured the western capital Tây Đô in 1543 and installed the Lê emperor and his court there. For the next 50 years Đại Việt was divided into two with the competing regimes launching indecisive attacks on each other. Nguyễn Kim, the key figure on the Lê side, was poisoned in 1545 and the war was left in the hands of his sons Nguyễn Uông and Nguyễn Hoàng, and also his son-in-law Trịnh Kiểm, the strongest among the three. Nguyễn Uông soon died, allegedly at the hand of Trịnh Kiểm. Fearing for his life, Nguyễn Hoàng asked Trịnh Kiểm in 1558 to allow him to go south, to develop the former Cham territories annexed to Đại Việt under the Trần. His request was accepted and he settled in the Thuận area of Thuận Hóa while remaining loyal to Trịnh Kiểm who controlled the Lê emperor in Thanh Hóa. For the next 40 years Nguyễn Hoàng, from his southern base, joined forces with Trịnh Kiểm in their war against the Mạc in the north.

Lê Trang Tông died in 1548 and was succeeded by his son who became Lê Trung Tông and bore the Lê crown for eight years under the direction of the all-powerful Trịnh Kiểm. When Lê Trung Tông died without issue, the throne was left vacant until Trịnh Kiểm found another Lê descendant who was crowned Emperor Lê Anh Tông. Trịnh Kiểm's death in 1570 triggered a power struggle between his two sons Trịnh Cối and Trịnh Tùng with the latter emerging victorious. Trịnh Cối changed sides and went over to the Mạc. Trịnh Tùng continued to direct the war against the Mạc and consolidated his power base in Thanh Hoá. The Lê emperor then fled to Nghệ An and was captured and killed while Trịnh Tùng crowned another juvenile Lê descendant as Emperor Lê Thế Tông at the age of eight. On the Mạc side in the north Mạc Phúc Nguyên had been succeeded by his son Mạc Mậu Hợp in 1561. He held onto power until the Lê/Trịnh finally won the war and beheaded him in Đông Kinh in January 1593. Remnants of the Mạc continued to claim legitimacy for another 84 years and operated along the border with China until their last 'king' Mạc Kính Vũ died in 1677. His followers were settled in Cao Bằng province with the approval of the Ming.

In Đông Kinh in 1593 Trịnh Tùng built new palaces for the Lê emperor and himself and sent for Lê Thế Tông to be formally crowned as the titular head of the second Lê dynasty, known as the Lê Trung Hưng period (restored Lê), that was to last 261 years. The Trịnh family remained the undisputed power behind the throne. The Lê restoration era was blighted by banditry and natural disasters, with droughts, floods and famines in 1595, 1596 and 1597. Relations with the Ming were awkward for the Chinese were reluctant to let go of the Mạc and recognize an independent Việt king. The Ming then demanded that Lê Thế Tông travel to the border to have his legitimacy examined. After twice sending envoys bearing gifts of gold and silver to the Ming, the Lê emperor travelled to the Nam Quan gate in 1596 but found no inspection team there. He returned home and made the same trip the following year with more gifts and the inspection formalities were completed. However, the Ming still denied him his full kingly status and awarded him the Mạc title of Commander of the Annam Commandery. The Ming emperor also requested that the Lê 'make arrangements for the Mạc in Cao Bằng, so that those few remaining Mạc can continue their ancestral sacrifices'.[9] When a Việt envoy protested the low rank awarded to the Lê king, the Ming replied that this Lê was too new and it remained to be seen if the people would accept him.[10] As soon as Lê Thế Tông was accepted by the Ming in 1599, Trịnh Tùng awarded himself the title of Nam Bình Vương (king of the Pacified South). He set the emperor's income and gave him 5,000 imperial guards. Lê Thế Tông died shortly thereafter aged 33 and was succeeded by his son Duy Tân who became the fifth Lê Trung Hưng emperor, Lê Kính Tông, at the age of eleven.

BOY EMPERORS AND FORCED SUICIDES: LÊ KÍNH TÔNG (1600–19) TO LÊ CHIÊU THỐNG (1787–88)

The 261 years of the Lê Trung Hưng period was a sorry succession of sixteen impotent Lê emperors being placed on the throne and removed in a murderous cycle of musical chairs. All state affairs were handled by the Trịnh Lords behind the throne. The emperors' duties were limited to foreign affairs until the period ended with the Trịnh–Nguyễn civil war. Most emperors were boys whose reigns were short and ended in forced suicides. The first emperor's reign ended in a disaster in 1619 when Trịnh Tùng discovered he was plotting to kill him with his own second son Trịnh Xuân. The emperor was forced to take his own life. The crown went to his eldest son Duy Kỳ who ascended to the throne as emperor Lê Thần Tông at the age of twelve. He had the distinction of reigning twice (1619–43 and 1649–62) after his preferred successor Lê Chân Tông died without issue at the age of twenty after a reign of six years (1643–49). Lê Thần Tông returned to rule for another thirteen years. Altogether Lê Thần Tông was on the throne for 37 years. When he died in 1662 his younger son Duy Vũ succeeded him at the age of nine as Lê Huyền Tông (1663–71). He too died young without an heir and aged only eighteen.[11] Another young son of Lê Thần Tông was crowned in 1672 as emperor Lê Gia Tông at the age of eleven. He died in three years. The tenth emperor of the period was also a son of Lê Thần Tông who reigned for 30 years as Emperor Lê Hy Tông before abdicating in favour of his eldest son, Duy Đường in 1705. The eleventh emperor Lê Dụ Tông ruled for 24 years before abdicating in 1729 for his son to become Emperor Lê Duy Phường. But then a tough new Trịnh Lord took power and demoted him in 1732, crowning his elder brother instead. The father of both, retired emperor Lê Dụ Tông, was forced to kill himself in 1735 and the next emperor, Lê Thuần Tông, ruled for just three years before suffering the same fate. The eleventh son of Lê Dụ Tông succeeded him as Emperor Lê Ý Tông at the age of seventeen and ruled for five years until the Lord Trịnh Doanh ordered him to abdicate in favour of a son of the late Emperor Lê Thuần Tông. This man became Emperor Lê Hiển Tông and ruled for 46 years, the longest of all the Lê. The next Lê emperor was the grandson of Lê Hiển Tông. He took the crown in 1787 as emperor Lê Chiêu Thống who ruled for only two years but became the most vilified of the Lê emperors because he went to Beijing to ask for support when he was threatened by the Tây Sơn rebellion in 1787. Lê Chiêu Thống's request brought the Chinese army back in Đại Việt in a brief war eventually won by the Tây Sơn, who established the Nguyễn-Tây Sơn dynasty in 1788. Lê Chiêu Thống fled to China with the defeated Qing army and remained there until his death.

The Lê dynasty of Vietnam spanned a total of 360 years, although the effective Lê period that turned Đại Việt into a powerful and independent state lasted only 100 years, until the Mạc usurpation of 1427. Yet despite this long chapter of short reigns and forced suicides, the Trịnh Lords put down some indigenous cultural roots, although the Confucian model remained the foundation of Việt society. The Hồng Đức period under Lê Thánh Tông (r. 1460–97), who annexed Champa, is recognized as a golden period when a distinct Việt identity with separate political and philosophical ideas developed. Their view of themselves, of their neighbours and of the world matured into a national consciousness that propelled the Việt through to the next centuries as they headed south towards the delta of the Mekong.

The disastrous rule of the Mạc resulted in the Việt returning to vassalage under the Ming. The next restored Lê era was not much better. The country was divided into two or more segments throughout and the first Mạc/Lê war lasted for 50 years. Even after the Lê captured the capital Đông Kinh in the north, the country would soon be divided between the two families who had worked together to restore the Lê – the Trịnh and the Nguyễn. With the Lê–Trịnh settled in Đông Kinh, the Nguyễn began to push south into what was viewed as a wild frontier of Thuận-Hóa and then further south to Quảng Nam, peopling the lands of the Cham with Việt settlers. It was only a matter of time before these powerful clans began to vie with each other for supreme power. The Trịnh–Nguyễn civil war exploded in 1600 and lasted for most of the next two centuries, until a third party, the Nguyễn-Tây Sơn, defeated both the Trịnh and the Nguyễn and deposed the last Lê emperor Lê Chiêu Thống in 1788.

10
Trịnh-Nguyễn Civil War
(1627–1788)

The 161-year-conflict between the two powerful clans serving the Lê courts was born of a north–south economic and political divide that opened when the Nguyễn made itself economically autonomous by stopping the sending of taxes to the older Trịnh regime in the north. The Lê emperors were token monarchs in this period with no role in realpolitik. War was triggered in 1627 when the Trịnh sent an army south to demand their dues, only to return empty-handed. An intermittent and indecisive civil war commenced that led to the partition of Đại Việt in 1672. The natural demarcation line was the Gianh River in Quảng Bình province, a major waterway running west–east to the north of today's Quảng Trị province. The conflict would ultimately result in the demise of both remnant Champa and the Khmer controlled part of the Mekong delta. The Nguyễn gradually pushed south and expanded the Việt-held territory to the Gulf of Siam resulting in the Cham kingdom of Panduranga (Phan Rang and Bình Thuận) and the ancient Khmer settlements in the Mekong Delta being digested by the descending Việt dragon. The population of what was to become modern Vietnam became more deeply intermixed with the infusion of these more or less assimilated minorities. The southernness of the Vietnamese south was much intensified as a consequence and would lay down a cultural base for the north–south divide that would impact on the world in the twentieth century. The southern Vietnamese are more insouciant, tolerant and darker in colour than their more austere, disciplined northern kinsmen. Keith Taylor concludes his *Birth of Vietnam* with: 'when they moved south, it became possible to relax and to indulge the senses'.[1] The southerners have a more casual way of speaking and organizing and they have developed a wholly different culinary palate, more complex and spicy than that of their counterparts in the north, and perhaps in some ways reminiscent of their distant Khmer and Cham origins.

ESTABLISHING THE VIỆT SOUTH (1558–1627 CE)

The Trịnh and the Nguyễn connected when the emperor Lê Trang Tông was in exile in Laos in 1533–43 under the protection of Nguyễn Kim. The protector's daughter Ngọc Bảo was married to Trịnh strongman Trịnh Kiểm, a man from a poor family who was physically powerful enough to be selected as an officer under Nguyễn Kim.[2] At the height of their war with the Mạc, Nguyễn Kim died of poisoning in 1545, leaving the management of the Lê emperor in exile in the hands of Trịnh Kiểm and Nguyễn Kim's two sons Nguyễn Uông and Nguyễn Hoàng. Trịnh Kiểm soon emerged as the strongest. Nguyễn Uông was killed, perhaps on the orders of Trịnh Kiểm, and the other Nguyễn brother headed south to the new lands acquired from the Cham.[3] Under the Lê, Thuận Hóa was under-developed and sparsely populated but rich in natural resources.[4] The frontier zone protected by mountains to the north and the west, with the sea to the east and the newly acquired land of Quảng Nam to the south, proved a fertile terrain for Nguyễn Hoàng. He settled in Triệu Phong district in 1558 with his followers. A great flood in the following year drove hundreds of families south to settle around him in Thuận Hóa, bringing the manpower and skills he needed. This *de facto* Nguyễn lord who commanded the garrison of Thuận Hóa nevertheless continued to profess loyalty to the Lê emperor and the Trịnh in the north. He gathered and forwarded taxes regularly and held the land in the name of the Lê. After ten years Nguyễn Hoàng was awarded the additional governorship of Quảng Nam to the south of Thuận Hóa.[5] He now ruled over a substantial tract of land from Hoành Sơn mountain to Cù Mông pass, on the border with the Cham land. For the next 50 years, under the rule of the diplomatic first Nguyễn Lord, Nguyễn Hoàng, Thuận Hóa was turned from frontier into a prosperous land with a flourishing foreign trade. Merchant ships from East and Southeast Asia, as well as from India and Europe called regularly to trade.[6] Nguyễn relations with the Lê emperors and the Trịnh lords behind the throne were kept cordial by regular payment of tax income and gifts of silk and other products. Nguyễn Hoàng paid several visits to Đông Kinh and stationed himself there for several years to help Lê against the Mạc.

As soon as the Lê armies disposed of the Mạc, Nguyễn Hoàng took his army south again in 1600 to focus on development. His departure from Đông Kinh marked the beginning of the north–south divide of the Việt. Northern historians branded Nguyễn Hoàng a rebel who was covertly working against the Lê–Trịnh in the north.[7] In the eighteenth-century Nguyễn account *Khâm Định Việt Sử Thông Giám Cương Mục*, he is a great hero who founded the Việt south later known as Đằng Trong ('the inner/lower side') as a viable alternative to Đằng Ngoài ('the outer/upper side') of the Lê–Trịnh. There was no open rift however as Nguyễn Hoàng acted as a fully subservient official of the Lê–Trịnh. Moreover the Trịnh in the north were preoccupied with their own internal power struggle following the death of Trịnh Tùng.

Nguyễn Hoàng's discreet creation of a prosperous and independent *de facto* state in the south coincided with a new age in international trade across the entire east–west maritime trading route and this 'Age of Commerce'[8] decidedly enriched the Nguyễn south. Advanced ship-building technology, perfected navigation and a burgeoning world market for expensive and exotic goods at both ends of the Maritime Silk Route encouraged new merchant fleets to sail further and more frequently between Europe and China, via the South China Sea. Đại Việt grew as a convenient stopover and a busy trading hub. Being more entrepreneurial than the Confucian aristocrats of the Lê–Trịnh north, the Nguyễn opened up their coast to international ships with the ports of Hội An and Đà Nẵng leading the way. The Chams had for centuries grown wealthy through their ports on this coast, their maritime skills and their pure deepwater wells were much appreciated by ships plying this maritime route. Hội An in Quảng Nam province, a riverine port at the mouth of the Thu Bồn River, provided the wealth through trade that made it possible to build their capital of Simhapura and major inland temple complexes at Mỹ Sơn and Đồng Dương. This port was partly overtaken by the Khmer-Cham deepwater port at Vijaya but continued to prosper until the crushing defeat of the Chams by Lê Thánh Tông in 1471. In the late sixteenth century, the Nguyễn further developed Hội An into a successful international city port to welcome Japanese, Southeast Asian, Dutch and Portuguese ships. Overseas trade became the engine propelling the Nguyễn into modern maritime commerce and became 'a matter of life and death' for the early Nguyễn in the new south.[9] Even the northern historian of the *Đại Việt Sử Ký Toàn Thư* felt obliged to note its impor-tance.[10] The Ming ban of foreign trade boosted rather than diminished the flow of trade in and out of the South China Sea during the second half of the sixteenth century. The Japanese came to buy lead and saltpetre as substitutes for Chinese commodities. Silk was another popular product for foreign merchants. The silk of Quảng Nam was soon reputed to be 'as fine as Guangdong silk',[11] and Việt blue and white ceramics were exported as Chinese. Trading with official Japan under Lord Tokugawa, founder and first shogun of the Tokugawa shogunate, from the beginning of the seventeenth century, brought Nguyễn Hoàng not only financial gain but also legitimacy, for he was treated as an equal Lord ruling over an independent state. The special relationship between the Việt and the

Japanese was further tightened when Japanese merchant Hunamoto was adopted as a son of Nguyễn Hoàng. Later, in 1619, his son Nguyễn Phúc Nguyên married one of his daughters to Japanese merchant Araki Sotaao who was ennobled. Both Hunamoto and Araki Sotaao were trusted men of Lord Tokugawa and between 1604 and 1635 they commanded seventeen ships between them.[12] The relationship between the Nguyễn and Tokugawa paid off militarily when the Trịnh-Nguyễn war broke out in 1627 and Tokugawa ceased trading with the Trịnh at the request of the Nguyễn.

Nguyễn Hoàng's hands-on involvement in trade is illustrated in an enormously detailed letter dictated by Dutch merchant Jeronimus Wonderaer in 1602 who was politely and personally authorized to buy pepper in Hội An by Nguyễn Hoàng. The ruler even lent him a pair of Portuguese scales for the transaction, before stepping back to allow Chinese merchants to set the commercial price. The merchant found the Nguyễn lord impeccably correct but blustered on for many pages about a 50 per cent price hike imposed by the Chinese.[13] Trading with China via Hội An flourished and Chinese merchants could benefit from indirect trade to circumvent a Ming trade ban with Japan. Key commodities were ivory, pepper, camphor and cardamom.[14]

Sailing in Southeast Asia depends on the monsoon winds, the north-easterly wind for the southbound voyages between late December and early March and the southeasterly wind in July for the northbound traffic. In between, the merchants waited in Hội An. The necessity of the long wait encouraged Chinese and Japanese traders to form clan associations and build communal houses and temples, several of which remain intact to this day. The Japanese and Chinese quarters were separated by an elegant covered bridge built in Japanese style. Hội An under the Nguyễn grew into a cosmopolitan urban centre and the most desirable trading port on the South China Sea, eclipsing Cambodia, Siam and Luzon in the Philippines.[15] The new residents brought with them their deities and religious practices. The Chinese brought their type of Pure Lands Buddhism, focusing on Amitābha (A Di Đà) and the mercy Goddess Quan Âm. They also added a God-like judge Quan Công and a Goddess Lady Thiên Hậu who found places in the Buddhism that the Nguyễn made into state religion, alongside their Confucianism that dominated under the Ming. The Europeans brought Roman Catholicism to Hội An, which was later used as a pretext for French interference.

European powers began to show interest in the Việt territory after an Italian Jesuit Cristoforo Borri settled in Đà Nẵng in 1618 and published a book on Cochinchina in Italian, French,[16] Latin and Dutch, in which he called the Việt 'superior to the Chinese in courage and in spirit [and] more polite and and more hospitable to Europeans'.[17] Other priests followed and one of them left a profound mark on the Vietnamese language. Alexandre de Rhodes studied the Vietnamese language intensively after he arrived in 1625 and 26 years later he published the first Việt-Latin dictionary in Rome, in which the tonal pronunciation of Việt speech was captured in diacritical marks above and below the letters of the Roman alphabet. This was a landmark development that greatly facilitated the preaching and conversion programmes of Catholic priests. It took until 1919 for this Romanized version to be made official as the national language, but it was rapidly adopted among the Catholic congregations and later by the Việt literati. With little modification, de Rhodes's Romanized script has today completely taken over as the national written script. De Rhodes's reception was not as favourable as this might seem to imply. After arriving in Cochinchina he soon moved north to the land of the Lê–Trịnh but was expelled after three years for converting too many members of the royal family, in violation of Confucian teaching.[18] He took refuge in Macao but was allowed to return to Đằng Trong a few times until he was banned altogether in 1645. The Portuguese arrived in the early seventeenth century and traded in silk, eaglewood and copper. They acquired the territory of Macao and found Hội An a convenient stopover on their trading route to Melaka.[19] But when the Nguyễn and Trịnh broke their long alliance and became firm enemies in 1627, the Portuguese switched to selling what the Nguyễn most coveted – cannon and ammunition from their foundry in Macao.

When Nguyễn Hoàng died in 1613 his chosen successor was his sixth son Nguyễn Phúc Nguyên, a talented general and even more skilful economist who has been credited as the founder of the new Hội An port. But he did not inherit the tactful diplomacy of his father and he saw the Lê administrative structure as obsolete.[20] Nguyễn Phúc Nguyên withheld all his taxes to the Lê court in the north, infuriating the Trịnh Lords. The prosperity of Hội An gave Nguyễn Phúc Nguyên the economic clout to stand up to the Trịnh politically and militarily and he prepared for war. By 1627 Trịnh Tráng had replaced his father as the new Lord behind the Lê throne and he sent a long memo to the Nguyễn offering benefits and promotion if Nguyễn Phúc Nguyên again submitted to the Lê–Trịnh.

SEVEN INCONCLUSIVE WARS ACROSS DIVIDING WALLS (1627–72 CE)

A large naval force sailed from the north in 1627 to wage war on the south under the command of Trịnh Tráng, the Lê emperor and a number of generals, but it was soon defeated by the Nguyễn at Nhật Lệ port. The fleet suffered heavy losses and withdrew north after hearing that Trịnh Tráng's relatives were again plotting against him there. This was the opening salvo in a civil war that would last 161 years. The Nguyễn erected a 10-km wall called *Lũy* Trường Dục across Quảng Bình province on the northern edge of their Thuận Hóa territory facing the Lê–Trịnh. A second wall 18 km long and five stories high was built across the narrowest section of the coastal strip at Nhật Lệ and it was called *Lũy Thầy* (the master's wall) after the advisor Đào Duy Từ who designed it. It was constructed with wooden stakes and filled with packed earth. Soldiers, horses and elephants were stationed on top.[21] Two more walls were built in 1634 and 1662, with the latter called Lũy Trấn Ninh,[22] ultimately to become the last bastion in the Trịnh-Nguyễn war. The walls were connected and guarded with heavy cannon set in turrets.[23] The Nguyễn kept the Trịnh at bay with these walls, even though they commanded a much smaller army.

The first phase of fighting lasted 45 years, in seven wars, until 1672 and involved tens of thousands of troops and hundreds of warships on the Trịnh side, but the engagements were all inconclusive. During the war of 1648 the Nguyễn captured 3,000 Trịnh soldiers.[24] Only one of the seven wars – the longest – was started by the Nguyễn, who in 1655 occupied land up to Nghệ An province. They fought for five consecutive years before the Nguyễn were pushed back south again.[25] By 1672 a truce was called and a demarcation line set on the Gianh River in Quảng Bình province. This held for the next 100 years. Each part of the divided state held their own mandarin recruitment exams, collected taxes, upheld the criminal code and conducted foreign affairs. The Lê emperors still reigned as the only monarch recognized by the newly established Qing in China,[26] but in 1736 the Nguyễn under lord Nguyễn Phúc Khoát began setting courtly procedures and their own costumes and rituals. From this time the south was a *de facto* state with its own legal system and royal court.[27] The Nguyễn lord proclaimed himself *vương* (royal) in 1744 and ruled as King Vũ Vương, establishing a line of royal Nguyễn lords who ruled as either Chúa (supreme lord) or *Vương* or both.

THE NGUYỄN SOUTHWARD MOVEMENT (NAM TIẾN)

Despite the civil war the Nguyễn continued their southward expansion. There were clashes on the border with the remaining Cham kingdoms under Nguyễn Hoàng in 1611. The Việt annals say this was necessary to keep the frontier area calm.[28] Cham records say Cham king Po Nit (r. 1603–13 CE) attacked Quảng Nam and the Nguyễn retaliated on the border. The Nguyễn won the exchange and expanded their territory

Khmer Buddha, Phú Sơn mound, Mekong Delta.

down to today's Phú Yên province, occupying the Cù Mông pass to Cape Varella, the northern part of the Cham kingdom of Kauthara.[29] Thousands of Trịnh prisoners of war were settled on this tract of land, called the Việt frontier post *Trấn Biên,* in 1648.[30] Skirmishes continued on the new border until 1653 when the Cham king Po Nraup (Bà Tấm) disastrously escalated the conflict and lost the rest of Kauthara to the Nguyễn. The Nguyễn set the new frontier at the River Phan Rang and demanded tribute from the Cham. King Po Nraup was taken in a cage back to Phú Xuân and is thought to have committed suicide along the way.[31] The only land the Cham still controlled was the southern kingdom of Panduranga, today's Bình Thuận province. King Po Nraup was either the half-brother or the same person – in conflicting Cham sources – of the admired Cham king Po Rome who ruled from 1627 to 1651 or 1653. Po Rome was considered by the Cham as a great king who united the lowland and highland Chams by virtue of his own ethnic origin, the son of a lowland Cham and a highland man of the Cru minority. The young Po Rome married Po Bia Sucih, the daughter of an ageing Jarai king in Panduranga who handed his throne to him when he passed away. Po Rome inherited the land, which at the time still included Kauthara, and ruled it successfully. Cham sources claim he then lost Kauthara because of the intrigues of his third queen, Việt princess Ngọc Khoa, the daughter of the Nguyễn lord Nguyễn Phúc Tần. The celebrated hilltop brick temple named after Po Rome in today's Ninh Thuận province remains the annual ceremonial rallying point for the Cham Brahmins and their diaspora followers.

THE FALL OF PANDURANGA

The death of Po Nraup in 1653 brought in a dark period in Cham history. Another war erupted in 1692 in Panduranga between Cham king Po Saut (Bà Tranh) and Minh Vương Nguyễn Phúc Chu. Po Saut built fortifications then attacked the Nguyễn's *Trấn Biên.* But within a year he was defeated[32] and imprisoned until his death in 1694 on the island of Hòn Chén on the Perfume River outside Huế. The Nguyễn seized Panduranga and changed its name to *Trấn* Thuận Thành. They appointed Po Saktiraydaputih as their administrative official (Khám Lý), who undertook to levy taxes for the Nguyễn and to oblige the Cham to wear Việt clothing and follow Việt traditions. Three years later the area was renamed as the Việt province of Bình Thuận but was still governed by Po Saktiraydaputih with the rank of *Phiên Vương* (local king). Sporadic Cham resistance in Panduranga and the nearby highlands continued until 1835 when their autonomy was finally ended by emperor Minh

Mạng. The first Cham resistance in early 1694 came from a Chinese resident called A Ban who took to the mountains and joined forces with Cham official Oc-nha Thát and launched attacks on Việt military posts in Thuận Thành. There was fighting in Phan Rí and Phan Rang that was stopped by the Việt authority threatening to kill Po Saktiraydaputih. However, after the death of Po Saut in Huế, A Ban laid siege to Phan Rang. The Chams were driven back by the Việt and retired higher into the mountains and settled along the Cambodian border. The rest of Po Saktiraydaputih rule was peaceful according to the Việt account until his death in 1728, although Cham sources indicate factional strife among the Chams.[33] There was constant friction between the Cham and the Việt, for the Cham living in leopard spot communities among the new Việt settlers, where they were disadvantaged in trade, taxes, labour contracts and a legal system which favoured the Việt.[34]

FROM FUNAN TO VIETNAM: THE MEKONG DELTA

The annexation of the Mekong Delta from the indigenous Khmers took another 100 years. This massive acquisition is not well documented and was probably a mix of gradual insertion and occupation and land purchase that later turned into an armed invasion. This happened as the Khmer royal family was more focused on the military threat from Siam. The lower Mekong Delta entered history as a polity called Funan by the Chinese at the beginning of the first millennium of the Common Era. It is assumed the Funanese were speaking a version of Old Khmer but there is no inscription to prove it. They built magnificent brick and stone temples bearing resemblances to Cham temples and they constructed a large canal system linking their cities. The literacy of Funan can be gauged from the fact that it sent two Buddhist scholars to the Wu capital to translate Mahayana texts from Sanskrit into Chinese.[35] The archaeological evidence shows Funan was trading on the East–West maritime route with a trading post of Oc Eo, in today's An Giang province. Religious artefacts and coins from the Roman Empire, Persia, Greece and India were found there.[36] Sometime in the sixth to the seventh century Funan was absorbed into a state the Chinese called Zhenla,[37] the predecessor of the Khmer state founded in Kulen, just north of Angkor, in 802.

At the beginning of the seventeenth century, the Mekong Delta was a vast, wild and sparsely populated zone of mangrove swamps and ruled by a Khmer king a good way north in Udong beside the Tonle Sap River that descends from ancient Angkor. Relations between the Khmer royals and the Nguyễn were cordial from the beginning of the seventeenth century.[38] They were strengthened further under the second Nguyễn

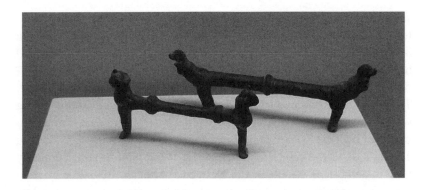

Oc Eo, Modelled animals, Historical Museum, Ho Chi Minh City.

lord Nguyễn Phúc Nguyên when he married his daughter Princess Ngọc Vạn to the Khmer King Chey Chettha II in 1620. Through this connection Nguyễn Phúc Nguyên obtained the Khmer king's agreement to establishing in 1623 two customs posts at the river ports of Prei Nokor (today's Saigon) and Kas Krobei (today's Bến Nghé in the Saigon vicinity). The terms of the five-year agreement created rest-over locations for merchants plying the land and river routes across Cambodia, Siam and Đại Việt. The provisional term was never mentioned again as both places became thriving and populated.

The Nguyễn connection became embroiled in a power struggle on the death of Chey Chettha II in 1627. His son Cau Bana Tu by his Việt queen reigned for a period in his own capital outside Udong before he was killed by mercenaries hired by his uncle in 1632. It was part of score-settling over a Khmer princess who was betrothed to the nephew but taken as wife by the uncle. There were assassinations in several branches of the royal family. Relations with the Nguyễn remained stable as the Việt former queen continued to reside at Udong and exert considerable influence at court while keeping the Nguyễn informed. But in January 1658 the situation turned grave with the Khmer royals divided in open conflict in which they were supported by armies from Malaya and Vietnam. The king Cau Bana Cand (Nặc Ông Chân/Ang Chan), who had converted to Islam, was supported by the Malays and the Muslim Cham, who were opposed by the princes Ang Sur and Ang Tan on the Việt former queen's side and her Việt backers. The Khmer royal chronicle claims that ex-queen Ngọc Vạn wrote to her nephew the Nguyễn lord asking for troops and promising that Cambodia would become a vassal. The Việt records claim their army was sent into Khmer territory on the pretext that 'the Khmer king Nặc Ông Chân encroached the common border'.[39] The Khmer-Việt common border resulted from the Việt seizure of the Cham territory of today's Khánh Hòa province in 1653. At the

141

same time Việt immigrants settled around and beyond the Nguyễn customs posts may have felt threatened by Ang Chan's forces manoeuvring in the power struggle. The Việt annals say when the Nguyễn army invaded it, they captured King Ang Chan at the Việt merchant settlement at Mô Xoài.[40] The king's fate is unrecorded and Ang Sur took the Khmer throne. Trouble at the Khmer court flared again in 1673 with one faction siding with Siam and the other with the Nguyễn. General Nguyễn Dương Lâm marched into the Khmer capital and appointed Khmer prince Nặc Ông Thu to rule in the capital and prince Nặc Ông Nộn to rule as deputy king in Saigon, as vassals of the Nguyễn.[41] Shortly thereafter in 1679 the area around Saigon became a reception centre for 3,000 Ming loyalists who had fled China in 50 ships and docked in Hội An to plead for help from the Nguyễn. They were settled in today's Biên Hòa and on the banks of the Mekong at what was to become the city of Mỹ Tho.[42] The Ming settlers, along with the Việt settlers and indigenous Khmers soon brought prosperity to the delta. Merchant ships from China, Europe, Japan and Java became regular callers. The Ming settlers intermarried and remained Chinese in culture though they assumed an official Việt identity. This was seen when they took refuge from the Tây Sơn rebels to establish the ethnically Chinese twin city of Saigon at Chợ Lớn ('great market'). In 1688 Ming rebel Hoàng Tiến killed the Ming loyalist leader Dương Ngạn Địch in Mỹ Tho and attacked the Khmer king Nặc Ông Thu. This incident prompted the lord Nguyễn Phúc Tần to send in his troops, taking over the lower Mekong and advancing to Phnom Penh, where the Khmer king Nặc Ông Thu surrendered.[43] The Khmer king offered regular tribute in elephant, gold and silver to the Nguyễn and the Khmer territory from Biên Hòa to the lower Mekong Delta was occupied by the Nguyễn. In 1693 Nguyễn Phúc Chu seized Panduranga, extending Nguyễn control over a huge tract of land stretching from Bình Thuận to the province of Long An in the Delta, which was renamed *Phủ Gia Định* under the governorship of Nguyễn Hữu Cảnh. He quickly organized administrative units in the area and appealed to people from the northern provinces to move south. The Ming loyalists were officially inscribed in the Việt population register and grouped into villages called the Minh Hương,[44] a term still in use today. Gia Định now numbered 40,000 households.

The Nguyễn southern advance pushed further in 1714 when the Ming immigrant Mạc Cửu invited the Nguyễn court to accept his claim to control the Gulf of Siam port of Hà Tiên. Mạc Cửu had emigrated from Guangdong and settled in Hà Tiên in 1708 where he first worked as an official for the Khmers and grew wealthy from running casinos in the port.[45] He built commercial links with Phú Quốc island and Cà Mau at the tip of the peninsula and decided to offer allegiance to the

Nguyễn cause rather than the Khmers, who were losing territory both to Siam and the Nguyễn.[46] Mạc Cửu was appointed governor of Hà Tiên and the Nguyễn acquired more Khmer land. The continuing power struggle at the Khmer court provided Nguyễn Phúc Trú with a pretext for sending his army in 1733 to take over the territory beyond Mỹ Tho that became today's Vĩnh Long province. In 1750 another Nguyễn lord Nguyễn Phúc Khoát attacked the Khmer who he claimed encroached on the border west of Bình Thuận province. The Nguyễn launched another attack on Phnom Penh, but failed to capture Khmer king Nặc Ong Nguyên. For the next fifteen years, the Nguyễn and a succession of Khmer kings fought repeated battles and each time the Nguyễn seized another tract of Khmer land. By 1779 the Nguyễn held the entire Mekong Delta.

The southward movement that finally took Việt rule to the Gulf of Siam deposited the rich ethnic melange that characterizes the Delta today. A local French survey in 1931 found there were 4.5 million Annamites (from the central part of Vietnam called Annam that is still nominally ruled by the Việt emperor) and half a million coastal 'Malaysians' and highland 'Indonesians'.[47] The Chams were classified as Malaysians and highland sub-groups included Ra Đê, Raglai, Jarai and others. The 'Indonesians' were said to be less mixed than the Malaysians and also numbered 300,000 on the Vietnamese side of the mountain chain. It said the Vietnamese called the highland people 'Mọi', meaning 'savage'. The French survey observed that the Việt moved southwards in the eleventh, fifteenth, sixteenth and eighteenth centuries to colonize and Vietnamize the indigenous peoples but did not massacre them. Today the Khmers of the delta are one of the largest minorities at 1.4 per cent of the total population of 82 million, according to the official and UN Population Fund census of 2009.[48] The Việt *kinh* (lowland/city) make up 86 per cent. Then come the Tày (Tai), Thái, Mường, Khmer, Hoa, Nùng, Hmông, Dao, Ja Rai and 34 smaller groups. Some 75 per cent of the ethnic minorities live in distinct groups on the highlands along the border with Yunnan southern China, including the Tày, Thái and Mường. Further south, along the spine of the central highlands, live the Ếđê, Bana, Hmông, Jarai and Raglai. The Raglai are the highland cousins of the Cham, who remain on the coastal lowland and number about 1 million. Vietnam's 54 ethnic minorities remain rural and live from small-scale agriculture and handicrafts. Most of them speak their own languages, in a variety of language family groups such as the Mon-Khmer, the Tay-Thai or Tibeto-Burman. Some, like the Chinese, are bilingual. The Tày and the Mường are closest to the Việt *kinh* and enjoy an economic social level comparable to the *kinh*. The ethnic minorities are in the lowest income bracket with severely limited education, especially among women, because they do not command the Vietnamese language of the teachers.[49] The UN states the Hmông live in the hardest conditions and the Khmer have the worst housing.[50] Such is the ethnic diversity that resulted from the Nguyễn's southward movement.

11

The Decline of the Lê–Trịnh and the Rise of the Tây Sơn

1735 was a year of unmitigated disaster in the north with flood, earthquake, famine and death turning citizens into robbers who would defy even the imperial guards in their will to survive, while the Lê–Trịnh court showed signs of collapse.[1] Lord Trịnh Giang's brutal dismissal and enforced suicide of the previous emperor Lê Duy Phường had undermined the confidence of those supporting his successor Lê Thuần Tông. Groups of Lê loyalists rose up in protest at the killing and rebel groups organized themselves in almost all provinces. It took until 1751 to suppress the uprisings, and by then the Trịnh court was in the grip of a group of eunuchs favoured by rival Trịnh Doanh. The eunuchs ruthlessly suppressed their rivals and there was much turmoil. Trịnh Doanh died in 1767 and lord Trịnh Sâm took over. When there were more food riots Trịnh Sâm sent in his elite troops without mercy. The court gradually weakened to the point where it was an easy prey for a new group of disaffected people, the Nguyễn Tây Sơn.

The Trịnh lords in the north and the Nguyễn lords in the south had accorded themselves *vương* (royal) status since the 1740s, with emperor Lê Hiển Tông a nominal monarch. The Nguyễn moved their capital as they expanded their territory and were now settled in Phú Xuân, today's Huế in Thừa Thiên province. In 1765 a boy of twelve called Nguyễn Phúc Thuần was crowned as the royal lord with the agency of mandarin Trương Phúc Loan, who was powerful but unpopular.[2] The association made the new lord a laughable figure and he was not fully respected. Disaffected groups challenged the Nguyễn power and among these was Nguyễn Nhạc from Quy Nhơn, the former Cham capital of Vijaya. He was a customs officer who 'spent the tax money that he collected' and had to escape to the highlands. Supported by his brothers Nguyễn Lữ and Nguyễn Huệ, he declared war on mandarin Trương Phúc Loan from a base in the central highlands called Tây Sơn ('Western Mountain'). The brothers raided the rich and gave to the poor in Robin Hood fashion that earned them instant wide support. They allied themselves with a former Cham queen in the highlands who brought her troops to fight against the Nguyễn.[3] Some think Nguyễn Nhạc got to know the Cham on the highlands as a tax collector. Following A Ban's and Oc-nha Thất's campaign in 1693, Cham resentment against the Nguyễn continued to fester and it was no surprise that some Cham highlanders allied with Nguyễn Nhạc to fight against the Nguyễn in 1771. The Cham had little choice about which side to fight on in a protracted war between the Tây Sơn and the Nguyễn over the control of their own former territory of Kauthara and Panduranga. But the Tây Sơn-Nguyễn war resulted in driving more Cham out of the former Kauthara-Panduranga up into the highlands of Kontum and Gia Lai and along the Cambodian border. From there they later moved into Cambodia to form exile villages like Kompong Cham. The Cham population in Cambodia was further swollen during the Tây Sơn-Nguyễn war when Cham king Po Cei Brei, a descendant from the Cru of Po Rome, fled with his court and thousands of followers to Kompong Cham in 1795. Po Cei Brei had supported Nguyễn rule in Phan Rang/Bình Thuận in 1783–6, but when the Tây Sơn captured his territory they appointed a new Cham king to replace him.[4] When Po Cei Brei went to Cambodia, his general Po Sau Nun joined forces with Nguyễn Ánh to fight the Tây Sơn. This led to a serious quarrel among Cham noblemen and these branches of the Cham nobility remained antagonistic through the nineteenth and twentieth centuries.

THE TÂY SƠN-NGUYỄN WAR AND NGUYỄN HUỆ'S TAKEOVER

In 1771 the Nguyễn Tây Sơn launched a successful attack against Quy Nhơn citadel and used it as their lowland base. From there they began preparations for a move on Phú Xuân.[5] Meanwhile the Trịnh exploited the problems the Nguyễn were facing with a major offensive in 1774. The Trịnh army broke through the demarcation line at Gianh River in 1774 and advanced on Phú Xuân. Nguyễn Phúc Thuần was soon defeated and escaped from Phú Xuân in ships that took him south to Quảng Nam,[6] where they found themselves also threatened by the Tây Sơn. They again took to their ships and headed south to the newly acquired *Phủ* Gia Định. With the Nguyễn fled, the Trịnh and the Tây Sơn clashed at Phú Xuân in March 1775 and the Trịnh forced the Tây Sơn back to their base in Quy Nhơn, where they offered to join the Trịnh in pursuing the Nguyễn. Nguyễn Nhạc became a Lê/Trịnh general with the title of Grand Duke.[7] A year later an epidemic broke out among the Trịnh army in the south, causing them to retreat to Phú Xuân, leaving Quảng Nam to the Tây Sơn. The Tây Sơn under Nguyễn Lữ attacked the remnants of the Nguyễn in today's Saigon. Meanwhile Nguyễn Nhạc proclaimed himself *Tây Sơn Vương* (royal Tây Sơn) at the former Cham capital of Vijaya. The Tây Sơn killed all the Nguyễn royals except a young warrior of fifteen years called Nguyễn Phúc Ánh, who managed to escape south.[8] In 1778 Nguyễn Nhạc went further and proclaimed himself emperor while his brother Nguyễn Lữ was given the title of *Đông Định Vương* (Eastern Pacification king) and his youngest brother Nguyễn Huệ was elevated to the rank of general (*Long Nhương*).

For the next 25 years Nguyễn Huệ and the last Nguyễn lord Nguyễn Ánh fought running battles across southern Vietnam. Their warships sailed between the Saigon area and Quy Nhơn following the monsoon winds while Saigon changed hands repeatedly. The Nguyễn and Tây Sơn governed by turn, changing laws and raising taxes. In January 1780 Nguyễn Ánh proclaimed himself king in Saigon and appointed the Khmer king Ang Eng in Cambodia. In Cambodia the Nguyễn first clashed with the Thai in 1782 under king Taksin. During this engagement Nguyễn Ánh got to know one of the Thai generals from the Chakri clan, whose family was then under threat from Taksin. Nguyễn Ánh became an ally and Chakri succeeded in founding the current Chakri dynasty as king Rama I.

In 1783 Nguyễn Ánh was chased out of Saigon and took refuge on Phú Quốc island with his troops in a dire state, living on grass and banana stalks. It was in these circumstances that a fateful encounter took place with the French. The Nguyễn leader turned to bishop Pigneau de Béhaine of Adran for help in Hà Tiên. They had known each other since 1777 when Nguyễn Ánh was driven to Hà Tiên by the Tây Sơn and he took shelter in Pigneau de Béhaine's seminary for three months. This founded a political alliance and the Bishop often helped Nguyễn Ánh during his years fighting the Tây Sơn. In 1783 the bishop and the lord fled from Phú Quốc island to an island in the Gulf of Siam, after which they reached the new Thai capital Bangkok. Nguyễn Ánh urged the bishop to travel to France to plead for help from King Louis XVI. He first signed a treaty with the Portuguese that came to nothing. Then he sent his four-year-old son Prince Cảnh to France with the bishop to negotiate with full authority.[9] With the help of King Rama I, Nguyễn Ánh returned to Gia Định the following year with 300 Thai ships and 20,000 Thai troops. But by 1785 the Nguyễn and the Thai were defeated by the Tây Sơn under the remarkable command of Nguyễn Huệ. Remnants of the Thai returned to Thailand, Nguyễn Phúc Ánh and his own remnants crossed back into Thailand with the beaten Thai forces. The Việt were allowed to stay in a Bangkok suburb. The soldiers farmed the land there while Nguyễn Ánh worked on a new plan to retake Gia Định. The Bangkok suburb is still a thriving Việt enclave today under the name of

Ban Yuon (Việt village). While in Bangkok Nguyễn Ánh helped Rama
I fight off an invasion from Burma and the Thai king again offered troops
to help the Nguyễn recover Gia Định. Nguyễn Ánh declined the offer
because he recalled how 'violent the Thai were to the Việt at large' during
their previous campaign.[10]

With remnants of the Nguyễn army in exile, the Tây Sơn prepared
to advance north, to confront the Trịnh, whose grip on power had been
weakened by popular discontent. In July 1786 under the command of
Nguyễn Huệ and another talented general, Nguyễn Hữu Chỉnh, the Tây
Sơn defeated the Trịnh and captured Thăng Long, declaring their loyalty
to the Lê emperor Lê Hiển Tông. The emperor married his young
daughter Ngọc Hân to Nguyễn Huệ, and died shortly thereafter, leaving
the throne to Lê Chiêu Thống, the last Lê emperor.[11]

With Nguyễn Huệ's victory in Thăng Long the relationship between
the three Tây Sơn brothers came under strain and Nguyễn Nhạc took
his army to Thăng Long to proclaim his own loyalty to the new Lê
emperor. Both Nguyễn armies then withdrew back south leaving the
capital to the Lê emperor, who was soon back under Trịnh control. The
rule of lord Trịnh Bồng was however opposed by various groups and
the emperor appealed for help to Tây Sơn general Nguyễn Hữu Chỉnh.
The general had formerly supported the Trịnh and was well known at
the Lê court. He moved his army into Thăng Long and made himself
the new authority behind the emperor. Emperor Lê Chiêu Thống ordered
the Trịnh's palaces to be burnt, effectively ending Trịnh control permanently. This act angered the Tây Sơn but only after the brothers had
divided the land into three fiefdoms did they respond. Nguyễn Nhạc
remained in Quy Nhơn as the central king, Nguyễn Lữ took over Gia
Định and Nguyễn Huệ was given the land north of Hải Vân pass and
the title of Bắc Bình Vương ('king for the pacification of the north').
From his capital in Phú Xuân Nguyễn Huệ sent a general north to dislodge
Nguyễn Hữu Chỉnh. This he achieved easily but when the general tried
to seize power, Nguyễn Huệ headed up to Thăng Long and made it his
own seat. In late 1787 Nguyễn Huệ proclaimed himself Emperor Quang
Trung and ended the Lê dynasty.

Lê Chiêu Thống escaped to the border and appealed to Qing China
for help. In 1788 emperor Qian Long sent in general Sun Shi Yi (Tôn Sĩ
Nghị). Nguyễn Huệ by then had moved back to Phú Xuân, leaving one
of his generals in Thăng Long. The Chinese force quickly took the capital
and reinstalled Lê Chiêu Thống under the protection of the Qing
general.[12] Nguyễn Huệ marched north and demanded that the Chinese
general withdraw to China, but Sun Shi Yi refused. This was the time
of the lunar new year festival and security was lax while soldiers celebrated. Nguyễn Huệ pressed on and devastated the Chinese force, which

withdrew across the border with Lê Chiêu Thống. Emperor Quang Trung was restored to power in the capital and became the new master of the Việt. To appease the giant neighbour he sought recognition from the Qing emperor. But when he was called to Beijing to pay his respects to the emperor, he sent an impostor instead, which seemed to satisfy the Qing, who awarded him the king of Annam title *An Nam Quốc Vương*. The ousted Lê emperor died in China in 1793 at the age of 28. But he outlived Quang Trung/Nguyễn Huệ who died suddenly in 1792 aged 41. He was succeeded by his ten-year-old son Nguyễn Quang Toản, while affairs of state were controlled by his unpopular regent uncle Bùi Đắc Tuyên.

THE NGUYỄN COUNTER-OFFENSIVE (1789–1802)

By 1787 Nguyễn Ánh and his troops had lived in Bangkok for two years. Portugal offered him guns and 56 warships but the offer was declined for fear of offending the Thai king.[13] Nguyễn Ánh however surreptitiously left Bangkok in the middle of the night with his family and his troops to sail back to Phú Quốc island. The Nguyễn army, now including Chinese seamen, or rather pirates, sailed to Long Xuyên and then swiftly attacked Nguyễn Lữ in Saigon. He retook Gia Định and established his capital in Saigon.[14] He consolidated his base for a long-term war with the Tây Sơn by fixing law and order, taxation and agricultural issues. Soldiers worked in army plantations to stock rice while he built up his army and navy. Nguyễn Ánh built ships and bought weapons and ammunition from Macao and prepared for a final assault on the Tây Sơn. In Saigon, his new capital, Nguyễn Ánh built a huge octagonal walled fortification to keep out the Tây Sơn. The new Nguyễn lord-become-king called it the Turtle Citadel (*Thành Quy*) after its shape. It was more commonly known as the *Bát Quái* (*Ba-gua*) and its design followed that of French architect Théodore Lebrun, and was fortified according to the Vauban principles of defence.[15] This citadel later inspired Nguyễn Ánh to create his much more famous citadel in Huế after he was crowned emperor Gia Long in 1802. The Huế Imperial Citadel differed in shape and size but was also in the Vauban style.

Nguyễn Ánh's ally Bishop Pigneau de Behaine, who had sailed to France via Pondicherry in 1786, finally returned in 1789. The bishop had to wait nine months at the court of Louis XVI but he finally signed the Treaty of Versailles with the minister of foreign affairs Montmorin on 28 November 1787. France promised four frigates and 1,650 well-equipped soldiers with an 'adequate' number of cannon. In return Nguyễn Ánh ceded the island of Côn Sơn (Poulo Condore) to France and gave the European power exclusive trading rights at the port of Đà Nẵng. The Treaty was never implemented as France had domestic problems in 1787. Pondicherry governor Baron de Conway, who was to provide the ships and troops, decided to ignore it. Pigneau de Behaine returned to Vietnam with Prince Cảnh but he did not return empty-handed. Following him were twenty French merchant captains and officers who offered their services privately. Captains Chaigneau, Vannier, Olivier, Dayot and de Forsans were the best known. Chaigneau was the most colourful character and was to stay longest in Vietnam with Vannier. Both became mandarins at the court of the celebrated emperor Gia Long, after Nguyễn Ánh took that title.[16]

Backed by this unusual force, Nguyễn Ánh launched his offensive against the Tây Sơn in their stronghold of Quy Nhơn in 1792. After a fierce naval battle that lasted 40 days in Thị Nại bay, Nguyễn Ánh was driven back.[17] Annual seasonal campaigns followed when the monsoon wind was favourable in April–October. The Nguyễn lord made his son Prince Cảnh crown prince in 1793.[18] He again laid siege to Quy Nhơn citadel for three months but retired when the wind turned. Nguyễn Nhạc in Quy Nhơn appealed to his nephew Emperor Cảnh Thịnh/Quang Toản in Phú Xuân for help and Cảnh Thịnh sent 18,000 men with 80 elephants and 30 warships to seize Quy Nhơn for himself. Nguyễn Nhạc died of rage soon after.[19]

The deaths of Quang Trung/Nguyễn Huệ in 1792 and of his brother Nguyễn Nhạc the following year dealt a heavy blow to the Tây Sơn. Generals of the two regions fought battles while also holding off Nguyễn Ánh. Gia Định prospered under Nguyễn rule, and Nguyễn Ánh even offered to help the king of Thailand against the Burmese. The Thais accepted and a Nguyễn fleet of 100 warships and 1,000 sailors sailed to Thailand but the war was over before the Nguyễn arrived. The monsoon wars with the Tây Sơn continued until Nguyễn Ánh gained a decisive victory at Quy Nhơn in 1799.[20] This was helped by French mercenaries who commanded a frigate and a corvette at the head of a fleet of 447 junks and 42,000 soldiers.[21] Two years later Nguyễn Ánh successfully attacked Phú Xuân and the young Tây Sơn king Quang Toản escaped to Bắc Hà, today's Hanoi. By 1802 Nguyễn Ánh proclaimed himself emperor Gia Long and marched north to launch the last offensive against the Tây Sơn. Within a month he captured Bắc Hà, the Tây Sơn king and his entourage. They were taken to Phú Xuân to the Nguyễn ancestral temple and executed. Emperor Gia Long had unified the country for the first time since Nguyễn Hoàng went south in 1600. Vietnam had grown much larger and now stretched from the Chinese border to the tip of Cà Mau peninsula on the Gulf of Siam.

THE TÂY SƠN LEGACY

The Tây Sơn fought against the Nguyễn in Đằng Trong in 1778 but only reigned over parts of Vietnam. During their fourteen years of power they were at war continuously with the Nguyễn and the Qing. Although Nguyễn Huệ is rightly hailed as a great hero of Vietnamese history for having repulsed the Qing invasion of 1788, the Tây Sơn left few significant marks on Việt society. The exception was Emperor Quang Trung who adopted *Nôm* as the national language. He embedded this script of modified Chinese characters by ordering the translation into *Nôm* of many classical Chinese works and he reformed the Buddhist temples and pagodas.[22]

The participation of Chinese pirates and French officers in the Nguyễn army is well documented in both Vietnamese and French records, but the role of the Cham in this war remains obscure, despite the fact that their territory of Kauthara-Panduranga was the scene of a major contest between opposing Việt forces. Furthermore, the Cham were crushed, dispersed and Vietnamized when the war was over.

During the Tây Sơn-Nguyễn war, a Cham general named Po Sau Nun Can joined forces with Nguyễn Ánh to fight the Tây Sơn. When Nguyễn Ánh established the Nguyễn dynasty in 1802 he created an

The nine Royal Urns, symbols of the Nguyễn Dynasty: Imperial Citadel, Huế.

autonomous Cham enclave and appointed Po Sau Nun Can as governor. The enclave covers the old Cham Kauthara-Panduranga region, today's Cam Ranh bay to the Upper Đồng Nai on Kontum-Gia Lai plateaux.[23] However, the creation of this autonomous zone led to a serious political problem under the second Nguyễn emperor Minh Mạng (r. 1820–40).

Although an official of the court in Huế, Po Sau Nun Can was more loyal to the viceroy of Gia Định, the powerful eunuch general Lê Văn Duyệt, who ruled over the region as if it was his own kingdom. The viceroy of Gia Định had jurisdiction over all southern Vietnam, the autonomous Cham enclave and Cambodia, which was then a vassal of Vietnam. Unlike his father who trusted Lê Văn Duyệt completely, emperor Minh Mạng viewed the viceroy with suspicion as Lê Văn Duyệt was thought to have advised Gia Long against him as successor. He decided on a purge to reduce Lê Văn Duyệt's power and some of Lê Văn Duyệt's staff and family lost their posts, including his adopted son Lê Văn Khôi, who was jailed for an unspecified offence. Gia Định was divided into six smaller administrative provinces and became known as Lục Tỉnh (six provinces), three on the east and three on the west.

Lê Văn Khôi rebelled in 1833 after Lê Văn Duyệt's death and it took the force sent from Huế three years to recapture the Turtle citadel, while Lê Văn Khôi had died during the siege. The citadel was razed to the ground and 2,000 people were captured and killed. The governor of the Cham enclave was implicated in the revolt and the emperor abolished this last Cham enclave in 1832–3. Minh Mạng then ordered a new and smaller citadel to be built on a corner of the old Turtle citadel which became the focus of the French invasion in the late nineteenth century.

12

Nguyễn Dynasty (1802–1945) Creates 'Việt Nam'

Just 28 years after the Nguyễn were chased out of their capital Phú Xuân, lord Nguyễn Ánh returned in triumph in 1802 and proclaimed himself the first Nguyễn emperor Gia Long. He renamed the now unified country Việt Nam and set up the Nguyễn dynasty.[1] The capital around the old citadel Phú Xuân later became known as Huế. Thăng Long in the north was renamed Bắc Thành (citadel of the north) and placed under the military governorship of the trusted general Nguyễn Văn Thành. The north was called Bắc Kỳ and *phủ* Gia Định was called Nam Kỳ with another general, the eunuch Lê Văn Duyệt, governing from its capital Saigon. This last dynasty is still the subject of hot debate in Vietnam. Did they sell out to France? Could they have helped prevent the devastating colonial and post-colonial wars? This chapter attempts an overview of their successes and failures as they appear in the official documents in Vietnamese and French.

THE FIRST NGUYỄN EMPEROR GIA LONG (r. 1802–19)

Gia Long sent envoys to the Qing court seeking recognition which came in 1804. The Qing awarded him the title *An Nam Quốc Vương* and a royal golden seal. Gia Long undertook to send to the Qing every three years 200 taels of gold, 1,000 taels of silver, 100 bolts of silk, two sets of rhino horns, ivory and cinnamon. The Chinese golden seal was to play a key role in 1884–5 in the delicate triangle of China, France and Vietnam. In the year he was recognized by China, Gia Long began rebuilding his capital in Huế. A high-profile, richly embellished complex of palaces, modelled on nothing less than the Forbidden City in Beijing, was built within a large square citadel surrounded by high walls and deep moats on the north side of the Hương (Perfume) River. The length of the surrounding walls was 10 km, the size of the huge Angkor Thom palace and temple complex in neighbouring Cambodia. Inside the fortress were

Thái Hòa Palace in the Nguyễn Imperial Citadel.

three layers of housing, one inside the other, with the Forbidden Purple City of the emperor being the innermost. Thái Hòa Palace (Palace of Supreme Harmony) was among the first constructed in order to house the bi-monthly court assemblies. Gia Long was crowned there in 1806. For his first nine years the country followed the Hồng Đức code of the Lê dynasty, with six ministries in charge of civil service recruitment, taxes and finance, courtly protocol, military recruitment, building works, criminal and civil justice. As under the Lê, a censor oversaw the public morality of the court and the emperor. Then in 1811 Gia Long ordered general Nguyễn Văn Thành to create a new code of laws for Vietnam, which was published in 22 books and 398 articles in 1815. Gia Long upheld the teaching of Confucius and established a Confucian Temple (Văn Miếu) in Huế as well as an imperial college for noble children (Quốc Tử Giám). Recruitment exams were held every six years and teachers were sent to remote areas to educate the population. Agriculture was accorded high priority, including the military plantations system (đồn điền) he set up in the Mekong Delta during the war, and a new atlas was compiled in 1806 with the title *Nhất Thống Địa Dư Chí*. In the north Gia Long was preoccupied with the upkeep of the dyke system and established a Dyke Department in Bắc Thành with a mandarin in charge.[2] Local industry was encouraged and was to attain its apogee under his successor Minh Mạng. Ship construction at shipyards along the southern coast grew rapidly. Specialized factories for guns, ceramics, decorative objects and silk were established in Huế and its suburbs. Sophisticated Chinese products were coveted and missions were often sent to China to place royal orders. Outside Huế a thriving pottery industry emerged to cater to all classes of domestic and export wares.

Asian trade has also a Nguyễn focus but trade with Europe slowed under Gia Long. In 1778 a British merchant ship was denied entry, and a later British trading mission of ships under the Marquis of Wellesley was again rejected. Between 1815 and 1817 French commercial ships were also refused permission to trade, despite Gia Long's special relationship with the Frenchmen who had helped him to obtain the crown.[3]

For seventeen years Gia Long reigned over a heterogeneous court that prominently featured his odd mix of French allies. Each French counsellor was allocated an escort of 50 soldiers and was exempted from the solemn rite of kowtowing in court. The most influential of the French mandarins was Jean-Baptiste Chaigneau, who had supported Gia Long in his long battles against the Tây Sơn. Before Gia Long's final victory, Chaigneau was ennobled with the title *Thắng Tài Hầu* (Marquis of Thắng Tài). Emperor Gia Long gave him the Vietnamese name Nguyễn Văn Thắng and allowed him to marry Vietnamese Catholic lady Benoîte Hồ-Thị-Huê.[4] Chaigneau and Vannier lived comfortably in Huế and had several children by their Vietnamese wives. Chaigneau's son Michel was named Nguyễn Văn Đức, who was so comfortable in the Vietnamese language that when he went to France for the first time in 1820 at the age of seventeen his French was judged 'behind'. Missionaries had been viewed with suspicion in the north and the south during the Nguyễn lord period, and some were banned like Alexandre de Rhodes. However, emperor Gia Long turned a blind eye to French and other European missionary activities and they built churches and converted citizens without hindrance from court or local authorities. All this changed dramatically on the death of Gia Long in 1819, when his successor Minh Mạng applied very different ideas on the running of the state, Christianity and the presence of the French in Vietnam.

MINH MẠNG (r. 1820–40)

The fourth son of Gia Long, Nguyễn Phúc Đảm, became emperor Minh Mạng, after his eldest half-brother crown prince Nguyễn Phúc Cảnh and his next two brothers died prematurely. By the time Minh Mạng took the crown at the unusually mature age of 30, Vietnam had been at peace for eighteen years and was politically and socially anchored. He changed the name of the country from Việt Nam to Đại Nam (Great South). From 1826 onwards, he faced a number of rebellions in both the north and the south for the restoration of the Lê. Some of these

Kham Van Chi Ti Gold Seal, Emperor Minh Mạng, 1827,
Hanoi Museum of History.

endured several months, such as the Phan Bá Vành rebellion in Nam
Định (1826–7), the Nông Văn Vân at the Sino-Việt border (1833–5) and
the Lê Văn Khôi (1833–4) in Gia Định. The Cham in Bình Thuận were
again drawn into the conflict, which led to their ultimate political demise.
But despite the revolts Minh Mạng held power firmly throughout his
reign. The changes he instigated included creating 31 provinces, including
the six provinces of Gia Định that covered the whole of southern Vietnam.
To regulate affairs at court, Minh Mạng established an Inner Cabinet in
1829 and a Privy Council in 1837. Minh Mạng upgraded the exams to
recruit mandarins at doctorate level and ordered them every three years
rather than six.[5] Externally Đại Nam under Minh Mạng occasionally
clashed with Siam and Laos mainly over the control of Khmer territory.
However, the realm achieved its largest extent under his reign, including
a large section of Laos from the Việt border up to Savannakhet.

Minh Mạng was more open to foreign trading than his father and
became personally involved in maritime commerce. Trade with China,
Europe and Southeast Asia operated smoothly at the main ports of Đà
Nẵng, Hội An and Saigon. By 1822 trade with Britain began after a visit
to Saigon, Đà Nẵng and Huế by diplomat John Crawfurd.[6] Minh Mạng
refused to meet him but after his mission it was decreed that all
Vietnamese ports were open on equal terms to the merchant ships of
France, Holland, the United States and Britain.[7] The French thus lost
the exclusive port access specified in the now defunct Treaty of Versailles.
Minh Mạng sent ships every year to Singapore, Cambodia, Batavia (Java),

Thái Hòa Palace, roof corner, Imperial Citadel, Huế.

Canton and Calcutta from 1835–9. They carried rice, raw silk, animal skins, oil, salt, salted fish, bird nests, shark fins, buffalo horn and elephant tusks. They bought in opium, wool, tea, silk, spices, paper, porcelain, copper, firearms and ammunition.

Minh Mạng undertook a massive construction programme in the Imperial Citadel, where the Thái Hòa palace and other old buildings were redesigned or moved to make room for new ones. All were redecorated and embellished in a unique Nguyễn style that was superficially Chinese but contained many Vietnamese motifs and materials. Craftsmen were brought in from China and Vietnamese workers attempted to take over their trade secrets. Gia Long had been used to a hard and casual lifestyle from a young age, but his son Minh Mạng had a strict Confucian upbringing. He was a learned scholar who engaged directly in state affairs and was a stern disciplinarian who punished opponents severely. The case of Lê Văn Khôi, the adopted son of Lê Văn Duyệt, Gia Long's trusted viceroy in Gia Định, is an example of Minh Mạng's belief in a strict social and political order. When the emperor considered Lê Văn Duyệt had become too powerful in Gia Định with the support of the Cham governor in the Cham autonomous zone in Bình Thuận, he began to instigate a change in both regions to break up such power. Lê Văn Khôi then tried to establish an autonomous region away from the influence of Huế court. With the support of the Christian community and others like the Cham he occupied all six provinces of the south and proclaimed himself the Great Commander, organizing a court as if he were king.[8] When a naval force was sent from Huế he entrenched himself in the Phiên An (former Turtle) citadel in Gia Định and sought aid from Siam. It took the emperor's troops nearly three years to drive out the Siamese and capture the citadel. Lê Văn Khôi died during the siege and 2,000 were killed or captured. The citadel was razed to the ground.[9] A French priest, père Marchand, was accused of being one of the ringleaders and was taken back to Huế to be killed in a gruesome manner along with six other 'leaders' who included Lê Văn Khôi's seven-year-old son.

The autonomous Cham Zone in Bình Thuận province was broken up early in the conflict and the land incorporated into the administrative system of the province. In 1832 Champa ceased to exist, even in its diminutive form.[10] Resistance from the Cham in the highlands, however, continued, causing the Huế court headache and expense, until it was suppressed by the army in 1835. Two Cham leaders of the Vietnamese names of Nguyễn Văn Thừa and Nguyễn Văn Nguyên were executed for having connections with the Lê Văn Khôi's uprising in Gia Định.[11] The Cham population scattered even further to the highlands along the Cambodian border, or into Châu Đốc in the Lower Mekong by the Cambodian border. Those who remained in the lowlands retained few Cham characteristics and disappeared into the Việt population of Ninh Thuận and Bình Thuận.[12]

MINH MẠNG TURNS ON CHRISTIANS

The demise of the Cham proved a minor problem for Minh Mạng compared with the impact of European Christian missionaries in the country. The seriousness of the incident in Gia Định in 1833–5 convinced Minh Mạng that the Catholic Church was at the root of his problems and he ordered a total ban of Christianity.[13] Churches were closed and Christians were ordered to renounce their faith or face punishment including death. From 1833–8 missionaries and their converts were imprisoned or killed on the emperor's orders.[14] Churches were searched and priests and laymen interrogated and tortured for confessions. In 1825 after a French ship called the *Thetis* surreptitiously brought a French missionary to Đà Nẵng, Minh Mạng decreed that all foreign ships were to be watched and all French priests brought to Huế for translation work rather than being left at large to preach to the population. None of these measures endeared the emperor to the Europeans and the killing of père Marchand for complicity in the 1833 rebellion in the Phiên An citadel remained a controversy that haunted Minh Mạng and the Nguyễn in later years.

European intervention in East and Southeast Asia intensified during Minh Mang's reign. The British took over Singapore and established colonial rule there in 1819. In China British trade escalated into the Opium War in 1840. The French also exerted pressure on China and obliged the Qing to open several ports to them by 1844. China signed treaty after treaty giving the United States and European countries more and more power inside China. The Spanish and the Dutch, meanwhile, continued to entrench themselves in the Philippines and Indonesia, while the Portuguese firmly held Macao. Emperor Minh Mạng viewed the onset of these events in China with alarm; if China, the powerful mentor of Vietnam, had such trouble dealing with the West, what would become of Vietnam? In 1840 Minh Mạng sent delegations to Penang, Batavia, Paris and London to explore possible accommodation, but to no avail and by the time they returned Minh Mạng had died. No audience was conceded with King Louis Philippe in Paris after *Société des Missions Étrangères* reported the hostility of Minh Mạng's court and advocated vigorous intervention in Vietnam to defend Catholics.[15]

The spread of Christianity was a cause of great concern throughout the reign of Minh Mạng because the promotion of an alternative God was seen as fundamentally inconsistent with the core Vietnamese traditional belief that the emperor was a Son of Heaven, chosen to govern the country with a Celestial Mandate. When European missionaries came to preach and encouraged Vietnamese citizens to serve a Christian God in heaven, it was seen as a direct challenge to the emperor's authority or an act equivalent to rebellion. This foreboding was intensifed by the perceived involvement of missionaries in actual rebellions and led to Minh Mang banning Christianity altogether. But even under the ban, French and other European priests continued to work clandestinely in Vietnam. A number of Europeans priests were executed for alleged involvement in anti-court plots.[16] The persecution of Christians was to be a key pretext for later French intervention. Minh Mang's actions against European missionaries were widely condemned outside Vietnam. As a devoted classical scholar Minh Mang viewed the preaching of European priests as rebellious intervention and a challenge to his Celestial Mandate. Minh Mang died aged 50 after a strong reign of 21 years during which he brought in many reforms, built a firm base for the independent state and left a large cultural legacy for the country. Independent Vietnam was at its strongest and most organized under him, but he will always be remembered for persecuting Christians.

THIỆU TRỊ (*r.* 1841–7) THE POET

The eldest son of Minh Mạng succeeded him as Nguyễn emperor Thiệu Trị at the age of 31 on 12 February 1841. He proved to be the most artistic and a prolific poet of the dynasty. His domestic policy was to pursue his father's work of developing Vietnam into a well-organized realm and to uphold traditional values. In foreign policy he also followed his father, but with less rigidity. In 1840 he went as far as welcoming the arrival in Đà Nẵng of a French warship commanded by captain Favin Levêque, who requested the release of five imprisoned missionaries. The emperor made this concession and similarly freed Bishop Dominique Lefèbvre in 1845 at France's request, despite his being condemned to death. With these gestures Thiệu Trị showed a less obdurate attitude towards foreign interference and from 1843 French warships docked in Đà Nẵng, often requesting better treatment for French missionaries, even though by then there were few French citizens left in Vietnam. Even the Chaigneau and Vannier families had gone back to France. Only missionaries were left.

The year 1847 saw an escalation after Bishop Lefèbvre reentered the country in secret and was again arrested. The French sent in two gunships under the command of Captain Lapière and Commander Charles Rigault de Genouilly with a letter from the French king demanding his release. While they awaited the bishop's release the French commanders said they detected unusual activity on Vietnamese ships and opened fire, sinking five ships.[17] The incident, known as the bombardment of Đà Nẵng, was said to have resulted from intelligence passed to the French by a Vietnamese Catholic.[18] The French version of the bombardment says the French ships interdicted the Vietnamese navy as it was preparing to attack them.[19] Emperor Thiệu Trị was enraged and he ordered handsome rewards for the capture and killing of all Christian missionaries in Vietnam. Thiệu Trị died shortly after this incident and was succeeded by his second son Nguyễn Phúc Hồng Nhậm, who was crowned Emperor Tự Đức at the age of nineteen. The first prince was said to be a playboy and unsuitable.

TỰ ĐỨC (r. 1847–83) AND 'VOLUNTARY HUMILIATION'

Tự Đức inherited a nation cocooned in Confucian values but on the brink of modernity in the form of war with France. He became the longest reigning monarch of the dynasty and presided over the transfer of large tracts of his realm to France. Tự Đức and the Nguyễn have been bitterly criticized in hindsight for the treaties they signed with the French. Tự Đức, a poet emperor, who built the most scenic tomb for his afterlife and retired to it constantly when still alive when the pressures at court became unbearable, described his treaties with the superior military power as a 'voluntary humiliation' performed 'for the sake of conserving the people and maintaining the peace for the country'.[20] Whether the emperor had a real alternative in the face of French military power and

Tomb of Emperor Tự Đức, Huế.

ambition is still debated, with the less generous blaming his loss of territory to France on his weakness and the extravagance of his court.

After the first bombardment of Đà Nẵng, Vietnamese ports faced constant visits and harassment from French gunboats, which resulted in more bans on European missionaries. Recent research however suggests the bans were ineffective and the persecution exaggerated. For example, in a letter to the Paris Directors at the *Missions Étrangères* on 2 May 1850, French Bishop Pierre André Retord of Acanthe, Vicar Apostolic of Western Tonkin, gives a glimpse of the actual situation:

> After the edict of our little king (*notre petit roi*) Tu-Duc against our religion, and especially against European missionaries, the pagan king did not seem to pay more attention to us; little by little, his mandarins did the same, and, after a frightening while, things went back to normal . . . That means, even though we were not allowed religious freedom, we took it back ourselves and we have been able to continue with ease up to now. We went back to work with renewed vigour, preaching and taking confessions day and night . . . We reaped a much better harvest than any year before.[21]

The considerable latitude afforded to Christians is illustrated in an incident ten years later when Catholic convert and reformist scholar Nguyễn Trường Tộ was given an audience with the emperor to present his reform suggestions for Vietnam. The court was so incensed by his ideas that the emperor had to send him home to Nghệ An with an armed escort.[22] Yet the fact remains that a well-known Catholic convert, who had travelled in Europe for some years to study European systems, was granted an audience at the imperial court. While pressure from France increased, Tự Đức faced internal rebellions, one of them involving his own family. Tự Đức faced constant opposition from his elder half-brother Hồng Bào, who had been passed over for the throne. In 1851 this Prince organized a plot with help from foreign priests to overthrow Tự Đức.[23] Hồng Bào was imprisoned and later committed suicide in captivity. The persecution of Christians intensified again after the failed Hồng Bào coup with the emperor issuing a decree calling on citizens to capture and kill European missionaries, which was repeated in 1855. Three French priests and many Christians were reported executed in 1851 and the scene was set for eventual international confrontation. But the new French emperor Napoleon III decided instead to create a Committee for Cochinchina in 1857 with the cabinet strongly opposing intervention in Vietnam – a country too few of them knew and too far away to risk spending large sums of expedition money on. Some said the priests were fabricating a crisis in collusion with naval officers.[24]

The uncertainties in Paris allowed French naval officers in the East a freer hand. In one incident the French ship *Catinat*, under Captain Le Lieur, arrived in Đà Nẵng in September 1856 and handed Vietnamese representatives a letter from the French emperor and said a French envoy would arrive shortly to establish relations. The Vietnamese opened the letter and left it on the beach; the insulted French captain directed a salvo of gunfire on the port and left. The envoy was M. de Montigny, the French consul in Shanghai, who arrived in January 1857 and presented the Huế court with a set of requests including the establishment of a consulate, a trading post in Đà Nẵng, free trade and free missionary activities in Vietnam. Tự Đức refused all and the French decision to intervene militarily appears to have been decided then. Spain would provide a support contingent because their nationals 'had been persecuted for over two centuries' in Vietnam.[25]

THE FRENCH INVASION (1858–85)

A fleet of twelve French warships under Vice-Admiral Rigault de Genouilly entered Đà Nẵng in late 1858 and bombarded the city. They captured two maritime posts of An Hải and Điện Hải. Two months later, the French fleet attacked both Đà Nẵng and Thị Nại in Quy Nhơn.[26] By the end of the year the French fleet was still in Đà Nẵng but unable to proceed to Huế. The popular revolution that they were promised by the missionaries did not materialize. They were enfeebled by dysentery and cholera and meeting strong Vietnamese resistance. The fleet left Đà Nẵng and proceeded south in January 1859.[27] In the south the French began their invasion on 2 February 1859 by entering the port of Vũng Tàu and travelling upriver to Biên Hòa, north of Saigon. They overwhelmed Saigon and captured Gia Định-Saigon. De Genouilly made three demands on the Huế court: cession of land, free trade and unhindered propagation of Christianity. The court was unanimous in refusing the first but wavered on the others. Senior minister Phan Thanh Giản advised the emperor to accept the demand to lift the ban on Christianity for the sake of peace.[28] The French fleet returned to Đà Nẵng for more bombardment before moving on to China in 1860 to increase their pressure on the Qing. When a ceasefire was reached in China the French Navy returned to Vietnam reinforced by 30 ships and 3,500 men from the French naval force in China.[29] The treaty with China was seen in Paris as an opening for a stronger French presence in Asia, where Vietnam would be a base to counter the influence of the British, who had now acquired Hong Kong and Singapore. Vice-Admiral Rigault de Genouilly advised his government that southern Vietnam and the Mekong would be of great importance to commerce and he won the support of the new Secretary for the Navy and Colonies, Marquis de Chasseloup-Laubat. The French fleet under Admiral Charner arrived in February 1861 and the French campaign in South Vietnam was relaunched.

The city of Mỹ Tho succumbed in April 1861,[30] followed by Biên Hòa and Bà Rịa. The Vietnamese asked for a truce, which the French accepted on condition that a twelve-point agreement was accepted. Tự Đức refused and the war resumed. By March 1862 the French had taken Vĩnh Long province and proposed a new treaty, which the emperor now accepted.[31] Senior minister Phan Thanh Giản was sent to Saigon to sign on behalf of the emperor with Admiral Bonard, who had replaced Charner. In this treaty Vietnam ceded to France the three eastern provinces Biên Hòa, Gia Định-Saigon, Định Tường-Mỹ Tho, and the island of Poulo Condore. France was accorded 4 million francs or 2.8 million taels of silver as war reparations, payable over ten years. The ports of Đà Nẵng, Bà Lạt on the Hồng River and Quảng Yên were open to free trade and the propagation of Christinity was granted.[32] France agreed to hand back the western province of Vĩnh Long. Vietnam was committed to inform France of any foreign diplomatic activities. It was to be the first of several treaties that the Nguyễn Court signed with France under heavy military pressure.

Emperor Tự Đức sent a mission to Paris a year later offering to buy back the three lost provinces. A French newspaper reported the offer as

85 million francs. The offer was also not known to the French representatives to the treaty of 1862, which was named after French governor Bonard. Bonard, de la Grandière and Marquis de Chasseloup-Laubat, secretary of state for the Navy and Colonies, were all kept in the dark.[33] The delegation was well received by the chief of protocol at the Foreign Office, Félix-Sébastien Feuillet de Conches. However, the audience with Napoleon III was postponed for a month because of the time it took to translate the complex protocols. The Vietnamese delegation was taken to visit museums, gardens, palaces, cathedrals, factories and was treated to a hot air balloon ride at the Champs de Mars, where their photographs were taken. They were visited by the ageing Michel Đức Chaingeau, son of French ex-mandarin Jean-Baptiste of the time of emperor Gia Long. Each day was recorded in precise detail by grand counsellor Phan Thanh Giản, head of the delegation, in his report for the court.[34] The audience with Napoleon III finally took place on 7 November 1863 at the Palais des Tuileries when ambassador Phan Thanh Giản presented his case to the French emperor, translated by French officer Captain Aubaret. His age, dignity and chanted presentation 'moved the court ladies to tears'.[35] The emperor agreed to a renegotiation and said he was only interested in 'civilizing through commerce'.

The Phan Thanh Giản's mission was judged a success and the Vietnamese delegation left France via Spain to return to Saigon. They were taken to Huế on the French ship *Écho* on 24 March 1863. Work on a renegotiated treaty began immediately between Phan Thanh Giản and Aubaret. However those in favour of French occupation did not wait long before they embarked on a diplomatic counter-offensive. From April 1864 the pro-colonial party led by Bonard, Rigault de Genouilly, Marquis de Chasseloup-Laubat and Henri Rieunier, the next secretary for the Navy and Colonies, launched a campaign to inform the French authorities of what they perceived as the facts of Cochinchina. Their campaign gained momentum and French public opinion began to favour an occupation of southern Vietnam. In June of 1864 Napoleon III issued an order to stop the negotiation for a new treaty and reverted to the former treaty of 1862. His reversal decree reached Huế on 21 July when the new draft treaty had been signed a week earlier. Under the new treaty France was to return to Vietnam the three occupied provinces in exchange for protectorate rights in all six provinces of South Vietnam. They were allowed to open three posts in Saigon and Vũng Tàu (Cap Saint-Jacques), to establish residences in Đà Nẵng, Bà Lạt, Quảng Nam and on the coast of central Vietnam. Each residential post was given 9 sq. km of land. Vietnam was to pay France 80 million francs in reparations. There was to be free propagation of Christianity, although the law of Vietnam forbade its citizens from straying from their national religion. This last clause would be important later. Marquis de Chasseloup-Laubat argued against the new treaty at the French court and it was not ratified. In January 1865 the treaty was officially repudiated by France and Emperor Tự Đức's offer to buy back the three provinces was abandoned.

The negotiation for the south took place when there was trouble on the Sino-Viet border, with ethnic minorities and Lê remnants fighting each other. Piracy meanwhile, flourished along the coast. Tự Đức continued to procrastinate over the strategic decisions regarding the French, and distracted himself with constructing his lavish tomb on the south side of the Hương River in Huế, which has since become a star tourist attraction in modern Vietnam. The building of imposing tombs with palatial buildings and vast landscaped gardens as palaces for the afterlife was a special feature of the Nguyễn dynasty. Earlier emperors built modest resting places for themselves and their ancestors but from Gia Long onwards the Nguyễn built huge palatial complexes with lakes and parks comparable in size and style to the Imperial Citadel. Tự Đức began to build his final resting place in 1864 when his dream of buying back lost territory from France was shattered. By 1866 the tomb was completed, despite anger from the conscripted labourers who received little from the depleted treasury while the country was at war on many fronts. Tự Đức was subsequently criticized for the luxury and grand scale of the tomb complex; but for him it was not only a resting place for the afterlife, it was a sanctuary from his highly pressured current life. Once completed, the emperor lived in his tomb with his wives and concubines for months at a time for his remaining sixteen years to escape the pressure of affairs as the French encroached.

COCHINCHINA

Admiral Louis-Adolphe Bonard, the first military governor of Cochinchina, formed a local army and invited local dignitaries to join his administration. Many refused and some rebelled against the French occupation, including Trương Định, the head of a military agricultural estate. He united local militia groups to fight the French, with the approval of Huế. After the 1862 treaty he gained more local support and fought against both the French occupation and 'the court who abandoned the people'. They kept up a guerrilla campaign for a year before Trương Định was killed in 1864. His two sons continued the fight along the Cambodia border for three more years.[36] Such unrest prompted the French to demand the court in Huế to take action, but when it continued they moved into the remaining three western provinces of southern Vietnam along the Khmer border. Unlike on previous occasions, the decision to

occupy the territory was taken in Paris, as the French former naval commander Rigault de Genouilly had been made secretary of the Navy and
Colonies, and he ordered Admiral de la Grandière to take the western
provinces of Vĩnh Long, An Giang and Hà Tiên in 1867. The elder states-
man Phan Thanh Giản was then general governor of the provinces and
when the French army and navy arrived in Vĩnh Long in June 1867 he
decided against resistance 'to avoid more bloodshed'. He took poison at
the age of 71 after handing over the provinces to Admiral Pierre de la
Grandière. Phan Thanh Giản was stripped of all titles posthumously
and his name was chiselled off the stelae of doctorates at the Temple of
Literature. (He was reinstated under the reign of emperor Đồng Khánh.)
His two sons joined the resistance and led a force in the western area
that managed to control Rạch Giá province for a while in 1868.[37] Many
other resistance groups were formed to fight the French and one brought
together Vietnamese, Cambodian, Cham and highlanders, but all were
small, ill-equipped and ineffective.

Before the French took over southern Vietnam they had planned to
use the Mekong as a transport route to Yunnan. In 1866 Admiral de la
Grandière ordered the exploration of the Mekong River up to Yunnan
and appointed Lt. Colonel de Lagrée and Captain Francis Garnier to
lead the expedition.[38] In 1863 the French had secured control of
Cambodia, and forced Thailand to pull back from Khmer territory,
giving them access to the Mekong below Laos. The mission charted the
river and discovered falls in Cambodia. The great variation in water flow
from its Himalayan source made the huge river impossible for ship
navigation throughout the year. They also found that the Hồng River in
North Vietnam was an important access route to China. This realization
was supported later by the first voyage of a French merchant, Jean Dupuis,
in 1870 and the French expedition switched to studying the Hồng, whose
flow was much more reliable. A plan was formed to secure the control
of this river.[39] Paris sanctioned no action in northern Vietnam at first,
for Napoleon III was fighting the Franco-Prussian war with Germany
that he lost in 1871. When Napoleon was captured and the Third French
Republic was founded, the French colonial authority in Vietnam was
left drifting without direction from Paris. French officers and businessmen
plotted their own course to control the weak court in Huế. On 26 January
1872 a Captain Senez was ordered by the French governor in Saigon to
take the frigate *Bourayne* to the port of Tourane (Đà Nẵng) with one
official mission and one secret. The official one was to find ways to fight
piracy in the Gulf of Tonkin and the secret one was to explore the Hồng
River and to find a way to navigate to Yunnan.[40] Senez reported back
to Saigon and returned to Hanoi to meet a French merchant Jean Dupuis,
who owned three commercial junks. Since 1868 Jean Dupuis had sailed

Captain Francis Garnier.

his junks up and down the Hồng River carrying goods between Vietnam and Yunnan without permission from the Vietnamese authorities. He sold cannons and ammunition to Yunnan and brought out salt and rice, both controlled products in Vietnam. When Vietnamese officials ordered him to stop these activities, he imprisoned the officials. The Huế court sent veteran mandarin Nguyễn Tri Phương to Saigon for negotiations with the French governor. The new governor of the south was Admiral Marie-Jules Dupré, who had lent 30,000 piastres of public money to Dupuis to pursue his commercial exploits. Dupré told Paris the River Hồng would be a major asset and when the Vietnamese delegation arrived in Saigon to raise the matter of Jean Dupuis, Dupré despatched Captain Francis Garnier to Hanoi with carte blanche authority to resolve the problem. Garnier joined forces with Jean Dupuis and demanded that the governor of Hanoi, Nguyễn Tri Phương, open the River Hồng to French navigation and trade with France. The Vietnamese refused but

Garnier posted a notice in Hanoi saying the River Hồng was open for shipping between the Gulf of Tonkin and Yunnan by all those who had treaties with Vietnam. He fixed the customs tariffs for foreign ships, according to which those travelling to and from Saigon paid only half dues. The notice was torn down by the Hanoi governor. On 19 November 1873 Garnier complained to Nguyễn Tri Phương that he was obstructing trade in north Vietnam and warned that he would take action. At dawn the next day Garnier stormed the Hanoi citadel with Dupuis and captured Nguyễn Tri Phương, who died from serious injury.[41] The citadel fell in three hours. Garnier took over Hanoi and launched attacks into the four adjacent provinces of Nam Định, Phủ Lý, Ninh Bình and Hải Dương, which all fell within days. Emperor Tự Đức called for a truce but while his envoys travelled to Saigon to negotiate with the French governor, a Vietnamese army led by local officials joined forces with a rebel Chinese militia called Black Flag. This group attacked a Hanoi suburb and killed Garnier when he arrived to confront them. He was 'decapitated and his heart ripped out'.[42] Garnier's death and the wild situation in the north prompted serious questioning in Paris about French policies in Vietnam,[43] while negotiations continued in both Hanoi and Saigon. Those in Hanoi were conducted by Captain Philastre, the French chief justice of Saigon and a senior mandarin from Huế called Nguyễn Văn Tường. They agreed that France would return to Vietnam all the provinces taken in the north, as well as the Hanoi citadel, and Dupuis would be expelled from Hanoi. In March 1874 a new treaty was signed between Governor Dupré and Tự Đức's representatives. This treaty of 22 clauses legalized the French control of the south and a protectorate in the north. According to the 1874 treaty, Vietnam would cede to France all six provinces in the south, follow French foreign policies, and open to trade the Hồng River, the Hanoi citadel and the ports of Hải Phòng in the north and Thị Nại in central Quy Nhơn. France would place consuls at these locations. French and foreign citizens in Vietnam would be judged by French authorities only.[44] Lastly, France would appoint an ambassador to Huế and Vietnam would send an ambassador to Paris.[45]

Tự Đức then looked to the Qing government for help with the situation on the Sino-Việt border where the Vietnamese army openly allied against the French with the powerful Black Flag, led by Liu Yung-fu (Lưu Vĩnh Phúc). This group was a mix of triad members and remnants from the visionary Christian Taiping revolution in China. The Qing responded and despatched a force from Guangxi and another from Yunnan but their effectiveness went unrecorded. Tension between the French and the Vietnamese armies saw flare-ups, as in April 1882, when Captain Henri Rivière launched an attack against the Hanoi Citadel. Governor Hoàng Diệu hanged himself on a tree as French soldiers entered the citadel.[46] Rivière also took locations in Nam Định, Hòn Gai and Sơn Tây. The Black Flag group meanwhile continued to fight against the French. They killed Rivière, along with 32 officers and men in an ambush at Cầu Giấy, outside Hanoi on 19 May 1883.[47] Paris was outraged at the demise of Rivière and the National Assembly angrily diverted civilian funding to military use. The French Navy arrived off Huế in August 1883 only to find that Tự Đức had passed away the previous month. But some members of his court were willing to reach an accommodation.[48]

THREE EPHEMERALS: DỤC ĐỨC (r. 1883), HIỆP HÒA (r. 1883), KIẾN PHÚC (r. 1883–4)

Tự Đức died childless but he had earlier adopted three of his nephews and appointed three regents to oversee the succession. One regent died and the other two, civil mandarin Nguyễn Văn Tường and military mandarin Tôn Thất Thuyết, would play key roles in the ensuing inept succession. The first adopted son was put on the throne as Emperor Dục Đức in 1883 but was dismissed in three days when he showed softness for the French. At the will-reading ceremony Dục Đức omitted certain sentences, which was judged lese-majesty and he was thrown in prison to die of starvation.[49] Tự Đức's youngest brother, the son of Thiệu Trị by a lesser queen, was then crowned Emperor Hiệp Hòa. But he too favoured turning Vietnam into a full French protectorate. On his order the mandarins Nguyễn Trọng Hợp (Hiệp) and Trần Đình Túc signed the 1883 treaty of Huế with French envoy Jules Harmand[50] ceding to France protectorate rights throughout Vietnam, including Huế. Before the treaty could be ratified in France Hiệp Hòa was dethroned and forced to take poison in November 1883. The regents then enthroned the youngest of Tự Đức's adopted sons as Emperor Kiến Phúc, aged fifteen, while they tried to unscramble the treaty.[51] Kiến Phúc's reign was almost as short as his predecessors as he died of unknown causes in July 1884. France sent a new treaty which was signed on 6 June 1884 by French envoy Jules Patenôtre and the two Vietnamese regents.

The Patenôtre treaty divided Vietnam north of the French-owned Cochinchina into two regions governed by different authorities. Tonkin in the north was governed by the French as Bắc Kỳ, and the Nguyễn Court governed the centre called Annam or Trung Kỳ. Both regions were under French protection and the French authority had the right to enter the Imperial Citadel at will. The French occupied Thuận An port, the gateway to Huế. The high drama of events at the Nguyễn court unfolded against a background of continuing war in the north along the border. There were regular clashes between the French army and navy under Admiral Amédée Courbet and the Chinese until France forced China to relinquish all rights over Vietnam in another treaty signed at Tianjin in May 1885. This recognized France's protectorate over Vietnam in article two. The French representatives in Huế then demanded that the Nguyễn Court hand over to France the royal seal that China gave to the first emperor Gia Long. The regent Nguyễn Văn Tường refused and proposed the seal be destroyed. In a solemn ceremony witnessed by French representatives and Vietnamese courtiers, the 6 kg gold seal was melted, ceremoniously ending the hold of China over Vietnam.

HÀM NGHI (r. 1884–5): THE REBEL WHO SHOULD HAVE STAYED?

On the death of Kiến Phúc his blood brother prince Nguyễn Phúc Ưng Lịch became the eighth Nguyễn emperor Hàm Nghi at the age of thirteen. This was the first test of the Patenôtre treaty and there was an instant reaction from Pierre Paul Rheinart, the French chargé d'affaires at Huế, who insisted on the French right to prior approval. He even offered his own candidate Nguyễn prince but the court refused. Paris turned down Rheinart's urgent request to use force to replace Hàm Nghi, but Rheinart still ordered the French army to point their heavy cannons at the citadel. After lengthy negotiation the Nguyễn court agreed to ask in writing for French permission to enthrone Hàm Nghi and he was re-crowned in the presence of French representatives. Military coercion would soon return. Regent Tôn Thất Thuyết accused the French of violating the Patenôtre treaty by stationing two battalions of riflemen in north Vietnam in 1885.[52] The French decided to remove him when events took another dramatic turn. Marshall Roussel de Courcy, the new French regional commander, declared a state of siege within ten days of his arrival and proposed using force against the Nguyễn court and this was approved. Marshall de Courcy reached Huế on 2 July 1885 to present his credentials to emperor Hàm Nghi. In the preliminary protocol negotiation de Courcy demanded that all his troops should enter the citadel by the central Ngọ Môn gate, which was strictly reserved for the emperor and the Chinese ambassador. When it was refused, de Courcy demanded that both regents call on him.[53] Perhaps because he had heard of the plan to remove him, Tôn Thất Thuyết excused himself and only Nguyễn Văn Tường went to de Courcy. The fragile relationship broke down and during the night of 4 July 1885, Tôn Thất Thuyết sent the Vietnamese army on a surprise attack on the French legation across the river and on their garrison at Mang cá fort, a few kilometres away at the northeast corner of the Imperial Citadel. But they soon ran out of ammunition and by dawn the French retaliated and assaulted the citadel. A large part of the citadel was burnt and thousands perished.[54] The royal treasury was looted and hundreds of chests of silver bars were confiscated as French troops pushed through the complex of palaces.[55] Tôn Thất Thuyết escaped with Hàm-Nghi and three senior queens to a secret base in Quảng Trị province while the regent Nguyễn Văn Tường stayed behind to negotiate peace terms. After the first stop on their escape the senior queens elected to return to Huế, but Tôn Thất Thuyết with his sons and the young emperor carried on to Tân-Sở, a remote base prepared in advance near the Lao border.[56]

Tân-Sở was constructed in 1883, when French pressure grew heavy on emperor Tự Đức, and the court saw the need for an alternative capital far from Huế in case the citadel had to be abandoned. The base was secretly built by 2,000 workers on a plateau close to the border with Laos and one third of the royal treasure was transported there for safekeeping. Like the Huế citadel, Tân-Sở had three levels of fortification in an area of 450 × 500 m hidden behind dense bushes and guarded by heavy guns, but it would not be able to withhold a serious assault and the royal fugitives soon abandoned it when the pursuing French got near.[57]

During his short stay at Tân Sở, emperor Hàm Nghi issued a royal decree calling on the people to help him fight the French, which set off what became known as the Cần Vương ('support the emperor') movement of groups ready to join him in exile and to ambush French forces. The royal party headed north on both sides of the Lao border. They travelled along a network of mountain tracks originally used as ancient trade routes and which in the twentieth century were known as the Hồ Chí Minh Trail or the Trường Sơn Route during the war in Vietnam. They were helped by the Mường minority who knew the terrain intimately and could avoid the pursuing French. The royal fugitive party eventually settled in Minh Hóa, Quảng Bình province, north of Quảng Trị and Huế, where they evaded the French for the next two years. A village elder Cao Lượng retold the sejour of Hàm Nghi in his village in great detail to French Inspector M. B. Bourotte in 1928. The young emperor arrived in December 1885 with regent Tôn Thất Thuyết and hundreds of soldiers. They carried 50 chests of valuables and they occasionally scattered into the jungle to avoid French troops. The French set up outposts throughout the region to try to box in the royal party. 'The French troops were merciless, they arrested many people, burned houses and took all that was good.' Some of the emperor's supporters were arrested and put to death.[58] When the situation became hopeless, Tôn Thất Thuyết left the emperor in the care of his sons and crossed into China to seek help; he never returned. Hàm Nghi was captured in November 1888 when he was betrayed by his Mường tribal officer Trương Quang Ngọc. Two months later Hàm Nghi was sent to Algiers where he lived a long and healthy life in exile. In Huế regent Nguyễn Văn Tường was imprisoned and then shipped into exile in Tahiti where he died only months later.[59]

ĐỒNG KHÁNH (r. 1885–9) THE CYPHER; THÀNH THÁI (r. 1889–1907) THE UNSTABLE; DUY TÂN (r. 1907–16) AND THE RESISTANCE

With the rebel emperor in the maquis, the French installed a cypher. When their two-month-deadline for the court to bring back Hàm Nghi expired Emperor Đồng Khánh was the first ruler appointed by the French. At his coronation on 19 September 1885 he went to the French governor general to salute him first, before being crowned as emperor.[60] He ruled only in name under French protection. He once travelled to Quảng Bình province in 1886 to try to meet Hàm Nghi but returned empty-handed. Court affairs were conducted by courtiers under French direction. For the next three years, Vietnam had two emperors, Hàm Nghi agitating against the French in Quảng Bình province and Đồng Khánh who fully collaborated with them in Huế. Đồng Khánh suddenly died aged 27 on 28 January 1889 and a ten-year-old prince was chosen to replace him as emperor Thành Thái.

Thành Thái was the son of Dục Đức, who was emperor for only three days before being ousted and dying in prison. Under Thành Thái the French governor general presided over the council of ministers at court and the Vietnamese emperor, though the son of heaven for his people, had no worldly power. Later he was judged to be mentally unstable and in 1907 he was asked to abdicate by the court and go into exile on Réunion. His youngest son was put on the throne at the age of seven as Emperor Duy Tân.[61] Duy Tân came to the Nguyễn court when colonial powers were under pressure in East Asia. The Vietnamese elite then saw Japan as the new ideal Asian state after its astounding naval victory over Russia in 1905. Anti-French activities in Vietnam quickened and secret societies were formed with links to those in exile in Japan and China. Dr Sun Yat Sen's success in founding the Republic of China and the Guomindang in 1911 fuelled anti-French activity in Vietnam. At the outbreak of the First World War, thousands of Vietnamese citizens were drafted to fight for France in Europe, and demonstrations and agitation continued in the cities. The young Emperor Duy Tân decided to join the anti-French resistance in 1916 when he was sixteen. He left the Forbidden Purple City but was captured immediately and sent to join his father in exile on Réunion.[62]

KHẢI ĐỊNH (*r*. 1916–25) 'THE PUPPET'

Last but one Nguyễn emperor Khải Định was the son of Đồng Khánh. He ascended the throne in 1916 at the age of 32 and showed himself to be mature, mild of character and accepting of the *status quo*. His court and the French governor general were on excellent terms, while anti-French groups continued to operate in the countryside. His intimate relationship with the French was heavily criticized, even in his lifetime. After his visit to France in 1922, Phan Chu Trinh, one of the most prominent revolutionary figures, published a letter criticizing him. The Paris trip was undertaken so he could put his son crown prince Vĩnh Thụy in school in Paris. Phan Chu Trinh's letter accused the emperor of seven major crimes – such as stealing from the people and living a life of luxury, favouritism and dressing inappropriately (in French-influenced clothes).

Khải Định's most significant act was his decree to replace the Chinese-based *chữ Nôm* with Romanized Vietnamese (*quốc ngữ*). *Quốc ngữ* had been in extensive use since 1861. Thus the language created for the propagation of Christianity became the national language of the realm that had so resisted it.

BẢO ĐẠI (*r*. 1926/1932–45) 'THE PLAYBOY'

When Khải Định died in November 1925, his heir crown prince Vĩnh Thụy was considered too young to rule so he continued his education in France while court matters were managed by regent Tôn Thất Hân. He returned to Huế when he was nineteen and was crowned in 1932 as Emperor Bảo Đại, the last Nguyễn emperor. Similar to his father's, his position was titular and all state affairs were in the hands of the French governor general. Even so, and to his credit in Vietnamese eyes, during the early years of his reign he appointed forward-looking intellectuals to his court, including the young mandarin and future president Ngô Đình Diệm.[63] Whether he was frustrated by his failure to engage the true literati, or because of his upbringing in France, Bảo Đại indulged himself in pleasure-seeking that brought much criticism in and out of the country and alienated the court from the population. Reality caught up with Bảo Đại in 1939 when the world entered a new global conflict and Vietnam became involved in the war in the Pacific. From 1940 to 1945 Vietnam suffered the fate of being the theatre of engagement of an expanding Japan and a weakened France. Japan overthrew the French authority in Vietnam and set up a Japanese protectorate within the 'Greater East Asia Co-Prosperity Sphere'.

Japanese troops entering Saigon in 1941.

Bảo Đại now headed a nation freed from France but under an Asian master, Japan. Through his cordial relationship with the Japanese ambassador Yokohama in Huế, Bảo Đại was allowed to form his own government. The Trần Trọng Kim's government under Bảo Đại was welcomed in Vietnam, but it was soon obvious that it was powerless to cope with the fast pace of the last phase of the Second World War. The government proved indecisive in August 1945 when the Japanese power collapsed after the bombing of Hiroshima and Nagasaki. Bảo Đại's friend Yokohama bid his farewell on 16 August 1945 and Bảo Đại was on his own. He frantically wrote to 'all the parties of the Potsdam Conference, President Truman, King George VI and General De Gaulle' to ask for the peoples of Inchochina to be given 'the same degree of peace enjoyed throughout the world'.[64] But no one answered. In this political vacuum the League for the Independence of Vietnam, commonly known as Việt Minh, emerged as the strongest party and formed a new government in Hanoi under the leadership of Hồ Chí Minh. Six days later, at the request of this government, Bảo Đại signed his abdication statement on 25 August 1945, ending 143 years of the Nguyễn dynasty.

From Gia Long to Bảo Đại, just 82 of the 143 dynastic years were truly independent. The rest were under the shadow of the French protectorate, when the Nguyễn court reigned in isolation, alienated from the people. Meanwhile the country at large was immersed in a war of resistance led by the literati and supported by the peasantry. Though uncoordinated and often fought with few means, this was to be a long-lasting war, sustained by little but hope, and manifested under many forms. It eventually led to the establishment of the revolutionary government in August 1945 and the end of monarchy in Vietnam. Far more war would ensue, creating a massive diaspora of the Việt people throughout the globe.

13

French Colony (1887–1945)

All pretence that Vietnam was an independent realm headed by a legitimate ruler was abandoned in 1885 when the emperor was appointed
by the French *Résident-Supérieur* and court affairs decided by a council
of ministers headed by the Resident. The emperor was the keeper of less
and less credited rituals with nothing much to do, as emperor Bảo Đại
discovered after his coronation in 1932.[1] The Patenôtre treaty of 1884
split Vietnam into three regions administered by three different types
of authority. The south was called Nam Kỳ and *Cochinchine* in French
and was run as a French overseas territory. The north was called Bắc Kỳ
or *Tonkin* and was a French protectorate run by a French-supervised
administration. The central region of Trung Kỳ or *Annam* was ruled by
the emperor and his court, under the protection and direction of the
French authority. Despite the different paper definitions, in reality, all
three regions were run by French authorities from administrative centres
in Hanoi, Huế and Saigon with each centre headed by a *Résident-
Supérieur*. From 1887 all three regions of Vietnam were integrated into
the French territory called *L'Union indochinoise,* which included
Cambodia and Laos. Though there was no real distinction between the
Vietnamese regions, the different status of each created bureaucratic
barriers to Vietnamese travel because of the documents required. The
resultant clampdown on inter-regional travel accentuated older differences
among the regions. As Marr says, it generated 'mutual ignorance for the
economic advantage and political expediency of the colonists'.[2]

Following the French occupation of Saigon in 1859, the first governor
of Cochinchina was Admiral Louis-Adolphe Bonard, who framed an
administration along the lines of the British system in India and the
Dutch in Java. However a Confucian elite of local literati declined to
cooperate with the new French regime that ruled the territory directly
under the 1862 treaty. The French established administrative machinery
to oversee finance and the judiciary. New taxes were imposed on opium,
salt, alcohol and a variety of imports. The French authority was also

responsible for issuing licences for new factories.[3] The management of the eastern provinces was in place by the time the three western provinces were taken in 1867. 'It took only five days to appoint all the administrative posts.'[4] Cochinchina was in the hands of a succession of French naval officers, making it the *gouvernement des amiraux*, until 1873 when a school was formed to train civil servants.[5] French became the official language of Cochinchina in 1903, although Romanized Vietnamese (*quốc ngữ*) had been in extensive use since 1861. Both *quốc ngữ* and French were made compulsory for official recruitment exams by 1903.[6] French vocabulary was Vietnamized for everyday use. The French words for rubber (*caoutchouc/cao-su*), soup (*soupe/súp*), spoon (*cuillère/cùi dzìa*), suitcase (*valise/va-li*), coolie (*cu-li*) entered the local dialect with many others. Such words made the language of the south incomprehensible for Vietnamese from other regions. For example, a popular cookbook published in Saigon in the 1950s has several pages devoted to translating ingredients and methods from southern to northern Vietnamese dialects. The separation of the regions would be emphatic for one generation from 1954 to 1975 when regional outlook, expectations and attitudes would lead to mutual hostility. In 1954, when a million people moved south at the end of the French war, and a large but lesser number of people moved north, the new arrivals in both areas were met with suspicion and sometimes hostility.

In 1897 French military rule was phased out and a civil administration under Governor-General Paul Doumer was put in charge of the whole of Indochina. The French *Résident-Supérieur* in Huế answered to him.[7] A council of fifteen French residents was elected to guard their financial and economic interests. The infrastructure of Vietnam and the rest of Indochina was transformed under Paul Doumer (1897–1902) who built ports, canals, roads, railroads and bridges. Gustave Eiffel's company built long iron bridges with distinctive latticed structures like the Long Biên bridge in Hanoi (Doumer bridge), the Tràng Tiền bridge in Huế and several smaller ones in the south. Vietnamese peasants were drafted into the construction work under the traditional compulsory corvée system that exacted work as a kind of tax levied on each Vietnamese. As the rich could buy their way out of the obligation, the burden fell on the peasants. In some cases rice farmers might have to leave their land fifteen times a year to fulfil corvée duties. Not only did they not get paid for this work, they had to sustain themselves from their own resources.[8] The farmers of Annam seemed to bear a heavier burden than their compatriots elsewhere, not just in the corvée duties but also by a rise in land and poll taxes. In 1897 poll taxes rose five times from 0.5 piastre to 2.5 piastres per head. Land taxes also rose 50 per cent.[9] The court in Huế had to pay its own employees. To administer such an extensive network

Currency of French Indochina.

of projects, more Frenchmen were brought into the colony to take up posts such as collectors of taxes, duties and excise, inspectors of works and issuers of contracts and permits to build plantations or to open factories. As the number of projects grew, so did the personnel. It was estimated in 1910 that 5,000 Frenchmen were working as government officials in Vietnam.

The new transport system helped the colonists to move their products out of Vietnam, and to bring in imports. By the turn of the nineteenth century some large French factories had been built in Đà Nẵng, Huế, Quy Nhơn and Nha Trang-Phan Rang. Later the colonists focused on areas where the soil was suitable for their products. The colonists who moved onto the central highlands were no longer individual planters but employees of large commercial concerns already established in France.[10] Some set up monopolies like the alcohol producer Fontaine.[11] The colonial power held a monopoly on salt and opium and locals were encouraged to consume more and more of both. French companies paid little or low tax. After five years under Doumer French companies operating in Vietnam were engaged in mining, textiles, water and electricity, distilleries and brick kilns. Rice farming remained a major part of the economy even though large tracts of land were confiscated for rubber, tea and coffee. The seizure of land hit the ethnic minorities hard on the high plateaux. The highlands, homeland of the Nùng, Thái, Mường, Hmong, Chinese and upland Cham, had previously been autonomous with little regard for any government. But now they were gathered up into French officialdom. Their cultural and linguistic autonomy was respected but the French now appropriated to themselves the right to

Money issued by the Banque de l'Indochine.

cover their land with plantations and they conscripted the highlanders under the corvée system. The presence of French settlers drew more and more missionaries to these areas, with the result that a large number of highlanders in the central region became Christians. Resentment at the loss of land, the imposition of a poll tax and the corvée duties broke out as an uprising in 1908.

RESISTANCE GROUPS

Starting in 1859, when the French army and navy first entered the south, armed militia groups were formed to fight them. The first named leader of such a group was Trương Định, who worked on one of the Vietnamese army plantations in Cochinchina and was killed in an uprising. Other groups carried out acts of sabotage or ambushed French individuals. One group had Cambodian, Vietnamese, Cham, Mường and Stiêng members and operated from 1866–8 in the southern highlands on the Cambodian border. It disintegrated with the death of its Khmer leader Pakumbo. Further south in the delta port of Rạch Giá there was another group led by the sons of Phan Thanh Giản, the counsellor who led the Nguyễn delegation to Paris in 1863. After the treaties of 1874, 1883 and 1884 were signed many more of such groups were formed, some of them supported by the literati who were particularly disatisfied with the court's succumbing to pressure from France. Among the group leaders were Nguyễn Trung Trực (1861–8), Nguyễn Hữu Huân (1868), Mai Xuân Thưởng (1886), Đinh Công Tráng (1886–7), Nguyễn Thiện Thuật and

Cao Thắng (1885–9), Phan Đình Phùng (1885–96) and Hoàng Hoa
Thám (1887–1913). Some have city streets named after them today. The
strongest and best organized were established after the storming of Huế
and the appeal of emperor Hàm Nghi in July 1885. They operated in
the Trường Sơn central highlands, in pockets of Nghệ An and Thanh
Hóa and along the Chinese border.

Hàm Nghi's appeal fell on responsive ears among the Vietnamese
literati. His Cần Vương ('support the emperor') movement produced
resistance groups in most provinces along the Trường Sơn chain of
mountains and the Chinese border, sometimes with cooperation from
local chieftains, such as the group of Tống Duy Tân in Thanh Hóa
province, who was supported by the ethnic Mường in 1892. Another
chieftain who joined the anti-French movement was a Thái who worked
with the poet and patriot Nguyễn Quang Bích in the Đà (Black) River
valley from 1889 to 1893. Scholar Phan Đình Phùng's group was the
best known to heed Hàm Nghi's call to arms. His area of operations from
1885–96 spanned the western side of four central provinces of Thanh
Hóa, Nghệ An, Hà Tĩnh and Quảng Bình where the emperor was
captured in 1888. His commander Cao Thắng manufactured home-
made rifles modelled on those captured from the French.[12] The resistance
continued unabated by the capture of the emperor. The group of Hoàng
Hoa Thám or Đề Thám was a another notable one. Hoàng Hoa Thám
was a commoner and man of action who formed the Yên Thế movement
in 1885 on the edge of the Hồng River delta of north Vietnam and
continued to operate there until 1909. He was supported by peasants
who lost land to the French.[13] The group attacked French installations
in Bắc Giang, Thái Nguyên and Hưng Hóa, ambushed trains and once
kidnapped a Frenchman for ransom. This group was operating relatively
close to Hanoi and the French twice negotiated a truce with them. Under
the first truce in 1894, Hoàng Hoa Thám was given the control of four
cantons, or 22 villages, with the right to levy his own taxes for three
years.[14]

The French violated the truce in 1895 by launching an attack, but
Hoàng Hoa Thám escaped and fought on. A second truce was agreed
in 1897 on unknown terms and it lasted twelve years. Outside this area
Hoàng Hoa Thám continued to support uprisings and assassinations.[15]
In 1909 the French launched a large operation against Yên Thế and
Hoàng Hoa Thám was forced back into the mountains of Tam Đảo after
taking heavy losses. He is presumed to have been betrayed and killed in
November 1913 when the French army put on display what it said was
his head.

Anti-French resistance also showed itself in tracts and newspaper
articles. One early reform movement was led by Phan Bội Châu, who

advocated better education among young men under an alternative king. He was a scholar from Nghệ An who gathered remnants of the Cần Vương movement and put them under the leadership of Nguyễn prince Cường Để. Phan Bội Châu saw the futility of small-scale armed struggle and tried to bring in reforms that would be supported internationally. He secretly travelled to Japan in 1905 to meet with revolutionaries from China as well as the Japanese who had just spectacularly defeated Russia in 1905. He formed his *Đông Du* (travel east) movement, convinced that Japan should be the model for young Vietnamese to follow, and that they should travel to Japan to study.

Phan Bội Châu left for Japan a second time to join Prince Cường Để and formed the Việt Nam Duy Tân Hội (association for the modernization of Vietnam). Four Vietnamese students were smuggled out of Vietnam to attend the Japanese Military Academy in 1906. In Tokyo, Phan Bội Châu met with the Chinese Guomindang leader Sun Yat-sen and other reformers from China, India, the Philippines and Korea. Châu joined forces with them to form a League of East Asians working for the reform of their homelands. Japanese politics however took a different turn in 1910 when Japan came to terms with the French, and Phan Bội Châu, Cường Để and all Vietnamese students were expelled from Japan. They took refuge in China while Phan Bội Châu went to Thailand then Hong Kong, Shanghai and Guangdong to further his campaign, while continuing to send back pamphlets to Vietnam.

In 1912 the French authority passed death sentences on the revolutionaries in exile and Governor-General Albert Sarraut travelled to Guangdong to negotiate their extradition. Phan Bội Châu was jailed but he continued to write and direct his movement.[16] He was freed during the warlord war in Guangdong in 1917 and travelled on through China, Japan and Thailand, making a living by writing newspaper articles. He now leant towards Marxism after the success of the Russian Revolution. The Đông Du movement continued to inspire young men to travel out of Vietnam to learn about what was suppressed at home. Phan Bội Châu was arrested during the protests against imperial powers in Shanghai in 1925 and extradited to Vietnam to stand trial and was condemned to death. However, under international pressure, he was allowed to live in Huế without the right to leave the city until he died there in 1940. Other Vietnamese reformers surfaced including the scholar Phan Chu Trinh and the young Emperor Duy Tân, who was quickly exiled to Réunion.

Phan Chu Trinh was from a wealthy family in Quảng Nam and still a young boy when Emperor Hàm Nghi launched his Cần Vương movement in 1885. He followed his father when he became an ardent follower and took his family into the mountains to answer the call to arms. Although his father was soon killed by a fellow compatriot,[17] the orphaned

Phan Chu Trinh continued his work. Together with several young men like Trần Quý Cáp and Hùynh Thúc Kháng he advocated for non-violent reforms and opposed Japanese militarism. They cut their hair short, dressed like westerners and travelled around Vietnam to speak out against the mandarin system, while raising money to send students to Japan. He was at first a great admirer of Phan Bội Châu but when they met in Hong Kong in 1906 he rejected the platform of Châu's Vietnam modernization movement. Phan Chu Trinh considered that a return to imperialism under prince Cường Để was unnecessary and he decided to return from Tokyo to Vietnam to persuade the French authority to reform their system. Phan Chu Trinh did not mince his words when he approached the French governor-general Paul Beau (1902–08), successor to Paul Doumer, to demand reforms. He wrote a letter praising the French modernization of Vietnam but was strongly critical of their policy of suppression, land seizure, taxation and corvée labour and he urged full respect for the Việt people. Whether or not he received a reply from Beau, his letter was published in newspapers in Paris.

Under Paul Beau, six new schools were opened in Hanoi in 1906 to add to the eighteen already established. These were run as private schools by Vietnamese scholars with a curriculum limited to teaching French, quốc ngữ and Chinese, with some geography and chemistry. In March 1907 a new school with a difference was granted permission to open in Hanoi under the name of Đông Kinh Nghĩa Thục (Tonkin free school), modelled after the Japanese egalitarian Keio Gijuku school for commoners. The Tonkin school was set up by a group of scholars led by Đào Nguyên Phố and Nguyễn Quyên and taught subjects in three languages – Chinese, quốc ngữ and French. History, literature, science and mathematics were taught to hundreds of students at eight levels. Aligned with Phan Chu Trinh's ideas, the school was against the old mandarin exams and advocated a modern lifestyle, the use of quốc ngữ and short hair. Nationalist ideas gradually entered the school with calls to support local products rather than French imports and resistance leaders were saluted as heroes. Phan Chu Trinh was one of the most popular guest speakers at the school. Some teachers were briefly arrested when they took their lectures outside the school to a wider public. Provincial scholars obtained materials from the school in order to open their own and short hair became the symbol of a reformer even though it could land the wearer in jail for showing dangerous political leanings. The colonial authority became alarmed when it heard that the exile writings of Phan Bội Châu were circulating and in January 1908 the school was closed.

HỘI AN TAX UPRISING (1908)

Despite the outward appearance of successful colonization the French only had firm control in the south. In central Vietnam the higher ground between the coast and the mountains was a no-man's land sometimes held by the resistance and sometimes by the French. Further up the mountains in the highlands there was unrest among the ethnic minorities who were obliged to pay tax, offer corvée labour and who felt possession of their land was under threat. In March 1908 there was a peasant uprising against taxation. This time protests in the rural and mountainous areas found an echo in the cities. Shouting the slogan 'no tax for the French' some 300 villagers from Đại Lộc district of Quảng Nam province marched to the office of the district chief to demand the release of three arrested people. When they were repelled they marched on to the French resident's headquarters at the picturesque port of Hội An. The crowd demanded that corvée duty be shared equally among the rich and the poor and they were told this would be looked into. But six of them were then arrested and the crowd camped outside the residence in protest. Thousands more villagers from surrounding areas quickly gathered. For several weeks thousands of villagers took turns to picket the Resident's compound in makeshift camps. Finally reinforcements arrived and the Resident ordered them to open fire on the demonstrators. He also promised to dismiss the local mandarin and not to increase taxes. By then, word had spread from Hội An and thousands of people came out to voice their grievances in Quảng Nam and Quảng Ngãi provinces. The protests spread to Phú Yên, Bình Định and Thừa Thiên. In Huế, large crowds converged on the compound of the French Resident. By mid-April the French authority decided to respond with a serious show of force and began dispersing the crowds with gunfire. Thousands were arrested while villages were razed. Some, like the scholar Trần Qúy Cáp, were executed. Phan Chu Trinh and Huỳnh Thúc Kháng were shipped to prison on Côn Sơn island.[18] It was perhaps the strength of this popular discontent that persuaded the French to attack Hoàng Hoa Thám in Yên Thế the next year. Yên Thế fell but there were other protests among the highland ethnic minorities like the Mường in Hòa Bình province (1909–10), the Hmong in Hà Giang (1911–12) in the north and the Hre, Cham and Raglai in the central highlands. There were also sporadic problems on the Chinese border during the First World War. In 1917 a mutiny at a garrison in Thái Nguyên on the border led to the occupation of the town for a month and after they were driven into the mountains there were flare-ups for six months.[19]

The First World War made serious demands on Vietnamese labour and manpower. 50,000 soldiers and an almost equal number of labourers were drafted into the war in Europe and many did not return. The treasury and rice depots were also depleted. When the war was over demand for raw materials like rubber increased sharply and the acreage under rubber increased threefold between 1917 and 1926.[20] In the south, rubber output increased tenfold with 86,000 workers engaged, according to 1929 statistics. In the highlands coffee and tea plantations were expanded, encroaching on traditional farming land and provoking unrest among the Nùng, Dao and Hmong. Mining also grew in the north with 53,000 workers working down the colleries.[21] Under the two terms of the governor Albert Sarraut (1911–14 and 1917–19) parts of the educational system were reformed. Many people now adopted western clothes, manners and lifestyle, which became the subject of vivid debate in journals like *Nam Phong* (southern wind).

The 1920s and 1930s also marked the beginning of Vietnamese feminism, at least in big cities like Hanoi and Saigon, where women attempted to break through restrictions of the traditional Confucian society by embracing the western way of life. They went out to meet their contemporaries in mixed groups, rode bicycles, discussed and debated with men on equal terms. In Hanoi, the traditional Vietnamese long dress *áo dài* was radically modified to incorporate western features like puff-sleeves. Sports became popular among men and women. The number of early feminists was small but their lifestyle was broadcast far and wide. At the same time many of those who were educated under the French colonial system became aware of their second-class status. Their ideas and aspirations eventually strengthened support for the ongoing anti-colonial movement.

THE RISE OF THE NATIONALIST MOVEMENT

In the new world order between the First and Second World Wars, major new political concepts were forged in the October Revolution in Russia, the rise of the nationalist Guomindang in China, the appearance of the Labour Movement in the United Kingdom and the establishment of communist parties across Europe. The Vietnamese observed these developments intently and engaged themselves. The compulsory use of Romanized Vietnamese became the chosen means of the new literati to express themselves in newspapers, tracts and pamphlets. Vietnamese newspapers now appeared alongside their French counterparts and publishing houses were set up in large cities of all three regions to print books, journals and guides to advocate modern life and science. With the spread of these political ideas, meetings, demonstrations and civil disobedience were organized throughout the country. Consequently writers, journalists and newspaper publishers were constantly harassed, arrested or imprisoned by the French authority.

The rise of the labour movement and communist ideals in Europe appealed to a young man known as Nguyễn Ái Quốc (the patriot Nguyễn), who lived in Europe in the 1910s and 20s. He later founded the Vietnamese Communist Party and took the pseudonym Hồ Chí Minh. He had been born Nguyễn Sinh Cung in the family of a classical scholar in Nghệ An province and grew up witnessing upheavals like the 1908 uprising in Hội An and elsewhere, as well as the ensuing repression. According to his official biography, his first pseudonym was Nguyễn Tất Thanh but he assumed the name Nguyễn Ái Quốc at the end of the First World War.[22] In 1911 he travelled to England as galley hand on a French ship and settled in London during the war. He moved on to Paris between 1917 and 1919, where he met Phan Chu Trinh, who had been released from prison. The two of them passed a difficult period working at retouching photographs. They at first shared many political ideas but later Nguyễn Ái Quốc took his own direction. He wrote articles for French newspapers, engaged actively with leftists and joined the 1920 French Socialist Congress as a delegate from Indochina.[23] That event set him on a new political career path that separated him from Phan Chu Trinh. He travelled extensively from Russia to China, India and Thailand, studying and working on his communist ideals. By the end of the Second World War, he began to use his new name Hồ Chí Minh, the meaning of which may be variously translated as 'bringer of light', 'utterly bright' or 'supreme sage', none of which has been officially preferred.

In Vietnam, three types of political parties were established to define the route to independence. The first group advocated reform within the French colonial system through constitutionalist and the socialist parties. The second were militant religious sects such as the Cao Đài and the Hòa Hảo. The third type advocated a revolutionary approach such as the Vietnam Nationalist Party, the Indochinese Communist Party and the Vietnam Restoration League. Nguyễn Ái Quốc founded the Thanh Niên Cách Mạng Đồng Chí Hội (Revolutionary Youth) in Guangzhou in 1925. This was soon followed by the non-communist Việt Nam Quốc Dân Đảng (Vietnam Guomindang) founded by Nguyễn Thái Học in 1927. In the south of Vietnam the Cao Đài religion gained support across many social strata and formed a sizeable political force working against the colonial power by 1926. It became best known in the early 1950s under the militant general Trình Minh Thế, who organized terrorist attacks against the French in the cities. The Vietnam Guomindang attempted a general uprising after a mutiny at a garrison in Yên Bái on 10 February 1930. The action spread to several areas but soon spluttered out. Popular support was not forthcoming, and Nguyễn Thái Học and the rest of the party leadership were arrested and later executed. The party disintegrated and its members joined other parties. Also in 1930 Nguyễn Ái Quốc was called to Hong Kong from his base in Thailand to join a meeting of representatives of different communist factions. He managed to unite the factions into the Việt Nam Cộng Sản Đảng (Vietnamese Communist Party) with a Marxist–Leninist leaning. The name of the party was changed back to Indochinese Communist Party (ICP) later that year. In 1930 the ICP mobilized up to 100,000 peasants to stage demonstrations and strikes. The French reaction was swift and brutal. The ICP was purged in Vietnam by 1931. Nguyễn Ái Quốc was arrested by the British in Hong Kong at the request of the French but was later released.

With the onset of the Second World War the French again cracked down on the ICP in Vietnam. Party members escaped to the countryside and mountainous regions. Nguyễn Ái Quốc modified his goals in July 1939 to promoting democratic rights, freedom of organization, speech, assembly and the press. He envisaged the goals being achieved by a broad democratic front.[24] In May 1941 such a front was realized under the name of Việt Nam Độc Lập Đồng Minh Hội (Vietnam Independence League), later shortened to become the Việt Minh. The League was formed during the eighth plenum of the ICP in South China and welcomed all nationalist groups working against both the French and the Japanese, who were then in control of the Pacific region. The general-secretary was Nguyễn Ái Quốc and under his umbrella came a number of nationalist parties such as the Tân Việt (New Vietnam) and new factions of the former Vietnam Guomindang.[25] Although the ICP dwarfed the other members in this alliance, this did not appear to be a problem as all nationalists at the time shared the same patriotic purpose of liberating Vietnam. They were encouraged by many indications of support from the population at large.

By 1943 the Việt Minh has gained much wider support, from the nationalists, the new literati and the peasants, and appealed to both men and women. By the end of 1944 it is estimated that the Việt Minh had half a million members in Vietnam.

When war broke out in the Pacific, Japan reached an accommodation with Vichy France, whereby the French continued to govern in Vietnam as a proxy for the Japanese. The Japanese demanded war materials and food that the French provided, thus generating an unprecedented nation-wide famine in 1944–5. Up to 2 million Vietnamese died of starvation. In Hanoi even wealthy families survived on thin porridge once a day

A British Lieutenant receiving the surrendered sword of a Japanese naval officer in
a ceremony in Saigon, 13 September 1945.

and student volunteers spent their mornings collecting cartloads of
bodies from the streets.[26]

On 9 March 1945, after the fall of the Vichy Government, Japan
took direct control of Vietnam and encouraged Emperor Bảo Đại to
proclaim independence for the country, within the Japanese Greater
East-Asia co-Prosperity Sphere. This move galvanized the Việt Minh
into action. On 6 April 1945 the Việt Minh formed an alternative
government and declared a liberation zone at the Sino-Viet border with
a village named Tân Trào as their 'capital'. Hồ Chí Minh and his general
Võ Nguyên Giáp worked along with the American Office of Strategic
Services (oss), whom Hồ believed would help him in his anti-French
resistance. The u.s. sought his cooperation in searching for downed
American pilots. This exchange was facilitated by a special group called
the Deer Team, led by an American, Major Allison Thomas. The

Americans had the task of providing arms and giving military training to the Việt, while the Việt would provide them with weather reports and information on their downed pilots. The secret exchange was to have a wide psychological impact in Vietnam, to the surprise of the American side. The cooperation ended with the Japanese surrender on 15 August 1945. The Việt Minh swiftly seized power from the now defeated Japan on 16 August 1945; Hồ Chí Minh and Võ Nguyên Giáp left Tân Trào village to return to Hanoi to form a new government. Within ten days, the new government persuaded Emperor Bảo Đại to sign his decree of abdication in Huế, ceding his power to the revolutionary Democratic Republic Government of Hồ Chí Minh. On 2 September 1945 Hồ Chí Minh declared the independence of Vietnam under the government of Democratic Republic of Vietnam to a rapturous audience in Hanoi. 'The joy was genuine, the people believed that their time has come.'[27]

The situation in Vietnam and the whole of Southeast Asia in September 1945, however, was extremely volatile and it was exacerbated by the way the Allies shared their territorial responsibility. On the same day that Japan surrendered, the Southeast Asia Command (SEAC) under General Douglas MacArthur was widened to include Indonesia and the former French Indochina south of parallel 16. Its task was to maintain law and order while civil governments were reintroduced. A line was drawn at the sixteenth parallel, dividing Vietnam into two zones with the Chinese in control north of the parallel and the British in control of the south. The post-war chaos with no internationally recognized government, no colonial power and severe famine left by the Japanese was a nightmare for all.

When the British Twentieth Indian Division under General Douglas Gracey arrived in Vietnam in September 1945, they found to their surprise that Vietnam already had a *de facto* government and they did not know in advance that organized anti-colonial movements had existed for some years. Gracey, with little manpower, found himself between a rock and a hard place. He had to protect the population, local and colonial and to restore the 'ruling rights' of the pre-Japanese powers, namely the French government in Vietnam.[28] Following the declaration of independence under Hồ Chí Minh there were riots and attacks on French property and lives; the French retaliated with attacks on the Vietnamese. The British now faced the challenge of how to restore order and decided, to the alarm of both the French and the Vietnamese, to employ the surrendered Japanese troops. Meanwhile, there was confusion everywhere, not just about who actually held power, but also about how the population was to survive the widespread famine. The situation was so volatile that even the revolutionary government under Hồ Chí Minh admitted that

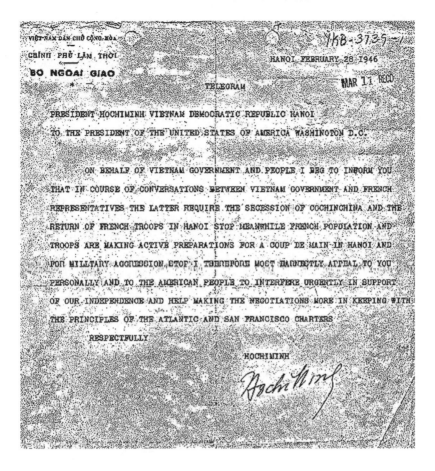

The telegram sent by Hồ Chí Minh to President Truman asking for
American support, 28 February 1946.

their hold on power was fragile, and that they needed international
recognition in order to survive.

In September 1945, with British and Japanese POW support, the
Vichy French military forces were reformed in the south of Vietnam.
When French paratroops finally arrived they were supporters of the
Free French, who had their own scores to settle with the Vichy. The
revolutionary government sent urgent pleas from Hồ Chí Minh to the
United States asking for help with the famine and recognition for the
Democratic Republic of Vietnam (DRV) as the sole legitimate authority
for Vietnam. The u.s. did not respond.[29] The DRV went it alone and
came to an agreement with France on 6 March 1946. Under this arrange-
ment, the DRV agreed to a return of France to North Vietnam, in
exchange for France recognizing the DRV as a free state within the
French Union.

The agreement turned out to be worthless as France reneged on its commitments and none of the agreed points came to fruition. Armed clashes soon occurred and the French response was a heavy naval bombardment of Hải Phòng port in November 1946 that caused much death and destruction. Thousands of people perished under the barrage and war broke out in the city streets. On the 28 November 1946 the Việt Minh withrew from Hải Phòng, leaving the city to the French.[30] Hải Phòng was the opening act of a renewed French war on the Việt Minh. When French troops reached Hanoi, the Việt Minh built defence posts throughout the city. On the 18 and 19 December 1946, the French authority demanded that the Việt Minh remove these posts and transfer the security control to them. The Việt Minh refused and decided to officially resume their resistance against the French. The then president Hồ Chí Minh issued a call to arms to the population at large.

In 1945 the struggle for survival, the disputed control of Vietnam, the inadequate temporary intervention of the British and Chinese, compounded by the indifference and ignorance of the United States, would combine to generate three more decades of war in Vietnam. The u.s. Pentagon Papers concluded with hindsight in 1967 that 'the u.s. had failed to recognise that the Việt Minh was the principle vehicle for Vietnamese nationalism and that, it, in fact, was in control of and effectively governing all of Vietnam.'[31] It was a comment born out of bitter recognition and lingering regret that a great opportunity had been lost to spare the Vietnamese people three more decades of bloodshed on a scale hitherto unknown.

14

French War (1947–54)

For many Vietnamese, the seven years between the renewed anti-French resistance and the signing of the Geneva Accords of 1954 was a time of extreme hardship and confusing loyalty. The call to arms by the government of Hồ Chí Minh on 19 December 1946[1] was answered by many Vietnamese, but not all. At 8 PM on that day the Việt Minh blew up Hanoi's electricity plant and other key installations and led an exodus of citizens out of the cities under the cover of darkness. Hanoi residents were told to make holes in the walls of their houses so that they could move through the interior, from house to house, to avoid travelling through the open streets.[2] On that night tens of thousands of Vietnamese left their homes in the cities to disperse into the countryside, facing a profoundly uncertain future. The anti-French feeling was running high but other city dwellers chose the rural areas for fear of more urban combat. Many joined the resistance fighters in the fervent belief that their cause was just, but many others were non-communist nationalists who could not contemplate the return of the French. The French quickly retook cities like Huế, Hanoi and provincial capitals and re-established themselves in most urban areas. At the same time, the Việt Minh controlled the villages and established liberation zones in the countryside. For the next seven years the French entrenched themselves in the cities while the Việt Minh embedded themselves in the countryside. The Việt Minh increased their military training programmes and honed their guerrilla tactics during these years. They continuously raided and sabotaged French bases and institutions. The French launched heavy sweeps into the liberated zones and in 1947 gained control of the Việt Bắc region, northwest of Hanoi along the Chinese border, with the objective of cutting off supply routes from China. They also captured villages in the Việt Minh zones.[3] The recapture of Việt Bắc became a priority for the Việt Minh under Võ Nguyên Giáp.

The year 1947 and the early months of 1948 were a dire time for most Việt people, regardless of their political affiliation. The most severe hardship fell on those in the liberated zones. The country was embroiled in a war without frontiers, the economy was in tatters and all human lives were under constant threat. In the liberated zones soldiers and civilians coped with frequent French attacks and shared a makeshift existence in utter poverty. Despite the efforts of village leaders it was a desperately hard life for both evacuees and local villagers, who had to share their homes and meagre rations with the newcomers. By 1948 the city people in the countryside were exhausted, physically, financially and morally and they started to leave the liberated zones to risk the consequences of returning to their homes in the cities to rebuild their lives. Another problem that emerged in the liberated zones was that of the presence of the fighters' families. It was one thing for the fighters to go off and campaign for their cause while their families stayed home, but it was quite different when their families were with them and subjected to the same dangers. And in the maquis they saw their elders weakened by hunger and hardship and their babies short of nourishment and medicine. Once back in the cities those with education had employment opportunities with the French authorities, but they could also provide useful information to the resistance.[4] By 1948 the situation improved for the Việt Minh, whose strength increased to 250,000 men, as support began to arrive from China and the Soviet Union.[5] They managed to retake a part of the Việt Bắc region and a number of villages in the liberated zones, in both north and south. By 1949 they were equipped to build rifles and mortars locally.[6] In January 1950 Hồ Chí Minh declared that his government was 'the only legal government of Vietnam' and said he was willing to cooperate with any nation that recognised his on the basis of 'equality and mutual respect of national sovereignty and territory'. China recognized them immediately on 18 January 1950. The Soviet Union followed suit on 30 January 1950.

France had been toying with a 'Bảo Đại Solution' since 1948, which aimed at creating three independent states of Laos, Cambodia and Vietnam within the French Union. The former emperor Bảo Đại was invited back from exile to be head of state for the Associated State of Vietnam – to the dismay of the nationalists and the Việt Minh under Hồ Chí Minh, who had long known Bảo Đại's pro-French attitude and lack of political weight. Nevertheless, many nationalists left the resistance to cross over to the Associated State of Vietnam, perhaps more to escape the hardening communist ideology of the DRV than for any respect for the ex-emperor. The three Associated States solutions were sanctioned by Paris on 2 February 1950. The only real result was a polarization in world politics. While the United States and the United Kingdom recognized this state of Vietnam in February 1950, China and the Soviet Union had already recognized the DRV. With this affirmation, the Việt Minh was further drawn into the sphere of international communism and away from its earlier relationship with the United States. As disclosed in the top secret *Pentagon Papers*,[7] the United States was following the situation in Indochina with great interest, tinged with alarm and a sense of impending doom. For them the 'loss' of China to communism in 1949 and the spread of communism in Eastern Europe was a calamity. The outbreak of war in Korea in the following year served as affirmation that if nothing was done, communism would spread to Southeast Asia and eventually threaten the security of the United States. The Soviet Union was considered the master of all communist action in the world, including China and if the USSR brought Indochina within its sphere of influence, the dominoes would topple across Asia in a chain reaction.

The domino theory had been advanced by General Claire Chennault in reference to the victory of the communists in China. It was repeated later in a memorandum by the U.S. joint chiefs of staff to the U.S. secretary of defense on the strategic importance of Southeast Asia.[8] It subsequently became a mantra repeated in all important U.S. policy papers. If Vietnam/Indochina fell to communism, Burma, Thailand and other states of Southeast Asia would fall too like a collapsing line of dominoes. If that happened, the USSR, in U.S. eyes, would control half of Europe and a huge part of Asia.

In a meeting of the National Security Council under President Truman on 27 February 1950, the U.S. Administration was advised that 'it is important to United States security interests that all practicable measures be taken to prevent further communist expansion in Southeast Asia. Indochina is a key area of Southeast Asia and is under immediate threat.'[9] Which measures were 'practicable' was to become a hotly debated subject in the U.S. government in the following years. The advice to the Truman administration was prompted by a request from France on 16 February 1950 asking the United States to provide military and economic assistance to the French Union forces so that they could pursue the war in Indochina. The request presented the U.S. government with a dilemma: should it assist a restoration of colonial power in order to stem the flow of communism in Southeast Asia, or stick to the Truman doctrine of 1949 that 'all nations and all peoples are free to govern themselves as they see fit'?[10] The choice was put into words by the then secretary of defense to President Truman in a memorandum of 6 March 1950: 'The choice confronting the United States is to support the legal governments in Indochina or to face the extension of Communism over the remainder of the continental area of Southeast Asia and possibly westward.'[11]

The fear of a communist takeover won over in the end. Following the Chinese communist invasion of Hainan island on 1 May 1950, President Truman approved U.S. $10,000,000 urgent military aid to

Indochina – meaning France and their Associated States whom they perceived as 'legal governments'. It was the beginning of a peculiar and contradictory relationship between the United States and France. The paradox is succinctly expressed in the *Pentagon Papers*:

> there was a basic incompatibility in the two strands of u.s. policy: (1) Washington wanted France to fight the anti-communist war and win, preferably with u.s. guidance and advice; and (2) Washington expected the French, when battlefield victory was assured, to magnanimously withdraw from Indochina. For France, which was probably fighting more a colonial than an anti-communist war, and which had to consider the effects of withdrawal on colonial holdings in Algeria, Tunisia and Morocco, magnanimous withdrawal was not too likely.[12]

France was unlikely to further clarify whether there was a convergence of these regional and global issues. Writing after the event, General Henri Navarre, architect of the final stage of the war in Vietnam, posed these contorted questions: 'Is it for the liberation of the Associated States from the Viet-Minh, and giving them independence to break away from France?' or 'to simply participate in the American politics of containment of communism in Southeast Asia?' 'Having renounced all national advantages in Indochina and accepted that we would withdraw once the war was over . . . is it normal then to undertake the sacrifices alone in a war that France no longer has an objective for itself?'[13] The possibility of a large-scale Chinese intervention in Indochina, like that in Korea in June 1950, continued as another obsession in the thinking of American policy-makers in the years to come. Following the outbreak of the Korean War, French outposts along the Chinese border had been heavily reinforced with u.s. assistance.[14] In December 1950 the u.s. even believed that the Chinese were amassing troops at the Vietnamese border for an imminent attack.[15] The u.s. saw either 'Yellow Peril' or 'Domino Theory'.

From 1947 public opinion in France began to turn against the French military activities in Vietnam. In 1950 42 per cent of those who answered questionnaires on the French involvement in Indochina were opposed to it.[16] In an attempt to reverse the unfavourable opinion at home, a new commander was sent to the Vietnamese battlefield. General De Lattre de Tassigny, a renowned strategist and a ruthless military commander, assumed control of the French Union forces. His arrival precipitated a period of brutal fighting, not just between the French army and the Việt Minh, but also between the Việt Minh and the newly French-trained Vietnamese forces mobilized by Bảo Đại in 1951. Thousands of new

French paratroopers landing on the Vietnamese east coast of Annam, 1952.

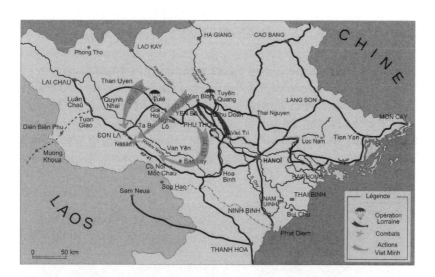

Battle of Nà Sản, the prelude to Điện Biên Phủ, 1952.

French outposts were set up all over the north and 'entire villages were razed to the ground, their farm animals and crops destroyed'.[17]

In 1951 the Indochinese Communist Party split into three national parties. The party in Vietnam became Đảng Lao Động Việt Nam (Vietnam Workers' Party) with Hồ Chí Minh as chairman and Trường Chinh as the general secretary. In the south a new Central Office for

South Vietnam (Trung Ương Cục Miền Nam) came into being to lead the communists in the south. It became known internationally by the acronym COSVN. Despite heavy fighting in 1951 the Việt Minh had regained the Việt Bắc region by 1952 and controlled more than half of the Hồng River delta.

In 1953 while negotiation for a Korean Armistice was going on, the new U.S. President Dwight D. Eisenhower, a former military commander and anti-communist hardliner, made clear his feelings about the spread of communism in his first State of the Union Message on 2 February. Eisenhower called the communist activities in Korea 'the most painful phase of Communist aggression throughout the world. It is clearly a part of the same calculated assault that the aggressor is simultaneously pressing in Indochina and in Malaya ... The working out of any military solution to the Korean war will inevitably affect all these areas.'[18] His view was echoed by his hardliner secretary of state John Foster Dulles, who went as far as saying that Korea and Indochina were two lines to contain China in the middle.[19]

ĐIỆN BIÊN PHỦ

In 1953 the Việt Minh joined forces with the Pathet Lao to launch an Upper Laos offensive in which they wrested the control of the Lao border region from the French and took over several towns in Laos. By January 1954 they had taken control of the mountain transit town Attopeu and the Boloven plateau in Laos.[20] Alarm bells were set ringing in Washington as communism was seen to spread to Laos. The U.S. immediately and

Currency of the Democratic Republic of Vietnam under Hồ Chí Minh, 1945–51.

French legionnaire going to war at Điện Biên Phủ, 1954.

substantially increased their military assistance to French Union forces. For the fiscal year of 1954 the administration proposed $460 million in military assistance to the French and Congress approved only $400 million. However, after the French put forward the so-called Navarre plan of action to achieve victory over the Việt Minh, an additional $385 million was secured by the National Security Council.

The Navarre Plan was strongly supported by U.S. secretary of defense General John O'Daniel. Henri Navarre was sent to Vietnam in Novmber 1953 with the aim of drawing out guerrilla forces into a conventional battle in a mountainous area named Điện Biên Phủ, 16 km from the

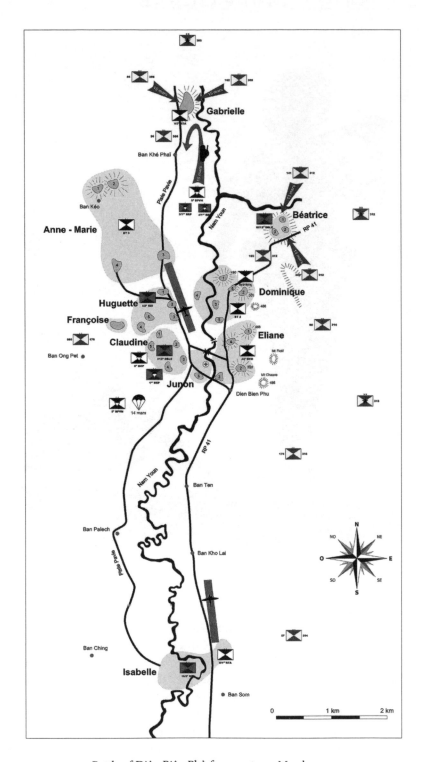

Battle of Điện Biên Phủ from 13 to 15 March 1954.

Laotian border. Under his command this valley was made a stronghold for French forces with 16,200 men, artillery, tanks and aircraft. What Navarre did not know was that his force was actually dwarfed by Vietnamese troops estimated to be 50,000 men, who were supported by an even larger force of labourer/transporters who hauled dismantled artillery pieces onto the high ground above the Điện Biên Phủ base.[21] The Vietnamese side was commanded by Võ Nguyên Giáp, the DRV minister of defence.[22] The geographical location of Điện Biên Phủ was a conscious but disastrous choice of the French commander who thought it would bring the Việt Minh within range of his heavy guns. But the choice of a valley surrounded by 1,000-m hills was turned to an advantage by the Việt who set up their heavy field guns in the hills and used them to cut off French supply routes and batter the French garrison on the plain below.

An international conference had been arranged in Geneva to discuss the Korean and Indochinese conflicts in May 1954 with the situation in Vietnam scheduled to be discussed on 8 May 1954. To increase his leverage at the conference table, Võ Nguyên Giáp attacked the Điện Biên Phủ garrison on 13 March. By 27 March the French were cut off by land and dependent on airlifted supplies. On 22 April the airstrip was lost to the Việt Minh and the French came under constant artillery bombardment from the surrounding hills. The French surrendered on 7 May, one day before the talks on Vietnam were scheduled to open in Geneva. By then, 25,000 Vietnamese and 1,500 French soldiers had been killed in the conclusive battle of the French Indochina war.

The failure of France in Indochina and the humiliation of Điện Biên Phủ in particular, were blamed on the lack of a political conviction in France. In his memoirs Henri Navarre tried to pin his disastrous battle strategy on the politicians: 'From beginning to end, our leaders never knew what they wanted, or, if they did know, they could not declare it. They never dared to tell the nation that there was a war in Indochina . . . Even worse, they allowed the army to be attacked from behind.'[23]

1954 GENEVA CONFERENCE

The scheduled Geneva Conference on Vietnam opened the next day in the presence of the United States, France, Britain, China, the Soviet Union, the Democratic Republic of Vietnam under Hồ Chí Minh, the State of Vietnam under Bảo Đại, Cambodia and Laos. Just two days earlier the U.S. was still working on a military solution to relieving the siege of Điện Biên Phủ by a 'united action' involving the U.S., the United Kingdom and France. The U.S. goal was to stop the spread of communism,

Actual fighting at Điện Biên Phủ, the French side, 1954.

Việt Mınh troops raise their victory flag at the Battle of Điện Biên Phủ, 1954.

Võ Nguyên Giáp and Việt Minh, c. 1944.

but France was only interested in immediate assistance to Điện Biên Phủ and the UK wanted first to await the outcome of the Geneva Conference. Just one day before the French surrender at Điện Biên Phủ, communist containment was weighing heavily in the thinking of the U.S. Secretary of State. At a meeting of the National Security Council in Washington, Dulles lamented the fact that 'there is no responsible French Government with which to deal' and asked: 'Is the U.S. prepared to acquiesce in the clearly engineered Communist aggression in Indo-China – with Red Chinese support – even though we evaluate this loss as very serious to the free world and even though we have the military means to redeem the situation?'[24]

The obstacles to agreement among the parties to the conference seemed insurmountable. The chief negotiators were General Walter Biddel Smith on the U.S. side, Anthony Eden for the UK side and Georges Bidault for France. Phạm Văn Đồng was the chief negotiator for the DRV and the State of Vietnam was represented by Trần Văn Đỗ. The USSR delegation was headed by Vyacheslav Molotov and the Chinese by Zhou Enlai. During the talks, the confrontational stances of the U.S. and Chinese delegations were so resolute that both Anthony Eden and Molotov had to frequently act as mediators. The delegation of the State of Vietnam of Bảo Đại, despite their independent status agreed in Paris on 18 April 1954, had little say in negotiating their own political future. French representatives avoided them and secretly negotiated with the DRV, then reported to the U.S. and it was then up to the U.S. to persuade the Vietnam delegation to accept the result.[25] The new prime minister Ngô Đình Diệm, who joined the government of Bảo Đại on 18 June 1954, proved obdurate on the question of a partition of Vietnam.[26] The U.S. and the

Young Võ Nguyên Giáp and Hồ Chí Minh during the anti-French period.

United Kingdom sometimes felt left out of the secret talks between France and the DRV and the U.S. then decided to adopt a 'dissociated' approach, in case they failed to exert enough influence to 'make the final terms compatible with American interests'.[27]

Thus did the Geneva Conference proceed in fractious and lopsided fashion. It seemed to be heading for a stalemate, when, in a sudden reversal of position, Phạm Văn Đồng proposed to the sixth restricted session on 25 May what amounted to the partitioning of Vietnam, possibly under pressure from the USSR and China. He proposed the idea that a temporary line of demarcation be drawn in a 'zonal re-adjustment', according to the official Vietnamese News Agency two weeks later.[28] The proposal was immediately rejected by the United States but gradually gained favour with France. It appalled the State of Vietnam who immediately urged Paris not to accept such a division. After two more months of deliberation, in eight plenary and twenty-two restricted sessions, on 21 July a two-part agreement was reached to form the Geneva Agreement of 1954 or the Geneva Accords.

There are two main parts of this agreement: a document on the ceasefire, signed by France and the DRV and a final declaration which was not signed. The bilateral ceasefire stipulated that a temporary demarcation line would be set up at parallel 17 and a demilitarized zone (DMZ) set up on either side of this line. All French forces would regroup south of the line and all DRV forces to the north of it. French forces would withdraw from Indochina and respect the sovereignty and independence of all three countries, Laos, Cambodia and Vietnam. The Accords called for all military forces to withdraw to their respective zones within 300 days. In addition, neither side was to enter military alliances, establish foreign military bases or supplement its army and armaments. An International Control Commission (ICC) consisting of Canada, India and Poland would supervise the ceasefire. During the 300-day period, all civilians were free to move from one zone to the other. After that national elections would be held in July 1956 to reunify the country. The final declaration was approved by the DRV, France, Britain, China and the Soviet Union but not the United States or the State of Vietnam. They both submitted separate reservations. On behalf of the State of Vietnam, Trần Văn Đỗ lodged his protest over the partition of Vietnam, and asked the conference to officially note that his government reserved the right to act to protect Vietnamese people. The United States 'noted the existence of the accords and promised not to disturb them by force'. Eisenhower and Dulles then reasoned with their critics at home that 'the accords provided the United States with an opportunity to build an

Actual meeting on Indochina: the Geneva Conference, 1954.

Soldiers of the anti-French Việt Minh force march with joy in Hanoi,
October 1954, after the French departure.

anticommunist, capitalist bastion in Southeast Asia free of the taint of
French colonialism'.[29]

As a conference started in hostile conditions and manned by hard-
liners, it was a wonder that there was an agreement at all. Nevertheless,
all sides immediately voiced loud reservations. The DRV admitted that
they had only attained part of their objective, and still feared that the
U.S. would intervene. The State of Vietnam was presented with an agreement they hardly negotiated and the U.S. felt faced with a lingering threat
of communist expansion across the seventeenth parallel. Barely two
months after the Accords were announced, President Eisenhower assured
Prime Minister Ngô Đình Diệm of forthcoming U.S. assistance to a non-
communist Vietnam. Diệm assured the U.S. that he would be their man
to stop the spread of communism in Southeast Asia.

The French began their withdrawal from Hanoi on 10 October 1954
and handed the city to the DRV. Before they left they destroyed a number
of installations and symbolic cultural sites such as the historical Chùa
Một Cột (One Pillar Pagoda), even though the Geneva Accords stipulated
'no destruction or sabotage of public properties or injuries to the life of
civilians'. The French officially declared the transfer to be 'without serious
incident' and the ICC said it was successful.

The grey areas regarding Việt civilians – who would protect them if they were prevented from leaving one zone for the other – had never been addressed. Initially it was estimated that 100,000 civilians would leave the north to head south, but this figure eventually swelled to 600,000–800,000.[30] It was an exodus, 'a passage to freedom' in Vietnamese and American public relations jargon and a 'coerced evacuation of Catholics' for the DRV.[31] At the same time 100,000 Việt Minh soldiers and civilians left the south to go north.[32] DRV said this figure was closer to 150,000.[33] Contrary to popular belief not all evacuees from the north were Catholics, although it has been suggested that 70–80 per cent of Catholics in the north headed south. A sizeable proportion of those going south were non-Catholic Vietnamese intellectuals, professionals, merchants, landowners and Chinese settlers. All expressed fear of what would happen once the DRV took over. Of the evacuees, 100,000 were from Hanoi alone.

The majority of the evacuees were airlifted by the French or transported in French naval ships. An estimated 200,000 people were converging on Hanoi and Hải Phòng, placing a huge strain on public utilities and generating hygiene problems at Gia Lâm airport and Hải Phòng port. Families with elderly people and babies squatted in makeshift areas in the long and gloomy wait. At Gia Lâm airport in Hanoi each family was allocated a straw mat to sit on.[34] It was a time of complete uncertainty for those who chose to go and those who stayed. No one knew what awaited them. Some families were split over the decision to stay or to leave, but none realized they would not see each other again for twenty years. Because of the unexpected number of refugees the U.S. West Pacific fleet was drafted in to carry out 'Operation Freedom'. They were reinforced by a few ships from the UK, Taiwan and Poland. They worked around the clock to make the six-day round trip between Hải Phòng and Saigon/Vũng Tàu, while encountering typhoons and containing outbreaks of disease. In the end 500,000 people were shipped from the north to the south by French aircraft and French and American ships. The 100,000 who headed north did so by their own means.

The question why so many Việt, who value above all ties to family and land, decided to uproot themselves and leave in droves remains puzzling. They must have felt forces stronger than their own traditional values, especially when the separation of the country was, in the Geneva Accords, to last only two years while elections were prepared. When the two-way evacuation ended, North Vietnam lost a large number of citizens and was left with the enormous problems of resettling displaced people, rebuilding the shattered infrastructure and relaunching an economy. The problems the south faced in providing for so many newcomers was cushioned by generous aid from the U.S. and international relief agencies.

Some 42 reception centres in Saigon and Vũng Tàu strained public funds, manpower, infrastructure and utilities but were allievated by readily available international assistance. Integrating northerners into southern society would take much longer. During a century of French occupation, the Việt people had lived in separated regions or *kỳ*, under different administrations, which accentuated cultural and linguistic differences. Inter-regional travel for Vietnamese had been all but impossible. In the south the arrival of such a large wave of northerners in 1954 was greeted with hostility.[35] Southerners who went north found they were viewed with suspicion and were not accorded the same status in any structure they were placed in. Marriages between northerners and southerners were often discouraged.

In the circumstances of a human tragedy of epic proportions, it is a wonder that Vietnam managed to overcome so much social upheaval in the wake of the Geneva Accords. But what people did not realize was that they were accommodating all these problems only to be plunged again into a bitter twenty-year war that ironically would involve many of the major parties to the Geneva Accords whose intention was to end all hostility in Vietnam. In January 1955 U.S. aid began to be sent to South Vietnam, accompanied by a number of American advisors for the training of the fledging army. After five years of feeling hostage to their own fear of communist expansion in Southeast Asia, the U.S. was taking the first small steps to directly intervene in Vietnam, steps that would have major repercussions throughout the world.

15

Vietnam–American War (1954–75)

The road to renewed hostility in Vietnam began with an agreement in Geneva in 1954 that nobody thought would happen, given the intransigence of the parties. It then became a volatile pack of cards that all parties played with high stakes in the run-up to a nationwide election. The stakes got higher and higher and almost all the states at the Geneva talks were drawn back into the endgame that was indeed the reunification of Vietnam, but by force not by election, after another twenty years of war. Many questions about the aftermath of the agreement still puzzle analysts. Among them are how did peace turn so quickly to war? Why did the United States show willingness to get so deeply involved in a war that contradicted 'all previous patterns of America's involvement abroad'?[1] In the end, in the analysis of Henry Kissinger, national security advisor and then secretary of state during 1969–77 under Richard Nixon and Gerald Ford, 'the once near-universal faith in the uniqueness of America's values – and their global relevance – was replaced by growing self-doubt.'[2] A related sentiment had been expressed a decade earlier by another key figure in the U.S. administration, Robert S. McNamara, secretary of defense (1961–8) under Kennedy and Johnson, who said he had no doubt that the war 'caused terrible damage to America'.[3] It was on his watch that events went out of control, both in Vietnam and within the Kennedy administration. The picture that eventually emerged, as painted by McNamara, was an alarming lack of knowledge of the situation in Vietnam, confusion and disunity in the U.S. government at a time when decisive actions were needed. The result was that America slithered down a road of no return in Vietnam. In McNamara's own words, in retrospect, they had been wrong but 'made an error not of values and intentions but of judgment and capabilities'.

The Vietnamese, north or south, on the other hand, were never in doubt about their objectives. The communist north wanted to reunify the country along the lines of the Geneva Agreement. The nationalist south wanted to retain its freedom and independence. The north said they believed unity in Vietnam could only be achieved by eliminating the American 'neo-colonial' design for the country. The south wanted to resist communist control of the south at all costs. At a strategic level that overarched these objectives, was the United States' determination to contain the spread of communism from China into Southeast Asia possibly 'engineered by the USSR'. The situation was further muddled by France's continuing role as guarantor of Vietnamese territorial integrity, unity and safety. The French cared greatly for their own investment, especially in the south, which had long been their overseas territory up to 1954. Both the communist north and the nationalist south, meanwhile, could not wait to be rid of them. These were criss-crossing conflicts that did not bode well for an agreement that everybody was unhappy with in the first place.

FIRST STEPS APART (1954–6)

In 1955 the U.S. became directly involved in a region McNamara later called 'terra incognita'.[4] The first steps towards American involvement were in fact taken a year before. In their discussions with France and the UK prior to the Geneva Conference, the U.S. broached the subject of 'united action' to stem the flow of communism through Asia. The position of France at the time was limited to military assistance to their troops currently under siege at Điện Biên Phủ, while the UK wanted to wait for the conference. When the Geneva Conference was over, the U.S. considered the outcome 'a disaster for the free world'; 'Geneva gave Communist China and North Vietnam a new base for exploitation of Southeast Asia.'[5]

With France and the UK on board, the Southeast Asia Treaty (SEATO) was signed in Manila on 8 September 1954. Under this treaty the states of Indochina were covered by separate protocols, which assured them of collective defence by SEATO nations, in case of subversion or aggression. South Vietnam was considered the most important component of the three states, yet the most vulnerable. The U.S. took direct steps to remedy this by supporting Prime Minister Ngo Đinh Điệm. In a letter handed to Điệm on 23 October 1954, President Dwight Eisenhower promised direct economic and military assistance in a package called 'an intelligent program of American aid given directly to your Government' in order to 'assist Viet Nam in its present hour of trial'. Eisenhower said the purpose was 'to build a strong government, that . . . will be respected both at home and abroad and discourage any who might wish to impose a foreign ideology on your free people'.[6] The new element in this was direct military aid, previously channelled through France. France's position declined massively in 1954 and was now disappearing. By the first half of 1955 France had handed police, local government and then army authority to the government in Saigon. By 1956 France had gone. The south was under pressure from a mass of evacuees who taxed the resources of the relief agencies. The government focused on securing the armed religious sects Hòa Hảo and Cao Đài. The Ngô Đình Diệm government also attempted to eliminate the Bình Xuyên, a powerful criminal organization who controlled gambling, prostitution and opium dens in Saigon and its contiguous Chinese twin-city of Chợ Lớn. The first Bình Xuyên campaign ended in an uneasy truce mediated by the French but it was resumed in April 1955 when the Vietnamese army managed to dislodge the Bình Xuyên elements from Saigon and Chợ Lớn.

Thanks to unwavering u.s. support power resided in 1955 with Ngô Đình Diệm. Emperor Bảo Đại was head of state only in name. Bảo Đại wrote to Diệm on 28 April 1955 from his residence in Cannes, summoning the prime minister for consultations. Ngô Đình Diệm ignored the request.[7] The following day representatives of eighteen political parties and 29 notable figures met in Saigon to decide on the future of South Vietnam. Hoà Hảo, Cao Đài and other armed groups were present. After five hours of deliberation, the meeting decided on three main points: the removal of Bảo Đại from the future government, the removal of the current government and a request for Ngô Đình Diệm to head a new provisional revolutionary government. A referendum was held on 24 October 1955 which duly ousted Bảo Đại and supported Ngô Đình Diệm being president of a new Republic of Vietnam. When Bảo Đại was informed, he remained in France, never to return to Vietnam.

It was clear to all that Ngô Đình Diệm had no intention of holding the nationwide election to reunify Vietnam as stipulated in Geneva. This was already implied in his refusal to start consultations with the north by 20 July. The southern hesitations about the accords had been signalled by ambassador Trần Văn Đỗ in Geneva when the State of Vietnam did not sign the final declaration. Ngô Đình Diệm declared that he would not consider an election until he was certain that it would be free. He may also have known about Eisenhower's estimate in 1954 that 80 per cent of the Vietnamese would vote for Hồ Chí Minh instead of Bảo Đại in any election.[8] By June 1956 u.s. assistant secretary of state for Far Eastern affairs Walter Robertson picked up Ngô Đình Diệm's theme: 'We support president Diem fully in his position that if elections are to be held, there first must be conditions which preclude intimidation or coercion of the electorate. Unless such conditions exist there can be no free choice.'[9] Meanwhile the north was already issuing a new guideline for their supporters in the 'revolution in the south' to 'combine the political struggle with a self-defence struggle'.[10]

In North Vietnam the picture was uniformly grey in the post-Geneva period. In their own assessment, 'agriculture was in a dire state, thousands of sq. km were left uncultivated, tens of thousands of farmers were home-less, the hydraulic system was damaged by the French, industry was out of date and in need of machinery, mining industry output was reduced to half the pre-war level, infrastructure was seriously damaged, few trained engineers and technicians stayed behind, health care was almost non-existent.'[11] Land reform was identified as a 'core objective in the efforts to consolidate peace for the north'.[12] The aim was to distribute land to landless farmers for them to increase food production. Land belonging to the French, the Catholic Church and individuals was confiscated. The crude methods employed turned the land reform pro-gramme into a nasty class struggle in which landowners, petit-bourgeois and intellectuals were persecuted, tortured, ridiculed and humiliated. Ten of thousands of landowners were killed in 1955–6. The ethnic minori-ties were not spared. General Võ Nguyên Giáp denounced at the tenth plenary session of the Central Committee in November 1956 the failure to respect freedom of worship and the status of tribal chiefs 'thus injuring, instead of respecting local customs and manners'.[13] The same Central Committee session heard that the disastrous start to land reform 'damaged the party apparatus, the government and the party policies'.[14] In reality the reform threatened the survival of the government. It fuelled hatred against the educated, who openly questioned the policies of the com-munist government. In Hanoi in 1955 three journals opened that strongly opposed the party line and challenged the 'validity of the government's policies on land reform, the economy and democratic freedom'.[15] Well-known writers appeared in the pages of *Nhân Văn*, *Giai Phẩm* and *Đất Mới* journals until they were closed down withinin a year and their editors arrested for 'causing bad feelings among the population over the political direction and the leadership of the party' and 'inciting work-ers to stage demonstrations against the government'. Some were given heavy sentences after a trial that became known as the infamous 'Nhân Văn–Giai Phẩm case'. Their opposition to the policies of the party and the land reform programme was officially blamed on the 'agents left behind by the American and South Vietnamese, who then cooperated with the writers and artists to create trouble'.[16] The horrors of the land reform programme have long achieved deserved notoriety. Today they are referred to obliquely in terms such as the following: 'Funda-mental mistakes were made in which the emphasis was put on '*đấu tố*' (denunciation),[17] and less on education . . . before the mistakes were acknowledged and remedial measures taken to restore honour to the wronged victims.'[18] One stated worry of the government in the north was that land reform would be exploited for propaganda in the south, and this proved justified when it was broadly hailed in the south as an example of what communists were capable of.

North Vietnam tried to revive the foreseen nationwide elections by contacting the south repeatedly in 1955–8. Ngô Đình Diệm's indifference prompted China in January 1956 to call for the Geneva Conference to be reconvened. Co-chairs USSR and UK demurred and the election deadline passed without mention. By early 1957 the partition of Vietnam was a hard fact nailed to the contested Demilitarized Zone (DMZ) and all negotiation doors were shut. Letters and postcards between the two regions took years to arrive by round-about routes.

Ngô Đình Diệm asserted his control in the south, after ejecting Bảo Đại and general Dương Văn Minh from the defence ministry, by taking the positions of president, prime minister and defence minister. He gave his brothers powerful positions in Saigon and in Huế. Ngô Đình Nhu was made chief advisor and security chief and he installed himself at the head of a political party called the *Cần Lao* (workers' party), which appeared to have no grassroots support. Diệm's failure to delegate soon earned him the labels 'autocratic' and 'despotic'. His reluctance to share power with other political groups like the Hòa Hảo and the Cao Đài contributed to his rising unpopularity. The U.S. now urged him to widen his political base to secure South Vietnam against a communist takeover. The settlement of hundreds of thousands refugees from the north was going well and security was established in large areas of the deep south, but land reform was a growing problem in the south – not created through zealous officials supporting brutal solutions as in the north, but through indifferent local administrations who did not settle northerners carefully, and through corrupt officials exacting money in transactions. By 1959 the land reform programme came to a standstill in the Mekong Delta and the highlands.

The government in Saigon meanwhile launched a new campaign to weed out 'communist elements'. In 1956 'being a communist' was outlawed and a 'denouncing the communists' (tố cộng) campaign led to farmers denouncing their neighbours, sometimes for personal reasons. Those who were labelled communists were then taken away to re-education centres. The glee, fear and loathing of the campaign was comparable to a witch-hunt. The campaign claimed early success when the number of detainees rose from 15,000 in 1956 to 50,000 in 1960 and the government officially judged many to be real supporters of the north. Harder to substantiate was Saigon's claim made to the U.S. that '100,000 former communist cadres rallied to the Government of Vietnam.'[19] The U.S. rejected this claim as exaggerated. The north however estimated it lost 90 per cent of its cadres in the south in 1955–8. They estimate that 60,000 communist party members in the Mekong Delta had crumbled to 5,000

Ngô Đình Diệm, Eisenhower and Dulles, Washington DC, 1957.

by 1958. In the province of Quảng Trị, immediately below the DMZ, only 176 party members survived from 8,400 members four years earlier.[20] These figures were of course unknown to the U.S. and South Vietnam at the time. The South Vietnamese government turned more and more to the military for support in disturbed rural areas. More military officers were appointed heads of local administrations, no doubt to the dismay of local citizens who would resent such an imposton on their traditional communal structures. In 1958 one-third of province chiefs were military and two years later this had risen to two-thirds.

Opposition to President Diệm could be heard in the Saigon media in 1957. Newspapers began to be harassed by the government and the largest closed in 1958. Nationalists who had worked under both Ngô Đình Diệm and Bảo Đại began to distance themselves from what they called his 'oppressive policies'. Eighteen former cabinet members, high-ranking officials and religious leaders got together in 1960 and issued a manifesto to say that the government had 'provoked the discourage-ment and resentment of the people'. Nationwide, the government called attacks on their installations and personnel 'acts of subversion by the *Việt Cộng*' (Vietnamese communists), a new name that was instantly embedded in the political jargon.[21] It would soon be familiar to Americans as VC, although they mistakenly applied the label exclusively to South Vietnamese communists.

INSURGENCY IN THE SOUTH

During the 300-day regroupment period in the Geneva Accords, over 100,000 men and women left the south to go north, while a small number of communist cadres remained. Among those living in South Vietnam in 1956–7 was Lê Duẩn, a staunch communist who was already a member of the Politburo and would become the DRV strongman as first secretary of the Party. At the end of 1956 Lê Duẩn formulated a draft plan for revolutionary subversion in South Vietnam which was tabled at a meeting of the Central Committee of South Vietnam in Phnom Penh in December 1956.[22]

The committee determined it would increase its activities through secret armed units and military bases in locations left over from the anti-French era along the Cambodian border from the Lower Mekong Delta to the central highlands.[23] The situation in South Vietnam was debated at the fifteenth plenum of the Central Party Committee of the DRV in January 1959 and a plan of action was formed for the south. The communists would 'carry out the revolution by violence, combining the political struggle with an armed struggle to overthrow the Southern administration'.[24] U.S. analysts assumed aid from both the USSR and China was behind this. The committee pointed to the U.S. as 'an enemy of peace'[25] and the terms 'American imperialism' and 'neo-colonialism' entered the vocabulary of North Vietnam. Getting rid of the Americans now became a 'just cause' for the people to pursue. The people of North Vietnam did not need much persuasion to buy this argument, for the hard times under the French and the Japanese were still in every memory and opposition to any foreign intervention had long been considered a noble cause. The north's 'anti-American war to save the country' (Chống Mỹ Cứu Nước) was launched in this vein with the U.S. identified as 'the principal colonial power'.

During 1959 and 1960, thousands of trained military personnel and political cadres were sent to the south to organize an insurgent force. They were able to occupy villages and towns for days and they conducted raids, assassinations and kidnappings against government officials in the countryside. The writ of the government of South Vietnam in rural areas was curtailed. On 20 December 1960 the National Liberation Front

Việt Cộng operating along the canals of South Vietnam.

for South Vietnam (NLF) was formed. It was said to have included all anti-government groups in South Vietnam, including the communists, who were working together 'to overthrow the government of Ngô Đình Diệm and the disguised colonial regime of the Americans'.[26] U.S. estimates said NLF membership doubled in a few months and 'doubled again by fall 1961, and then redoubled by early 1962. At that time an estimated 300,000 were on its rolls.'[27]

U.S. ENTANGLEMENT

President Eisenhower viewed the situation in South Vietnam with increasing alarm, although he thought it less urgent than Laos. North Vietnam now began creating a military supply route from north to south that encroached on Lao territory. The Soviet Union meanwhile started to airlift supplies from North Vietnam to Viet-Pathet Lao units in Laos. Following the resolution of the fifteenth plenum the DRV military began to open such a supply land route along the natural border with Laos, i.e. the Trường Sơn mountain chain.[28] The route was later called the Hồ Chí Minh trail, a network of jungle and mountain tracks crisscrossing the border and heading south. It was not a new system of roads but an ancient web of tracks that had long served as trade routes. From 1959 this system of tracks and roads was constantly enhanced under dense jungle foliage. The land route was followed by shipping and other supply routes but in 1960–61 it was the land route that caused the most concern among policy-makers in the u.s. The u.s. now saw Laos and this network of supply trails as a key brick in the line of dominoes. This was Eisenhower's legacy bequeathed to the newly elected President John F. Kennedy. The situation in Laos was given high priority in Eisenhower's briefing to President-elect Kennedy on his last day of office in January 1961. Eisenhower stated clearly his belief that 'if Laos were lost to the communists, it would bring unbelievable pressure to bear on Thailand, Cambodia and South Vietnam.'[29] However, no clear course of action was proposed to prevent this. Some of those present later said Eisenhower advocated unilateral action in Laos but McNamara got the opposite impression. Kennedy had already made known his own position on the spread of communism in Asia as a senator, when he saw Vietnam as 'a crucial link in America's overall geopolitical position.'[30] He considered South Vietnam as the United States' own creation that could not be abandoned. Furthermore, beside his committed focus on Vietnam, Kennedy's own credibility was under pressure from following through with Eisenhower's Cuban Bay of Pigs invasion fiasco in April 1961. According to Henry Kissinger, Kennedy ignored Eisenhower's analysis of the situation in Laos and instead 'drew the line in South Vietnam.'[31]

By the time Kennedy took over, the Eisenhower administration had given more than a billion u.s. dollars in aid to South Vietnam and had 1,500 Americans attached to the u.s. embassy in Saigon, making it the largest u.s. mission in the world.[32] Kennedy also inherited from his predecessor a counter-insurgency programme that would require developing 'middle war' technologies for policing Asian hotspots. By March 1960 Washington saw 'the Viet Cong were making significant headway' and that the threat from inside was greater to South Vietnam than an invasion from outside.[33] A counter-insurgency plan (CIP) was formed in which the South Vietnamese government would organize a civic force to deal with insurgency, advised by u.s. military personnel down to battalion level. In June 1960 u.s. Army special forces arrived in Vietnam, followed by long-range specialist Ranger battalions for counter-guerrilla operations. The American presence was growing larger and deeper under Kennedy. Barely ten days after he assumed office, the new president accepted the CIP and authorized a u.s.$41 million increase in aid for South Vietnam to help train the civic force.

In an attempt to separate civilians from guerrilla-combatants, a massive relocation programme was launched under the 'strategic hamlets' (Ấp Chiến Lược) campaign. This aimed at gathering civilians into controllable hamlets, where they were housed with government assistance and their children could go to school in a secure environment. It failed miserably in practice for it ignored the attachment of the Vietnamese farmers to their land, their ancestoral graves and to the local spiritual deities they venerated. They resented and resisted being moved. Later on the guerrillas infiltrated the hamlets and often outwitted the defence forces. Villagers' lives became harder and more dangerous than before. Resentment grew ever stronger until the programme was abandoned.

Since 1960 internal support for the government under Ngô Đình Diệm had steadily eroded in the cities and the rural areas. Even the military became impatient with the president's aloofness and his delegation of power to family members, especially to the unpopular Ngô Đình Nhu. On 11 November 1960 a botched military coup attempt was launched by paratroopers. Brutal retaliation measures did not improve the image of the already unpopular regime. In February 1962 two dissident airforce pilots bombed the presidential palace but Ngô Đình Diệm and his family survived.

In the first two years of the Kennedy administration a good deal of effort went into finding out what was going on in South Vietnam and how to 'save it'. Several fact-finding missions were sent to see Ngô Đình Diệm and on visits around the country. Kennedy maintained his soft position on Laos but the U.S. assured the South Vietnamese there would be no compromise in Vietnam. The possibility of stationing regular U.S. forces in South Vietnam was raised for the first time with Ngô Đình Diệm in May 1961 during Vice-President Lyndon Johnson's visit. This was rejected out of hand. Ngô Đình Diệm instead sent a letter to Kennedy within a month asking for funding to increase the Vietnamese army from 170,000 to 270,000. He also asked for 'selected elements of the American Armed Forces' to establish training centres in South Vietnam and 'to be a symbol of American commitment to Vietnam'.[34] His first request was accepted in part but the second was left open.

General Maxwell Taylor and Walt Rostow, political advisor to Kennedy, then visited South Vietnam and recommended a military commitment to South Vietnam because 'the communist strategy of taking over Southeast Asia by guerrilla warfare was well on the way to success in Vietnam'. Their report was endorsed in a memo from defense secretary Robert McNamara, his deputy Roswell Gilpatric and the joint chiefs of staff on 8 November 1961, who went further, asking whether the U.S. had the 'willingness to attack (or threaten to attack) North Vietnam?' McNamara later recalled feeling worried and being over-hasty in this.[35] Three days later McNamara and secretary of state Dean Rusk sent another memo to the president advising him on the contrary to defer, 'at least for the time being, the dispatch of combat units'. At this time the figure of 40,000 American troops was mooted in another report as being 'necessary to get rid of the Viet-Cong'. An air attack on North Vietnam was

Front to back: Ngô Đình Diệm, Lady Bird Johnson, Madame Ngô Đình Nhu,
Lyndon B. Johnson, Nguyễn Ngọc Thơ, Jean Kennedy Smith, Stephen Smith
and others, Breakfast at Independence Palace, Saigon, 13 May 1961.

also considered in November 1961 but was rejected as counter-productive
in that it would invite strong reactions from both the USSR and China.

On 14 November 1961 Frederick Nolting, U.S. ambassador to Saigon,
was sent a telegram from the defense ministry informing him in private
that they were 'preparing plans for the use of U.S. combat forces in SVN
under various contingencies, including stepped up infiltration as well
as organized . . . (military) intervention. However, the objective of our
policy is to do all possible to accomplish this purpose without use of

u.s. combat forces.'[36] The following month the number of u.s. military personnel in South Vietnam was increased to 3,200. In February 1962 they came under the umbrella of a new institution called 'The United States Military Assistance Command, Vietnam (MACV)'. The years 1961–2 were clearly a time of u.s. indecision over Vietnam, with confusing messages passing back and forth between Saigon and Washington. No major decision was made despite strong recommendations from the u.s. military to intervene with regular forces. With hindsight, the indecisiveness of the Kennedy administration owed much to the problems of coping with manifold pressing problems in a rapidly changing world. The Berlin wall was going up in the final politico-military crisis of the Cold War, the fiasco of the Bay of Pigs had unfolded and civil war broke out in Laos. For a time Vietnam was sidelined.

By 1962 the NLF grouping of mixed opponents of the unpopular Saigon regime was consolidating under its new president Nguyễn Hữu Thọ, a South Vietnamese lawyer. They called the u.s. involvement 'the American armed invasion'. The communist fighters intensified their actions in the south with longer engagements but the u.s. military was sending back optimistic reports and McNamara saw it as a local problem: 'many of us – including the president and me – came to believe that the problem was such that only the South Vietnamese could deal with it . . . the u.s. should only play a support role to South Vietnam'.[37] This thinking prevailed until mid-1962 when the number of u.s. military advisors in the country numbered 16,000.[38] McNamara even made plans in March 1963 to withdraw 1,000 of these advisors. But then Ngô Đình Diệm stirred up a Buddhist hornet's nest in the former royal capital of Huế that would push open the door to escalation.

THE BUDDHIST CRISIS

In May 1963 in Huế a serious challenge arose to the authority of Ngô Đình Diệm's regime. It began with the celebration of the twenty-fifth anniversary of the ordination of Archbishop Ngo Đinh Thục, another brother of the president. Yellow and white papal flags and festive buntings were displayed throughout the city, despite a long-term ban on flying religious flags in the country. An order was issued afterwards to reinforce the ban on religious flags just before the most important event in the Buddhist calendar, the Birthday of Buddha (Lễ Phật Đản), which fell on 8 May. After the mass display of Catholic flags for the archbishop, the Huế Buddhists decided to fly their own multi-coloured flag at the main religious centre of Thiên Mụ or Linh Mụ pagoda. Thousands of people gathered to celebrate, to the alarm of the local security police. When they refused to disperse, the province chief ordered his troops to fire into the crowd and then ordered in tanks. Nine people were killed and fourteen injured. Some of the victims were children. The authorities quickly tried to blame the incident on communist agents, but an estimated 10,000 citizens demonstrated the next day to protest the killings. This was to be the first of many public demonstrations held in the next four months to protest against the actions of the central government – in Huế and also in Saigon. The number of people joining in the protests steadily rose and included university students, members of the opposition and a large number of monks. The brutal action against a religious gathering in the presence of monks during a Buddhist festival in Huế, the centre of national Buddhism since the nineteenth century, inflamed Buddhist discontent with the regime of their Catholic president. The protest soon became the political focus for all opposition parties and the growing unrest encouraged ever more overt expressions of resentment at the policies of the regime. Each demonstration was met with tear gas and rough charges by the police. The tense situation was not helped by insensitive remarks by Madame Ngô Đình Nhu, who publicly claimed that communist agents had infiltrated the Buddhist ranks. She soon earned notoriety as 'dragon lady' and figured on the cover of the u.s. news magazines.

On 11 June 1963 a hitherto little-known monk, the venerable Thích Quảng Đức, travelled from Thiên Mụ pagoda to perform self-immolation at a busy Saigon intersection in protest at the ban on Buddhist flags. The photographs taken by Malcolm Browne of the Associated Press, who had been alerted by the Buddhists, were flashed around a horrified world. President Kennedy later commented: 'No news picture in history has generated so much emotion around the world as that one.' In an attempt to defuse the situation, an agreement was reached between the government and the Buddhist monks on the 16 June, but it did not address the question of who was to blame for the killings in Huế. The protests grew stronger and more dramatic. By October six more monks had set themselves on fire in protest.

Throughout the summer a group of armed forces officers had been plotting the overthrow of Ngô Đình Diệm, but when they approached the u.s. for support, the u.s. only agreed to warn Ngô Đình Diệm to rid himself of his brother Nhu, his detested security chief. On 21 August 1963, following the declaration of martial law, Ngô Đình Nhu ordered his security force to attack pagodas throughout South Vietnam. They sacked and burned buildings, injured 30 monks and arrested 1,400. The Kennedy Administration watched these events with dismay and sent the usual fact-finding missions to Saigon. The last in September 1963 was led by McNamara himself and General Maxwell Taylor. Their report a month later optimistically affirmed that 'the war was being won, [and] it would be successfully concluded in the northern and central areas of South Vietnam by the end of 1964, and in the Delta by 1965, thereby permitting the withdrawal of American advisors.' It also recommended withholding some economic aid and cutting funding for the special force Nhu used in the raids on the pagodas. The u.s. announced the withdrawal of 1,000 American troops by the end of the year. McNamara's main recommendation however was that 'we do not take any initative to encourage actively a change in government'.[39] Kennedy approved the report and the press was told about the projected withdrawal, but not about the other recommendations. McNamara's stern advice against the 'active encouragement of a coup' in October would look farcical in November when the actual coup against Ngô Đình Diệm took place.

Since 1960 some in the Eisenhower Administration were questioning the credibility of Ngô Đình Diệm, but he was still considered the strongest known candidate for keeping Southeast Asia free of communism. When McNamara entered the scene he quickly lamented that Diệm's personality was an enigma to all. The u.s. had little idea of Diệm's long-term plans.[40] After Ngô Đình Nhu's brutal suppression of opponents and monks, carried out with Ngô Đình Diệm's approval, the u.s. administration quietly concluded they had to abandon him. How to do it and who could be a replacement however remained unanswered questions, according to McNamara's recollections. He later regretted that when Nhu's raids were launched against the pagodas. In his own words, 'all key decision-makers on Vietnam, president Kennedy, Dean Rusk, McGeorge Bundy, John McCone and I (McNamara), were out of Washington.' While the principals were on summer holiday, the affairs of state were left in the hands of deputies and when reports about the raids began to arrive in Washington on 24 August 1963 these officials 'saw an opportunity to move against the Diem regime. Before the day was out, the United States had set in motion a military coup.'[41] The main instigator was later identified as Roger Hilsman Jr, deputy secretary of state for Far Eastern affairs. According to McNamara, Hilsman drafted a cable to the new u.s. ambassador in Saigon, instructing him to tell the Vietnamese military commanders that 'the u.s. would give them direct support in any interim period of breakdown central government mechanism'. This draft cable went on its rounds for approval among available u.s. officials and some did approve it. When it got to Kennedy at his holiday home in Hyannis Port 'Kennedy said he would approve if his senior advisors concurred'. The draft was passed to Dean Rusk in New York, along with a note that 'the president already approved'. Dean Rusk endorsed it 'reluctantly'. The cia deputy chief also agreed 'because the president already approved'. The cable then went to McNamara's deputy, who also approved 'with misgiving' and it was sent to the ambassador in Saigon. Thus two days after becoming u.s. ambassador in South Vietnam, Henry Cabot Lodge went about looking for ways to organize a coup against the government of Ngô Đình Diệm. When the cable came to the knowledge of General Maxell Taylor, he declared himself 'shocked'. Kennedy also came to regret it, calling it 'a major mistake'.

In Saigon there was another turn in the situation. The army generals got in touch with the u.s. to say they were ready for a coup. On 5 October the u.s. government repeated its decision not to encourage a coup. However, Ambassador Lodge in Saigon felt they were by then already committed. Even as late as 29 October 1963, officials in Washington cabled that they felt that it was not too late to call off the coup because they did not know 'who among our officials in Saigon headed coup planning'. Cabot Lodge, on the other hand, told them that he 'do[es] not have the power to delay or discourage a coup'.[42]

On 1 November 1963 Ambassador Lodge called on President Diệm in the morning to press demands that earlier missions had put forward. At the same moment the coup plotters, led by generals Dương Văn Minh, Trần Thiện Khiêm and Trần Văn Đôn, gathered at the headquarters of the Joint General Staff (jgs) to finalize the coup operation, while army units were deployed around Saigon. By mid-afternoon these units occupied key installations including the radio station. The only resistance left was at the presidential palace. That afternoon Ngô Đình Diệm and Nhu called to ask Lodge where the u.s. stood but Lodge was evasive. That evening the Ngô brothers escaped out of the palace through a secret tunnel and got to the sister city/Chinatown Chợ Lớn and hid in a church. They telephoned the coup leaders from there to announce their surrender and they were captured at 6.50 AM on 2 November. Both were later found killed inside an armoured personnel carrier that had been provided to take them to the jgs headquarters. Nobody was ever held responsible for the double assassination.

General Dương Văn Minh became chief of state and chairman of the Military Revolutionary Council that included most of the coup leaders, and things seemed to return quickly to normal. Both deaths were officially described as 'suicide'. Later one of the coup leaders let slip that he felt they had to eliminate the Ngô brothers because they feared them. According to General Dương Văn Minh, 'Diệm had too much respect among ordinary people, they would make a comeback'.[43] When news of the coup reached Washington it was accepted as inevitable, but when Kennedy heard of the 'suicides' soon thereafter he was appalled. Kennedy looked for ways to fill the 'political vacuum' and again ordered a report. The purpose was 'to attempt to assess the situation: what American policy should be, and what our aid policy should be, how we can intensify the struggle, how we can bring Americans out of there'.[44]

Ngô Đình Diệm's body, 2 November 1963.

McNamara recollected later that with hindsight he believed this meant the president would act on his stated view that this was a South Vietnamese war that the Việt had to fight, and that the Americans would be brought home. McNamara said in retrospect that Kennedy accepted that 'a withdrawal would cause a fall of the dominoes but staying in would ultimately lead to the same result, while exacting a terrible price in blood.'[45] Kennedy's contribution ended with that, for on 22 November 1963 he was assassinated in Dallas.

JOHNSON AND ESCALATION

Incoming president Lyndon B. Johnson held discussions on Vietnam with his top aides in Honolulu and on 24 November he made his policy clear: 'win the war!'[46] To achieve this the U.S. would basically follow up Kennedy's policies with a new element added in Honolulu to strengthen a covert action force, manned by South Vietnamese but trained and supported by the CIA. This was to become Operation Plan 34A. Such covert action against North Vietnam by infiltration, propaganda, intelligence collection and sabotage had been underway for several months, but the new president wanted it intensified. Johnson's Honolulu meeting reinforced U.S. support for the new government in Saigon, emphasized the security of the Mekong Delta and authorized operations up to 50 km inside Lao territory.[47]

In the north the Saigon assassinations and the rapidly changing situation in both the United States and South Vietnam were intensely debated at the ninth plenum of the Communist Party Central Committee held in December 1963. The committee resolved to carry on the war by 'gathering all forces against imperialism led by the United States'.[48] In January 1964 the NLF held its own congress to outline a war plan for South Vietnam. Two months later in Hanoi, Hồ Chí Minh urged that 'each person should double his efforts for the sake of his Southern kin'. The reputed North Vietnamese 325th infantry division began moving south. The U.S. soon concluded that the number of North Vietnamese regulars moving south would 'take up a large percentage of the communist force in the south'.[49] North Vietnamese records confirm this escalation: 'apart from arms and military equipment, the movement of a great number of troops from North to South along the Trường Sơn Trail was for the first time successful . . . 40,000 regular cadres and soldiers from the north, which comprised 50 per cent of the army throughout the south and 80 per cent of cadres in directive organs of different fields [were sent]. This force was of great importance, creating new strength in the South'. With the arrival of regular North Vietnamese army units in South Vietnam, in the words of Kissinger: 'both sides crossed their Rubicons'.[50]

The North Vietnamese army and the NLF intensified their activities in South Vietnam, establishing a liberation zone in the central highlands and on the western edge of the Mekong Delta. Saigon meanwhile was obsessed with coup frenzy. In the sixteen months since the coup that toppled Ngô Đình Diệm, eight more coup attempts took place. The last in February 1965 brought to power another military government under the leadership of generals Nguyễn Văn Thiệu and Nguyễn Cao Kỳ, who were to remain in power for the south's final decade.

During this leadership crisis in the south, representatives of the largely autonomous ethnic minorities of the high plateaux of central Vietnam met in 1964 to form a resistance group opposed to the strategic hamlet programme. Their banner *Front Unifié pour la Lutte des Races Opprimées* (FULRO)[51] brought together representatives of the Bà Ná, Cham, Ê đê, Hre, Jarai, Raglai, Stieng and other minority groups to jointly demand their right to live in their traditional ways. The Front soon split into two groups, one militant and one pacific. The militant wing was later groomed by the United States to be a counter-insurgency force during the intensifying war.

Johnson approved the expansion of covert action against North Vietnam for a four-month period from 1 February 1964. The aim was 'to show North Vietnam that it would be in their interest to desist in South Vietnam.'[52] North Vietnam had decided two months earlier to intensify the war to show the u.s. that they could not win in South Vietnam. The question of whether to bomb North Vietnam, by then, hovered over top-brass meetings in Washington and Saigon. The u.s. joint chiefs of staff officially proposed bombing, as well as the possibility of a nuclear strike and a naval blockade, in a memo to McNamara on 2 March 1964. In May the covert plan against the north was extended for another four months and the u.s. administration was preparing to seek Congressional approval for an 'expansion of military action in Indochina.'[53] Johnson personally drafted a plan of action envisaging an initial two-prong approach. One was to get Congressional approval for an expansion of military action, the other was to initiate a series of secret communications with North Vietnam, via a Canadian representative of the International Control Commission (ICC), J. Blair Seaborn. Seaborn was to relay in secret meetings with North Vietnamese leaders that the u.s. would provide the north with economic and diplomatic support if they 'stopped supporting the Vietcong and end the conflict', otherwise the u.s. would begin air and naval attacks. Prime Minister Phạm Văn Đồng replied that the u.s. should withdraw from South Vietnam and accept the NLF in a neutral coalition government.[54] No agreement was reached and the scene was set for escalating confrontation, when a naval incident occurred off the coast of North Vietnam.

GULF OF TONKIN INCIDENT

On 2 August 1964, in the first of two incidents in the Gulf of Tonkin reported by the u.s. government, the destroyer uss *Maddox* reported it was engaged by three North Vietnamese torpedo boats. The *Maddox* was part of a covert action plan numbered 34-Alpha under which ships were putting ashore South Vietnamese intelligence agents or dropping off other agents to carry out acts of sabotage against North Vietnamese installations. Secret u.s. documents, declassified by the National Security Agency (NSA) in 2005, say the crew of the *Maddox* reported firing on North Vietnamese vessels identified as torpedo boats as they appeared to take up attack positions to launch torpedoes. Two days later the *Maddox* and uss *Turner Joy* were in the area monitoring radio and radar signals when they radioed that they were under threat from hostile vessels in international waters off North Vietnam. Based on reports of these incidents in the Gulf of Tonkin, President Lyndon B. Johnson ordered air strikes on North Vietnam and Congress soon passed a resolution authorizing wider military action. Whether the American pretext

President Johnson signing the Gulf of Tonkin resolution, 10 August 1964.

for action was based on real naval encounters in the Gulf, or on wrong readings of signals by the U.S. Navy, has been hotly disputed ever since among historians.

The incident intensified the Cold War. Krushchev had been replaced by Leonid Brezhnev as first secretary of the Soviet Communist Party and Brezhnev's response was to increase military aid to North Vietnam and openly support the NLF. With the Soviet Union now directly engaged, North Vietnam stepped up its activities in the south. The Hồ Chí Minh trail was strengthened so it could take trucks in key sections. North Vietnamese regulars joined in sabotage acts with the NLF and one of these – an attack against an American advisors' barrack in Pleiku in the central highlands – triggered the start of a systematic U.S. bombing campaign over North Vietnam code-named Rolling Thunder. The bombing started on 26 February 1965 and in March the U.S. sent in two battalions of marines to land on Đà Nẵng beach. After Johnson decided to Americanize the war, the Army of the Republic of Vietnam (ARVN) took on a secondary role; the military power that came to support them took over the frontline. The ultimate war aim remained the containment of communism in Southeast Asia.

From mid-1964 to early 1969 the number of U.S. military personnel in Vietnam grew from 16,000 to 550,000.[55] South Vietnam, Laos and at times eastern Cambodia were the field of battle. Australia, New Zealand, the Philippines, South Korea and Thailand were drawn into the war. Previously unheard of Vietnamese locations became known internationally as the sites of battles. Some proved to be hellish destinations for young U.S. army draftees and all were destined to become places of sad remembrance for fallen soldiers of all sides. North Vietnam, the Hồ Chí Minh trail and many areas in South Vietnam came under unremitting bombardment and toxic defoliation. With technology and firepower identified as the major assets of the U.S., the bombing campaign was stepped up from 25,000 sorties in 1965 to 108,000 in 1967. The tonnage of bombs dropped went up from 63,000 in 1965 to 226,000 in 1967.[56]

Tensions between the USSR and China blocked the overland passage of Soviet weaponry through China and the sea supply route from North to South Vietnam. The alternative route was through the hitherto island of neutrality that was Cambodia. Head of state Norodom Sihanouk was approached by the North Vietnamese and he agreed to let them use Sihanoukville on the Gulf of Siam to ship supplies and people. From eastern Cambodia North Vietnamese soldiers and supplies were moved in trucks overnight along what was named by the Americans the 'Sihanouk trail' into South Vietnam.[57] Tây Ninh province, only 100 km northwest of Saigon, became the headquarters for communist leaders in the south that was now styled Central Office for South Vietnam (COSVN). Set in the jungle somewhere on the border between Cambodia and South Vietnam, COSVN was a constant target of bombing raids but was still able to operate until the end of the war in 1975. The Sihanouk trail survived all efforts to cut it until 1970, when Sihanouk was overthrown in a military coup while travelling abroad. By then the north had moved an estimated 22,000 tonnes of arms, military equipment and supplies, and nearly 71,000 tonnes of rice and salt along this route. The eastern section of the Sihanouk trail became a battlefield when Cambodian coup leader General Lon Nol gave permission for secret bombing by B52s.

Henry Kissinger claims that by mid-1967 the Johnson administration was desperate to end the war.[58] At that time Kissinger was still a private citizen and he came to know a Frenchman, Raymond Aubrac, who knew

Hồ Chí Minh when he was living in Paris. McNamara says he authorized a trip by Aubrac and his companion Herbert Marcovich to North Vietnam in July[59] with the proviso that they went as private citizens. Kissinger met with the two Frenchmen on their return to Paris in July and relayed their message to McNamara in Washington. They said Hồ Chí Minh 'hinted that he would be willing to negotiate if the u.s. stopped bombing North Vietnam'.[60] The two Frenchmen then met for a lengthy discussion with Prime Minister Phạm Văn Đồng, who sought 'an unconditional end of bombing'.[61] Both sides were keen to keep the communication channel open and Mai Văn Bộ, the North Vietnamese consul general in Paris, was designated the Vietnamese official contact, while Kissinger was the unofficial contact on the u.s. side.[62] In August 1967, with Johnson's approval, McNamara told Kissinger the u.s. was ready to have immediate private contact with North Vietnam and was ready to stop the aerial and naval bombardment. In return, North Vietnam would undertake not to 'take advantage of the bombing cessation'. On 19 August 1967 Johnson ordered a bombing halt over Hanoi from 24 August to 4 September. The presidential order, in a diplomatic blunder, was not immediately made known to the American command in Vietnam and the bombing was actually intensified to make up for sorties lost during the bad weather.[63] Kissinger's unofficial contacts came to nothing.

THE 1968 TẾT OFFENSIVE

On 30 January 1968, while Vietnamese of both north and south prepared to celebrate the Tết Lunar New Year, North Vietnamese and NLF forces launched attacks throughout the south. The eve of Tết is a joyful occasion when firecrackers are set off to chase away bad spirits and to welcome in the new year at midnight. After years of prohibiting the firecrackers on security grounds, the ban was lifted in 1968 and they resounded throughout South Vietnam. In Saigon, where life had not yet been directly touched by the fighting, residents wondered why the firecracker barrages continued on through the night. By the next morning it was clear that the firecrackers were in fact gunfire and mortar explosions and Saigon was for the first time on the frontline. During the night, communist forces entered Huế and Saigon, attacking key installations and entrenching themselves in populated sectors. In Saigon the u.s. embassy, the presidential palace, the radio station, the airport, the JGS headquarters and police stations were all under attack. In a surreal drama Saigon citizens stood on their balconies or on rooftops watching helicopter gunships strafing their boroughs with rockets while huge fires and explosions turned the sky red.[64]

The Tết offensive was soon crushed in Saigon but the fighting continued elsewhere. Huế was the worst affected with 26 days of hand-to-hand combat in the old imperial citadel.

Thousands of citizens were killed by insurgents and northern soldiers in executions. Mass graves were being uncovered months after the fighting ended. The Huế imperial palace buildings, the Nguyễn tombs outside the city and the Cham monuments of Đồng Dương and Mỹ Sơn were bombed flat. Overall losses on the North Vietnamese side were estimated at 30,000 killed and thousands more captured. The communist forces lost all city battles but the psychological impact on the West was immense.

Public opinion in the United States turned sharply against the war after seeing daily TV network broadcasts of the U.S. embassy in Saigon penetrated by sappers and the Nguyễn dynastic citadel of Huế battered in a zone of extended artillery and hand-to-hand combat. Marches for peace were soon organized in the United States and Europe to demand an American withdrawal from Vietnam. The slogan 'Hey! Hey! LBJ, how many kids have you killed today?' is said to have really pained Johnson. On 31 March 1968 Johnson announced that he would not run for another term of office. He ordered a unilateral halt to the bombing above the twentieth parallel and urged Hanoi to come to the negotiating table.[65] North Vietnam and the U.S. began meetings in Paris on 10 May 1968. The talks immediately ran into deadlock, for the Vietnamese demanded a complete bombing halt over North Vietnam and the U.S. insisted on a withdrawal of North Vietnamese troops from South Vietnam. President Johnson eventually ordered a bombing halt on 1 November and the Paris talks restarted, then stopped and then restarted for the next three years, while fierce fighting continued in Vietnam.

ATROCITIES AND 'KATM'

The most visceral published atrocity story of the war occurred at the village of Mỹ Lai on the morning of 16 March 1968 when U.S. soldiers from the 20th Infantry's 1st Battalion (Charlie Company) flew into the village in helicopters and found only women, children and old men cooking their breakfast rice. At a briefing the evening before when a soldier had asked: 'Are we supposed to kill women and children?', Captain Ernest Medina replied: 'Kill anything that moves' ('KATM').[66] Charlie Company under Lieutenant William Calley shot chickens, pigs and water buffalo then gunned down old men and children who ran for cover. After four hours they had slaughtered more than 500 unarmed civilians.

The slaughter was first reported by the army as a battle in which 128 enemy troops were killed for no loss of American life.[67] Lieutenant

Johnson reading press reports on the bombing halt of 1968.

East gate Đông Ba of Huế Tết Offensive, 1968.

Calley was eventually tried by a military court and convicted of the premeditated murder of 22 Vietnamese civilians. He was sentenced on 31 March 1971 to life imprisonment with hard labour but he served only three years of this before being effectively pardoned by President Nixon and released.

Journalist Nick Turse has recently challenged the u.s. army case that Mỹ Lai was an exception in a 2013 book *Kill Anything that Moves: The Real American War in Vietnam* that has reignited the deep latent feelings about Vietnam among the u.s. veterans and the military. Turse argues that American atrocities like Mỹ Lai were not random acts of violence but a standard part of a large and coordinated policy by the American military. Turse says the military created a culture for its young conscripts, from boot camp to jungle camp, that encouraged wanton violence against Vietnamese civilians to achieve 'step-on' body count targets required by the chain of command since this was identified by McNamara as the key indicator for winning the war. General William Westmoreland's chosen weapon for killing more hostile Vietnamese than could be recruited and trained into soldiers was 'firepower'. Turse claims that what was different about Mỹ Lai was that the usual cover-up was broken. He built up his account from hundreds of documents collected by a Pentagon task force called the Vietnam War Crimes

My Lai massacre.

Working Group set up for investigating reports of atrocities. He followed up the data by going through reports of military trials of soldiers indicted for actions in Vietnam, with interviews with veterans, and by field visits to Vietnam to some of the scenes mentioned in the documentation. Turse has difficulty proving a direct link between the war strategists and the attitudes of individual soldiers to daily civilian deaths on a significant scale, but he found much corroboration from veterans on routine breaching of the rules of engagement with Vietnamese civilians by U.S. units in the field.

NIXON'S 'PEACE WITH HONOUR' OR 'DECENT INTERVAL'

In January 1969 Richard M. Nixon became the thirty-seventh president of the United States. By then the American involvement had led to 540,000 U.S. soldiers being stationed in South Vietnam. Some 31,000 had been killed in action and the Paris talks were getting nowhere.[68] Nixon promised to bring the Americans home and to secure 'peace with honour'. His assistant for national security affairs was Henry Kissinger. One of Nixon's first acts as president was a long memo to the secretaries of state and defense and the director of the CIA, ordering them to prepare answers to his 28 questions on the situation in Vietnam. The questions covered the strength and capability of all involved and 'possible alternative interpretations to existing data'.[69] As it turned out his view of Vietnam was very different from that of his predecessors. Nixon wanted to rapidly Vietnamize the war, taking him closer to Kennedy than Johnson. On 3 November 1969 Nixon made a speech on how he was going to extract Americans from South Vietnam and turn the war into a Vietnamese affair. The Vietnamization plan was already in place following an earlier visit to Vietnam by his defense secretary Melvin Laird. Nixon announced an increase in the training and equipment deliveries for South Vietnamese forces and a withdrawal of over 60,000 Americans from South Vietnam by December. He said he had worked out with the South Vietnamese government a timetable for a complete withdrawal of all u.s. combat ground forces and their replacement by South Vietnamese.[70] By this time 90,000 South Vietnamese soldiers had been killed in action. The South Vietnamese army was said to number 826,000.[71]

PARIS PEACE TALKS AND THE 1972 OFFENSIVE

By January 1969 the Paris talks were widened to include representatives of both the NLF and South Vietnam. In June 1969 the NLF transformed itself into the Provisional Revolutionary Government of the Republic of South Vietnam (PRG) and was put forward by Hanoi as the legal government of South Vietnam and became the official representative of the NLF at the talks. Several discreet channels were now used to bring the sides closer. Nixon sent a private letter to Hồ Chí Minh in July and a secret meeting was arranged between Kissinger and northern envoy Xuân Thủy in Paris in August. In his reply to Nixon's letter Hồ Chí Minh wrote a week before his death that the Vietnamese people were 'determined to fight to the last breath, through difficulty and sacrifice, to protect the Fatherland and national rights'.[72] Secret talks did get underway as the formal Paris talks went through the formalities and on 21 February 1970 Kissinger met Hanoi Politburo member Lê Đức Thọ secretly behind an antiquities shop opposite the Louvre in Paris. The secret talks got nowhere for two years.

Following the widening of the war into Cambodia in March 1970, the u.s. Congress voted to repeal the Gulf of Tonkin resolution, effectively curtailing the president's powers to wage war without the approval of Congress. Perhaps encouraged by this and motivated by a desire to test the strength of South Vietnamese forces, as well as the American resolve to support them, North Vietnam on 30 March 1972 launched a frontal, tank-led offensive through the DMZ into South Vietnam. They made significant territorial gains at first but then the u.s. airforce and navy launched massive airstrikes in support of ARVN units and also directly

American search operation in a village in South Vietnam.

on North Vietnam. Hải Phòng harbour was blocked with mines and North Vietnam backed off in mid-June. Kissinger and Lê Đức Thọ returned to their private negotiations. By October 1972 Kissinger and Lê Đức Thọ had agreed a draft peace accord. But when this was presented to President Nguyễn Văn Thiệu in Saigon, he demanded major changes and protested at not being consulted during the talks. In November Kissinger took back to Lê Đức Thọ a list of 69 changes inspired by Nguyễn Văn Thiệu, which was rejected. Lê Đức Thọ then tabled a counter-proposal that Kissinger considered 'outrageous'.[73] The two men met again on the 13 December in an explosive session and the negotiation was halted.

Frustrated, Nixon ordered a Christmas bombing campaign with B52 bombers on Hanoi that was the longest and most destructive yet experienced. According to Vietnamese statistics 2,380 people were killed, 1,356 were wounded, and seven out of nine railway stations and four out of five key bridges were destroyed. Half a million people were evacuated from Hanoi. Some 81 aircraft were shot down and 43 American pilots captured.[74] After twelve days and nights of relentless bombing, Hanoi agreed to return to the Paris talks. On 9 January 1973 Kissinger and Lê Đức Thọ accepted a draft agreement.[75] After 202 open sessions and 24 private meetings over a period of four and a half years, on 27 January 1973 an 'Agreement on Ending the War and Restoring Peace in Vietnam' was signed in Paris by secretary of state William Rogers and ambassador Henry Cabot Lodge for the U.S., foreign minister Nguyễn

Duy Trinh for the Democratic Republic of Vietnam, Mme Nguyễn Thị Bình for the PRG and ambassador Trần Văn Lắm for the Republic of Vietnam. A ceasefire went into effect the following day throughout North and South Vietnam and within 60 days all residual U.S. forces were to be withdrawn, all U.S. bases dismantled, and all prisoners of war released. An international force would keep the peace, the South Vietnamese would have the right to determine their own future, and North Vietnamese troops could remain in the south but would not be reinforced. The seventeenth parallel would remain the dividing line until the country could be reunited by 'peaceful means'.

The two men who brought about the agreement were later jointly awarded the Nobel Peace Prize. Kissinger accepted, but Lê Đức Thọ declined on the grounds that a 'true peace does not yet exist in Vietnam'. Hanoi viewed the agreement as only a partial success, for though it 'made the Americans leave', South Vietnam had still not 'succumbed'.[76] On 29 March 1973 the last U.S. military unit left Vietnam. The war had been fully Vietnamized, as promised by Nixon in 1969.

Throughout 1973 and 1974 fighting continued in many areas of South Vietnam while both sides accused each other of violating the Paris agreement. The United States remained largely mute and by 1974 Nixon was embroiled in the 'Watergate' scandal. In July 1974 Lê Duẩn, first secretary of the Vietnamese communist party, met with his army chiefs at Đồ Sơn beach resort near Hải Phòng to discuss a 'plan to liberate South Vietnam and reunify the country by 1975–6'.[77] Nixon resigned in August to be replaced by his vice-president, Gerald Ford, and North Vietnamese leaders judged it unlikely that the United States would again come to the assistance of South Vietnam. The Politburo met in December 1974–January 1975 to finalize their '1975–6 strategic plan' to attack South Vietnam. The first target was the central highlands.

THE FINAL DAYS

On 4 March 1975 the North Vietnamese army rolled into the highlands and within a week was threatening its largest city, Ban Mê Thuột. South Vietnamese president Nguyễn Văn Thiệu, an experienced army general, then made a fatal mistake and ordered the ARVN to abandon the highland cities of Pleiku and Kontum and come to the rescue of Ban Mê Thuột. When that failed, he ordered the army to draw back to the coast to defend Đà Nẵng and Huế. Kissinger later recorded that U.S. analysts thought this 'made sense as a war college exercise' but 'in terms of Vietnamese realities, it ushered in catastrophe'.[78] The so-called strategic withdrawal from the highlands was carried out along route 7B, a small road with

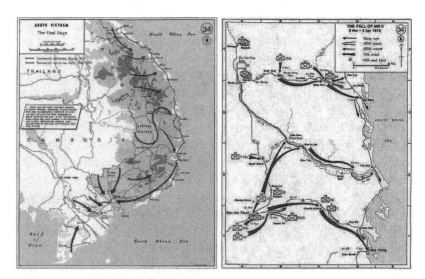

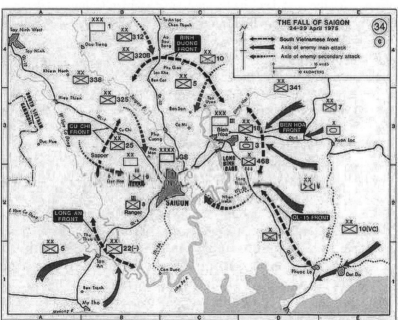

Maps of troop deployments in South Vietnam, the final days, April 1975.

broken bridges that was heavily mined. As the withdrawal began an estimated 400,000 civilians followed the 60,000 retreating troops, while the
indigenous highlanders rioted to protest against being left behind to
face the communists they had worked against. The exodus from the
highlands was chaotic. Food was scarce, thousands of the fleeing people
were killed both by hostile and friendly fire with the North Vietnamese
army in hot pursuit. Kissinger wrote that when they reached the coast
the 'Vietnamese divisions that had defended the Central Highlands
evaporated'. The North Vietnamese Politburo met on 18 March and reset
their target as taking the south by the end of 1975 with the first targets
Đà Nẵng and Huế.[79] This proved too conservative. As the communist
troops moved down towards the coast, the ARVN and civilians began
fleeing south from Huế to Đà Nẵng. The airports and the beaches of
both cities became scenes of a hasty and disorderly evacuation. By 25
March Huế was controlled by the northern army and the surrounding
province fell the next day. The Politburo met again in Hanoi and decided
the time was right to aim for Saigon. Within days Đà Nẵng fell, followed
by a string of coastal cities. North Vietnamese troops then entered Xuân
Lộc town, a short drive north from Saigon. General Võ Nguyên Giáp
publically urged the army to move even faster.

In Washington the collapse in South Vietnam was the subject of a
number of meetings that Kissinger later described as 'bizarre', given the
urgency. Evacuation plans for the residual 6,000 U.S. personnel and for
Vietnamese who had strong connections with the U.S. were now desperately needed, yet discussion in the U.S. administration was about what
could be done to send U.S. military equipment without violating the
Congress's War Powers Act passed the previous year.[80] By 5 April 1975
the ARVN had lost a vast amount of military equipment and replacement
equipment deliveries had been stopped for two years.[81] The Vietnamization
programme was way behind. President Ford acknowledged this in a
speech to Congress on 10 April, in which he referred to 'a vast human
tragedy that has befallen our friends in Vietnam and Cambodia' because
the U.S. was unable to 'provide adequate economic and military assistance
to South Vietnam' as restricted by law. 'Next, we reduced our economic
and arms aid to South Vietnam. Finally, we signalled our increasing reluctance to give any support to that nation struggling for its survival.'[82] Ford
disclosed the extraordinary fact that North Vietnam was now violating
the Paris agreement to the extent of having twenty army divisions –
'virtually their entire army' – in South Vietnam. He said letters had been
sent to all involved, including the USSR and China, to request a halt to
the fighting and enforcement of the 1973 agreement. Ford also asked
Congress to act quickly to approve an additional aid of $722 million for
South Vietnam and for an evacuation of U.S. and South Vietnamese as

South Vietnamese helicopter pushed over the side of USS *Okinawa* to make room for more helicopters to land during Operation Frequent Wind, 29–30 April 1975.

a last resort. The Ford administration then intensely debated evacuation and within days the Senate Foreign Relations Committee called on the president to get the Americans out fast, and never mind the South Vietnamese. They would give money for the evacuation, but not for aid.[83] Ford considered leaving key Vietnamese associates behind as unacceptable.

The battle for Saigon intensified. Faced with a force three times their own strength, the ARVN fought on for ten days but finally collapsed on 20 April 1975. The northern divisions were within 30 km from Saigon

Air Vice-Marshal and Vice-President Nguyễn Cao Kỳ arrive on uss *Midway* during Operation Frequent Wind, 29 April 1975.

Helicopters on uss *Midway*, Operation Frequent Wind, 29–30 April 1975.

Helicopter landing at the U.S. Defense Attaché Office compound to pick up
the last evacuees during Operation Frequent Wind, 30 April 1975.

when Thiệu resigned and flew out of Vietnam, handing over to his deputy
Trần Văn Hương. The scramble to evacuate Americans and South
Vietnamese was underway through the heavily shelled airport Tân Sơn
Nhất. In Kissinger's words, 'twenty years of hope, frustration and discord
over Vietnam has now been reduced to a single objective, to save the
maximum number of Vietnamese potential victims from the conse-
quences of America's abandonment'.[84] On 28 April, with the North
Vietnamese army at the city gates, General Dương Văn Minh took over
as president. Two days later, he ordered the ARVN to surrender as North
Vietnamese troops entered the city.

THE LOSSES

Some 21 years after the signing of the Geneva agreement, Vietnam was
once again unified by force. In 1976 the country was officially defined
as the Socialist Republic of Vietnam and Saigon was renamed Hồ Chí
Minh City. The war costs were extremely high with millions killed or
maimed and infrastructure shattered in the north and south. Vietnamese
historians judged that the 'total war' devised by the U.S. 'made life

South Vietnamese refugees landing on a u.s. aircraft carrier,
Operation Frequent Wind, 29–30 April 1975.

impossible across vast areas and destroying all life in regions controlled by the NLF and PRG'. The bombing campaigns from 1965 to 1972
'destroyed almost every industrial establishment, numerous towns and
cities, thousands of villages, all the bridges, most of the dams and
hundreds of schools, colleges and hospitals in North Vietnam'.[85] Nearly
72 million litres of herbicides were sprayed from 1961–72 on Vietnamese
soil[86] to destroy foliage and deprive North Vietnamese troops of cover,
including along the Hồ Chí Minh Trail. Vietnam today has an abnormally
high incidence of birth defects – for example around Đà Nẵng – of the
kind that can be linked to the use of defoliants like Agent Orange that
contains dioxin. The CIA estimated the bombing of North Vietnam killed
2,800 a month and these were 'heavily weighed with civilians'.[87] Over
150 billion dollars were spent on arms, military equipment and other
expenses.[88] A total of 2,594,000 u.s. soldiers served in Vietnam from
1965–73 and 58,220 lost their lives; over 300,000 were wounded. Over
2,000 went missing in action, while 766 were taken prisoner, many of
them downed pilots. In captivity 114 of these died.[89] The toll was much
higher on the Vietnamese side but exact figures will never be known.
Vietnamese government figures released in 1995 estimated there were

1.1 million military and almost 2 million civilian deaths from 1954–75.[90] In the south for the period of 1965–75, the official figure of military deaths for the ARVN was about 200,000.[91] The U.S. estimated North Vietnamese combat deaths as 950,000. Other sources, including some American ones, suggest half this figure.

When the fighting was over, the suffering continued. A million former ARVN soldiers, including retired ones, and government officials were rounded up and sent to re-education camps throughout Vietnam. High-ranking officers and officials were taken to labour camps in the north where they spent an average of ten years as prisoners for the crime of serving or being conscripted into a war their government lost. Many died in these camps and many left them with their health permanently damaged. The Vietnamese government does not consider these camps as labour or concentration camps but as institutions for re-educating 'war criminals'. Hanoi has reassessed the 're-education' and decided 'the government erred in carrying it out indiscriminately'. But the policy was justified because 'while it was possible to let over 1 million soldiers, policemen and officials of the old regime return quickly to civilian life, it would have been impossible to prevent civil war if all these former officers and cadres had had freedom of movement'.[92] This assessment reveals how the north was very unsure of its control of the south in 1975.

The consequences of the war have weighed heavily on Vietnam and the U.S. for decades. A massive exodus of between one and two million 'boat people' fled the new regime in often barely seaworthy craft. UNHCR estimates between 200,000 and 400,000 perished in storms or at the hands of pirates as they sailed for Hong Kong, Malaysia, Thailand and Australia. The other painful residues of the war include the U.S. troops and pilots missing in action, the resettling in the U.S. of former ARVN soldiers and the children of American fathers; the treatment and land rights of highlanders who joined FULRO and helped the U.S. during the war; the effects of herbicides on the Vietnamese environment and people, as well as on Americans; and the ongoing sufferers on all sides from post-traumatic stress disorder (PTSD) remain as haunting as ever, even to this day.

Epilogue:
Rising Tiger

Driving along the newest, smoothest and most comfortable north–south national highway running along the west side of Vietnam these days, not many people under the age of 40 could remember that this is, in part, the once notorious Hồ Chí Minh trail. Looking out at a beautiful leafy landscape, it is hard to imagine that the area has been subjected to intense spraying with herbicides containing dioxin for many years. Travelling around Hà Nội, Hải Phòng, the Mekong Delta, the central highlands, or, indeed, anywhere in Vietnam, one finds oneself wondering whether these really were the scenes of so many tragic deaths and such extreme destruction in the last century. They were. And even after the war ended in 1975, both North and South Vietnam remained 'battlefields' for an economic war of two decades against poverty and destitution.

The rapid victory of the Democratic Republic of Vietnam in capturing the south by force in 1975 turned into a social and economic nightmare for all Vietnamese. No post-war plan had been prepared to attempt to harmonize the socialist and capitalist economies and the country entered a decade of economic stagnation.[1] The party and government in Hanoi admitted some of the problems: 'In the north the economy was essentially at low-level and depended on small-scale production; the management was cumbersome, bureaucratic and centralised. The effects of the war further exacerbated the non-economic economy . . . After the end of the war in 1975 the shortcomings became even more clearly defined.' In the south 'the capitalist economy was unbalanced by the fact that it traditionally relied on foreign aid. When the aid was no longer there, the economy of the south immediately reached crisis point.'[2] Faced with such difficulties the fourth party congress in December 1976 decided on a classic five-year plan to achieve high growth and integrate reconstruction under a single socialist model. In the north the emphasis was on reconstruction and recovery while in the south the former capitalist society underwent violent changes. Millions of people were shipped out of urban areas to support an intense programme of agricultural development. The peasants who had flocked to the cities to escape the fighting were sent back to their land and jobless people were moved to remote 'new economic zones'. Conditions in these areas were harsh with diseases rampant and many died. Young people who were not in school and had no job were drafted into dredging thousands of kilometres of canals and ditches under a compulsory corvée. A large number of these later either bribed their way back to urban areas, or paid for others to do their corvée duty.

In December 1978, amid its unforeseen and mounting social and economic struggles, Vietnam suddenly invaded Cambodia to oust the horrendous human devastation of the Maoist Pol Pot regime. Vietnam's installation of its own Khmers Rouges faction brought rapid retaliation from China, which drove across Vietnam's mountainous northern border in February 1979. China had already stopped all aid to Vietnam and withdrew its experts.[3] The Vietnamese attack on Pol Pot's Chinese-oriented leadership of the Khmers Rouges was deemed by China as worthy of punishment in a short border incursion into a socialist neighbour. Vietnam was condemned around the world for invading Cambodia. The Association of Southeast Asian Nations (ASEAN), which had been viewing Vietnam with reservation since the end of the war, fearing expansion by its huge armed forces, now urged world opinion to condemn Vietnam for its action in Cambodia. ASEAN sponsored resolutions at the United Nations calling for the withdrawal of Vietnamese troops. Hanoi eventually admitted that 'relations between Vietnam and ASEAN and many countries in the world ran into many problems that affected our revolutionary path'.[4]

The combination of a brutally applied city exodus and agricultural plan and the invasion of Cambodia generated an extraordinary exodus from Vietnam of 'boat people' – economic and political migrants desperate enough to risk sea and storm to find a more viable life. Some 204,600 people left the country surreptitiously in small fishing boats and arrived in neighbouring countries in 1979 alone.[5] Many perished at sea or were killed by pirates in the Gulf of Siam. Economically the pace of collectivization in the south was accelerated from 1978 and the majority of private enterprises collapsed. Agricultural products were sold through state cooperatives at low prices, which destroyed the incentive for increasing production. In 1979 the central committee admitted complete economic failure: 'all fifteen main objectives [of the plan] were not fulfilled, some agricultural and industrial products . . . did not even reach the level of 1976 . . . the terrible consequences of the war, though real, could no longer explain everything'.[6] During the next plan of 1981–5 problems with centralized management became ever clearer and the leadership acknowledged that 'after two 5 year plans, the Vietnamese economy was in crisis'.[7] By 1985 per capita income dropped to U.S.$239 per annum,[8] making Vietnam the fifteenth poorest country in the world. Bangladesh and thirteen African countries ranked below Vietnam.

The effect of southern capitalism on communist cadres posted to the south was to create networks of corruption. Instead of tough old landlords and capitalist employers there appeared a new class of cadres and government officials who seized the fruits that their positions offered. They gave up performing official duties but held on to positions that allowed them privileges and ration cards, and worked elsewhere for cash. The party severely criticized 'negative effects . . . a euphemism often used to refer to corruption, which rapidly spread to officials of the State and Party'.[9] The fifth party congress declared: 'social justice has been violated, law and regulations were not adhered to' and 'acts of power abuse and corruption by cadres and officials occurred without being timely punished'.[10] According to party documents beween 1975–85 190,000 party members were expelled, mostly for 'morality',[11] another term for corruption. The departure of the boat people became a lucrative business for some officials who would accept bribes to look the other way. By 1986 there was not enough rice to feed the population. Households were issued with a low-grade wheat flour ration which was alien to most Việt. A black market for rice and other products thrived in both the north and south and inflation soared. The lack of food was officially described as 'chronic hunger' among the population.[12]

At the second plenum in April 1987 a new party leadership announced a plan that would give greater incentive to the private sector. It turned out to be a miracle drug for the ailing Vietnamese economy. Both Vietnamese and foreign investors responded quickly to a new liberalizing policy called Đổi Mới (renovation). This was the first crucial step that turned Vietnam from poverty to an Asian tiger economy. The Vietnamese, especially in the south, could now begin to follow their entrepreneurial bent and abandon the hated cooperatives, while foreign investors built factories manned by a skilled work force working at low labour costs.

Another crisis loomed for Vietnam in 1989 when communism collapsed in the Soviet Union and the international socialist umbrella folded. 'The changes in the Soviet Union and Eastern Europe brought about a sudden and enormous upset in our export-import markets and also changes in our economic cooperation agreements and labour contracts'. Vietnam had no choice but to brave capitalist markets. Vietnam's debts rose and foreign loans were drying up. The open market exposed Vietnam to repeated condemnations for its human rights record – which remains a major ongoing issue today. But the country rose in spectacular fashion to the challenge to become more competitive in its 1991–5 plan as noted by the World Bank and other economic institutes.

Modern Ho Chi Minh city skyline, view from Saigon River.

RISING TIGER

In 1994 president Bill Clinton lifted the nineteen-year u.s. trade embargo against Vietnam. The next year they restored diplomatic relations and investment increased by 50 per cent per annum. In 1995 alone total foreign investment in Vietnam was u.s.$19 billion. The new service industry expanded by 80 per cent in the 1990s.[13] The u.s. dollar became the preferred currency in all activities, high and low. The Russians, once prized clients in Vietnam's shops and businesses, became known as 'tây nghèo' (poor westerners). Membership of ASEAN was finally achieved in 1995 as Southeast Asian states showed fear of Chinese expansion. ASEAN membership opened the door to world markets and Vietnamese GDP growth averaged 6.8 per cent per year from 1997 to 2004, despite the Asian financial crisis of 1997 and a global recession. The World Bank stated: 'Between 1990 and 2010, Vietnam's economy has grown at an annual average rate of 7.3 per cent, and the per capita income almost quintupled.'[14] The transformation from a centralized economy to a market economy soon lifted Vietnam in just twenty years from the ranks of the poorest countries on earth to the status of lower-middle-income country.[15]

Membership in the ASEAN Free Trade Area (AFTA) later expanded regional economic opportunities and the u.s.–Vietnam bilateral trade agreement of December 2001 futher accelerated growth in Vietnam. Exports from Vietnam to the United States alone increased 900 per cent from 2001 to 2007. World Trade Organization membership in 2007 finally and firmly established Vietnam as a full partner in the global market. The country's current GDP per capita now stands at u.s.$2,600. Vietnam's own assessment of its progress from 1996 to 2000 declares that it has managed to 'consolidate the state, improve the lifestyle of the population and uphold the status and prestige of Vietnam in a global context'.[16] Yet it 'still has many problems to be addressed, such as inflation, high unemployment and lack of jobs, low training and education capacity' and it is still afflicted with deeply rooted 'corruption, waste, bureaucratic administration and degenerated cadres and officials'. These must be addressed if Vietnam is to fully achieve its potential as a rising economic tiger of Asia.

Appendix:
Dates and Dynasties

FROM ±85,000 BCE – PREHISTORY

2879–258 BCE	Hồng Bàng era under Hùng Vương
±600 BCE to ±100 CE	Đông Sơn culture
278–179 BCE	An Dương Vương Thục Phán and the Âu Lạc realm
179–130 BCE	Zhao To established Giao Chỉ and Cửu Chân.
111 BCE	Han take Giao Chỉ and Cửu Chân

111 BCE–939 CE – HAN PROVINCE

40–43	Trưng Sisters
187–226	Shi-xie and assimilation policies
248	Bà Triệu's uprising
468–85	Lý Trường Nhân uprising
541–7	Lý Bí and the Early Lý
548–70	Triệu Việt Vương
571–602	Lý Phật Tử – Hậu Lý Nam Đế
713–22	Mai Thúc Loan uprising
?–801?	Phùng Hưng uprising
906–38	Dawn of independence

INDEPENDENCE

939–65	Ngô dynasty
967–80	Đinh dynasty
980–1009	Early Lê
1009–1225	Lý dynasty

1009–28	Lý Thái Tổ
1028–54	Lý Thái Tông
1054–72	Lý Thánh Tông
1072–1127	Lý Nhân Tông
1128–38	Lý Thần Tông
1138–75	Lý Anh Tông
1175–1210	Lý Cao Tông
1211–26	Lý Huệ Tông
1225	Lý Chiêu Hoàng

1226–1413 TRẦN DYNASTY

1226–58	Trần Thái Tông
1257–8	The first Mongol invasion
1258–78	Trần Thánh Tông
1278–93	Trần Nhân Tông
1283–5	The second Mongol invasion
1287–8	The third Mongol invasion
1293–1314	Trần Anh Tông
1314–29	Trần Minh Tông
1329–41	Trần Hiến Tông
1341–69	Trần Dụ Tông
1370–72	Trần Nghệ Tông
1372–7	Trần Duệ Tông
1377–88	Trần Phế Đế
1389–98	Trần Thuận Tông
1400–1413	Hồ interlude

1407–27 MING INVASION

1407–13	Trần revival
1418–27	Rise of Lê Lợi

1428–1527 LÊ DYNASTY – THE FIRST 100 YEARS

1428–33	Lê Thái Tổ
1433–42	Lê Thái Tông
1442–59	Lê Nhân Tông
1460–97	Lê Thánh Tông

1497–1504	Lê Hiến Tông
1504–09	Lê Túc Tông and Lê Uy Mục
1510–16	Lê Tương Dực
1516–27	Lê Chiêu Tông and Lê Cung Hoàng

1527–92 MẠC USURPATION

1527–37	Mạc Đăng Dung and Mạc Đăng Doanh under the Ming
1540–93	Mạc Phúc Hải, Mạc Phúc Nguyên, Mạc Mậu Hợp

1533 1788 LÊ REVIVAL

1533–48	Lê Trang Tông
1548–56	Lê Trung Tông
1556–73	Lê Anh Tông
1573–99	Lê Thế Tông
1600–1619	Lê Kính Tông
1619–43 & 1649–62	Lê Thần Tông
1643–49	Lê Chân Tông
1663–71	Lê Huyền Tông
1672–5	Lê Gia Tông
1675–1705	Lê Hy Tông
1706–29	Lê Dụ Tông
1729–32	Lê Duy Phường
1732–5	Lê Thuần Tông
1735–40	Lê Ý Tông
1740–86	Lê Hiến Tông
1787–8	Lê Chiêu Thống

1627–1788 TRỊNH-NGUYỄN CIVIL WAR

1558–1627	Establishment of the Việt South
1627–72	Seven inconclusive wars

1771–1801 TÂY SƠN-NGUYỄN WAR

1789–1801	The Nguyễn counter-offensive

1802–1945 NGUYỄN DYNASTY

1802–19	Gia Long
1820–40	Minh Mạng
1841–7	Thiệu Trị
1847–83	Tự Đức

1858–85 FRENCH INVASION

Nguyễn emperors under French 'protection'

1883	Dục Đức (three days)
1883	Hiệp Hòa
1883–4	Kiến Phúc
1884–85/88	Hàm Nghi
1885–9	Đồng Khánh
1889–1907	Thành Thái
1907–16	Duy Tân
1916–25	Khải Định
1926/1932–45	Bảo Đại

1887–1945 VIETNAM AS FRENCH COLONY

1908	Hội An tax uprising

1947–54 FRENCH WAR

1954	Điện Biên Phủ
1954	Geveva conference – Partition of Vietnam

1954–75 VIETNAM–AMERICAN WAR

1954–6	First steps apart
1960	National Liberation Front for South Vietnam (NLF)
1963	Buddhist crisis

1963	Assassinations of Ngô Đình Diệm and John F. Kennedy
1964	Gulf of Tonkin Incident
1964–9	Escalation of the war
1968	Tết offensive
1969	Nixon's Vietnamization of the war
1968–73	Paris peace talks
1975	Last offensive
1976	Re-unification of Vietnam
1976–86	Economic and social difficulties; Boat people
1987–today	Renovation, modernization and economic success.

References

Introduction

1 K. W. Taylor, *A History of the Vietnamese* (Cambridge, 2013), p. 3.

1 Prehistory

1 Stephen Oppenheimer, *Out of Eden: The Peopling of the World* (London, 2004), p. 211.
2 Pedro Soares et al., 'Climate Change and Postglacial Human Dispersals in Southeast Asia', *Molecular Biology and Evolution*, xxv/6 (2008), pp. 1209–18.
3 S. W. Ballinger et al., 'Southeast Asian Mitochondrial DNA Analysis Reveals Genetic Continuity of Ancient Mongoloid Migrations', in *Genetics*, cxxx/1 (1992), pp. 139–52.
4 'Thời Cổ Đại', www.lichsuvietnam.vn, accessed September 2011.
5 Nguyễn Khắc Viện, *Vietnam: A Long History*, 7th edn (Hanoi, 2007), pp. 13–14; 'Thời Cổ Đại', www.dictionary.bachkhoatoanthu.gov.vn, accessed September 2011.
6 Oppenheimer, *Out of Eden*, p. 192.
7 *Một Thế Kỷ Khảo Cổ Học Việt Nam* [A Century of Archaeology in Vietnam], vol. II (Hanoi, 2005).
8 K. W. Taylor, *The Birth of Vietnam* (Berkeley, CA, 1983), p. XIX.
9 'Sunda Shelf', www.britannica.com, accessed 6 October 2011.
10 S. W. Solheim, 'Northern Thailand, Southeast Asia and World Prehistory', in *Asian Perspectives*, XIII/1 (Honolulu, 1972), p. 150.
11 'Thời Cổ Đại', www.lichsuvietnam.vn; Hà Văn Tấn, ed., *Khảo Cổ Học Việt Nam* (Hà Nội, 1999), vol. II.
12 Hà Văn Tấn et al., *Văn Hóa Sơn Vi* [Sơn Vi Culture] (Hanoi, 1999).
13 M. Colani, *L'Âge de La Pierre dans La Province de Hoa-Binh (Tonkin)* (Hanoi, 1927); 'Stations Hoabinhiennes dans La Region de Phu-Nho-Quan Province de Ninh Binh', in *Bulletin du Service Geologique de L'Indochine*, vol. XVII (Hanoi, 1928); 'Thời Cổ Đại'.
14 Hoàng Xuân Chính and Nguyễn Ngọc Bích, *Di Chỉ Khảo Cổ Học Phùng Nguyên* (Hanoi, 1978).
15 Ủy ban khoa học xã hội Việt Nam–Viện khảo cổ học (Vietnam Academy of Social Sciences, VASS), *Hùng Vương dựng nước* (Hanoi, 1974), vol. IV, part 3.

16 'Thời Cổ Đại'.

17 Hà Văn Tấn et al., *Văn Hóa Sơn Vì* (Hanoi, 1999), pp. 123 and 128.

18 S. W. Solheim, 'New Light on a Forgotten Past', *National Geographic*, CXXXIX/3 (1971), p. 333.

19 Solheim, 'Northern Thailand', p. 150.

20 Đỗ Đức Hùng et al., *Việt Nam những sự kiện lịch sử (từ khởi thủy đến 1858)* (Hanoi, 2001), p. 8.

21 Oppenheimer, *Out of Eden*, p. 211.

22 Solheim, 'New Light', p. 333.

23 Hà Văn Tấn and Trịnh Năng Chung, *Khảo Cổ Học Việt Nam*, ed. Hà Văn Tấn, et al., *Văn Hóa Sơn Vì*, p. 145.

24 'Thời Cổ Đại'.

25 Hà Văn Tấn Nguyễn Khắc Sử and Trịnh Năng Chung, *Khảo Cổ Học Việt Nam* (Hanoi, 1999), vol. II, p. 11.

26 Lam Thi My Dzung, 'Some Aspects of Vietnamese Bronze Age', in *The Final Research Results Supported by the KFAS International Scholar Exchange Fellowship program, 2001 2002*.

27 Hoàng Xuân Chính and Nguyễn Ngọc Bích, *Di Chỉ Khảo Cổ Học Phùng Nguyên*, p. 41.

28 'Thời Cổ Đại'.

29 Solheim, 'New Light', p. 339.

30 Stephen Oppenheimer, *Eden in the East: The Drowned Continent of Southeast Asia* (London, 1998), pp. 10 and 108.

31 Đào Duy Anh, *Đất Nước Việt Nam qua Các Đời* (Hanoi, 2005).

32 'Sunda Shelf'.

33 Nguyễn Việt, 'The Đa Bút Culture: Prehistoric Occupation During the Middle Holocene Sea Transgression', SEAS *Bulletin*, VII/2, presented at the 17th Congress of the IPPA (Taipei, 2002).

34 'Thời Cổ Đại'.

35 Ủy ban khoa học xã hội Việt Nam, *Hùng Vương dựng nước*, vol. IV, part 3; Taylor, *The Birth of Vietnam*, p. 312.

36 Trần Thế Pháp, *Lĩnh Nam Chích Quái*, trans. Lê Hữu Mục, 1st edn (Saigon, 1961), p. 44; *Đại Việt Sử Ký Toàn Thư: Ngoại Kỷ*, trans. Viện Khoa Học Xã Hội Việt Nam (Hanoi, 1992), vol. I, pp. 3–5; *Khâm Định Việt Sử Thông Giám Cương Mục: Tiền Biên*, trans. Viện Sử Học (Hanoi, 1998), vol. I, pp. 3–5.

37 Taylor, *The Birth of Vietnam*, pp. 1–2.

38 Hà Văn Tấn, *Khảo Cổ Học Việt Nam*, vol. II, p. 59.

39 Taylor, *The Birth of Vietnam*, pp. 1–2.

40 'Thời Cổ Đại', accessed October 2011.

41 *Đại Việt Sử Ký Toàn Thư*, trans. Viện Khoa Học (Hanoi, 1992), p. 4.

42 Taylor, *The Birth of Vietnam*, pp. 12–13.

43 Hà Văn Tấn, *Văn Hóa Sơn Vì*, pp. 415–17.

44 Lê Tắc, *An Nam Chí Lược* (Huế, 1961), p. 12.

45 Trần Thế Pháp, *Lĩnh Nam Chích Quái*, p. 44.

46 K. W. Taylor, *A History of the Vietnamese* (Cambridge, 2013), p. 5.

47 V. Goloubew, 'Le Tambour Métallique de Hoang-Ha', *Bulletin de l'Ecole Française d'Extrême-Orient* (BEFEO), XL/40–42 (1940), pp. 383–409; H. Parmentier, 'Anciens Tambours de Bronze', BEFEO, XVIII (1918), pp. 1–30; Helmut Loofs-Wissowa, 'Dongson Drums: Instruments of Shamanism or Regalia?' in *Arts Asiatiques*, XLVI (1991), pp. 39–49; K. Imamura, 'The

Distribution of Bronze Drums of the Heger I and Pre-I Types: Temporal Changes and Historical Background', http://hdl.handle.net/2261/35637, accessed October 2011.

48 Phạm Huy Thông et al., *Đông Sơn drums in Vietnam* (Hanoi, 1990).

49 Taylor, *The Birth of Vietnam*, appendix D, p. 313.

50 Taylor, *A History of the Vietnamese*, p. 18.

51 Ibid., pp. 5 and 19.

52 Nguyễn Duy Hinh, 'Dòng chữ Hán khắc trong lòng trống Cổ Loa' in *Những phát hiện mới Khảo cổ học 1995'* (Hanoi, 1995), pp. 157–8; Trịnh Sinh, 'Thử giải mã minh văn trên trống Cổ Loa (Hanoi), *Khảo cổ học*, vol. II (Hanoi, 2006); Nguyễn Việt, 'Minh văn chữ Hán trên đồ đồng Đông Sơn', in *Khảo cổ học*, vol. V (Hanoi, 2007).

53 *Đại Việt Sử Ký Toàn Thư*, trans. Viện Khoa Học (Hanoi, 1992), p. 6; *Đại Việt Sử Lược* [Historical Annals of Great Viet], book 1, trans. Nguyễn Gia Tương (Ho Chi Minh City, 1993), vol. I, p. 9.

54 *Cương Mục*, vol. I, p. 9.

55 Lương Ninh, 'Thời kỳ dựng nước Văn Lang – Âu Lạc', in *Lịch sử Việt Nam giản yếu* (Hanoi, 2000), pp. 37–48.

56 Đào Duy Anh, *Lịch Sử Việt Nam: từ nguồn gốc đến thế kỷ XIX* (Hanoi, 2002), pp. 54–5.

57 Nguyễn Quang Ngọc, 'Việt Nam từ thời tiền sử đến thời dựng nước', in *Tiến trình Lịch sử Việt Nam* (Hanoi, 2006), pp. 30–5.

58 *DVSKTT*, p. 6.

59 Ibid., pp. 8–9.

60 Communist Party of Vietnam online newspaper, www.cpv.org.vn, accessed October 2011.

61 'Cổ Loa - Giải mã huyền thoại', www.lichsuvietnam.vn, accessed October 2011; Phạm Như Hổ, '100 năm nghiên cứu khảo cổ học thời Bắc thuộc', in *Một thế kỷ khảo cổ học* (Hà Nội, 2005), pp. 18–19.

62 Communist Party of Vietnam online newspaper.

63 Lê Tắc, *An Nam Chí Lược*, p. 40; Taylor, *The Birth of Vietnam*, pp. 23–4.

64 Taylor, *The Birth of Vietnam*, p. 24.

65 Ibid., pp. 16–17.

66 *DVSKTT*, p. 14.

67 Lê Tắc, *An Nam Chí Lược*, p. 40.

2 Han Province (111 BCE–40 CE)

1 *Giao Châu Ký*, in Lê Tắc, *An Nam Chí Lược* (Huế, 1961), p. 40.

2 H. Maspéro, 'Etudes d'histoire d'Annam', BEFEO, XVI/1 and XVIII/3 (1916), p. 11.

3 Lê Tắc, *An Nam Chí Lược*, p. 50.

4 K. W. Taylor, *The Birth of Vietnam* (Berkeley, CA, 1983), p. 30.

5 Maspéro (1916), p. 11, n. 1.

6 Taylor, *The Birth of Vietnam*, p. 30.

7 *Đại Việt Sử Ký Toàn Thư*, trans. Viện Khoa Học (Hanoi, 1992), p. 20.

8 Trần Đình Luyện, 'Một thế kỷ nghiên cứu Luy Lâu và những vấn đề đặt ra', in *Một thê kỷ khảo cổ học Việt Nam*, vol. II (Hanoi, 2005), pp. 47–52.

9 Nishimura Masanari, 'Thành Lũng Khê: nhận xét mới từ những điều tra khảo cổ học', in *Một thê kỷ khảo cổ học Việt Nam*, vol. II (Hanoi, 2005), p. 54.

10 Trần Đình Luyện (2005), pp. 47–52.
11 *Hou Hanshu*, k. 54, 4.b in Maspéro (1916), BEFEO, XVIII/18 (1918), p. 27.
12 Lê Tắc, *An Nam Chí Lược*, p. 66.
13 Taylor, *The Birth of Vietnam*, pp. 33–4.
14 Lê Tắc, *An Nam Chí Lược*, p. 66.
15 Đào Duy Anh, *Lịch Sử Việt Nam* (Hanoi, 2006), p. 108.

3 Tutelage and Dissension (40–939)

1 Maspéro, 'Etudes d'histoire d'Annam', BEFEO (1916), p. 13.
2 DVSKTT, p. 21; *Khâm Định Việt Sử Thông Giám Cương Mục: Tiền Biên*, trans. Viện Sử Học (Hà Nội, 1998), p. 23.
3 Maspéro (1916), p. 13.
4 Lê Tắc, *An Nam Chí Lược* (Huế, 1961), p. 40.
5 *Shuijing zhu*, 37; 6a, in *The Birth of Vietnam*, K. W. Taylor (Berkeley, CA, 1983) p. 38.
6 DVSKTT, p. 21; *Hou Hanshu*, 8, 9 and 24, 12 in Taylor, *The Birth of Vietnam*, p. 39.
7 *Hou Hanshu*, 116, 3b; *Shuijing zhu*, 37, 9a in Maspéro (1916), pp. 14, n.7.
8 DVSKTT, p. 21, *Cương Mục*, p. 24.
9 Lê Tắc, *An Nam Chí Lược*, p. 85.
10 DVSKTT, p. 21; *Cương Mục*, p. 24; Taylor, *The Birth of Vietnam*, pp. 39–40.
11 Maspéro (1916), pp. 15–16.
12 Lê Tắc, *An Nam Chí Lược*, p. 13.
13 Maspéro (1916), pp. 16–17.
14 DVSKTT, pp. 20–21; *Cương Mục*, pp. 24–5.
15 Taylor, *The Birth of Vietnam*, p. 46; Đào Duy Anh, *Lịch Sử Việt Nam: từ nguồn gốc đến thế kỷ XIX* (Hanoi, 2002), p. 109.
16 Lê Tắc, *An Nam Chí Lược*, p. 15.
17 Maspéro (1916), p. 27.
18 Taylor, *The Birth of Vietnam*, p. 60.
19 G. Coedès, *The Indianised States of Southeast Asia*, trans. Susan Brown Cowing (Honolulu, 1968), p. 60.
20 Taylor, *The Birth of Vietnam*, p. 60.
21 S. O' Harrow, 'Men of Hu, Men of Han, Men of the Hundred Man', BEFEO, LXXV, n. 75 (1986), pp. 252–3; Taylor, *The Birth of Vietnam*, p. 130.
22 Taylor, *The Birth of Vietnam*, p. 53.
23 Lê Tắc, *An Nam Chí Lược*, pp. 50 and 70.
24 DVSKTT, p. 25 and note 1.
25 The Hu people were Indian and central Asian monks who lived in Luy Lâu; Lê Tắc, *An Nam Chí Lược*, p. 70.
26 *Cương Mục*, p. 31.
27 DVSKTT, pp. 26–7, *Cương Mục*, p. 33; Lê Tắc, *An Nam Chí Lược*, p. 70.
28 *Cương Mục*, p. 36.
29 Trần Trọng Kim, *Việt Nam Sử Lược* [Concise History of Vietnam] (Hanoi, 2002), pp. 55–6; Taylor, *The Birth of Vietnam*, p. 90.
30 Lê Tắc, *An Nam Chí Lược*, p. 41.
31 DVSKTT, pp. 34–7; *Cương Mục*, pp. 45–9.
32 Taylor, *The Birth of Vietnam*, pp. 135–6 and Appendix H.

33 *Cương Mục*, pp. 45–9.

34 Kim, *Việt Nam Sử Lược*, p. 56.

35 Taylor, *The Birth of Vietnam*, pp. 142–3.

36 *DVSKTT*, pp. 35–7; *Cương Mục*, pp. 45–9.

37 *Cương Mục*, p. 51; *DVSKTT*, p. 38.

38 Taylor, *The Birth of Vietnam*, p. 152, n. 26, pp. 143–4.

39 *DVSKTT*, pp. 35–7; *Cương Mục*, pp. 45–52; Lê Tắc, *An Nam Chí Lược*, p. 41.

40 Taylor, *The Birth of Vietnam*, p. 153 and appendix M, pp. 342–3.

41 *DVSKTT*, p. 39; *Cương Mục*, p. 53.

42 Taylor, *The Birth of Vietnam*, pp. 156–7.

43 Kim Sơn, *Thiền Uyển Tập Anh*, Book 1[1337], trans. Lê Mạnh Thát [from 1715 edition] (Saigon, 1999), pp. 94–5, n. 1.

44 Taylor, *The Birth of Vietnam*, pp. 156–7.

45 Lê Tắc, *An Nam Chí Lược*, p. 41; *DVSKTT*, p. 40; *Cương Mục*, p. 54.

46 Taylor, *The Birth of Vietnam*, p. 166.

47 Đào Duy Anh, *Lịch Sử Việt Nam*, p. 140, citing Sui's sources.

48 Taylor, *The Birth of Vietnam*, p. 167.

49 *DVSKTT*, p. 43.

50 Taylor, *The Birth of Vietnam*, p. 171.

51 *Tiến trình Lịch Sử Việt Nam*, ed. Nguyễn Quang Ngọc (Hanoi, 2001), pp. 54–64.

52 Taylor, *The Birth of Vietnam*, p. 188.

53 Lê Tắc, *An Nam Chí Lược*, p. 42; *DVSKTT*, p. 44; *Cương Mục*, p. 57, Maspéro (1916), p. 29; Taylor, *The Birth of Vietnam*, p. 192.

54 Taylor, *The Birth of Vietnam*, p. 193.

55 Charles Benn, *China's Golden Age: Everyday Life in the Tang Dynasty* (Oxford, 2004), p. 9.

56 *DVSKTT*, p. 44; *Cương Mục*, p. 58.

57 Taylor, *The Birth of Vietnam*, p. 208; Edward H. Schafer, *The Vermilion Bird: T'ang Images of the South* (Berkeley, CA, 1967), p. 28; Charles Benn, *China's Golden Age*, p. 11.

58 Taylor, *The Birth of Vietnam*, p. 208; Edward H. Schafer, *The Golden Peaches of Samarkand: A Study of T'ang Exotics* [1963] (Berkeley, CA, 1989), p. 16.

59 H. Maspéro, 'Le Protectorat Général d'Annam Sous Les T'ang: Essai de Géographie Historique, I', *BEFEO*, vol. X (1910), pp. 555–6.

60 Taylor, *The Birth of Vietnam*, p. 199.

61 *DVSKTT*, pp. 44–7; *Cương Mục*, pp. 57–66.

62 Lê Tắc, *An Nam Chí Lược*, p. 42.

63 *DVSKTT*, pp. 48–9; Lê Tắc, *An Nam Chí Lược*, p. 42; Maspéro (1910), p. 556.

64 Taylor, *The Birth of Vietnam*, p. 251–4 (Taylor calls this the Peaceful Sea Army). *DVSKTT*, pp. 48–50.

65 Đào Duy Anh, *Lịch Sử Việt Nam*, p. 152, Trần Trong Kim, *Việt Nam Sử Lược*, p. 73.

66 Maspéro, 'Le Protectorat Général d'Annam Sous Les T'ang', p. 557.

67 *DVSKTT*, p. 50, Lê Tắc, *An Nam Chí Lược*, pp. 84–7.

68 Đào Duy Anh, *Lịch Sử Việt Nam*, p. 153.

69 Lê Tắc, *An Nam Chí Lược*, pp. 42, 84–7, *Cương Mục*, pp. 71–2.

70 Taylor, *The Birth of Vietnam*, p. 259.

71 *Cương Mục*, p. 73.

72 *DVSKTT*, pp. 51–2.

73 Lê Tắc, *An Nam Chí Lược*, p. 42.

74 *DVSKTT* listed this date as the twelfth moon of 938.

75 *DVSKTT*, pp. 53–4; Lê Tắc, *An Nam Chí Lược*, p. 42; *Cương Mục*, p. 75.

76 Nguyễn Thế Anh, 'Attraction and Repulsion as the Two Contrasting Aspects of the Relations between China and Vietnam', in *China and Southeast Asia: Historical Interactions – An International Symposium*, University of Hong Kong, 19–21 July (2001).

77 K. W. Taylor, *A History of the Vietnamese* (Cambridge, 2013), p. 621.

78 Taylor, *The Birth of Vietnam*, p. XVII.

4 Independence

1 *DVSKTT*, vol. I, pp. 147–9; *Khâm Định Việt Sử Thông Giám Cương Mục: Tiền Biên*, trans. Viện Sử Học (Hanoi, 1998), p. 76.

2 *Cương Mục*, p. 77.

3 O. W. Wolters, 'Historians and Emperors in Vietnam and China: Comments Arising Out of Lê Văn Hưu's History, Presented to the Trần in 1272', in *Perceptions of the Past in Southeast Asia*, ed. Anthony Reid and David Marr (Singapore, 1979).

4 *DVSKTT*, vol. I, p. 153; *Cương Mục*, p. 82.

5 K. W. Taylor, *The Birth of Vietnam* (Berkeley, CA, 1983), pp. 280–81.

6 *DVSKTT*, vol. I, p. 154; *Cương Mục*, p. 82.

7 Ngô – Đinh - Tiền Lê displays at the National History Museum, Hanoi, http://baotanglichsu.vn, accessed March 2012.

8 See http://baotanglichsu.vn.

9 *DVSKTT*, vol. I, p. 155; *Cương Mục*, p. 82.

10 See http://baotanglichsu.vn.

11 On display at Hoa Lư.

12 Lê Tắc, *An Nam Chí Lược* (Huế, 1961), p. 34.

13 *DVSKTT*, vol. I, pp. 155–6; *Cương Mục*, pp. 82–3.

14 Taylor, *The Birth of Vietnam*, pp. 280–81; Lê Tắc, *An Nam Chí Lược*, p. 25.

15 *DVSKTT*, vol. I, p. 156.

16 According to the director of the Ninh Binh museum, the inscription was translated by the eminent Vietnamese historian Hà Văn Tấn.

17 Lê Tắc, *An Nam Chí Lược*, pp. 25 and 43.

18 *DVSKTT* vol., pp. 157–61; *Cương Mục*, pp. 84–7.

19 Lê Tắc, *An Nam Chí Lược*, pp. 34, 43.

20 *DVSKTT*, vol. I, pp. 165–9; Lê Tắc, *An Nam Chí Lược*, pp. 43–52; *Cương Mục*, pp. 89–90.

21 Lê Tắc, *An Nam Chí Lược*, pp. 35–43.

22 *DVSKTT*, vol. I, p. 170; *Cương Mục*, p. 91; Lê Tắc, *An Nam Chí Lược*, p. 25.

23 *Cương Mục*, pp. 90–96.

24 *DVSKTT*, vol. I, pp. 178–85; *Cương Mục*, pp. 99 and 103.

5 The Lý Dynasty (1009–1225)

1 *DVSKTT*, vol. I, p. 189; *Khâm Định Việt Sử Thông Giám Cương Mục: Tiền Biên*, trans. Viện Sử Học (Hanoi, 1998), p. 104; Kim Sơn, *Thiền Uyển Tập Anh*, trans. Lê Mạnh Thát (Saigon, 1976), p. 27, n.1.

2 *Tiến trình Lịch Sử Việt Nam*, ed. Nguyễn Quang Ngọc (Hanoi, 2001), pp. 70–76.

3 DVSKTT, vol. I, pp. 187–8; *Cương Mục*, p. 104, Sơn, *Thiền Uyển Tập Anh*, p. 112.

4 DVSKTT, vol. I, pp. 191–3; Lê Tắc, *An Nam Chí Lược* (Huế, 1961), p. 101; *Cương Mục*, pp. 106–9.

5 Sơn, *Thiền Uyển Tập Anh*, p. 48.

6 Cuong Tu Nguyen, 'Rethinking Vietnamese Buddhist History: Is the Thien Uyen Tap Anh a "Transmission of the Lamp" Text?', *Essays Into Vietnamese Pasts*, ed. J. K. Whitmore and K. W. Taylor (Ithaca, NY, 1995), pp. 113–14.

7 Đào Duy Anh, *Lịch Sử Việt Nam* (Hanoi, 2002), p. 188.

8 DVSKTT, vol. I, pp. 195–9; *Cương Mục*, p. 114.

9 *Cương Mục*, p. 115.

10 K. W. Taylor, 'The Rise of Dai Viet and the Establishment of Thang Long', in *Explorations in Early Southeast-Asian History: The Origin of Southeast-Asian Statecraft*, ed. Kenneth R. Hall and J. K. Whitmore (Ann Arbor, MI, 1976), p. 175.

11 Lê Tắc, *An Nam Chí Lược*, pp. 102–3; DVSKTT, vol. I, pp. 213–17; *Cương Mục*, pp. 116–21.

12 Trần Trọng Kim, *Việt Nam Sử Lược* (Hanoi, 2002), p. 105.

13 Hoàng Xuân Hãn, *Lý Thường Kiệt* (Saigon, 1967), pp. 101–2 and 62.

14 On display in the Vietnamese National History Museum in Hanoi.

15 Lê Tắc, *An Nam Chí Lược*, p. 14.

16 DVSKTT, p. 151.

17 Hoàng Xuân Hãn, *Lý Thường Kiệt*, p. 106 (citing Song-shi).

18 DVSKTT, vol. I, pp. 225–8; *Cương Mục*, pp. 126–33.

19 Lê Tắc, *An Nam Chí Lược*, pp. 26, 102–3; DVSKTT, p. 230; *Cương Mục*, p. 133.

20 Hoàng Xuân Hãn, *Lý Thường Kiệt*, pp. 135–42 (citing Song-shi); DVSKTT, p. 230; *Cương Mục*, p. 133.

21 DVSKTT, pp. 230–32.

22 Trần-văn Giáp, 'Le Bouddhisme en Annam, des Origines au XIIIe Siècle', in BEFEO, n. 32, vol. XXXII (1932), pp. 191–268.

23 Hoàng Xuân Hãn, *Lý Thường Kiệt*, p. 437, n.2.

24 Ibid., pp. 45–6.

25 DVSKTT, pp. 233–4; *Cương Mục*, pp. 136–7; Claude Jacques, *Études Épigraphiques Sur Le Pays Cham* (Paris, 1995), p. 23.

26 Lê Tắc, *An Nam Chí Lược*, pp. 102–3.

27 DVSKTT, p. 235; *Cương Mục*, p. 138.

28 Hoàng Xuân Hãn, *Lý Thường Kiệt*, pp. 200–230 (citing Song-shi).

29 DVSKTT, pp. 237–8; *Cương Mục*, p. 140; Lê Tắc, *An Nam Chí Lược*, p. 43.

30 Hoàng Xuân Hãn, *Lý Thường Kiệt*, pp. 221–30 (citing Song-shi)

31 DVSKTT, pp. 239–60; *Cương Mục*, pp. 141–9, 156; Lê Tắc, *An Nam Chí Lược*, p. 43.

32 DVSKTT, p. 267, *Cương Mục*, pp. 154–9, 161.

33 E. Aymonier, 'Première Étude sur les Inscriptions Tchames: Note d'Épigraphie, Po Nagar', *Journal Asiatique*, 409 (1891), p. 48.

34 DVSKTT, pp. 131–40, 274 ; *Cương Mục*, p. 163.

35 DVSKTT, pp. 280–89; Lê Tắc, *An Nam Chí Lược*, p. 104; *Cương Mục*, pp. 168–74 (DVSKTT recorded that the northern ambassador was Yuan but from the date he can only have been Jin, as recorded in *Cương Mục*).

36 *Cương Mục*, p. 176.

37 DVSKTT, pp. 294–9; George Coedès, 'Stèles de Prasat Chrung d'Angkor Thom', in *Inscriptions du Cambodge* (Paris, 1937–66), p. 245.

38 George Coedès, *Histoire Ancienne Des États Hindouisés* (Hanoi, 1944), p. 223.

39 Đào Duy Anh, *Lịch Sử Việt Nam*, p. 214; *Cương Mục*, p. 181.

40 J. K. Whitmore, 'The Rise of the Coast: Trade, State and Culture in Early Đại Việt', in *Journal of Southeast Asian Studies*, XXXVII (2006), pp. 104–7.

41 *DVSKTT*, pp. 301–2; *Cương Mục*, pp. 183–6.

42 *DVSKTT*, pp. 238, 308; *Cương Mục* p. 186.

43 *DVSKTT*, p. 299.

6 The Trần Dynasty (1226–1413)

1   *DVSKTT*, trans. Hoàng Văn Lâu, ed. Hà Văn Tấn (Hanoi, 2004), vol. II, p. 7.

2   *Khâm Định Việt Sử Thông Giám Cương Mục: Tiền Biên*, trans. Viện Sử Học (Hanoi, 1998), pp. 189–94.

3   *DVSKTT*, p. 12; Lê Tắc, *An Nam Chí Lược* (Huế, 1961), p. 27.

4   Đào Duy Anh, *Lịch Sử Việt Nam: từ nguồn gốc đến thế kỷ XIX* (Hanoi, 2006), p. 224.

5   Victor Lieberman, *Strange Parallels: Southeast Asia in Global Context, c. 800–1830* (Cambridge, 2003), vol. II, p. 354.

6   *DVSKTT*, vol. II, p. 41; *Cương Mục*, p. 199.

7   *Cương Mục*, p. 202.

8   *DVSKTT*, pp. 16–25; *Cương Mục*, pp. 196–206.

9   *Cương Mục*, p. 197 (Phan Phu Tiên's comment).

10 Lê Tắc, *An Nam Chí Lược*, p. 5.

11 Rashid-uddin, *Jami'u't-Tawarikh: Compendium of Chronicles*, part 1 and 2, trans. W. M. Thackston (Cambridge, MA, 1998), p. 211; David Nicolle, *The Mongol Warlords* (Poole, 1990), pp. 211–12.

12 Yuanshi, 'Uriyangkhadai Biography' and 'Annam Chapter', in *Đại Việt Sử Ký* vol. II, p. 259, n. 48.

13 *DVSKTT*, p. 261, n. 69.

14 Lê Tắc, *An Nam Chí Lược*, p. 37; *Những Trang Sử Vẻ Vang Của Dân Tộc Việt Nam Chống Phong Kiến Xâm Lược*, vol. I (Hanoi, 1984), p. 355.

15 Yuanshi, 'Annam Chapter', p. 259, n. 48.

16 Trần Quốc Vượng and Hà Văn Tấn, *Lịch Sử Chế Độ Phong Kiến Việt Nam* (Hanoi, 1961), p. 382; Lê Tắc, *An Nam Chí Lược*, p. 37; Yuanshi, 'Annam Chapter', p. 27 and p. 259, notes 47–8.

17 Lê Tắc, *An Nam Chí Lược*, p. 37.

18 Yuanshi, 'Annam Chapter', p. 260, n. 49.

19 Lê Tắc, *An Nam Chí Lược*, p. 37.

20 *Đại Việt Sử Ký*, vol. II, p. 260 n. 52.

21 *DVSKTT*, p. 173.

22 Trần Trọng Kim, *Việt Nam Sử Lược* (Hanoi, 2002), p. 132; Đào Duy Anh, *Lịch Sử Việt Nam*, p. 236.

23 Paul Ratchnevsky, *Un Code des Yuan*, vol. II (Paris, 1972), p. 55.

24 Hà Văn Tấn and Phạm Thị Tâm, *Cuộc Kháng Chiến Chống Xâm Lược Nguyên Mông Thế Kỷ XIII* (Hanoi, 2003), p. 71.

25 Morris Rossabi, *Khubilai Khan: His Life and Times* (Berkeley, CA, 1988), p. 78.

26 John F. Brundage, 'Conserving the Fighting Strength: Milestones of Operational Military Preventative Research', in *Military Preventive Medicine:*

Mobilization and Deployment, vol. I, ed. Dave E. Lounsbury (Falls Church, VA, 2003), pp. 118–21.

27 *Yuanshi*, 'Book 209', in *Đại Việt Sử Ký*, vol. II, note 51, p. 260.

28 *DVSKTT*, p. 174.

29 Rashid-uddin, *Jami'u't-Tawarikh*, p. 447.

30 *Yuanshi*, 'Annam book', in *Đại Việt Sử Ký*, vol. II, p. 35.

31 David Morgan, *The Mongols* (Oxford, 1990), p. 156.

32 For a full account and analysis of the Mongol invasions in Đại Việt, see Vu-Hong-Lien Warder, 'Mongol Invasions in Southeast Asia and Their Impact on Relations Between Đại Việt and Champa (1226–1326)', unpublished PhD thesis, SOAS (London, 2008).

33 *Yuanshi*, 'Annam chapter' in *Đại Việt Sử Ký*, vol. II, p. 261, n. 69. In this account, *Yuanshi* counts this year as the eighth of Möngke's reign because the Chinese and Vietnamese tend to include the very first moment of any event as the first year in their accounting, for instance, a child is one year old as soon as it's born. Rashid-uddin counts this Möngke's reign as the seventh, when he later died.

34 *DVSKTT*, p. 174.

35 *Cương Mục*, pp. 213–14.

36 *DVSKTT*, p. 176; Lê Tắc, *An Nam Chí Lược*, p. 5.

37 Lê Tắc, *An Nam Chí Lược*, pp. 18–19.

38 O. W. Wolters, 'Historians and Emperors in Vietnam and China: comments arising out of Lê Văn Hưu's history, presented to the Trần in 1272', in *Perceptions of the Past in Southeast Asia*, eds. Anthony Reid and David Marr (Singapore, 1979), pp. 69–89.

39 *DVSKTT*, p. 181.

40 Lê Tắc, *An Nam Chí Lược*, p. 19.

41 *DVSKTT*, p. 184.

42 Lê Tắc, *An Nam Chí Lược*, pp. 19–20.

43 *DVSKTT*, p. 187.

44 Paul Pelliot, *Mémoires Sur Les Coutumes du Cambodge de Tcheou Ta-Kouan: Version Nouvelle* (Paris, 1951), pp. 103–4; Rashid-uddin, *Jami'u't-Tawarikh*, part. 2, p. 439; Billy K. L. So, *Prosperity, Region, and Institutions in Maritime China* (Cambridge, MA, 2000), p. 117.

45 R. C. Majumdar, *The Inscriptions of Champa*, Book III (New Delhi, 1985), pp. 216–18.

46 Rossabi, *Khubilai Khan*, p. 216.

47 Pelliot, *Mémoires*, pp. 105–6.

48 *Yuanshi*, 'Annam chapter' in Hà Văn Tấn and Phạm Thị Tâm, *Cuộc Kháng Chiến* (Hanoi, 2003), p. 160.

49 Ibid., p. 111. Pelliot came to the same conclusion but cited his source as *Jingshi dadian*.

50 Ch'i-Ch'ing Hsiao, *The Military Establishment of the Yuan Dynasty* (Cambridge, MA, 1978), note 365, p. 205.

51 Ratchnevsky, *Un Code des Yuan*, p. 62 n. 1; *Yuanshi*, 'Annam Chapter' and 'Sodu's biography', in *Đại Việt Sử Ký*, vol. II, p. 263 n. 93; *Yuanshi*, 'Champa chapter' in *Cuộc Kháng Chiến*, p. 145.

52 Pelliot, *Mémoires*, pp. 110–11, n. 7.

53 Hà Văn Tấn and Phạm Thị Tâm, *Cuộc Kháng Chiến*, p. 146.

54 Pelliot, *Mémoires*, p. 119.

55 *Yuanshi*, 'Champa chapter', pp. 149–62; Georges Maspéro, *Le Royaume de Champa* (Paris and Bruxelles, 1928), pp. 178–81.

56 *Yuanshi*, 'Annam Chapter', p. 160.

57 Lê Tắc, *An Nam Chí Lược*, pp. 28 and 37.

58 Ratchnevsky, *Un Code des Yuan*, p. 60, n. 5.

59 Đào Duy Anh, 'Cuộc Kháng Chiến Của Nhà Trần Đã Ngăn Chặn Đà Bành Trướng Của Mông Cổ Xuống Đông Nam Á', in *Nghiên Cứu Lịch Sử*, 42 (Hanoi, 1962), pp. 16–20.

60 *Yuanshi*, 'Sodu biography', in Anh, *Lịch Sử Việt Nam*, p. 240.

61 *Yuanshi*, 'Principal Annals', in *Cuộc Kháng Chiến*, pp. 169–70 n. 1.

62 *DVSKTT*, p. 189.

63 Lê Mạnh Thát, *Toàn Tập Trần Nhân Tông* (Ho Chi Minh City, 2000), p. 454.

64 Ch'i-ching Hsiao, *Military Establishment*, p. 203 n. 352, p. 204 n. 359.

65 *Yuanshi*, 'Annam Chapter', in *Đại Việt Sử Ký*, vol. II, pp. 262–3.

66 Đào Duy Anh, *Lịch Sử Việt Nam*, p. 243.

67 *Những Trang Sử Vẻ Vang*, vol. I, p. 390.

68 *DVSKTT*, pp. 191–2.

69 Lê Tắc, *An Nam Chí Lược*, pp. 37–8.

70 Đào Duy Anh, *Lịch Sử Việt Nam*, p. 244.

71 *DVSKTT*, p. 192.

72 Lê Tắc, *An Nam Chí Lược*, p. 38.

73 Hà Văn Tấn and Phạm Thị Tâm, *Cuộc Kháng Chiến*, pp. 223–4.

74 *Những Trang Sử Vẻ Vang*, vol. I, p. 397.

75 Lê Tắc, *An Nam Chí Lược*, p. 38.

76 *Yuanshi*, 'Principal Annals', in *Toàn Tập Trần Nhân Tông*, ed. Lê Mạnh Thát, p. 99.

77 *Cương Mục*, pp. 231–2.

78 *Yuanshi*, 'Annam Chapter', p. 252.

79 Lê Tắc, *An Nam Chí Lược*, p. 38.

80 Ch'i-ching Hsiao, *Military Establishment*, p. 204, n. 358.

81 For more detail on this invasion, see Warder, 'Mongol Invasions'.

82 Ratchnevsky, *Un Code des Yuan*, p. 61, n. 1.

83 *Cương Mục*, p. 232.

84 Ratchnevsky, *Un Code des Yuan*, p. 62, n. 1.

85 *DVSKTT*, p. 195.

86 *Cương Mục*, pp. 20 and 234.

87 Lê Tắc, *An Nam Chí Lược*, p. 38.

88 *DVSKTT*, 'Auto-Biography Section', pp. 167–8.

89 Lê Tắc, *An Nam Chí Lược*, p. 38; *DVSKTT*, p. 197; *Yuanshi*, 'Principal Annals', p. 290; *Cương Mục*, p. 235.

90 *Yuanshi* 'Principal annals', p. 267 n. 113.

91 Lê Tắc, *An Nam Chí Lược*, p. 39; *DVSKTT*, p. 198.

92 Đào Duy Anh, *Đất Nước Việt Nam: từ nguồn gốc đến thế kỷ XIX* (Hanoi, 2002), pp. 253–4.

93 Lê Tắc, *An Nam Chí Lược*, p. 39; *DVSKTT*, p. 198; *Cương Mục*, p. 236.

94 *DVSKTT*, p. 198.

95 Louis Hambis and Paul Pelliot, *Le Chapitre CVII du Yuan Che: Les Genealogies Imperiales Mongoles Dans L'histoire Chinoise Officielle De La Dynastie Mongole (T'oung Pao, XXXVIII)* (Leiden, 1945), p. 126.

96 *Yuanshi*, 'Principal Chapter' in *Cuộc Kháng Chiến*, p. 334, n. 3.

97   Lê Tắc, *An Nam Chí Lược*, p. 39.
98   *Yuanshi*, 'Principal annals', p. 326.
99   Lê Tắc, *An Nam Chí Lược*, pp. 20–21, DVSKTT, p. 199, *Cương Mục*, p. 238.
100 O. W. Wolters, *Two Essays on Dai Viet in the Fourteenth Century* (New Haven, CT, 1988), p. 16.
101 Ibid., p. 5.
102 DVSKTT, p. 209.
103 *Cương Mục*, p. 253.
104 Jean Boisselier, *La Statuaire du Champa: Recherches Sur Les Cultes et l'Iconographie* (Paris, 1963), p. 333.
105 *Cương Mục*, p. 255–8; Warder, 'Mongol Invasions', pp. 220–29.
106 Étienne Aymonier, 'L'Inscription Čam de Po Sah', in *Extrait du Bulletin de la Commission Archéologique de l'Indochine* (Paris, 1911), p. 9.
107 DVSKTT, p. 225.
108 Ch'i-Ch'ing Hsiao, *Military Establishment*, pp. 147 n. 5, 150 n. 39.
109 Boisselier, *La Statuaire du Champa*, p. 350.
110 DVSKTT, pp. 219–25.
111 *Cương Mục*, pp. 263–4.
112 Lê Tắc, *An Nam Chí Lược*, pp. 46–7.
113 *Yuanshi* XXVIII 53a, in Maspéro, *Le Royaume de Champa*, p. 199.
114 DVSKTT, p. 235–6.
115 Geoff Wade, *The Mingshi Account of Champa*, ARI working paper, no. 3 (2003), www.ari.nus.edu.sg/pub/wps.htm, pp. 4–6, accessed July 2012.
116 DVSKTT, p. 243.
117 Lê Tắc, *An Nam Chí Lược*, p. 23.
118 DVSKTT, pp. 238–9.
119 John Whitmore, 'The Last Great King of Classical Southeast Asia: "Chế Bồng Nga" and fourteenth-century Champa', in *The Cham of Vietnam: History, Society and Art*, ed. Trần Kỳ Phương and Bruce M. Lockhart (Singapore, 2011), p. 186.
120 Ibid., p. 190.
121 DVSKTT, pp. 268–71; John K. Whitmore, *Vietnam: Hồ Quý Ly and the Ming (1371–1421)* (New Haven, CT, 1985), pp. 10–20.
122 DVSKTT, pp. 270–71.
123 Whitmore, 'The Last Great King', p. 192.
124 Ibid., p. 195.
125 Wade, *The Mingshi Account of Champa*, p. 6.
126 DVSKTT, pp. 273–4, 294–5.
127 *The Cambridge History of China, Vol. 71 The Ming Dynasty, 1368–1644, part 1*, ed. Frederick W. Mote and Denis Twitchett (Cambridge, 1988), p. 316.
128 John W. Dardess, *Ming China, 1368–1644: A Concise History of a Resilient Empire* (Lanham, MD, 2011), pp. 4–5.
129 DVSKTT, p. 305; Geoff Wade, trans., *Southeast Asia in the Ming Shi-lu: An Open Access Resource*, Asia Research Institute and the Singapore E-Press, Singapore, http://epress.nus.edu.sg/msl/entry/875, accessed 17 August 2012; DVSKTT put this number at 10,000 men but *Ming Shi-lu* recorded only 5,000 men.
130 Trần Trọng Kim, *Việt Nam Sử Lược* (Hanoi, 2002), pp. 305–6.
131 Geoff Wade, *Tai-zong shi-lu, juan 58.1a*, in 'The Ming Shi-lu as a source for Southeast Asian History', Asia Research Institute, published online at http://epress.nus.edu.sg/msl (Singapore, 2005), pp. 30–31, accessed August 2012.

132 Wade, entry 859.
133 Shih-Shan Henry Tsai, *Perpetual Happiness: The Ming Emperor Yongle* (Seattle, 2011), p. 179.
134 *DVSKTT*, p. 307; in Dardess's account, the number of men under Zhang Fu and Mu Sheng was 215,000.
135 Wade, entries 1104, 902, 858.
136 *DVSKTT*, p. 307; Edward L. Dreyer, *Early Ming China: A Political History, 1355–1435* (Stanford, CA, 1982), p. 208.
137 Wade, entries 1087, 1102, 1057; *DVSKTT*, p. 311.
138 Dardess, *Ming China: 1368–1644*, pp. 4–5.
139 Wade, entry 1263.
140 *DVSKTT*, p. 312.
141 Wade, entry 1268.
142 *DVSKTT*, p. 311.
143 Wade, entries 1444 and 1445.
144 *DVSKTT*, p. 322.

7 Ming Invasion and the Rise of Lê Lợi (1407–27)

1 Geoff Wade, 'Southeast Asia in the Fifteenth Century', in *Southeast Asia in the Fifteenth Century: The China Factor*, ed. Geoff Wade and Sun Laichen (Singapore, 2010), pp. 3–33.
2 Sun Laichen, 'The Ming Role in China's Southern Expansion' in *Southeast Asia*, ed. Wade and Laichen, pp. 44–82.
3 John Whitmore, 'Paperwork: The Rise of the New Literati and Ministerial Power and the Effort toward Legibility in Đại Việt', in *Southeast Asia*, ed. Wade and Laichen, pp. 104–25.
4 K. W. Taylor, *A History of the Vietnamese* (Cambridge, 2013), p. 179.
5 Trần Trọng Kim, *Việt Nam Sử Lược* (Hanoi, 2002), p. 216.
6 John W. Dardess, *Ming China, 1368–1644: A Concise History of a Resilient Empire* (MD, 2011), p. 4.
7 *DVSKTT*, p. 322.
8 Đào Duy Anh preferred to use the term 'Mắm' for this, which makes more sense as Mắm is a product made with lots of salt to preserve whatever the bottle contains, such as vegetables, meat or fish, whereas Nước Mắm is a liquid extract of salted fish that does not have such a high level of salt in it.
9 Alexander Ong Eng Ann, 'Contextualising the Book-Burning Episode' in *Southeast Asia*, ed. Wade and Laichen, pp. 157–9.
10 Ibid., citing *Yu qiao shu* [Book on the mountains of Vietnam] written by sixteenth-century private historian Li Wenfeng, Assistant Surveillance Commissioner in Yunnan.
11 Geoff Wade, trans., *Southeast Asia in the Ming Shi-lu: An Open Access Resource*, Asia Research Institute and the Singapore E-Press, National University of Singapore, http://epress.nus.edu.sg/msl/entry/916, accessed 17 August 2012.
12 Ann, 'Book-Burning Episode', pp. 157–8, citing Li Wenfeng, *Yueqiao shu*.
13 Trần Trọng Kim, *Việt Nam*, pp. 214–15.
14 Taylor, *A History of the Vietnamese*, p. 180.
15 Ann, 'Book-Burning Episode', p. 162.

16 Đinh Công Vĩ, 'Thử tìm hiểu phương pháp sưu tầm chỉnh lý thư tịch của Lê
   Quý Đôn', *Tạp Chí Hán Nôm*, no. 1 (Hanoi, 1986). In his preface to *Nam Ông
   Mộng Lục*, Lê Trừng explained that even though the southern country was so
   far away, it was not without talented people or valuable recorded stories, 'it
   would be regrettable if we did not know about them, since books were burned
   and lost during the war.' He said he managed to search and take notes of 'old
   affairs' to write this book but could only gather 1 or 2 per cent of the entire
   collection.
17 Wade, entries 1763, 2254; *DVSKTT*, p. 323.
18 Dardess, *Ming China: 1368–1644*, pp. 4–5.
19 Wade, entries 2337, 2425, 2435.
20 *DVSKTT*, trans. Cao Huy Giu, ed. Đào Duy Anh (Hanoi, 1968), vol. III, p. 6.
21 Wade, entry 2501.
22 *DVSKTT*, vol. III, p. 7.
23 Wade, entries 2698, 2704, 2929.
24 *DVSKTT*, pp. 18–9.
25 Wade, entry 37.
26 *DVSKTT*, vol. III, p. 21.
27 Wade, entries 153, 185; *DVSKTT*, vol. III, pp. 21, 27–8.
28 *DVSKTT*, vol. III, pp. 44–6; Wade, entry 382.
29 Lê Quý Đôn, *Đại Việt Thông Sử (1759)*, trans. Lê Mạnh Liêu (Saigon, 1973),
   trans. Viện Sử Học (Hanoi, 1877), p. 20.
30 *DVSKTT*, vol. III, p. 47; Wade, entry 389.
31 Wade, entries 392, 393.
32 Lê Quý Đôn, *Đại Việt Thông Sử*, pp. 20–21; *DVSKTT*, vol. III, p. 56.
33 Wade, entry 1073.
34 Li Tana, 'The Ming Factor and the Emergence of the Việt', in *Southeast Asia*,
   ed. Wade and Laichen, p. 96, note 70, citing Wang Hongxu, et al., *Ming Shi
   Gao: Huan Guan Zhi (A Draft of Ming History: Biographies of eunuchs)*
   (Taipei, 1962), vol. 178, pt 1.
35 *The Cambridge History of China*, p. 319.

8 Lê Dynasty: The First 100 Years (1428–1527)

1 Nguyễn Quang Ngọc, ed., *Tiến trình Lịch Sử Việt Nam* (Hanoi, 2006),
   pp. 110–16.
2 *DVSKTT*, vol. III, p. 61.
3 Geoff Wade, *Southeast Asia in the Ming Shi lu. An Open Access Resource*,
   Singapore. http://epress.nus.edu.sg/msl/entry/, 652, 655, 678, 683, 1122, 1125,
   1304 and 1310.
4 *DVSKTT*, p. 70; Trần Trọng Kim, *Việt Nam Sử Lược* (Hanoi, 2002), pp. 251–2.
5 Trần Trọng Kim, *Việt Nam*, p. 254.
6 John Whitmore, *The Development of the Lê Government in Fifteenth Century
   Vietnam* (Ann Arbor, MI, 1969), pp. 25–7.
7 *DVSKTT*, p. 76.
8 Trần Trọng Kim, *Việt Nam*, p. 254.
9 Trần Hàm Tấn, 'Étude sur le Văn-miêu de Hanoi', *BEFEO*, vol. XLV (Hanoi,
   1951), p. 108.
10 *DVSKTT*, vol. III, pp. 100–03, 112, 120, 125; Wade, entries 1821, 223, 1801.

11 Đào Duy Anh, *Lịch Sử Việt Nam*, p. 321; Nguyễn Quang Ngọc, ed., *Tiến trình Lịch Sử*, pp. 116–130.
12 *DVSKTT*, vol. III, pp. 148, 151, 156, 244, 184; Wade, entry 1373.
13 *DVSKTT* vol. III, pp. 224, 228, 237; Wade, entries 2560, 1702.
14 Wade, entry 1704; *DVSKTT* vol. III, pp. 240–5; *DVSKTT*, trans. Cao Huy Giu, ed. Đào Duy Anh (Hanoi, 1973), vol. IV, p. 49.
15 Đào Duy Anh, *Lịch Sử Việt Nam*, p. 327.
16 *DVSKTT*, vol. IV, pp. 7, 12, 45.
17 *DVSKTT*, vol. IV, pp. 68 and 84.
18 *Ô Châu Cận Lục*, trans. Dương Văn An (Saigon, 1961), p. 8.
19 *DVSKTT*, vol. IV, p. 106.

9 Mạc Usurpation (1527–92)

1 *Tiến trình Lịch Sử Việt Nam*, ed. Nguyễn Quang Ngọc (Hanoi, 2005), pp. 131–7.
2 Trần Hàm Tân, 'Étude sur le Văn-miêu de Hanoi', *BEFEO*, vol. XLV (Hanoi, 1951), pp. 114–16.
3 John Whitmore, 'Chung-hsing and Cheng T'ung in Texts of and on Sixteenth-Century Vietnam', in *Essays Into Vietnamese Past*, Cornell Southeast Asia Program (Ithaca, NY, 1995), p. 123.
4 *DVSKTT*, pp. 121–4; Wade, entries 2471, 2566.
5 Wade, entries 2561, 1562, 2563 and 2564.
6 Phan Huy Chú, *Lịch Triều Hiến Chương Loại Chí* (Hanoi, 1992), pp. 216–17; Lê Quý Đôn, *Đại Việt Thông Sử*, trans. Lê Mạnh Liêu (Hanoi, 1973), p. 48.
7 Wade, entry 2861, *DVSKTT*, pp. 131–2; Chú, *Lịch Triều Hiến Chương Loại Chí*, pp. 216–7.
8 *DVSKTT*, vol. IV, p. 130.
9 Wade, http://epress.nus.edu.sg/msl/entry/3034.
10 *DVSKTT*, vol. IV, p. 225.
11 Phan Huy Chú, *Lịch Triều Hiến Chương Loại Chí*, pp. 207–8.

10 Trịnh-Nguyễn Civil War (1627–1788)

1 K. W. Taylor, *The Birth of Vietnam* (Berkeley, CA, 1983), p. 297.
2 Phan Huy Chú, *Lịch Triều Hiến Chương Loại Chí* (Hanoi, 1992), p. 211.
3 *DVSKTT*, vol. IV, p. 144.
4 Phan Huy Chú, *Lịch Triều Hiến Chương Loại Chí*, pp. 157–60.
5 Lương Ninh, *Lịch sử Việt Nam giản yếu* (Hanoi, 2000), pp. 244–50.
6 Keith Taylor, 'Nguyen Hoang and Vietnam's Southern Expansion', in Anthony Reid, ed., *Southeast Asia in the Early Modern Era: Trade, Power and Belief* (New York, 1993), pp. 49–50; Li Tana, *Nguyễn Cochinchina* (New York, 1998), p. 60.
7 *DVSKTT*, vol. IV, p. 231.
8 Anthony Reid, *Southeast Asia in the Age of Commerce, 1450–1680* (New Haven, CT, 1988).
9 Li Tana, *Nguyễn Cochinchina*, p. 63.
10 Taylor, 'Nguyen Hoang and Vietnam's Southern Expansion', p. 49.
11 Phan Huy Chú, *Lịch Triều Hiến Chương Loại Chí*, p. 165.
12 Li Tana, *Nguyễn Cochinchina*, p. 64.

13 'The Trials of a Foreign Merchant: Letter by Jeronimus Wonderaer from Hội An, 1602', trans. Ruurdjer Laarhoven, in *Southern Vietnam Under the Nguyên: Documents on the Economic History of Cochinchina (Đàng Trong), 1602–1777*, ed. Li Tana and Anthony Reid (Singapore, 1993), pp. 6–26.

14 Li Tana, *Nguyễn Cochinchina*, p. 69.

15 Ibid., p. 63.

16 'Indochine Annamite: La Connaissance du Pays Jusqu'en 1900', *BEFEO*, vol. XXI (1921), pp. 197–278.

17 Cristoforo Borri, 'Les Européens qui ont vue le vieux Huế', in *Bulletins des Amis du Vieux Huế (BAVH)* (1931), p. 308.

18 Lê Thanh Khôi, *Le Vietnam: Histoire et Civilisation* (Paris, 1955), pp. 290–91.

19 Taylor, 'Nguyen Hoang and Vietnam's Southern Expansion', p. 50.

20 *DVSKTT*, vol. IV, p. 360, n. 25.

21 Phan Huy Chú, *Lịch Triều Hiến Chương Loại Chí*, pp. 161–2.

22 *Đại Nam thực lục Tiền Biên*, vol. 1, trans. Viện Sử Học (Hanoi, 1961), p. 108.

23 Phan Huy Chú, *Lịch Triều Hiến Chương Loại Chí*, pp. 161–2.

24 *Đại Nam thực lục Tiền Biên*, pp. 76–8.

25 Trần Trọng Kim, *Việt Nam Sử Lược* (Hanoi, 2002), pp. 318–28.

26 *Cương Mục*, p. 728.

27 Trịnh Hoài Đức, *Gia Định Thành Thông Chí*, vol. 3, trans. Lý Việt Dũng, ed. Huỳnh Văn Tới (Saigon, 2004), pp. 4–5.

28 *Đại Nam thực lục Tiền Biên*, p. 43.

29 Po Dharma, 'The History of Champa', in Emmanuel Guillon, *Cham Art* (London, 2001), p. 22.

30 *Đại Nam thực lục Tiền Biên*, p. 78.

31 Dharma, 'The History of Champa', p. 22.

32 *Đại Nam thực lục Tiền Biên*, pp. 147–8.

33 Po Dharma, 'Vấn đề khủng hoảng xã hội Campa', in *Champaka* (San Jose, CA, 1999), pp. 116–17.

34 Danny Wong Tze Ken, 'Vietnam-Champa Relations and the Malay-Islam Regional Network in the Seventeenth–Nineteenth Centuries', *Kyoto Review of Southeast Asia*, 5 (2004).

35 Paul Pelliot, 'La Dernière Ambassade du Fou-Nan en Chine sous Les Leang', *BEFEO*, III/3 (1903), pp. 671–2.

36 Lương Ninh, *Vương quốc Phù Nam: lịch sử và văn hóa* (Hanoi, 2005).

37 Paul Pelliot, 'Le Fou-nan', *BEFEO*, III/3 (1903), pp. 248–303.

38 Mak Phoeun and Po Dharma, 'La Première Intervention Militaire Vietnamienne au Cambodge (1658–1659)', *BEFEO*, LXXIII/73 (1984), pp. 285–318.

39 Đức, *Gia Định Thành Thông Chí*, p. 2.

40 Other sources spoke of a naval battle on the Tongle Sap between the Khmer king Cau Bana Cand and the Nguyễn navy. Cau Bana Cand was captured here.

41 Đào Duy Anh, *Đất nước Việt Nam qua các đời* (Thuan-Hoa, 1994), p. 239.

42 *Đại Nam thực lục Tiền Biên*, p. 125; Đức, *Gia Định Thành Thông Chí*, pp. 3–4.

43 Đào Duy Anh, *Đất nước Việt Nam*, p. 240; *Đại Nam thực lục Tiền Biên*, pp. 135–41.

44 Đức, *Gia Định Thành Thông Chí*, pp. 4–5.

45 *Đại Nam thực lục Tiền Biên*, vol. II, trans. Nguyễn Ngọc Tỉnh, ed. Đào Duy Anh (Hanoi, 1962), p. 167.

46 Đào Duy Anh, *Đất nước Việt Nam*, p. 375.

47 'Chapitre Premier: Ethnographie', *BAVH*, 1 and 2 (1931), pp. 71–91.

48 UNFPR, factsheet, 2009.
49 World Bank, 'Country Social Analysis: Ethnicity and Development in Vietnam',
   Summary Report vol. I and II (Washington, 2009), www.worldbank.org/en/
   country/vietnam/research.
50 UNFPR, factsheet.

11 The Decline of the Lê–Trịnh and the Rise of the Tây Sơn

1 Đào Duy Anh, *Lịch Sử Việt Nam: từ nguồn gốc đến thế kỷ XIX* (Hanoi, 2006),
   pp. 392–401.
2 *Đại Nam thực lục Tiền Biên*, vol. I, trans. Viện Sử Học (Hanoi, 1961),
   pp. 236–7; Trần Trọng Kim, *Việt Nam Sử Lược* (Hanoi, 2002), pp. 369–70.
3 Đào Duy Anh, *Lịch Sử Việt Nam*, pp. 411–13; Kim, *Việt Nam*, p. 370.
4 Dharma, 'Vấn đề khủng hoảng xã hội Campa', in *Champaka* (San Jose, CA,
   1999), p. 117.
5 Trần Trong Kim, *Việt Nam*, p. 370.
6 *Đại Nam thực lục Tiền Biên*, pp. 248–51.
7 Trần Trong Kim, *Việt Nam*, p. 373.
8 *Đại Nam thực lục Tiền Biên*, vol. II; *Đại Nam thực lục Chính Biên*, trans.
   Nguyễn Ngọc Tỉnh, ed. Đào Duy Anh (Hanoi, 1963), p. 28.
9 Pierre-Yves Manguin, 'Les Nguyen, Macau et Le Portugal : Aspects Politiques
   et Commerciaux d'une Situation Privilégiée (1773–1802)', in *École Pratique
   des Hautes Études : 4e Section Sciences Historiques et Philologiques, Annuaire
   1977–1978* (Paris, 1978), pp. 1305–8.
10 *Đại Nam thực lục Tiền Biên*, pp. 55 and 61.
11 Trần Trong Kim, *Việt Nam*, p. 388.
12 Trần Trong Kim, *Việt Nam*, pp. 390, 396–406; Phan Huy Chú, *Lịch Triều Hiến
   Chương Loại Chí* (Hanoi, 1992) pp. 211–6.
13 *Đại Nam thực lục Tiền Biên*, pp. 64–5.
14 Trần Trong Kim, *Việt Nam*, p. 414–18.
15 This style was made famous by the French military engineer Sébastien Le
   Prestre, Marquis de Vauban (1633–1707), who was hailed in his time as the
   most skilled architect of unbreachable fortifications.
16 A. Salles, 'Jean-Baptiste Chaigneau et sa Famille', BEFEO, XXIII/23 (1923), pp. 51–3.
17 Cao Xuân Dục, *Quốc Triều Chánh Biên Toát Yếu*, trans. Quốc Sử Quán Triều
   Nguyễn (Hanoi, 1972), p. 14.
18 *Đại Nam Thực Lục*, p. 165.
19 Lê Thanh Khôi, *Le Vietnam: Histoire et Civilisation* (Paris, 1955), p. 318.
20 *Đại Nam Thực Lục*, p. 316.
21 A. Salles, 'Jean-Baptiste Chaigneau', p. 53.
22 Trần Trong Kim, *Việt Nam*, pp. 408–9, 429–31.
23 Dharma, 'The History of Champa', p. 25.

12 Nguyễn Dynasty (1802–1945) Creates 'Việt Nam'

1 Trần Trọng Kim, *Việt Nam Sử Lược* (Hanoi, 2002), p. 437.
2 Đào Duy Anh, *Lịch Sử Việt Nam* (Hanoi, 2002), p. 456.
3 J. H. Peyssonnaux, 'Carnets d'un Collectionneur: Anciennes Ceramiques

Anglaises en Annam', *BAVH*, no. 2 (1922), p. 107.

4 A. Salles, 'Jean-Baptiste Chaigneau', p. 103.

5 Trần Trọng Kim, *Việt Nam*, p. 462.

6 John Crawfurd, *Journal of an Embassy from the Governor-General of India to the Courts of Siam and Cochin China: Exhibiting a View of the Actual State of Those Kingdoms*, 2nd edn, vol. 1 (London, 1830), pp. 424–5 .

7 Peyssonnaux, 'Carnets d'un Collectionneur', p. 107.

8 *Đại Nam thực lục, Chính Biên*, trans. Nguyễn Ngọc Tỉnh, ed. Đào Duy Anh (Hanoi, 1963), vol VI, p. 90.

9 Lê Thanh Khôi, *Le Vietnam: Histoire et Civilisation* (Paris, 1955), pp. 340–41.

10 Po Dharma, 'The History of Champa', in Emmanuel Guillon, ed., *Cham Art* (London, 2001), p. 26–7.

11 *Quốc Triều Chính Biên Toát Yếu*, trans. Quốc Sử Quán Triều Nguyễn, ed. Cao Xuân Dục (Hanoi, 1972), vol. 3, p. 103.

12 Dharma, 'The History of Champa', pp. 26–7.

13 Choi Byung Wook, *Southern Vietnam Under the Reign of Minh Mạng, 1820–1841* (New York, 2004), pp. 86–7.

14 Trần Trọng Kim, *Việt Nam*, p. 492.

15 A. Delveaux, 'Ambassade Minh Mang à Louis Philippe', *BAVH*, 4 (1928), pp. 257–64.

16 Lê Thanh Khôi, *Le Vietnam*, pp. 340–41.

17 Trần Trọng Kim, *Việt Nam*, pp. 497–8.

18 Oscar Chapuis, *The Last Emperors of Vietnam* (Westport, CT, 2000), p. 5.

19 L. Cadière, 'La Dynastie des Nguyen', *BAVH*, 1 and 2 (1931), p. 105.

20 E. Delamarre, trans., 'La Stèle du Tombeau de Tu-Duc', *BAVH*, 1 (1918), pp. 25–42.

21 Extract of a letter by Monseigneur Retord, Bishop of Acanthe and Vicar of Tonkin, in *Annales de la Propagation de la Foi* (Lyon, 1851), vol. XXIII, p. 271 (author's translation).

22 Đào Duy Anh, *Lịch Sử Việt Nam*, pp. 488 and 491.

23 Lê Thanh Khôi, *Le Vietnam*, p. 366.

24 Chapuis, *The Last Emperors of Vietnam*, p. 6.

25 Cadière, 'La Dynastie des Nguyen', p. 105.

26 *Quôc Triều Chính Biên Toát Yếu*, vol. v, pp. 160–61.

27 Paul Antonini, *L'Annam: Le Tonkin et L'Intervention de la France en Extrême-Orient* (Paris, 1889), pp. 188–9.

28 *Quôc Triều Chính Biên Toát Yếu*, vol. v, p. 162.

29 Lê Thanh Khôi, *Le Vietnam*, p. 368.

30 Antonini, *L'Annam*, p. 189.

31 *Quôc Triều Chính Biên Toát Yếu*, vol. v, p. 167.

32 Antonini, *L'Annam*, p. 189; Khôi, *Le Vietnam*, p. 369.

33 A. Delvaux, 'L'Ambassade de Phan-Thanh-Gian en 1863, d'après les Documents Français', *BAVH* (1926), pp. 69–80.

34 Trần Xuân Toàn, trans., 'L'Ambassade de Phan Thanh Gian, 1863–1864', *BAVH* (1919), pp. 161–216.

35 A. Delvaux, 'L'Ambassade de Phan-Thanh-Gian', p. 73.

36 Đào Duy Anh, *Lịch Sử Việt Nam*, pp. 514–15.

37 Lê Thanh Khôi, *Le Vietnam*, pp. 371–2.

38 'Indochine Annamite: La Connaissance du Pays Jusqu'en 1900', *BAVII*, vol. XXI/21 (1921), p. 206.

39 Lê Thanh Khôi, *Le Vietnam*, pp. 371–2.

40 Antonini, *L'Annam*, pp. 218–21.

41 Lê Thanh Khôi, *Le Vietnam*, pp. 373–4.

42 Antonini, *L'Annam*, p. 245; 'Un Missionnaire [by a Missionary]', *Les Expeditions Francaises au Tonkin* (Paris and Lille, 1890), pp. 142–50.

43 David G. Marr, *Vietnamese Anticolonialism: 1885–1925* (Berkeley, CA, 1971), pp. 39–40; Jean Dupuis, *Le Tonkin de 1872 à 1886 Histoire et Politique* (Paris, 1910), pp. 367–75.

44 H. Peyssonneaux and Bùi Văn Cung, 'Le Traité de 1874: Journal du Secrétaire de l'Ambassade Annamite', *BAVH*, 3 (1920), pp. 365–81.

45 Antonini, *L'Annam*, pp. 259–60.

46 Marr, *Vietnamese Anticolonialism*, pp. 41–3.

47 Antonini, *L'Annam*, pp. 274–5.

48 Marr, *Vietnamese Anticolonialism*, pp. 41–3.

49 Trần Trong Kim, *Việt Nam*, p. 562.

50 Antonini, *L'Annam*, p. 277.

51 Trần Trong Kim, *Việt Nam*, pp. 570–71.

52 A. Delvaux, 'La Prise de Huế par les Français 5 Juillet 1885', *BAVH*, 2 (1920), pp. 265–7.

53 A. Delveaux, 'Quelques Précisions Sur Une Période Troublée De l'Histoire d'Annam', *BAVH*, 3 (1941), p. 262.

54 Ant. Poupard, 'Souvenirs d'un Troupier: La Prise de Huế', *BAVH*, 3 (1929), pp. 237–8.

55 Delveaux, 'La Prise de Huế', pp. 291–2.

56 Trần Trong Kim, *Việt Nam*, pp. 580–83.

57 H. de Pirey, 'Une Capitale Ephémère: Tân Sở', *BAVH* (1924), pp. 211–20.

58 M. B. Bourotte, 'L'Aventure du Roi Ham-Nghi', *BAVH*, 3 (1929), pp. 138–42.

59 Delveaux, 'La Prise de Huế', p. 293.

60 Trần Trong Kim, *Việt Nam*, p. 584.

61 Lich Su Vietnam, www.lichsuvietnam.vn, accessed 24 January 2013.

62 Marr, *Vietnamese Anticolonialism*, pp. 231–3.

63 Bảo Đại, *Le Dragon d'Annam* (Paris, 1980), pp. 59–61.

64 Ibid., pp. 114–15.

13 French Colony (1887–1945)

1 Bảo Đại, *Le Dragon d'Annam* (Paris, 1980), pp. 34–5.

2 David G. Marr, *Vietnamese Anticolonialism: 1885–1925* (Berkeley, CA, 1971), p. 79.

3 Lê Thanh Khôi, *Le Vietnam: Histoire et Civilisation* (Paris, 1955), p. 370.

4 Paulin François Alexandre Vial, *Les Premières Années de La Cochinchine: Colonie Française* (Paris, 1874), pp. 49–51.

5 Lê Thanh Khôi, *Le Vietnam*, p. 370.

6 Nguyễn Khắc Viện, *Việt Nam: A Long History* (Hanoi, 2007), pp. 151–2.

7 A. Bonhomme, 'Administration', *BAVH* (1931), pp. 114–16.

8 Marr, *Vietnamese Anticolonialism*, p. 186.

9 Nguyễn Khắc Viện, *Việt Nam*, p. 153.

10 J.-D. Fangeaux, 'Le Service Forestier de l'Annam', *BAVH* (1931), pp. 238–9.

11 Nguyễn Khắc Viện, *Việt Nam*, p. 153.

12 Lê Thanh Khôi, *Le Vietnam*, pp. 383–4.

13 Marr, *Vietnamese Anticolonialism*, pp. 73–5.
14 Lê Thanh Khôi, *Le Vietnam*, p. 383–4.
15 Marr, *Vietnamese Anticolonialism*, pp. 73–5.
16 Lê Thanh Khôi, *Le Vietnam*, p. 386–90.
17 Marr, *Vietnamese Anticolonialism*, p. 87.
18 Nguyễn Khắc Viện, *Việt Nam*, pp. 162–3; Marr, *Vietnamese Anticolonialism*, pp. 188–93.
19 Nguyễn Khắc Viện, *Việt Nam*, p. 165.
20 Marr, *Vietnamese Anticolonialism*, p. 261.
21 Nguyễn Khắc Viện, *Việt Nam*, pp. 168–9.
22 Ho Chi Minh biography, www.marxists.org, accessed February 2013.
23 Marr, *Vietnamese Anticolonialism*, pp. 250–51 .
24 'Part one (1920–1945): The Party's line in the period of the Democratic Front (1936–1939)', http://dangcongsan.vn/cpv/Modules/News_English/News, accessed 18 June 2014; and http://countrystudies.us/vietnam/21.htm, accessed 18 June 2014.
25 Nguyễn Khắc Viện, *Việt Nam*, pp. 209–10.
26 Interviews with eyewitnesses.
27 Claude G. Berube, 'Ho, Giap and oss Agent Henry Prunier', www.historynet.com, 24 May 2011; 'Những chuyện cảm động về Bác Hồ qua lời kể của thành viên nhóm tình báo Con Nai (Mỹ)', *Quân Đội Nhân Dân* [People's Army Newspaper] (19 May 2007).
28 War Office record wo 203/2336, South East Asia Command: Military Headquarters Papers, Second World War. Allied Land Forces South east Asia, British National Archives.
29 'Truman and the Occupation of Indochina: 1945' in *United States – Vietnam Relations 1945–1967* (*The Pentagon Papers*) (Washington, 1967), pp. A.3 and A.23. Top-secret documents declassified in 2011, prepared by the Department of Defense in 1967 and declassified in 2011 but widely available since 1971, when leaked to the press.
30 Nguyễn Quang Ngọc, 'Việt Nam trong chín năm kháng chiến chống thực dân Pháp và xây dựng chế độ dân chủ mới (1945–1954)', chapter 11, *Tiến trình Lịch sử Việt Nam* (Hanoi, 2006), pp. 307–8.
31 'The Character and Power of the Viet-Minh', in *United States – Vietnam Relations 1945–1967*, p. B.1.

14 French War (1947–54)

1 Nguyễn Khắc Viện, *Việt Nam: A Long History* (Hanoi, 2007), p. 234.
2 Interviews with eyewitnesses.
3 Nguyễn Quang Ngọc, 'Việt Nam trong chín năm kháng chiến chống thực dân Pháp và xây dựng chế độ dân chủ mới (1945–1954)', chapter 11, *Tiến trình Lịch sử Việt Nam* (Hanoi, 2006), pp. 315–24.
4 Interviews with eyewitnesses.
5 Nguyễn Quang Ngọc, 'Việt Nam', pp. 315–24.
6 Nguyễn Khắc Viện, *Việt Nam*, p. 241.
7 *The Pentagon Papers* (Boston, 1971).
8 *Pentagon Papers*, vol. I, pt. 4, 'U.S. and France in Indochina, 1950–56', pp. 179–214.
9 'Report by the National Security Council on the Position of the United States

with Respect to Indochina', NSC 64, 27 February 1950.

10 Harry Truman, inauguration speech, 20 January 1949.

11 Top Secret Memorandum for the President from the Secretary of Defense, in *Pentagon Papers*, vol. I, p. 4, pp. 179–214.

12 'U.S. Involvement in the Franco–Viet Minh War, 1950–1954' in *Pentagon Papers*, vol. I, p. 2, Section. 1, pp. 53–75.

13 Henri Navarre, *Agonie de L'Indochine: 1953–1954* (Paris, 1956).

14 Nguyễn Khắc Viện, *Việt Nam*, p. 244.

15 'United States – Vietnam Relations 1945–1967' *Pentagon Papers*, vol. I, p. 4, pp. 179–214.

16 Alain Russio, 'L'Opinion Française et La Guerre d'Indochine (1945–1954) Sondages et Témoingnages', *Vingtième Siècle: Revue d'Histoire*, XXIX/29 (1991), p. 41.

17 Nguyễn Khắc Viện, *Việt Nam*, p. 245.

18 Eisenhower, Annual Message to the Congress on the State of the Union, 2 February 1953.

19 'U.S. Involvement in the Franco–Viet Minh War, 1950–1954', *Pentagon Papers*, pp. 179–214.

20 Nguyễn Khắc Viện, *Việt Nam*, p. 254.

21 Vietnamese sources put these figures in the hundreds of thousands.

22 Phan Ngọc Liên, ed., *Chiến Thắng Điện Biên Phủ 1954* (HCM, 2009), p. 43.

23 Navarre, *Agonie de L'Indochine*, p. 319.

24 Report by Mr Dulles on Geneva and Indo-china, NSC 195th Meeting, 6 May 1954.

25 Dulles to the American Delegation in Geneva, 17 June 1954.

26 Dulles to American Delegation in Geneva, 28 June 1954.

27 'The Geneva Conference: May–July 1954' in *Pentagon Papers*, vol. I, p. 3, pp. 108–78.

28 Vietnam News Agency (VNA) broadcast in English to Southeast Asia, 7 June 1954.

29 'Geneva Accords of 1954', *Dictionary of American History*, www.encyclopedia. com, accessed 12 April 2013.

30 James R. Reckner, in Ronald Frankum Jr., *Operation Passage to Freedom: The United States Navy in Vietnam, 1954–1955* (Lubbock, TX, 2007), p. XVI. In this, the figure 800,000 was mentioned although the lower figure was advanced by the official Commissariat of Refugee with reservation.

31 Lương Ninh, 'Việt Nam từ năm 1954 đến năm 1965', in *Lịch sử Việt Nam giản yếu* (Hanoi, 2000), pp. 549–53.

32 'Origins of the Insurgency in South Vietnam, 1954–1960', in *Pentagon Papers*, vol. I, p. 5, pp. 242–314.

33 Lương Ninh, 'Việt Nam', pp. 569–72.

34 Eyewitness account.

35 Eyewitness interviews.

15 Vietnam–American War (1954–75)

1 Henry Kissinger, *Ending the Vietnam War: A History of America's Involvement in and Extrication from the Vietnam War* (New York, 2003), p. 13.

2 Ibid., p. 9.

3 Robert S. McNamara, *In Retrospect: The Tragedy and Lessons of Vietnam* (New York, 1995), p. XVI.

4 Ibid., p. 32.
5 'U.S. and France in Indochina, 1950–56', in *Pentagon Papers* (Boston, 1971), pp. 179–214.
6 *Department of State Bulletin*, vol. 31 (1954), pp. 735–6.
7 Lâm Lễ Trinh, 'Truất phế Bảo Đại và khai sinh Đệ Nhất Cộng Hòa, ký ức 50 năm sau', 16 October 2005, www.vietnam-vrf.net, accessed April 2013. Lâm Lễ Trinh was Deputy-Minister and then Minister of Interior in Ngô Đình Diệm government (1955–9).
8 'Origins of the Insurgency in South Vietnam, 1954–1960' in *Pentagon Papers*, pp. 242–69.
9 Ibid., pp. 242–69.
10 Nguyễn Khắc Viện, *Việt Nam: A Long History* (Hanoi, 2007), p. 497.
11 Lương Ninh, 'Việt Nam từ năm 1954 đến năm 1965', in *Lịch sử Việt Nam giản yếu* (Hanoi, 2000), pp. 569–72.
12 Hoàng Quốc Việt, 'Đẩy mạnh cải cách ruộng đất để củng cố hoà bình, thực hiện thống nhất và xây dựng đất nước: Năm 1954', Dossier 3908, Ministry of Interior, National Archives III, in *The Vietnam Communist Party's Views of the Land Reform Process as seen from the Resolution of the Party Central Committee (1945–1956)*, ed. Le Thi Quynh Nga.
13 'Origins of the Insurgency in South Vietnam, 1954–1960' in *Pentagon Papers*, vol. I, pp. 242–314.
14 Communist Party of Vietnam (Đảng Cộng sản Việt Nam), *Văn kiện Đảng toàn tập*, [1956] (Hanoi, 2002), vol. XVII, p. 540.
15 *Đại Cương Lịch Sử Việt Nam*, ed. Trương Hữu Quýnh et al. (Hanoi, 2010), p. 969.
16 Ibid., pp. 963–9.
17 This term is translated as 'denounce' but means far more: a denunciation is followed by a mob trial and lynching.
18 *Đại Cương Lịch Sử Việt Nam*, p. 963.
19 'Origins of the Insurgency in South Vietnam, 1954–1960', in *Pentagon Papers*, pp. 242–314.
20 *Đại Cương Lịch Sử Việt Nam*, p. 984.
21 'Origins of the Insurgency in South Vietnam, 1954–1960' in *Pentagon Papers*, pp. 242–314.
22 Nguyễn Khắc Viện, *Việt Nam*, p. 480.
23 *Đại Cương Lịch Sử Việt Nam*, p. 984.
24 Nguyễn Khắc Viện, *Việt Nam*, p. 480.
25 'Origins of the Insurgency in South Vietnam, 1954–1960' in *Pentagon Papers*, pp. 242–314.
26 Manifesto of the National Liberation Front.
27 'Origins of the Insurgency in South Vietnam, 1954–1960' in *Pentagon Papers*, pp. 242–314.
28 Nguyễn Khắc Viện, *Việt Nam*, pp. 482–3; Đặng Phong, *Five Ho Chi Minh Trails* (Hanoi, HCM, 2012), p. 55.
29 McNamara, *In Retrospect*, p. 35.
30 Kissinger, *Ending the Vietnam War*, p. 27.
31 Ibid., p. 30.
32 Ibid., p. 26.
33 'Origins of the Insurgency in South Vietnam, 1954–1960' in *Pentagon Papers*, pp. 242–314.

34 'The Kennedy Commitments and Programs: 1961,' in *Pentagon Papers*, vol. II (Boston, 1971), pp. 1–39.

35 McNamara, *In Retrospect*, pp. 38–9.

36 Telegram DEPTEL 619 to Saigon, 14 November 1961, in *Pentagon Papers*, vol. II, p.1, pp. 1–39.

37 McNamara, *In Retrospect*, p. 40.

38 Ibid., p. 49.

39 Ibid., pp. 78–9.

40 Ibid., p. 40.

41 Ibid., pp. 52–5.

42 Ibid., p. 82 .

43 Ibid., p. 84.

44 John F. Kennedy, 'The President's News Conference', 14 November 1963, online by Gerhard Peters and John T. Woolley, *The American Presidency Project*, www.presidency.ucsb.edu, accessed May 2013.

45 McNamara, *In Retrospect*, p. 47.

46 Ibid., pp. 102–3.

47 National Security Council Memo NSAM 273, LBJ Library, www.lbjlib.utexas.edu, accessed May 2013.

48 Nguyễn Khắc Viện, *Việt Nam*, p. 492.

49 Kissinger, *Ending the Vietnam War*, pp. 36–7.

50 Đặng Phong, *Five Ho Chi Minh Trails*, p. 82. Trường Sơn was the official North Vietnamese name for this Trail.

51 Unified Front for the Struggle of Oppressed Races.

52 McNamara, *In Retrospect*, p. 105.

53 Ibid., p. 120.

54 Ibid., p. 121.

55 Kissinger, *Ending the Vietnam War*, p. 38.

56 George C. Herring, *America's Longest War: The United States and Vietnam, 1950–1975*, 2nd edn (New York, 1986), p. 146.

57 Đặng Phong, *Five Ho Chi Minh Trails*, pp. 311–24.

58 Kissinger, *Ending the Vietnam War*, p. 41.

59 McNamara, *In Retrospect*, pp. 296–7.

60 Kissinger, *Ending the Vietnam War*, p. 41.

61 McNamara, *In Retrospect*, pp. 296–7.

62 Kissinger, *Ending the Vietnam War*, p. 41.

63 McNamara, *In Retrospect*, pp. 298–9.

64 Author's eyewitness account.

65 Kissinger, *Ending the Vietnam War*, p. 47.

66 Nick Turse, *Kill Anything that Moves: The Real American War in Vietnam* (New York, 2013), p. 2.

67 Many detailed accounts have been published. Details of the massacre were first collected by U.S. veteran Ron Ridenhour who was not an eyewitness but had seen similar incidents. Investigative journalist Seymour Hersh published newspaper articles and the first book *Cover-Up* in 1972; Turse, *Kill Anything that Moves*, p. 5.

68 President Nixon's Speech on 'Vietnamization', 3 November 1969.

69 National Security Study Memorandum 1, 21 January 1969, www.nixonlibrary.gov, accessed May 2013.

70 Nixon on 'Vietnamization', 1969.

71 Kissinger, *Ending the Vietnam War*, p. 49.
72 Nguyễn Khắc Viện, *Việt Nam*, p. 512.
73 Kissinger, *Ending the Vietnam War*, pp. 406–8.
74 Nguyễn Khắc Viện, *Việt Nam*, p. 529.
75 Kissinger, *Ending the Vietnam War*, p. 422.
76 Lương Ninh, 'Việt Nam', pp. 590–92.
77 Nguyễn Khắc Viện, *Việt Nam*, p. 538.
78 Kissinger, *Ending the Vietnam War*, p. 533.
79 Nguyễn Khắc Viện, *Việt Nam*, p. 541.
80 Kissinger, *Ending the Vietnam War*, p. 534.
81 Ibid., p. 537.
82 Gerald Ford, 'Foreign Policy Address', Joint Session of Congress, 10 April 1975.
83 Kissinger, *Ending the Vietnam War*, p. 541.
84 Ibid., p. 544.
85 Nguyễn Khắc Viện, *Việt Nam*, pp. 304–5.
86 'Agent Orange' www.military.com, accessed May 2013.
87 Herring, *America's Longest War*, p. 147.
88 Gerald Ford, 'Foreign Policy Address'.
89 See www.mrfa.org/vnstats.htm, accessed May 2013.
90 Ministry of Labour, War Invalids and Social Affairs, 1995.
91 Charles Hirschman et al., 'Vietnamese Casualties During the American War: A New Estimate', *Population and Development Review*, xxi/4 (1995), pp. 783–812.
92 Nguyễn Khắc Viện, *Việt Nam*, pp. 341.

Epilogue: Rising Tiger

1   World Bank country data.
2   Nguyễn Quang Ngọc, 'Việt Nam từ 1975 đến nay' in *Tiến trình Lịch sử Việt Nam* (Hanoi, 2006), pp. 365–79.
3   Trương Hữu Quýnh et al., *Đại Cương Lịch Sử Việt Nam Toàn Tập* (Hanoi, 2010), pp. 1127–8.
4   Ibid., p. 1119.
5   UNHCR, 'Assistance to refugees', *Yearbook of the United Nations 1979: Part 1*, p. 915.
6   Nguyễn Khắc Viện, *Việt Nam: A Long History* (Hanoi, 2007), p. 347.
7   Nguyễn Quang Ngọc, 'Việt Nam', pp. 365–79.
8   See http://data.worldbank.org, accessed May 2013.
9   Nguyễn Khắc Viện, *Việt Nam*, p. 348.
10 Trương Hữu Quýnh, *Đại Cương Lịch Sử Việt Nam Toàn Tập*, pp. 1124–5.
11 Nguyễn Khắc Viện, *Việt Nam*, p. 346.
12 Trương Hữu Quýnh, *Đại Cương Lịch Sử Việt Nam Toàn Tập*, p. 1131.
13 Ibid., pp. 1136–48.
14 World Bank Vietnam Development Report 2012, overview.
15 Vietnam Country Data, World Bank.
16 Trương Hữu Quýnh, *Đại Cương Lịch Sử Việt Nam Toàn Tập*, pp. 1136–48.

Historical Sources

This book has been written to paint a concise but comprehensive picture of the land we call Vietnam from the arrival of *Homo sapiens* on the Hồng River plain, through a millennium as a province of the advanced Chinese empire to the north, until the Việt fused their form of Chinese language with indigenous Mon-Khmer language and formed a long chain of independent dynasties. This powerful new hybrid culture expanded south into the lands of the Cham and Khmer until it became the focus of French colonialism in the Orient, and then the battleground of international ideological conflict. Finally it engaged in world markets with a socialist-capitalism not unlike that of its big Chinese neighbour. To encompass the long span of time we have at times stepped beyond the strictly historical, as in the mention of the human DNA trail and the Recent Single Origin Hypothesis (RSOH) in chapter One. We have also traced the archaeological study of the early inhabitants of the Hồng River from Madeleine Colani's 1927 book *L'Âge de La Pierre dans La Province de Hoa-Binh (Tonkin)*, and Vietnamese language works like the 1978 volume *Di Chỉ Khảo Cổ Học Phùng Nguyên [Archaeological Site of Phùng Nguyên]* by Hoàng Xuân Chính and Nguyễn Ngọc Bích.

For the nearly sixteen centuries of history, we rely inevitably on Chinese and Chinese-style dynastic chronicles translated into French, Vietnamese and English. The main texts in Chinese and Nôm, a vernacular, character-based Vietnamese script, are grouped in works such as *Đại Việt Sử Ký Toàn Thư [Complete Book of the Historical records of Great Viet]*, vol. I, trans. Cao Huy Giu, ed. Đào Duy Anh (Hanoi, 1967); vols. II–IV, trans. Hoàng Văn Lâu, ed. Hà Văn Tấn (Hanoi, 2004). These four volumes form the annals of events in Vietnam from the time of Hồng Bàng in the third century BCE to 1675 under the Lê dynasty. The original set was written by the historian Lê Văn Hưu, who was commissioned by the Trần court to compile the first comprehensive history of Vietnam. His 30 volumes called *Đại Việt Sử Ký* cover the period from 207 BCE to 1225 CE. They were written in Chinese characters and followed Chinese scholarly conventions, but achieve unprecedented Vietnamese insights. O. W. Wolters reads them as a way to assert Vietnam's recent independence in a delicate period when the Trần faced Kublai Khan's wrath.

Next came Phan Phu Tiên who continued Lê Văn Hưu's account up to 1446. Both chronicle sets were subsequently lost. Under the Lê dynasty and Emperor Lê Thánh Tôn in 1479 courtier Ngô Sĩ Liên was commissioned to reproduce the volumes of *Đại Việt Sử Ký*. He used sources from China, local records and eyewitness accounts of events in Vietnam and peppered his text with his own comments. The four volumes of *Đại Việt Sử Ký Toàn Thư* in existence today were translated into Romanized

Vietnamese by the Vietnamese Sinologist Cao Huy Giu and edited and annotated by the historian Đào Duy Anh in 1967 and further edited by Hà Văn Tấn in 2004. They are historical documents commissioned by various Vietnamese political powers to promote Vietnamese identity and nationalism, and therefore bring both elucidation and patriotic predilection, especially to the crucial relationship with China. A balanced historical view sometimes emerges from comparing Vietnamese and Chinese accounts of the same events, but sometimes we are left with unresolved contradiction.

Modern Vietnamese scholarship includes translation works such as *Đại Việt Sử Lược [Historical Annals of Great Viet]*, trans. Nguyễn Gia Tường (HCM, 1993); *Đại Nam thực lục Tiền Biên [Chronicle of the Great South, Version 1]*, vol. I, trans. Viện Sử Học, (Hanoi, 1961); *Đại Nam Thực Lục, Chính Biên [Chronicle of the Great South, Official Version]*, vol. 2, trans. Nguyễn Ngọc Tỉnh, ed. Đào Duy Anh (Hanoi, 1963); Trần Thế Pháp's *Lĩnh Nam Chích Quái [The Wonders (or Extraordinary Things) from Lĩnh Nam]*, trans. Lê Hữu Mục, 1st edn (Saigon, 1961). Eminent contemporary historians include Vietnamese scholars Đào Duy Anh, Hà Văn Tấn and Trần Quốc Vượng, and international scholars John Whitmore, O. W. Wolters and Keith Taylor. The works of the Vietnamese scholars have only been made available to an audience outside Vietnam in recent years. Paris-based Vietnamese historians like Lê Thành Khôi and Nguyễn Thế Anh add a new dimension to the common historical pursuit. A 1920 book *Việt Nam Sử Lược [Concise History of Vietnam]* by Trần Trọng Kim defines the historical contour of Vietnam up to the twentieth century. The most comprehensive and decidedly patriotic account of the Mongol invasions of Vietnam in the late thirteenth century is found in *Cuộc kháng chiến chống xâm lược Nguyên Mông Thế Kỷ XIII* by Hà Văn Tấn and Phạm Thị Tâm and was published in Hanoi in 2003. Rashid-uddin's *Jami'u't-Tawarikh*, translated from Persian by W. M. Thackston in 1998, is another document relevant to the period 1226–36, which is known as a primary source on the Mongols in Europe, the Middle East and Central Asia, but deserves recognition too on Mongol activities in China and Southeast Asia. Eyewitness data on the Mongol invasion appears in the 1961 Hue University translation of *An Nam Chí Lược* by mandarin Lê Tắc, who served the Trần court for ten years before defecting to the Mongol side with his master Trần Kiện. Lê Tắc composed his work in Chinese in China in the late thirteenth–early fourteenth centuries. This work is known from nineteen of the twenty manuscript chapters that are held in the British Library in what is probably an eighteenth-century copy.

The authors' own experience of modern Vietnam was extended by Daniel Ellsberg's leaking the *Pentagon Papers*, by the memoirs of Robert McNamara and Henry Kissinger, and by Nick Turse's recent *Kill Anything That Moves*. Another recent work that is rich in material on the Vietnamese Communist Party is *Việt Nam, a Long History* by Nguyễn Khắc Viện, who was an insider responsible for providing information to the outside during the last war.

Select Bibliography, Archives and Websites

Bibliography

Antonini, Paul, *L'Annam: Le Tonkin et L'Intervention de la France en Extrême-Orient* (Paris, 1889)

Aymonier, E., 'Première Étude sur les Inscriptions Tchames, Note d'Épigraphie, Po Nagar', *Journal Asiatique*, 409 (1891)

Bảo Đại, *Le Dragon d'Annam* (Paris, 1980)

Bùi Vinh, *Văn Hóa Tiền Sử Việt Nam* [Pre-historic Culture of Vietnam] (Hanoi, 2011)

Byung Wook, Choi, *Southern Vietnam Under the Reign of Minh Mạng (1820–1841)* (New York, 2004)

Cao Xuân Dục, *Quốc Triều Chánh Biên Toát Yếu*, trans. Quốc Sử Quán Triều Nguyễn (Hanoi, 1972)

Coedès, G., *The Indianised States of Southeast Asia*, trans. Susan Brown Cowing (Honolulu, 1968)

Colani, Madeleine, *L'Âge de La Pierre dans La Province de Hoa-Binh (Tonkin)* (Hanoi, 1927)

Crawfurd, John, *Journal of an Embassy from the Governor-General of India to the Courts of Siam and Cochin China: Exhibiting a View of the Actual State of Those Kingdoms*, 2nd edn, vol. I (London, 1830)

Đại Nam thực lục Tiền Biên [Chronicle of the Great South, Version 1], vol. 1, trans. Viện Sử Học (Hanoi, 1961)

Đại Nam Thực Lục, Chính Biên [Chronicle of the Great South, Official Version], vol. 2, trans. Nguyễn Ngọc Tỉnh, ed. Đào Duy Anh (Hanoi, 1963)

Đại Việt Sử Lược [Historical Annals of Great Viet], book 1, trans. Nguyễn Gia Tường (Ho Chi Minh city, 1993)

Đặng Phong, *Five Ho Chi Minh Trails* (Hanoi, 2012)

Đào Duy Anh, *Lịch Sử Việt Nam, từ nguồn gốc đến thế kỷ XIX* (Hanoi, 2006)

Dardess, John W., *Ming China, 1368–1644: A Concise History of a Resilient Empire* (Lanham, MD, 2011)

Hà Văn Tấn Nguyễn Khắc Sử and Trịnh Năng Chung, *Khảo Cổ Học Việt Nam*, vol. II (Hanoi, 1999)

Hà Văn Tấn, Nguyễn Khắc Sử and Trịnh Năng Chung, *Văn Hóa Sơn Vì* [Sơn Vì Culture] (Hà Nội, 1999)

Herring, George C., *America's Longest War: The United States and Vietnam. 1950–1975*, 2nd edn (New York, 1986)

Hoàng Quốc Việt, 'Đẩy mạnh cải cách ruộng đất để củng cố hoà bình, thực hiện

thống nhất và xây dựng đất nước, năm 1954' ['Moving the Land Reform
Forward in Order to Consolidate Peace, Achieve Unification and Nation
Building, year 1954'], Dossier 3908, Ministry of Interior, National Archives
III, in Le Thi Quynh Nga, *The Vietnam Communist Party's Views of the Land
Reform Process as Seen From the Resolution of the Party Central Committee
(1945–1956)*

Hoàng Xuân Chính and Nguyễn Ngọc Bích, *Di Chỉ Khảo Cổ Học Phùng Nguyên*
[Archaeological Site of Phùng Nguyên] (Hà Nội, 1978)

Hoàng Xuân Hãn, *Lý Thường Kiệt* (Saigon, 1967)

Kissinger, Henry, *Ending the Vietnam War: A History of America's Involvement
in and Extrication from the Vietnam War* (New York, 2003)

Lê Tắc, *An Nam Chí Lược*, Dossier 3908, (Vietnamese) Ministry of Interior,
National Archives III, accessed May 2013 (Huế, 1961)

Lieberman, Victor, *Strange Parallels: Southeast Asia in Global Context, c. 800–1830*,
vol. I (Cambridge, 2003)

Lương Ninh, *Lịch sử Việt Nam giản yếu* [Concise History of Vietnam] (Hanoi,
2000)

McNamara, Robert S., *In Retrospect: The Tragedy and Lessons of Vietnam* (New
York, 1995)

Marr, David G., *Vietnamese Anticolonialism, 1885–1925* (Berkeley, CA, 1971)

Mote, Frederick W., and Denis Twitchett, eds, *The Cambridge History of China*,
vol. 7: *The Ming Dynasty, 1368–1644, Part 1* (Cambridge, 1988)

Ngô Sĩ Liên, *Đại Việt Sử Ký Toàn Thư* [Complete Book of the Historical Records
of Great Viet], vol. I, trans. Cao Huy Giu, ed. Đào Duy Anh (Hanoi, 1967)

Ngô Sĩ Liên, *Đại Việt Sử Ký Toàn Thư* [Complete Book of the Historical Records
of Great Viet], vol. II, trans. Hoàng Văn Lâu, ed. Hà Văn Tấn (Hanoi, 2004)

Nguyễn Khắc Viện, *Việt Nam: A Long History* (Hanoi, 2007)

Nguyễn Thế Anh, 'Attraction and Repulsion as the Two Contrasting Aspects
of the Relations between China and Vietnam', in *China and Southeast Asia:
Historical Interactions – An International Symposium* (University of Hong
Kong, 19–21 July 2001), www.vninfos.com

Nguyễn Việt, 'The Đa Bút Culture, Prehistoric Occupation During the Middle
Holocene Sea Transgression', *SEAS Bulletin*, VII/2, presented at the 17th
Congress of the IPPA (Taipei, 2002)

Nguyễn Việt, 'Minh văn chữ Hán trên đồ đồng Đông Sơn' ['Chinese characters
on Đông Sơn bronze objects'], *Khảo cổ học [Archaeology] journal*, 5 (2007)

Những chuyện cảm động về Bác Hồ qua lời kể của thành viên nhóm tình báo
Con Nai (Mỹ)' [Moving Stories about Uncle Ho as Told by Intelligence Agents
of the Deer Unit (USA)'], *Quân Đội Nhân Dân* [People's Army Newspaper]
(19 May 2007)

Những Trang Sử Vẻ Vang Của Dân Tộc Việt Nam Chống Phong Kiến Xâm Lược
[Glorious Chapters in the History of the Viet in their Resistance against
Feudal Invaders], vol. I (Hanoi, 1984)

Nicolle, David, *The Mongol Warlords* (Poole, 1990)

Nishimura Masanari, 'Thành Lũng Khê: nhận xét mới từ những điều tra khảo cổ
học' ['Lũng Khê Citadel: A New Assessment From Archaeological
Investigations', in *Một thế kỷ khảo cổ học Việt Nam* [A Century of Archaeology
in Vietnam], vol. II (Hanoi, 2005)

O'Harrow, S., 'Men of Hu, Men of Han, Men of the Hundred Man', in *BEFEO*,
LXXV/75 (1986)

Ô Châu Cận Lục [Recent Records of the Ô territory], trans. Dương Văn An (Saigon, 1961)

Ong Eng Ann, Alexander, 'Contextualising the Book-Burning Episode', in *Southeast-Asia in the Fifteenth Century*, ed. Geoff Wade and Sun Laichen (Singapore, 2010)

Oppenheimer, Stephen, *Out of Eden: The Peopling of the World*, revd edn (London, 2004)

Pentagon Papers, Gravel Edition (Boston, MA, 1971)

—, 'U.S. Involvement in the Franco-Viet Minh War, 1950–1954', in *The Pentagon Papers*, Gravel Edition (Boston, MA, 1971)

Phạm Huy Thông et al., *Đông Sơn drums in Vietnam* (Hanoi, 1990)

Phạm Như Hồ, '100 năm nghiên cứu khảo cổ học thời Bắc thuộc' [100 Years of Archaeological Research on the Chinese Colonial Period], in *Một thế kỷ khảo cổ học* [A Century of Archaeology] (Hà Nội, 2005)

Phan Huy Chú, *Lịch Triều Hiến Chương Loại Chí* [Chart of Court Rituals and Protocols According to Categories] (Hanoi, 1992)

Po Dharma, 'The History of Champa', in *Cham Art*, ed. Emmanuel Guillon (London, 2001)

Poupard, Ant., 'Souvenirs d'un Troupier: La Prise de Hue', *BAVH*, 3 (1929)

Rashid-uddin, *Jami'u't-Tawarikh: Compendium of Chronicles*, parts 1–2, trans. W. M. Thackston (Cambridge, MA, 1998)

Ratchnevsky, Paul, *Un Code des Yuan*, vol. II (Paris, 1972)

Rossabi, Morris, *Khubilai Khan: His Life and Times* (Berkeley, CA, 1988)

So, Billy K. L., *Prosperity, Region, and Institutions in Maritime China* (Cambridge, MA, 2000)

Soares, Pedro et al., 'Climate Change and Postglacial Human Dispersals in Southeast Asia', *Molecular Biology and Evolution*, XXV/6 (2008)

Solheim, Stephen W., 'Northern Thailand, Southeast Asia and World Prehistory', in *Asian Perspectives*, XIII/1 [12] (Honolulu, 1972)

Sun Laichen, 'The Ming Role in China's Southern Expansion', in *Southeast-Asia in the Fifteenth Century*, ed. Wade and Laichen (Singapore, 2010)

Sun Xiang Jun et al., 'Vegetation and Climate on the Sunda Shelf of the South China Sea during the Last Glaciation-Pollen Results from Station 17962', *Journal of Integrative Plant Biology*, XLIV/6 [Beijing] (2002)

Tana, Li, 'The Ming Factor and the Emergence of the Việt', in *Southeast-Asia in the Fifteenth Century*, ed. Geoff Wade and Sun Laichen (Singapore, 2010)

Tana, Li and Anthony Reid, eds, 'The Trials of a Foreign Merchant: Letter by Jeronimus Wonderaer from Hội An, 1602', trans. Ruurdjer Laarhoven, in *Southern Vietnam Under the Nguyên: Documents on the Economic History of Cochinchina (Đằng Trong, 1602–1777)* (Singapore, 1993)

Taylor, K. W., *The Birth of Vietnam* (Berkeley, CA, 1983)

—, 'Nguyen Hoang and Vietnam's Southern Expansion' in *Southeast Asia in the Early Modern Era: Trade, Power and Belief*, ed. Anthony Reid (New York, 1993)

—, *A History of the Vietnamese* (Cambridge, 2013)

Trần Thế Pháp, *Lĩnh Nam Chích Quái* [The Wonders (or Extraordinary Things) from Lĩnh Nam], trans. Lê Hữu Mục (Saigon, 1961)

Trần Trọng Kim, *Việt Nam Sử Lược* [Concise History of Vietnam] (Hanoi, 2002)

Trịnh Hoài Đức, *Gia Định Thành Thông Chí* [Complete Geographical History of Gia Định Region], vol. 3, trans. Lý Việt Dũng, ed. Huỳnh Văn Tới (Saigon, 2004)

Trương Hữu Quýnh, Đinh Xuân Lâm, Lê Mậu Hãn, *Đại Cương Lịch Sử Việt Nam Toàn Tập* [Complete Collection of an Outline of Vietnamese History] (Hanoi, 2010)

Tsai, Shih-Shan Henry, *Perpetual Happiness: The Ming Emperor Yongle* (Seattle, 2011)

Turse, Nick, *Kill Anything That Moves: The Real American War in Vietnam* (New York, 2013)

Wade, Geoff, trans., *Southeast Asia in the Ming Shi-lu: An Open Access Resource*, Asia http://epress.nus.edu.sg/msl

Warder, Vu-Hong-Lien, 'Mongol Invasions in Southeast Asia and their Impact on Relations Between Đại Việt and Champa (1226–1326 CE)', PhD thesis, SOAS, University of London, 2008

Whitmore, John, *Vietnam, Hồ Quý Ly and the Ming, 1371–1421* (New Haven, CT, 1985)

—, 'The Rise of the Coast: Trade, State and Culture in Early Đại Việt', *Journal of Southeast Asian Studies*, 37 (2006)

—, 'Paperwork: The Rise of the New Literati and Ministerial Power and the Effort toward Legibility in Đại Việt', in *Southeast Asia in the Fifteenth Century*, ed. Geoff Wade and Sun Laichen (Singapore, 2010)

—, *The Development of the Lê Government in Fifteenth Century Vietnam* (Ann Arbor, MI, 1969)

Wolters, O. W., 'Historians and Emperors in Vietnam and China: Comments Arising Out of Lê Văn Hưu's History, Presented to the Trần in 1272', in *Perceptions of the Past in Southeast Asia*, ed. Anthony Reid and David Marr (Singapore, 1979)

World Bank, 'Country Social Analysis: Ethnicity and Development in Vietnam', Summary Report (Washington, DC, 2009)

Archives and Collections

Hanoi: Đông Sơn Collection, National History Museum
London: National Archives, War Office record WO 203/2336, South East Asia Command: Military Headquarters Papers, Second World War. Allied Land Forces South East Asia

Websites

www.ari.nus.edu.sg: Wade, Geoff, *The Mingshi account of Champa*, ARI working paper no. 3 (June 2003)
www.cpv.org.vn: Communist Party of Vietnam online newspaper
http://data.worldbank.org
www.dictionary.bachkhoatoanthu.gov.vn
http://epress.nus.edu.sg: Research Institute and the Singapore E-Press
www.lichsuvietnam.vn: 'Cổ Loa – Giải mã huyền thoại' [Cổ Loa - Decoding the Legend]
www.lichsuvietnam.vn: *Thoi Co Dai*
www.marxists.org/reference/archive/ho-chi-minh/biography.htm: *Biography of Ho Chi Minh*

Acknowledgements

We would like to acknowledge with thanks a fellowship awarded by the British Academy – ASEASUK-ECAF, notably for the research contained in chapter Ten. The book owes an immense debt to Lien's parents, Col. Vũ Công Định and Mrs Nguyễn Thị Ân, for their firsthand accounts of life under the French occupation, the resistance and the last war in Vietnam.

Photo Acknowledgements

The author and publishers wish to express their thanks to the below sources of illustrative material and/or permission to reproduce it.

Photos courtesy of authors: pp. 23, 24, 25, 26, 27, 30, 33, 40, 48, 73, 100, 138, 141, 151, 154, 156, 157, 161, 178, 196; photo courtesy Chùa Thầy: p. 41; photo courtesy Fine Arts Museum, Ho Chi Minh City: p. 138; photo courtesy Guimet Museum, Paris: p. 23; photos courtesy History Museum, Hanoi: pp. 30, 100, 156; photo courtesy Hue Monument Conservation Centre: p. 230; photo courtesy Imperial War Museum, London: p. 187; photo courtesy Lưu Ly: p. 97; photos courtesy Lyndon B. Johnson Presidential Library, Austin, Texas: pp. 217, 225, 229; photos courtesy Museum of Ethnic Minorities, Vietnam: pp. 26, 27; photos courtesy Museum of Ethnology, Hanoi: pp. 24, 26, 27; photos courtesy Museum of Vietnamese History, Ho Chi Minh City: pp. 141, 178, 196; photo courtesy National Archives and Records Administration, Washington, DC: p. 212; photos courtesy National Museum of Vietnamese History, Hanoi: pp. 25, 30, 100, 156; photo courtesy Nguyễn Thanh Quang: p. 109; photo courtesy Petr and Bara Ruzicka: p. 121; photo courtesy Thành Viên: p. 58.

Index